MRI Bankers' Guide to™
Foreign Currency

32nd Issue III-1999

Table of contents

New in this issue...

Barbados: A modified $2 note has been issued recently. Improved notes of $5 and $10 will follow.

Belarus: A new note of 1,000,000 rubliei was issued in April.

Belize: "Short" notes of $2 and $5 have been issued recently. These two notes complete the new series.

Bulgaria: The monetary unit was changed to the "new" leva equal to 1,000 old ones. Notes in the new unit were issued in July. Older notes remain valid.

Cayman Isl.: The $25 and $100 notes issued by the Cayman Islands Monetary Authority were placed in circulation in July.

Cuba: The Central Bank has issued its own notes of 20 and 50 pesos. Those of the Banco Nacional are still used.
The 1 peso notes commemorative of the 45th anniversary of the Banco Nacional were not issued for circulation.

England: A new £20 note honoring Sir Edward Elgar, the musician, was issued in June. It has many improvements.

Indonesia: A new note of 50,000 rupiah has been issued. It will gradually replace the "Soekarno" notes. A 100,000 rupiah note may be issued soon.

Luxembourg: The recent notes of 100 francs issued by the Banque Internationale has ceased to be legal tender. They can be redeemed until 28 February 2002.

Mauritius: The legal tender status of the previous notes has been restored. Notes of the new type with the modified language order will be issued soon.

New Zealand: The current notes will be gradually replaced by polymer ones. The $20 was already issued, and the others planned for release soon. A $10 note will be issued to commemorate the millennium.

Nigeria: Larger notes will be issued in 2000. The values are 100; 200 and 500 naira, to be released between 1999 and 2000.

Northern Ireland: The First Trust Bank has issued improved notes. The Northern Bank will issue notes of the Inventor Series in October .

Norway: A new 500 kroner note was issued in June.

Scotland: Clydesdale Bank plc issued a £20 note honoring Alexander "Greek" Thomson. The Royal Bank of Scotland issued a note to commemorate the opening of the Scottish Parliament.

Sri Lanka: Plans for the issue of new polymer notes have been postponed.

Uruguay: A new note of 10 pesos uruguayos was issued in May.

Venezuela: Coins will replace small denomination notes.

This note will soon lose all value:
Malta: 10 liri Cat.#36 . . . . 15 Dec 1999

"MRI Bankers' Guide to Foreign Currency" ™

Copyright ©1999 by Monetary Research, Inc.,
Arnoldo Efron, Director.
Luisa Kluger, Marketing and International Sales
Gabriel A. Leichen, Operations
Elma A. Ramírez, Administration

Catalog numbers from "Standard Catalog of World Paper Money"
Vols. 2 and 3, used by permission of Krause Publications, Inc.

Published quarterly in the United States of America by
Monetary Research Institute
1223 Witte Road (77055)
P.O. Box 3174
Houston, Texas 77253-3174

Telephone (713) 827-1796
Telefax (713) 827-8665
e-mail: aefron@mriguide.com

ISSN 1055-3851

Yearly subscription (4 numbers) $200 or Euros 200 including First Class
postage in the United States, and Airmail delivery elsewhere.

Multiple subscription discounts as follows:
2 to 9 copies: 15 percent, 10 to 24 copies: 20 percent, 25 copies and up: 25 percent.
Library discount: 25% on single copies or yearly subscription(s.)

Single copy: $60.00 or Euros 60 (plus State Sales Tax for Texas addresses)
Back issues: $60.00 or Euros 60 (plus State Sales Tax for Texas addresses).

Printed in the United States of America

Multilingual Index

NOTE: slightly similar spellings are omitted for the sake of brevity.

Identification Guide

Use this section to identify currency written in exotic languages.

Afghanistan

Algeria

Armenia

Belarus

Bulgaria

Cambodia

Georgia

Greece

Kazakhstan

D.P.R. of Korea

D.P.R. of Korea

Kyrgyzstan

Laos

Libya

Macedonia

Mongolia

Nepal

Pakistan

Russia

Taiwan

MRI BANKERS' GUIDE TO FOREIGN CURRENCY
P.O.Box 3174 HOUSTON TX 77253 USA

Tajikistan

Thailand

Transdniestria

Ukraine

Uzbekistan

Yugoslavia

How to recognize worthless currency

Currency can be worthless because of:

Alteration or raised value: Genuine notes of low value are altered to pass for a higher value. In good notes the value in letters and numbers match. Compare a suspected note with a known good one.

Mismatched pieces: A note put together with pieces of different bills is worthless. Verify on taped bills that serial numbers match, and that all fragments belong to the same note.

Mutilation: Notes missing portions may be worthless. Rules for the redemption of mutilated currency vary. If a bill is missing a little bit of a corner, it may be valid, but the loss of 25% or more may render it worthless. If the mutilation is caused by fire or accident, some central banks will redeem the currency. Bills intentionally mutilated or defaced may not be redeemable.

Robberies: When large sums are stolen, and the serial numbers of the notes are known, these may not be negotiable. If a quantity of red stained circulated notes is presented for exchange, these may be stolen, as banks use a "bomb" which stains the currency once the robbers are away. In many cases there are rewards for information leading to the recovery of stolen money.

Inscriptions: Political or commercial writings may make a note worthless. Initials or numbers usually are not a problem.

Counterfeiting: To recognize counterfeit money it is necessary to know the security features found in real money.

You cannot rely on counting machines equipped with "Anticounterfeit" sensors. The machines recognize certain elements in the ink. Counterfeiters add the same chemicals to the ink, foiling the device.

Paper

Most banknotes are printed on good quality paper. To increase protection against forgery, the paper may have one or more of the following:

Threads: Small fibers of silk or other materials are mixed with the paper. Forgers imitate them with thin color pencils or pens.

"Confetti" or planchettes: Little pieces of paper or thin metallized disks of different colors are mixed in the paper paste.

Some planchettes are embedded inside the paper, while others are seen on the front or back surfaces. They can be flaked-off with a pin. Forgers copy them by making dots with color markers.

Embedded wire: A metallic or plastic wire or thread is embedded inside the paper. It can be seen by holding the note against the light. Counterfeiters try to imitate it by folding the note many times where the wire should be, or by printing

a thick line in the back, creating an illusion of a thread. If a tear is made where the thread should be, the metallic or plastic wire can be seen inside the paper.

Many plastic threads have writings which can be seen with a magnifying lens.

Segmented embedded wire: An embedded wire appears as segments of silver on the front of the note. Forgers imitate the segments with metallic ink. When a real note is seen through the light, the thread is continuous.

Watermark: Perhaps the oldest anti-forgery device, it consists of legends or figures visible when the note is held against the light. Variations in the thickness of the paper create the illusion of an image. Watermarks are imitated with wax, light yellow ink or grease imprints.

Pseudo watermarks: In notes of little value, where the risk of forgery is small, a lightly lithographed image gives the illusion of a watermark.

Holograms: Silvery designs applied to the note. Their images and colors change depending on the angle of observation.

Printing

When checking a note look for:

High relief: Most notes are printed with engraved plates, creating high relief which can be felt with the tip of your fingers. Copies made with a laser color printer will have some raised feel, but colors will not match exactly. When seen with a magnifying glass, thin lines in real bills look full. Forgeries made with laser copiers or commercial color printing will show instead little round or rectangular dots, which create the illusion of a line.

Color: Combinations of light and bright colors are used to make forgery difficult. When in doubt, compare with a known genuine bill.

Perfect register: A design in the front is mirrored in the same position in the back of the note. When seen through the light, both sides match exactly. Printing with perfect register requires sophisticated equipment hard to obtain. Front and back designs may be partial. When seen together a complete picture appears.

Serial numbers: In genuine notes are of even alignment and thickness.

Vertical serial numbers, or of increasing size are produced with special machines, and are harder to counterfeit.

Microlettering: Wording printed in very small type looks like a plain solid line to the naked eye, but under magnification it can be read.

Invisible printing: Designs are printed with ink which can only be seen under quartz or ultraviolet light.

Optical devices: Silvery or golden seals on which two or more images are visible when the note is tilted.

Latent impression: Some portions of the note have sculptured engraving. When

looking at the note at a given angle some legends or designs become visible.

Color shifting inks: Small seals printed with special inks change color as the note is tilted.

Raised marks: High relief marks help blind people recognize different denominations. In fake notes these marks may be flat.

Printer's name: If the name of the printer appears, it is usually in tiny print at the bottom of the back the note. Lettering is even; in fake ones it is not.

Signers titles: The titles of signing officers are written in small print. Forgers often use uneven letters to imitate them.

Useful tools:

The tools most useful to recognize forgeries are:

- ▸ a magnifying glass of 10X or more,
- ▸ a UV light.

These are inexpensive and available from local stamp dealers.

Current, outmoded and redeemable notes

Current: A widely used note.

Outmoded: A note which is still legal tender, but because it's old or not usually found in circulation, in practice is not accepted by the public. If you sell it to travelers, they may have problems.

See the "Outmoded and redeemable notes" section for each country.

Redeemable: After a note is retired, time is given for its exchange. It may be a few days or many years. Some countries set no time limit.

The redemption of obsolete currency is not an absolute right. Some central banks reserve the right to refuse to redeem notes, even if presented in time, but this is very rare.

On the other hand, after time limits expired, and given special circumstances, other central banks will exchange it.

Demonetization of currency can be sudden, borders may be closed to prevent its repatriation during the very short time allowed for its exchange.

Depending on currency restrictions or regulations, outmoded and redeemable notes may be sent for redemption to the issuing bank; or to any of the redemption services advertised in this guide.

No responsibility whatsoever, express or implicit, is assumed for any losses resulting from errors or changes in the current status of banknotes or any other reason.

Collectors notes: There is great demand for currency for collectors. Some notes may be highly valuable, even if legally worthless.

Collector's notes are valued according to rarity, condition and demand.

We welcome enquiries about the disposal of obsolete currency. Send us the notes by registered mail. We will evaluate them, and submit an offer subject to your approval. If not accepted, your notes will be returned at our expense.

Currency import and export restrictions

There may be restrictions to the amounts and kinds of local or foreign currency travelers may take in or out. The rules published apply to foreign non-resident visitors.

We contacted all monetary authorities, asking for copies of their currency regulations. Not all answered, forcing us to seek unofficial information. Consulates, embassies and government tourist offices do not always give reliable answers.

The information given here was obtained from sources considered reliable. However it must be stressed that no express or implied responsibility whatsoever is assumed for its correctness, or for the consequences of violations of import-export laws, rules or regulations.

Common sense indicates that arriving or leaving with small amounts of cash should not create problems, while carrying large amounts may raise suspicions of drug dealing or tax evasion.

A prudent traveller will not enter a country carrying money of their enemies.

Some countries have peculiar laws which make it illegal to bring in some currencies but not others. Others may limit how much local or foreign currency can be held, and force visitors to change a fixed amount of hard currency.

Others yet forbid holding any foreign currency at all. On arrival you must convert it into local money. When you leave you may reconvert. If banks are closed at departure you cannot do it, and since it is illegal to export their currency, you may as well give it away.

Do not think of tearing it up. Since money is one of the attributes of sovereignty, its destruction may be considered a crime.

Official and parallel rates of exchange

The rates in the first column apply to tourists exchanging at official banks or exchanges. The second column is for parallel market.

If there are restrictions for the sale of hard currency, a parallel market develops, usually with higher rates. This "black" market may range from open and free, to persecuted and dangerous.

Using the parallel market may entail risks of being cheated, or getting into trouble with the law.

Rates in the parallel market may be slightly higher than the official, or much higher, as in Iraq where it was around 1,000 times higher than the bank rate.

Most banknote trading is based on free or parallel rates of exchange.

Large and small notes

Money changers may quote different rates for larger and smaller bills. Due to import-export restrictions, it may be illegal to repatriate large notes. Their rate will be lower. Or smaller notes may be discounted due to the high cost of repatriation.

During the travel season dealers import small notes and sell them at a premium to recover their shipping cost.

Comment reconnaître les billets de banque sans valeur.

Les billets de banque peuvent ne plus avoir de valeur pour différentes raisons:

Billet retouché ou valeur augmentée: Un vrai billet de faible valeur est modifié pour le faire passer à une valeur plus élevée. Vérifier que la valeur en lettres et en chiffres correspondent, et que le dessin et la couleur soient identiques à la description.

Morceaux dépareillés: Des morceaux provenant de différents billets sont assemblés. Vérifier que le numéro de série soit le même sur les deux moitiés et que tous les morceaux proviennent du même billet.

Billets déchirés: Les billets auxquels il manque des fragmentes peuvent perdre leur valeur. Tous les pays n'ont pas les mêmes règles pour le remplacement des billets déchirés. S'il manque un angle du billet, il n'y a aucun problème mais s'il manque 25% ou plus de la surface, le billet peut perdre sa valeur. Cependant, si la perte intervient lors d'un incendie, certaines banques centrales remplacent les billets. Des billets déchirés ou dégradés intentionnellement ne sont pas remplacés.

Billets comportant des inscriptions: Beaucoup de banques centrales n'acceptent pas les billets avec inscriptions surtout s'il s'agit de propagande politique ou de publicité. Des initiales ou des chiffres ne posent généralement pas de problème.

Fausse monnaie: pour reconnaître de la fausse monnaie, il faut connaître les différents systemes de sécurité utilisés pour la vraie monnaie.

Les machines à compter équipées de détecteurs"Anti-fausse-monnaie"peuvent être déjouées. Elles reconnaissent certains éléments de l'encre. Les faux-monnayeurs ajoutent des produits chimiques à l'encre, ce qui trompe l'appareil.

Papier

La plupart des billets de banque sont imprimés sur du papier de bonne qualité. Afin d'augmenter la protection contre l'imitation, le papier possede une ou plusieurs de ces caractéristiques:

Filaments: Des petits morceaux de soie ou d'autres fibres sont mélangés avec la pâte à papier. Les faux-monnayeurs les imitent avec de fins crayons.

Confettis ou planchettes: Des petits morceaux de papier ronds et de différentes couleurs sont mélangés avec la pâte quand le papier est fait. C'est le cas des billets canadiens.

Certaines planchettes sont enlacées à l'intérieur de la trame du papier. D'autres sont à la surface du billet, et peuvent être ôtées avec une aiguille. Les planchettes sont imitées par un point fait au crayon de couleur.

Fil de sécurité: Un fil ou filament de plastique ou de métal est inséré dans la trame du papier. On le voit en tenant le billet à contre-jour. Les faux monnayeurs essaient de les imiter en pliant le billet un grand nombre de fois à l'endroit ou devrait se trouver le fil, ou en imprimant une ligne épaisse au verso afin de donner une impression de filament. Si le billet est déchiré à l'endroit du filament, on peut voir le fil de métal ou de plastique.

Beaucoup de filaments de plastique ont des inscriptions visibles à la loupe.

Fil de sécurité segmenté: Le fil de sécurité présente des segments de plastique argenté visible sur le billet. Les copies ont des segments imprimés avec de l'encre de couleur métallique. Sur un vrai billet, le filament est continu quand on le regarde à la lumière.

Filigrane: Sûrement la plus ancienne méthode anti-imitation, est un dessin ou un chiffre visible lorsque le billet est tenu à contre-jour. Des différences dans l'épaisseur du papier créent l'image.

Les filigranes son imités avec de la cire, de l'encre jaune clair ou des impressions huileuses.

Pseudo filigrane: Sur des petites coupures où le risque de contrefaçon est faible, le filigrane est remplacé par une legère impression qui donne l'illusion d'un filigrane.

Hologrammes: Des motifs argentés sont appliqués sur le papier ou le plastique. L'image et les couleurs changent en fonction de l'angle de vue.

Impression

Lorque vous pensez qu'un billet pourrait être contrefait, vérifiez les details suivants:

Relief: La plupart des planches à billets sont gravées, ce qui crée sur le billet des reliefs qui peuvent être sentis avec le bout des doigts. Les copies faites avec une imprimante laser couleur auront le même toucher mais les couleurs ne correspondront pas exactement. Quand on observe un vrai billet à la loupe, on voit de fines lignes. Les imitations faites en copie laser ou impressions couleurs laissent apparaître de petits poinçons

MRI BANKERS' GUIDE TO FOREIGN CURRENCY
P.O.BOX 3174 HOUSTON TX 77253 USA

ronds ou rectangulaires pour donner l'impression de lignes.

Couleur: L'alternance de couleurs légères et soutenues est utilisée pour rendre l'imitation plus difficile. Pour vérifier comparer le billet douteux avec un vrai.

Image parfaite: Un petit dessin sur une face possède sa replique sur l'autre face. Lorsqu'on regarde le billet à la lumière, les deux images correspondent parfaitement. Il est difficile de réussir une image parfaite sans un équipement sophistiqué que la plupart des faux-monnayeurs ne peuvent pas acquérir. Les deux images sont souvent incomplètes mais, à la lumière, le dessin entier apparaît.

Numéro de série: Les numéros de série des vrais billets sont de même alignement et épaisseur.
Les numéros de série verticaux et de taille grossissante sont faits avec des machines spéciales et sont difficiles à contrefaire.

Micro-impression: Les mots écrits en très petits caractères ressemblent à un trait plein, mais à la loupe on peut les lire.

Caractères invisibles: Ils sont faits avec de l'encre visible uniquement au quartz ou aux ultraviolets.

Effets d'optique: Il s'agit de parties argentées ou dorées sur lesquelles une ou plusieurs images sont visibles lorsque le billet est incliné.

Impression latente: Certaines portions du billet ont des sculptures gravées. En regardant le billet de biais, ces dessins deviennent visibles.

Marques pour aveugles: Des marques en relief aident les aveugles à distinguer les différentes coupures. Sur les faux billets, ces marques peuvent être lisses.

Nom de l'imprimeur: Si le nom de l'imprimeur apparaît, il est souvent en petits caractères en bas au verso du billet. Sur les vrais billets l'écriture est régulière, alors que sur les faux elle ne l'est pas.

Rang des signataires: Le rang des fonctionnaires signataires est écrit en petits caractères. Les faux-monnayeurs ne les imitent pas souvent soigneusement. Les lettres ne sont donc pas régulières.

Instruments utiles

Voici les outils les plus utiles pour reconnaître les faux billets:

Loupe d'au moins 10X.
Lampe à UV (ultra-violets)

Les deux peuvent être achetées à un prix peu élevé chez un philatéliste.

Billets courants, démodés et échangeables

Courant: Billets largement utilisés.

Démodés: Ce sont les billets qui ont un cours légal mais que l'on ne trouve pas souvent en circulation car ils ont été remplacés. Théoriquement, ils ont cours, mais dans la pratique, il sont refusés. Vendre ce type de billets à des voyageurs peut créer des problèmes car ils vont être

refusés, les gens pensant qu'il sont sans valeur.

Voir la partie "Outmoded and redeemable notes" pour chaque pays.

Échangeables: Lorsqu'un billet est retiré de la circulation, il y a un délai pour l'échanger. Ce délai peut être de quelques jours comme de trente ans. Certains billets peuvent être échangeables sans limite de temps.

L'échange de billets périmés n'est pas un droit absolu. Certaines banques centrales se réservent le droit de refuser d'échanger les billets pendant le délai légal mais ceci est très rare.
D'autre part, après l'expiration des délais légaux et dans des circonstances spéciales, certaines banques centrales échangent toujours les billets périmés.

La démonétisation d'une émission peut être soudaine, avec fermeture des frontières pour empêcher le rapatriement des billets durant le court délai autorisé pour l'échange.

En fonction des restrictions ou de la réglementation monétaire, les billets hors-circulation ou échangeables peuvent être envoyés à la banque émettrice ou n'importe quel autre service mentionné dans ce guide pour l'échange.

Aucune responsabilité, expresse ou implicite, n'est engagée pour des pertes de change dues à des erreurs, à la variation du cours légal, ou a quelque autre raison que ce doit.

Billets de collection: Il existe un vaste marché de billets pour collectionneurs. Certains billets peuvent garder de la valeur même après avoir perdu leur cours légal. Cette valeur numismatique est basée sur la rareté, l'état de conservation, l'offre et la demande.

Veuillez consulter l'éditeur pour la vente de vieux billets. Nous vous conseillons de nous envoyer les billets par lettre recommandée. Après réception, nous les évaluerons et vous ferons une offre. Si celle-ci ne vous convient pas, nous vous renverrons les billets à nos frais.

Restrictions pour l'importation et l'exportation de billets.

Beaucoup de pays ont des lois et réglementations ayant pour but de contrôler les sommes et types de monnaie locale ou étrangère que les voyageurs peuvent faire rentrer ou sortir du territoire. Nous indiquons les règles applicables aux visiteurs étrangers non-résidents.

Pour cela, nous avons contacté les autorités monétaires de chaque pays pour avoir connaissance de leurs règlementations. Toutes n'ont pas répondu, ce qui nous a obligé à poursuivre des recherches non-officielles.

Les consulats, ambassades et offices nationaux de tourisme ne donnent pas toujours des réponses fiables.

Les informations fournies dans ce guide proviennent de sources considérées comme fiables. Cependant, nous ne prenons pas de responsabilité expresse ou

implicite quant à l'exactitude des renseignements, ou les conséquences de violation des règles, lois et règlement de circulation de la monnaie.

Arriver ou repartir avec des montants de devises raisonnables ne devrait pas poser de problèmes alors que de grosses sommes peuvent être suspectes (trafic de drogue, fuite de capitaux.) Le voyageur prudent évitera d'aller dans un pays avec des devises d'un pays ennemi.

Certains pays ont des lois particulières, comme rendre illégale l'introduction de certaines devises, mais pas d'autres. Un pays africain avait une loi, abrogée depuis, qui considérait comme un délit le fait d'avoir plus de USD 150 en monnaie locale.

D'autres pays forcent les voyageurs à changer un certain montant d'une monnaie forte à l'arrivée. D'autres encore interdisent de garder une quelconque monnaie étrangère. Lors de l'arrivée, vous devez tout convertir en monnaie locale et reconvertir en monnaie étrangère au moment du départ. Si les banques sont fermées le jour de votre départ, vous devez abandonner votre argent, car il est illégal de l'exporter.

Surtout ne déchirez pas vos billets. La monnaie étant un attribut de la souveraineté d'un pays, sa destruction peut être considérée comme un délit.

Cours officiel et marché parallèle

Les taux publiés s'appliquent aux touristes qui échangent leurs devises auprès de banques ou organismes officiels.

Lorsqu'il y a des restrictions pour l'échange de monnaies fortes, un marché parallèle se développe et propose des taux plus avantageux. Ce marché noir peur être ouvert et libre ou combattu et dangereux.

Utiliser le marché parallèle peut exposer à des risques de fraude et vous mettre hors la loi.

Le cours du marché parallèle peut être légèrement supérieur au cours officiel ou le dépasser largement, comme en Iraq où le cours du marché noir est 1,000 fois supérieur au cours bancaire.

La majorité des échanges de monnaie dans le monde se fait sur la base du marché libre ou parallèle.

Grosses et petites coupures.

Les bureaux de change utilisent différents taux en fonction de la valeur du billet. A cause des restrictions douanières, il se peut que les grosses coupures ne soient pas rapatriables. Cependant, les bureaux de change les accepteront, mais à un cours légèrement inférieur. Il en est de même pour les petites coupures car il faut couvrir les coûts d'expédition.

Pendant la saison touristique, les cambistes importent des petites coupures, et doivent les vendre à un taux légèrement supérieur pour couvrir les frais d'envoi.

MRI BANKERS' GUIDE TO FOREIGN CURRENCY
P.O.BOX 3174 HOUSTON TX 77253 USA

Wie man wertlose Währungen erkennt.

Währungen können aus verschiedenen Gründen wertlos sein:

Veränderte Banknoten: Eine echte Note von niedrigem Nennwert wird geändert, um sie als höherwertigeren Schein weiterzureichen. Überprüfen Sie, daß der Nennwert in Buchstaben und Ziffern übereinstimmt, und daß der Entwurf und die Farben mit dem Nennwert übereinstimmen.

Fragmente von verschiedenen Banknoten: Fragmente von verschiedenen Noten sind zusammengeklebt worden.

Falls Sie einen reparierten Geldschein einhandeln, überprüfen Sie, daß die Seriennummern übereinstimmen, und daß alle Stücke zur gleichen Banknote gehören.

Beschädigte Währung: Unvollständige Geldscheine können wertlos sein. Jedes Land hat seine eigenen Regelungen zur Einlösung von beschädigten Banknoten. Wenn nur eine Ecke eines Geldscheins fehlt, dann ist die Einlösung kein Problem. Wenn mehr als 25% der Note fehlen, dann ist sie unter Umständen wertlos.

Obwohl Zentralbanken sich das Recht vorbehalten, beschädigte Geldscheine nicht einzulösen, werden im Falle eines Feuers oft Ausnahmen gemacht.

Banknoten mit Inschriften: Der Großteil der Zentralbanken akzeptiert keine Geldscheine mit Inschriften. Besonders solche mit politischer Propaganda oder kommerzieller Werbung werden abgelehnt. Initialen oder Nummern stellen normalerweise kein Problem dar.

Falschgeld: Um Falschgeld zu erkennen, ist es notwendig, mit den verschiedenen Merkmalen der Banknoten vertraut zu sein.

Geldzählmaschinen, die sogar mit Sensoren gegen Falschgeld ausgerüstet sind, bringen nicht immer das richtige Ergebnis. Nur bestimmte Chemikalien können im Farbstoff erkannt werden. Gute Fälschungen enthalten die Chemikalien im Farbstoff und lassen dadurch das Falschgeld nicht erkennen.

Papier
Banknoten werden üblicherweise auf Hochqualitätspapier gedruckt. Um Fälschungen vorzubeugen, hat das Papier eines oder mehrere der folgenden Merkmale:

Fasern: Kleine seidenähnliche Fasern werden bei der Herstellung in das Papier gemischt. Diese Fasern sind unter dem Vergrößerungsglas sichtbar. Geldfälscher versuchen, diese Fasern mit feinen Buntstiften nachzuahmen.

Planchetten: Kleine verschiedenfarbige Konfettistückchen werden in das Papier eingearbeitet. Sie werden hauptsächlich in kanadischen Banknoten verwendet. Sie sind entweder im Papier eingebettet oder können auch auf beiden Seiten des Geldscheins gefunden werden. Planchetten können mit einer Nadel vom

Papier gelöst werden und werden mit Filzstiftpunkten imitiert.

Sicherheitsfaden: Ein Faden aus Metall oder Plastik ist vertikal in das Papier eingearbeitet. Er ist gut sichtbar, wenn man die Geldnote gegen das Licht hält.

Geldfälscher versuchen, durch mehrmaliges Falten der Note den Eindruck eines Sicherheitsfadens zu imitieren. Ein kleiner Riß an der Kante einer Banknote zeigt, ob sie echt oder gefälscht ist. Der Plastikfaden in der 1989-92 erschienenen deutschen Banknotenserie trägt eine Inschrift, die nur unter dem Vergrößerungsglas sichtbar ist.

Teilweise eingearbeiteter Sicherheitsfaden: Der Faden ist in kleinen "Fenstern" auf der Vorderseite der Banknote als unterbrochene silberne Linie sichtbar.

Wasserzeichen: Sie sind eine der ältesten Maßnahmen gegen Fälschungsversuche. Wenn man die Banknote ins Licht hält, wird eine Inschrift oder eine Figur sichtbar.

Wasserzeichen werden hergestellt, indem man die Dicke des Papiers während der Herstellung verändert. Dickere Teile erscheinen dunkler, dünnere Schichten erscheinen heller und schaffen so das gewünschte Abbild.

Fälscher imitieren Wasserzeichen mit Wachs oder Fetteindrücken an den gewünschten Stellen.

Pseudo Wasserzeichen: In Banknoten mit kleinerem Nennwert, bei denen das Fälschungsrisiko gering ist, wird das Wasserzeichen durch Lichteindrücke ersetzt. Auf diese Weise erscheint die Illusion eines Wasserzeichens.

Hologramme: Hologramme sind im Material, auf welchem die Banknote gedruckt wird, eingearbeitet. Das Abbild und die Farben verändern sich mit dem Blickwinkel.

Druckqualität
Bei einer verdächtig aussehenden Banknote beachten Sie bitte die folgenden Merkmale:

Stichtiefdruck: Die meisten Banknoten sind auf eingravierten Platten gedruckt, wodurch im fertigen Druck ein reliefartiges Bild entsteht, das man mit den Fingerspitzen fühlen kann.
Kopien von einem LaserFarbdrucker geben auch das Reliefgefühl, aber die Farben können nicht 100%-ig nachgeahmt werden. Auch feine Linien können von einem Laserdrucker nicht nachgeahmt werden. Anstelle von Linien produziert diese Maschine kleine runde oder rechteckige Punkte, die die Illusion einer Linie ergeben.

Farbe: Helle und dunkle Farbkombinationen werden verwendet um das Fälschen zu erschweren. Bitte vergleichen Sie die Farben einer verdächtigen Banknote mit einer echten.

Durchsichtregister: Teile des Musters auf der Vorderseite sind als perfektes Spiegelbild auf der Rückseite sichtbar. Extrem teure Maschinen sind notwendig, um eine exakte Inschrift zu erhalten. Diese Maschinen sind für Fälscher nicht

verfügbar.

In neueren Banknoten sind nur Teile des vollständigen Musters auf der Vorderseite sichtbar. Hält man die Banknote gegen das Licht, dann wird das komplette Muster sichtbar.

Seriennummern: Die Seriennummern echter Banknoten sind in Abstand und Druckstärke gleichmäßig. Fälschungen sind sehr selten gleichmäßig. Vertikale Seriennummern und Nummern mit zunehmender Größe werden mit speziellen Numerierungsmaschinen produziert und sind sehr schwer zu fälschen.

Mikrodruck: Das sind sehr klein gedruckte Inschriften. Das bloße Auge sieht nur eine gerade Linie. Unter dem Vergrößerungsglas kann man die Inschrift lesen.

Fluoreszenz: Mit einer speziellen Farbe aufgedruckte Inschriften, die bei normalem Licht unsichtbar sind, werden unter UV-Licht (z.B. Quarzlampe) sichtbar.

Optische Muster: Das sind gold- oder silberfarbige Siegel, die bei Blickwinkeländerung ein oder mehrere Abbilder zeigen.

Kippeffekt: Teile der Banknote weisen skulpturierte Farbreliefs auf, die nur bei bestimmten Blickwinkeln Inschriften oder bestimmte Bilder zeigen.

Blindenschrift: Viele Länder verwenden leicht fühlbare Muster, um Blinden das Unterscheiden verschiedener Nennwerte zu erleichtern. In Fälschungen sind diese Zeichen flach und nicht fühlbar.

Name der Druckerei: Üblicherweise findet man den Namen der Druckerei am unteren Teil der Rückseite der Banknote. Auf echten Geldscheinen sind die Buchstaben gleichmäßig gedruckt; auf Fälschungen nicht.

Titel der Signatoren: Die Titel der unterschreibenden Beamten sind in sehr kleinen Buchstaben gedruckt. Fälscher imitieren diese oft nicht perfekt genug, was zu ungleichmäßigen Buchstaben führt.

Nützliche Hilfsmittel:
Hier sind die besten Hilfsmittel zur Erkennung von Falschgeld:
▸ Ein gutes Vergrößerungsglas
▸ Eine UV-Lampe
Beide sind recht preiswert beim örtlichen Briefmarkenhändler erhältlich.

Im Umlauf befindliche, ausgelaufene und einlösbare Banknoten
Im Umlauf: Eine Banknote, die legales Zahlungsmittel ist und weitverbreitet verwendet wird.

Ausgelaufen: Eine Banknote, die legales Zahlungsmittel ist, aber weil sie durch eine neue Serie ersetzt wurde, nicht im täglichen Gebrauch ist. In der Theorie ist die Banknote aktuell, in der Praxis jedoch wird sie abgelehnt. Beim Einlösen dieser Banknoten können Reisende Schwierigkeiten bekommen, weil sie für wertlos gehalten werden.

In dieser Publikation können diese Banknoten im Teil "Outmoded and Redeemable Notes" gefunden werden.

Einlösbar: Wenn Banknoten aus dem Umlauf genommen werden, dann wird üblicherweise eine gewisse Zeitfrist zur Einlösung gegeben. Diese Einlösungsfrist kann von ein paar Tagen bis 30 Jahre dauern. Einige Hersteller lösen alte Währungen unbegrenzt ein.

Das Einlösen veralteter Banknoten ist kein absolutes Recht. Zentralbanken können die Einlösung verweigern, aber unter gewissen Umständen werden Banknoten noch eingelöst, nachdem alle rechtlichen Zeitgrenzen abgelaufen sind.

Abhängig von Währungsbeschränkungen und anderen Regelungen, können ausgelaufene und einlösbare Banknoten zur Herkunftsbank oder zu jedem in dieser Publikation genannten Einlösezentrum zur Einlösung gesendet werden.

Banknoten mit Sammlerwert: Es existiert ein großer Markt für alte Währungen zum Sammelzweck. Das heißt, daß einige Banknoten recht wertvoll sein können, obwohl sie als Zahlungsmittel wertlos sind.

Der numismatische Wert hängt von der Seltenheit, der Erhaltung der Banknote und Angebot und Nachfrage ab. Als zusätzlicher Service für unsere Abonnenten können die Herausgeber über die Verfügbarkeit alter Währungen konsultiert werden.

Wir empfehlen Ihnen, die Banknoten per Einschreiben zu schicken. Nach Erhalt prüfen wir die Banknoten und unterbreiten Ihnen ein Angebot für Ihre Zustimmung. Falls das Angebot abgelehnt wird, dann senden wir die Ware auf unsere Kosten wieder zurück.

Import- und Export-Beschränkungen.

Viele Länder haben Regeln und Vorschriften über Beträge und Arten von einheimischen und Fremdwährungen, die Touristen bei der Ein- und Ausreise beachten müssen.

Die hier publizierten Regeln treffen nur für ausländische Besucher zu.

Wir setzten uns mit den Fremdwährungs-Autoritäten jedes Landes in Verbindung, um die zutreffenden Beschränkungen zu erhalten.

Da nicht alle Länder antworteten, sind wirgezwungen, auch inoffizielle Informationsquellen zu verwenden. Konsulate, Botschaften und Touristenbüros haben leider nicht immer aktuelle Informationen.

Die in dieser Publikation gegebenen Informationen können jedoch als sehr zuverlässig gelten.

In jedem Falle muß man hervorheben, daß keine Verantwortung irgendeiner Art für die Richtigkeit der gebotenen Informationen oder für etwaige Folgen von Verletzungen der zutreffenden Import- und Exportgesetze, Beschränkungen und Regeln übernommen wird.

Man kann auf jeden Fall annehmen, daß der Besitz einer kleinen Menge Fremdwährung keine Probleme verursachen wird. Nimmt man aber einen großen Betrag mit auf die Reise, läuft man Gefahr, des Drogenschmuggels oder der Steuerhinterziehung verdächtigt zu werden.

Der erfahrene Reisende wird auch nicht versuchen, in ein Land die Währung verfeindeter Staaten einzuführen, z.B. den Irak mit israelischem Geld zu besuchen.

Einige Länder finden es ungesetzlich, bestimmte Fremdwährungen einzuführen, aber andere nicht. Ein altes, mittlerweile außer Kraft gesetztes Gesetz in einem afrikanischen Staat verbot z.B. den Besitz von mehr als $150 in der nationalen Währung.

In anderen Ländern sind Besucher verpflichtet, bei der Ankunft einen bestimmten Betrag in harter Währung umzutauschen. Andere wiederum erklären es für ungesetzlich, jegliche Fremdwährung zu besitzen. So muß man bei der Ankunft das gesamte Geld in die örtliche Währung umwechseln. Bei der Abreise darf man sein Geld wieder zurücktauschen. Ist die Bank zum Zeitpunkt des Rückflugs geschlossen, dann macht man sich strafbar, wenn man versucht, das Geld mit nach Hause zu nehmen. In diesem Falle ist es am besten, das Geld zu verschenken. Die Landeswährung stellt nämlich eines der Attribute der nationalen Souveränität dar. Deshalb kann die Zerstörung des Geldes

als Beleidigung der Nation angesehen und geahndet werden.

Offizielle und parallel Wechselkurse

Der veröffentlichte Kurs gilt für Touristen, die Währungen bei offiziellen Banken oder Wechselstuben wechseln.

Sobald es Beschränkungen für den Verkauf harter Währung gibt, entwickelt sich ein paralleler Markt (Schwarzmarkt), und ein höherer Kurs ist die Folge. Dieser parallele Markt kann sich frei und in der Öffentlichkeit entwickeln, aber er kann auch verfolgt werden und als gefährlich gelten.

Man muß betonen, daß der Geldwechsel auf dem parallelen Markt ein hohes Betrugsrisiko oder Schwierigkeiten mit dem Gesetz mit sich bringt.

Normalerweise liegt der Schwarzmarktkurs etwas höher als der offizielle Kurs, oder aber, wie es der Fall im Irak ist, der inoffizielle Kurs ist fast 1,000 Mal höher als der Bankkurs.

Der Großteil des Banknotenhandels wird auf der Basis von freien oder parallelen Wechselkursen abgehalten.

Währungen mit großem und kleinem Nennwert

Im Banknotenhandel gelten manchmal unterschiedliche Kurse für verschiedene Nennwerte. Aufgrund von Import- und Exportbeschränkungen kann man Banknoten mit großem Nennwert nicht wieder ins Ursprungsland einführen.

Deshalb diskontieren Händler große Banknoten. Andererseits können auch Banknoten mit kleinem Nennwert aufgrund hoher Rückführungkosten diskontiert werden.

Üblicherweise bringen Touristen Scheine mit großem Nennwert zurück, während Reisewillige eher Noten mit kleinem Nennwert für den Erstkontakt im fremden Land benötigen. Das ergibt die große Nachfrage für kleinere Banknoten.

Aus diesem Grund müssen Händler in der Reisesaison die kleineren Scheine importieren und verkaufen diese zu einen höheren Preis, um die Lieferungskosten auszugleichen.

MRI BANKERS' GUIDE TO FOREIGN CURRENCY
P.O.BOX 3174 HOUSTON TX 77253 USA

Como reconhecer cédulas sem valor.

O papel moeda pode ser invalidado por várias razões.

Notas alteradas: uma nota autêntica, de denominação baixa, é alterada para passar por nota de valor mais alto. Verifique se as quantias em palavras e cifras são iguais.

Fragmentos desemparelhados: uma nota reconstruída com pedaços de diferentes notas carece de valor. Quando receber uma nota remendada, verifique se a numeração de ambas metades são iguais e se todos os fragmentos pertencem a mesma nota.

Notas mutiladas: Notas às quais faltam pedaços talvez sejam total ou parcialmente inválidas. Se o que falta é apenas um canto da nota, geralmente não ha problema, mais se a perda é de 25% ou mais, é provavel que esta nota não tenha valor. Quando a perda ocorrer por fogo ou acidente, alguns bancos centrais poderão remir as notas em questão.

Os bancos centrais talvez se recusem a remir notas intencionalmente desfiguradas ou mutiladas.

Notas com inscrições: Alguns bancos centrais não aceitarão notas com inscrições, especialmente de propaganda política ou comercial. Iniciais ou números não costumam apresentar nenhum problema.

Dinheiro falsificado: Para reconhecer dinheiro falsificado é preciso estar familiarizado com os elementos de seguridade presentes numa nota. As máquinas de contar dinheiro, equipadas com um sensor "anti-falsificação" podem enganar-se. Elas detectam a presença de certos elementos existentes na tinta das notas genuínas. Os falsificadores acrecentam estes elementos à tinta, e as máquinas não são capazes de detectar a falsificação.

Papel

O dinheiro é geralmente impresso em papel de boa qualidade. Para aumentar a proteção contra falsificações, o papel tem uma ou mais das seguintes características:

Fios: pequenos fios de seda ou de outras fibras são misturadas ao papel. Podem ser vistas com lente de aumento. Os falsificadores as imitam usando lápis de cores claras.

Confetes: Pequenos confetes ou pedaços de papel de cores diferentes, incorporados à pasta do papel no processo de fabricação. Podem ser vistas nas notas canadenses.

Podem ser removidos com un ãlfinete. Os falsificadores os imitam pintando-os.

Fios de seguridade: Um fio metálico ou plástico, visível à contraluz, é engarçado no papel durante a fabricação. Os falsificadores tentam imitá-lo dobrando as notas muitas vezes no lugar onde deveriao estar o fio, criando assim a ilusão de uma linha mais grossa. Se um pequeno rasgão é feito no borde de uma nota

autêntica pode-se ver o fio. Muitas notas recentes incorporam no fio plástico uma inscrição visível com uma lente.

Fio de seguridade segmentado: Partes do filamento aparecem na cara da nota como segmentos prateados. Os falsificadores as imitam imprimindo os segmentos con tinta metálica prateada. Nas notas autênticas, pode-se ver uma linha contínua, à contra-luz.

Marca de agua ou filigrana: Um dos mais antigos recursos contra a falsificação, consiste em legendas ou figuras visíveis à contra-luz. Elas são criadas variando a espessura do papel durante a fabricação. As partes mais espessas parecem mais escuras e as mais finas parecem mais claras, criando desta maneira uma imagem. São imitadas com impressões de elementos gordurosos, de cera ou tintas opacas.

Pseudo-marcas de agua: Em notas de denominação baixa, onde o risco de falsificação é mínimo, a marca de agua é substituída por uma leve impressão que dá a ilusão de uma marca de agua.

Hologramas: Imagens metalisadas incorporadas ao papel, cujas figuras e cores variam segundo o ângulo de visão.

Impressão

Numa nota suspeita, verifique os seguintes detalhes:

Alto-relevo: A maioria das notas são impressas em chapas gravadas, que produzem um relevo sensível ao tacto. As cópias feitas em copiadoras "Laser" poderão dar esta sensação de relevo, mas as cores não combinarão exatamente.

Cor: Combinações de cores leves e brilhantes são usadas para dificultar as falsificacões. Compare as cores de uma nota suspeita com as de uma nota autêntica.

Registro perfeito: Uma parte do desenho da cara é reproduzido no verso da nota. Quando olhado à contra-luz, ambos coincidem completamente. Para obter um registro perfeito é necessário dispor de máquinas extremamente caras, que estão fora do alcance dos falsificadores.

Númeração das séries: os números das séries das notas autênticas tem uma espessura e alinhamento perfeitos. As séries de numeração vertical ou com números em progressão crecente são produzidas em máquinas especiais, e são difíceis de serem falsificadas.

Impressãõ microscópica: Algumas inscrições são impressas em um tipo muito pequeno, que a olho nu parece uma linha contínua, no entanto podem ser lidas com uma lente de aumento.

Impressões invisíveis: são impressões feitas com uma tinta visível somente à luz de quartzo ou ultravioleta.

Elementos óticos: Selos dourados ou prateados contendo imagens visíveis segundo o ângulo de observação.

Impressões latentes: Parte do desenho é esculpido de tal forma que, quando se olha a nota enviesadamente, legendas e figuras tornam-se visíveis.

Marcas em relevo: muitos países incluem marcas em relevo para ajudar os cegos a distinguirem as diferentes denominações. Nas notas falsificadas essas marcas talvez não sejam en relevo.

Nome do impressor: o nome do impressor, quando aparece, está geralmente no reverso da nota, em pé de imprensa. Nas notas autênticas a escrita é uniforme; nas falsas, não.

Títulos dos assinantes: os títulos dos funcionários que assinam as notas são escritos em letras muito pequenas. Muitas vezes os falsificadores não as imitam cuidadosamente, disto resultando letras desiguais.

Instrumentos úteis: para examinar cédulas bancárias recomendamos usar:
uma lente de 10x o más de aumento
uma lâmpada de quartzo.
Ambas podem ser obtidas a prezo razoável, através de filatelistas.

Notas corrente, fora de circulação e remíveis

Correntes: tem circulação legal e está em uso.

Fora de circulação: nota que do ponto de vista legal é corrente, mas por ter sido substituída por outra, não se encontra na circulação diária. Teoricamente pode ser corrente, mas na prática será recusada. Se uma delas é vendida a um turista, ele/ela talvez tenha dificuldade em gastá-la, porque em alguns lugares será recusada. Nesta publicação, a informação sobre estas notas pode ser encontrada na seção "Obsolete and redeemable notes".

Remíveis: quando as notas são postas fora de circulação, os bancos estabelecem um prazo para que sejam trocadas. Este período pode ser tão breve como alguns dias ou tão longo como trinta anos, ou mesmo ilimitado.

A remição de dinheiro obsoleto não é direito inalienável. Alguns bancos centrais talvez se recusem a remir determinadas notas, à sua discrição.

Por outro lado, depois de ter expirado todas as datas legais, em circunstâncias especiais, alguns bancos centrais ainda trocarão notas obsoletas.

Dependendo das restrições e regras, as notas obsoletas e remíveis podem ser enviadas ao banco emissor ou a qualquer dos centros de remição anunciados nesta publicação.

Notas colecionáveis: existe um amplo mercado para notas obsoletas com o fin de colecioná-las. Isto significa que algumas notas talvez sejam de alto preço ainda que tenham perdido o seu valor legal.

O valor numismático é baseado na raridade, estado de preservação, oferta e procura. Como um serviço adicional aos nossos leitores, o editor desta publicação pode ser consultado sobre como dispor de moedas ou notas obsoletas. Sugerimos que nos envie as notas por correio registrado. Uma vez recebidas serão avaliadas e uma oferta será submetida para aprovação, ao proprietário. Se a oferta não for aceita, as notas serão devolvidas.

Importacão e exportacão de dinheiro

Casa país tem seu próprio regulamento e condições sobre a quantidade e espécie de moeda local ou estrangeira com que os viajantes podem entrar ou sair do país.

As regras publicadas aqui são as que se aplicam aos estrangeiros não residentes, ou seja, visitantes.

O fato de consultar consulados, embaixadas e escritórios governamentais de turismo nem sempre produz respostas dignas de fé.

A informação dada nesta publicação foi obtida através de fontes consideradas de confiança. No entanto é preciso sublinhar que não aceitamos nenhuma responsabilidade expressa ou implícita, pelo que for entendido enquanto à precisão da informação dada, nem pelas consequências da violação de leis, regulamentos ou condições de importação-exportação de dinheiro.

O sentido comúm indica que qualquer pessoa que viaje a um país estrangeiro com uma quantidade razoável de dinheiro não deve ter nenhum problema; enquanto que, si levar uma grande quantidade corre o risco de ser suspeito de evasão de moeda ou impostos ou de tráfico de drogas. Um viajante prudente não visitará o Iraque levando moeda de Israel, por exemplo.

Alguns países tem leis peculiares, como considerar ilegal entrar com certas moedas, e outras não. Ha um país africano que tinha uma lei, hoje em dia revogada, que considerava um crime possuir mais do que o equivalente a US$ 150 em moeda local.

Outros países requerem que os visitantes troquem uma determinada quantia, ao contado, quando entram no país. Outros ainda, consideram ilegal possuir qualquer quantidade de moeda estrangeira. Ao chegar deve-se trocar tudo o que se leva à moeda local e ao sair, reconverte-se à moeda estrangeira. Se o banco estiver fechado no dia dã saída, não se poderá fazer a reconversão e, desde que é ilegal exportar a moeda do país em questão, o melhor que se faz é dá-lo de presente. *Nem pense em rasgá-lo.* O dinheiro é um dos atributos de soberania de um país e destruí-lo constitui um insulto à nação.

Cambio oficial e paralelo

As cotações nesta publicação se aplicam aos turistas que troquem dinheiro estrangeiro em bancos e casas de câmbios oficiais.

Um mercado paralelo se desenvolve quando ha restrições para a compra de moeda estrangeira e um preço mais alto Este mercado paralelo pode ser livre e aberto ou perseguido e perigoso.

Convem prevenir que trocar dinheiro no mercado paralelo supõe um grande risco de ser roubado, além de problemas com as autoridades.

O mercado paralelo pode oferecer preços um pouco mais altos que o mercado oficial, ou pode ser muitas vezes mais alto, como no Iraque, onde o preço não-oficial é mais ou menos 1,000 vezes maior do que o preço do banco.

Notas grandes e pequenas

Diferentes preços talvez sejam aplicados no câmbio de notas, de acordo com suas denominações.

Devido às restrições de importação e exportação, notas de denominação muito alta talvez não possam ser legalmente reintroduzidas no país de origem. Portanto, no estrangeiro a cotação é mais baixa. Por outro lado, as notas de pouco valor tambem podem ter uma cotação mais baixa por causa do custo muito alto de repatriá-las.

Os visitantes estrangeiros geralmente trazem notas de alta denominação, e os viajantes locais pedem notas de pequena denominação para custear suas despesas iniciais no estrangeiro, o que causa uma demanda de notas de baixa denominação.

Durante a temporada turística os cambistas devem importá-las e vendê-las com uma comissão para recuperar o custo de importação.

Como reconocer billetes sin valor

El papel moneda puede carecer de valor por varias razones:

Alteración: Un billete auténtico de poco valor es alterado para pasarlo por uno mayor. Verifique que los importes en palabras y cifras coincidan, y que el color y diseño correspondan.

Fragmentos híbridos: Un billete reconstruido con trozos de billetes diferentes carece de valor. Al recibir un billete pegado, verifique que la numeración de ambas mitades coincida, y que todos los fragmentos sean del mismo billete.

Dinero dañado: Faltándole un trozo, un billete puede perder parte o todo su valor. Faltando muy poco, generalmente no hay problema, pero si falta el 25% o más, el billete puede perder su valor.

Sin embargo, algunos bancos centrales aceptan billetes dañados en incendios o accidentes aunque estén incompletos.

La mayoría de los bancos centrales rehusan redimir billetes dañados intencionalmente.

Dinero robado: En algunos robos de dinero se conocen los números de serie de los billetes robados, los cuáles pueden entonces ser no negociables. De presentarse un lote de billetes nuevos o usados

manchados de rojo, hay que tener en cuenta que en caso de robo algunos bancos ponen una "bomba" que mancha con tinta roja el dinero una vez que los ladrones huyen. Pueden haber recompensas para quienes quienes ayudan a recuperar dinero robado.

Inscripciones: Muchos bancos centrales no redimen billetes con inscripciones de propaganda política o comercial. Las iniciales o cifras casi nunca presentan problemas.

Dinero falso: Para detectar falsificaciones es necesario conocer los elementos de seguridad presentes en el papel moneda.

Las máquinas contadoras con un sensor para reconocer billetes falsos no son totalmente confiables. Detectan ciertos elementos presentes en la tinta de los billetes genuinos. Los falsificadores agregan esos elementos, y las máquinas ya no pueden reconocerlos.

Papel

La mayoría de los billetes se imprimen sobre papel de alta calidad. Para aumentar la protección contra las falsificaciones, el papel tiene varias elementos:

Hebras: A la pasta del papel se agregan hebras de seda u otras fibras. Se pueden ver con una lupa. Los falsificadores las imitan con lápices de colores.

Confetti: Pequeños discos de color agregados a la pasta del papel durante su

fabricación. Se ven en los billetes canadienses. Con un alfiler se los puede remover. Los falsificadores los imitan pintándolos sobre el papel.

Hilo de seguridad: Durante la fabricación del papel se introduce en su trama un hilo metálico o plástico, visible al trasluz. Los falsificadores los imitan doblando el billete muchas veces para que el doblez parezca una línea gruesa, o imprimiendo una línea negra en el reverso.
Rompiendo el borde de un billete genuino es posible ver el hilo de metal o plástico. Algunos filamentos tienen inscripciones.

Hilo de seguridad segmentado: Partes del filamento aparecen en el frente del billete como segmentos plateados. Los falsificadores los imitan imprimiendo los segmentos con tinta metálica plateada. En los billetes genuinos, mirando al trasluz se ve un línea llena.

Marca de agua o filigrana: Uno de los mas antiguos elementos de seguridad. Diferencias de espesor en el papel crean zonas oscuras y claras, las que generan una imagen al trasluz. Se imitan con impresiones grasas, de cera o tinta amarilla.

Seudo filigrana: En billetes de poco valor, donde el riesgo de falsificación es mínimo, la filigrana es reemplazada por una lígera impresión.

Hologramas: Imágenes plateadas incorporadas al papel, cuyas figuras y colores varían según el ángulo de observación.

MRI BANKERS' GUIDE TO FOREIGN CURRENCY
P.O.BOX 3174   HOUSTON TX 77253   USA

Impresión

Si un billete es dudoso, verifique los siguientes detalles:

Relieve: Casi todos los billetes son impresos con planchas grabadas, que producen un relieve que puede sentirse al tacto. Las copias hechas con copiadoras a color "Laser" tienen relieve, pero los colores no coinciden perfectamente.

Bajo lupa las líneas en los billetes auténticos se ven nítidas, mientras que las falsificaciones hechas con "laser" o tricromía se ven como puntitos que crean la ilusión de una línea.

Color: Los billetes auténticos tienen combinaciones de colores pálidos y vivos, muy difíciles de copiar. Compare los colores con un billete genuino.

Registro perfecto: Pequeños diseños del frente y reverso coinciden cuando son vistos al trasluz. Para obtener registro perfecto hacen falta máquinas muy complejas que están fuera del alcance de los falsificadores.

El diseño de cada lado puede ser parcial, pero vista al trasluz, la imagen aparece completa.

Numeración: Los números de serie en los billetes auténticos son parejos y bien alineados.

Las numeraciones verticales o de tamaño escalonado se imprimen con máquinas especiales, y son difíciles de falsificar.

Impresión microscópica: Leyenda en tipo muy pequeño, que a simple vista parece una línea llena, pero que se puede leer con una lente.

Impresión invisible: Hecha con tinta que sólo se puede ver bajo luz ultravioleta o de cuarzo.

Elementos ópticos variables: Sellos plateados o dorados, que presentan imágenes variables según el ángulo de observación.

Impresión latente: Parte del diseño es esculpido de tal forma que cuando se mira el billete al sesgo, se pueden ver letras o diseños latentes.

Marcas para ciegos: Marcas en alto relieve para ayudar a los ciegos a reconocer los distintos valores. En los billetes falsos falta el relieve.

Pie de imprenta: El nombre del impresor, cuando aparece, generalmente es en el borde inferior del reverso. Las letras son pequeñas, bien alineadas y de espesor parejo. En los falsos son desparejas, y a veces con errores.

Títulos de los firmantes: Igual que en el pie de imprenta, las letras deben ser muy parejas.

Herramientas útiles:

Para examinar billetes recomendamos usar:

▸ Una lupa de 10X o mas aumento.
▸ Una lampara de cuarzo.
Ambas pueden conseguirse a precio razonable a través de filatelistas.

Billetes corrientes, fuera de uso y canjeables

Corriente: Tiene curso legal, y se usa ampliamente.

Fuera de uso: Billete que desde el punto de vista legal es corriente, pero como es poco usual en circulación, el público lo rechaza, pensando que carece de valor.

No es aconsejable vender estos billetes a viajeros, pues pueden tener problemas.

Estos billetes estan listados en la sección "Outmoded and Redeemable notes".

Canjeable: Al retirar billetes de circulación, los bancos centrales dan plazo para su canje, desde unos pocos días hasta muchos años, o aun sin límite.

La información proporcionada en esta guía se basa en comunicaciones oficiales, y de no ser posible, en consultas con bancos locales y otras fuentes.

No asumimos ninguna resposibilidad expresa o implícita por las pérdidas o problemas que puedan ocurrir por la desmonetización de billetes, o por errores en la información publicada.

El retiro de billetes puede ser súbito, con cierre de fronteras para evitar su repatriación durante los pocos días en que se pueden canjear, o limitado a una pequeña cantidad por persona.

El canje de billetes fuera de circulación no es un derecho absoluto, y algunos bancos centrales pueden rehusarlo aun dentro del plazo legal.

Por otra parte, después que éste expiró, otros bancos centrales siguen canjeando billetes desmonetizados si hay una buena razón por la cual no fueron presentados a tiempo.
Si las disposiciones aduaneras lo permiten, los billetes retirados pueden ser enviados para su canje al banco emisor, o a alguno de los servicios de canje que anuncian en esta publicación.

Billetes para coleccionistas: Hay un mercado amplio para billetes de colección. Muchos billetes vencidos tienen valor, de acuerdo con su rareza, estado de conservación y oferta y demanda.

Invitamos a nuestros suscriptores a consultarnos sobre el valor de billetes desmonetizados que posean.

Restricciones sobre el movimiento de dinero

Muchos paises limitan las cantidades y tipos de dinero que los viajeros pueden traer o llevar consigo, o lo prohiben totalmente. La información publicada se refiere a normas que se aplican a viajeros no residentes.

Hemos pedido información oficial a las autoridades monetarias de todos los paises, pero no todas contestaron, por lo que tuvimos que buscar otras fuentes de información.

Las consultas a consulados, embajadas y oficinas nacionales de turismo no siempre

La información publicada fué obtenida de fuentes consideradas buenas, pero no asumimos ninguna responsabilidad expresa o implícita por errores o consecuencias que puedan surgir de las violaciones de esas reglas, o cualquier otra pérdida de cualquier naturaleza.

Algunas paises prohiben la importación de ciertas monedas. Cierto país africano tenía una ley que penaba poseer más del equivalente de US$150 en moneda local.

El sentido común indica que arribar o partir con una cantidad grande de dinero puede despertar sospechas de tráfico de drogas o evasión impositiva.

Igualmente, no es prudente visitar ciertos paises llevando dinero de sus enemigos.

En algunos paises los visitantes están obligados a canjear un mínimo de moneda fuerte. Otros requieren que el viajero cambie tòdo su dinero al llegar. Al salir puede reconvertir. Si en ese momento los bancos están cerrados no puede, y como es prohibido exportar dinero local, no lo puede sacar.
Ni pensar en romperlo, pues como el dinero es un atributo de soberanía nacional, destruirlo es considerado un crimen de insulto a la nación.

Tipos de cambio oficiales y paralelos

Publicamos la cotización que se aplica a turistas cambiando dólares en bancos o cambios oficiales.

Las restricciones para la compra de moneda fuerte, crean un mercado paralelo o negro, con cotización más alta. Ese mercado puede ser abierto y libre, o clandestino y perseguido.

Cambiar en el mercado negro lleva el riesgo de ser engañado, robado, o de tener problemas con las autoridades.

El mercado paralelo puede ser apenas 5 o 10% más alto que el oficial, o mucho más alto, como en Iraq, donde fué cerca de 1,000 veces superior al tipo bancario.

Los cambistas basan sus cotizaciones para billetes extranjeros en el mercado paralelo.

Billetes grandes y pequeños

Para algunas divisas se aplican cotizaciones diferentes según se trate de billetes pequeños o grandes.

Las cotizaciones mas bajas se aplican porque la repatriación de billetes grandes puede estar prohibida, o porque cuesta mucho enviar billetes pequeños.

Durante la temporada de turismo los cambistas importan billetes pequeños, por los que cobran premio para recuperar su costo de importación.

MRI BANKERS' GUIDE TO FOREIGN CURRENCY
P.O.Box 3174 HOUSTON TX 77253 USA

Currency codes and abbreviations

(⋆) ISO Codes

$	Bermuda / dollar
$	Brunei / dollar
$	Cape Verde / escudo
$	Chile / peso
$	Colombia / peso
$	Cuba / peso
$	Liberia / dollar
$	Malaysia / ringgit
$	México / peso
$	New Zealand / dollar
$	Portugal / escudo
$	Singapore / dollar
$	Solomon Islands / dollar
$	Tonga / pa'anga
$	USA / dollar
$	Samoa / tala
$A	Australia / dollar
$F	Fiji Isl / dollar
$U	Uruguay / peso uruguayo
AED⋆	United Arab Emirates / dirham
Af	Afghanistan / afghani
AFA⋆	Afghanistan / afghani
Afl	Netherlands Antilles / guilder
AFL	Aruba / guilder
ALL⋆	Albania / lek
AMD⋆	Armenia / dram
ANG⋆	Netherlands Antilles / guilder
AOR⋆	Angola / kwanza reajustado
ARS⋆	Argentina / peso
A$	Australia / dollar
ATS⋆	Austria / schilling
AUD⋆	Australia / dollar
AWG⋆	Aruba / florin
AZM⋆	Azerbaijan / manat
B	Panamá / balboa
B	Thailand / baht
B/	Panamá / balboa
BAD⋆	Bosnia-Hercegovina / dinar
BAM⋆	Bosnia-Hercegovina / Convertible mark
BBD⋆	Barbados / dollar
BD	Bahrain / dinar
BD$	Bermuda / dollar
BDS$	Barbados / dollar
BDT⋆	Bangladesh / taka
BEF⋆	Belgium / franc
BF	Belgium / franc
BGL⋆	Bulgaria / lev
BGN⋆	Bulgaria / (New) lev
BHD⋆	Bahrain / dinar
BIF⋆	Burundi / franc
BMD⋆	Bermuda / dollar
BND⋆	Brunei / dollar
BOB⋆	Bolivia / boliviano
Br	Ethiopia / birr
BRL⋆	Brazil / real
BR$	Brunei / ringgit
Bs	Bolivia / boliviano
Bs	Venezuela / bolívar
BSD⋆	Bahamas / dollar
B$	Bahamas / dollar
B$	Brunei / ringgit
BTN⋆	Bhutan / ngultrum
BWP⋆	Botswana / pula
BYB⋆	Belarus / ruble
BZD⋆	Belize / dollar
BZ$	Belize / dollar
C/	Costa Rica / colón
C/	El Salvador / colón
C/	Ghana / cedi

C/	Nicaragua / córdoba
CAD⋆	Canada / dollar
Can$	Canada / dollar
CDF⋆	D.R. Congo / franc congolais
CDN	Canada / dollar
CF	Comoros / franc
CFA Fr	Fr. CFA / franc
CFAF	CFA / franc
CFPF	CFP / franc
Ch$	Chile / peso
CHF⋆	Switzerland / franc
CI$	Cayman Islands / dollar
CLF⋆	Chile / unidades de fomento
CLP⋆	Chile / peso
CNY⋆	China / yuan Renminbi
Col$	Colombia / peso
COP⋆	Colombia / peso
CR	Cambodia / riel
CRC⋆	Costa Rica / colón
CRD	Croatia / dinar
CR$	Brazil / cruzeiro real
C$	Nicaragua / córdoba
Cub$	Cuba / peso
CUP⋆	Cuba / peso
CVE⋆	Cape Verde / escudo
C.V.	Cape Verde / escudo
CYP⋆	Cyprus / pound
CZK⋆	Czech Republic / koruna
D	Gambia / dalasi
D	Tunisia / dinar
D	Vietnam / dong
Đ	Vietnam / dong
DA	Algeria / dinar
Db	São Tome & Principe / dobra
DEM⋆	Germany / Deutsche Mark
DF	Djibouti / franc
Dfl	Netherlands / guilder
DH	Morocco / dirham
Dh	United Arab Emirates / dirham
Din.	Yugoslavia / dinar
DJF⋆	Djibouti / franc
DKK⋆	Denmark / krone
DKr	Denmark / krone
DM	Germany / Deutsche Mark
DOP⋆	Dominican Rep. / peso
Dr	Greece / drachma
Δρ	Greece / drachma
DZD⋆	Algeria / dinar
E	Swaziland / emalangeni
€	Euro
ECU	European currency unit
EEK	Estonia / kroon
EGP⋆	Egypt / pound
ECS	Ecuador / sucre
EC$	East Caribbean / dollar
EEK	Estonia / kroon
ERN	Eritrea / nakfa
Esc	Portugal / escudo
ESP⋆	Spain / peseta
ETB⋆	Ethiopia / birr
EUR⋆	Euro
F	Burundi / franc
F	Comoros / franc
F	Djibouti / franc
F	France / franc
F	Luxembourg / franc
f	Rwanda / franc
f	Netherlands / guilder
FBu	Burundi / franc
FF	France / franc
FIM⋆	Finland / markka
FJD⋆	Fiji / dollar
FKP⋆	Falkland-Malvinas / pound
FKr	Faroes / krone
fl	Netherlands / guilder
FMG	Madagascar / franc
Fmk	Finland / markka
Fr	Switzerland / franc
FRF⋆	France / franc

FRW	Rwanda / franc
F$	Fiji / dollar
Ft	Hungary / forint
G	Haiti / gourde
G	Netherlands / guilder
G/	Paraguay / guaraní
GBP⋆	United Kingdom / pound
GEL⋆	Georgia / lari
GF	Guinea-Conakry / franc
GHC⋆	Ghana / cedi
GIP⋆	Gibraltar / pound
GMD⋆	Gambia / dalasi
GNF⋆	Guinea-Conakry / franc
GNS⋆ (obsolete)	Guinea-Conakry / syli
GRD⋆	Greece / drachma
G$	Guyana / dollar
GTQ⋆	Guatemala / quetzal
GWE⋆ (obsolete)	Guinea-Bissau / escudo
GWP⋆ (obsolete)	Guinea-Bissau / peso
GYD⋆	Guyana / dollar
Hfl	Netherlands / guilder
HKD⋆	Hongkong / dollar
HK$	Hongkong / dollar
HNL⋆	Honduras / lempira
HRD⋆ (obsolete)	Croatia / dinar
HRK⋆	Croatia / kuna
HTG⋆	Haiti / gourde
HUF⋆	Hungary / forint
I/.	Perú / inti (obsolete)
ID	Iraq / dinar
IDR⋆	Indonesia / rupiah
IEP⋆	Ireland / punt
IKr	Iceland / króna
ILR⋆ (obsolete)	Israel / old sheqel
ILS⋆	Israel / sheqel
INR⋆	India / rupee
IQD⋆	Iraq / dinar
IR	India / rupee
IR£	Ireland / punt
IRR⋆	Iran / rial
ISJ⋆ (obsolete)	Iceland / old krona
ISK⋆	Iceland / króna
ITL⋆	Italy / lira
JD	Jordan / dinar
JMD⋆	Jamaica / dollar
JOD⋆	Jordan / dinar
JPY⋆	Japan / yen
J$	Jamaica / dollar
K	Czech Rep. / korun
K	Lao / kip
K	Myanmar (Burma) / kyat
K	Papua New Guinea / kina
K	Slovakia / korun
K	Zaïre / nouveau makuta
K	Zambia / kwacha
KD	Kuwait / dinar
KES⋆	Kenya / shilling
KGS⋆	Kyrgyzstan / sum
KHR⋆	Cambodia / riel
KMF⋆	Comoros / franc
KN	Lao / new kip
Kp	Lao / kip
KPW⋆	Korea P R / won
Kr	Denmark / krone
Kr	Iceland / króna
Kr	Norway / krone
Kr	Sweden / krone
KRW⋆	Korea, Rep / won
KSh	Kenya / shilling
KWD⋆	Kuwait / dinar
KYD⋆	Cayman / dollar
KZR	Angola / kwanza reajustado
£	Falkland-Malvinas / pound
£	Gibraltar / pound
£	Ireland / pound
£	Saint Helena / pound
£	United Kingdom / pound

MRI Bankers' Guide to Foreign Currency
P.O.Box 3174 Houston TX 77253 USA

£C . . . . Cyprus / pound
£Ir . . . . Ireland / punt
£m . . . . Malta / lira
L . . . . Albania / lek
L . . . . Honduras / lempira
L . . . . Italy / lira
L . . . . Lebanon / livre
L . . . . Romania / leu
LAK★ . . . . Lao / kip
LBP★ . . . . Lebanon / livre
LD . . . . Libya / dinar
LE . . . . Egypt / pound
Le . . . . Sierra Leone / leone
Lemp . . . . Honduras / lempira
Lit . . . . Italy / lira
LKR★ . . . . Shri Lanka / rupee
LL . . . . Lebanon / livre
Lm . . . . Malta / lira
Lps. . . . . Honduras / Lempira
LRD★ . . . . Liberia / dollar
Ls . . . . Latvia / lats
LS . . . . Syria / pound
LSL★ . . . . Lesotho / loti
LSM★ (obsolete) . . . . . . Lesotho / maloti
LT . . . . Turkey / lira
LTL★ . . . . Lithuania / litas
LUF★ . . . . Luxembourg / franc
LuxF . . . . Luxembourg / franc
Lv . . . . Bulgaria / leva
LVL★ . . . . Latvia / lats
LVR★ (obsolete) . . . . Latvia / rublis
LYD★ . . . . Libya / dinar

M . . . . Lesotho / maloti
M . . . . Mozambique / metical
M$ . . . . Macao / pataca
MAD★ . . . . Morocco / dirham
MAF★ (obsolete) . . . . Mali / franc
Mau . . . . Rs Mauritius / rupee
MDL★ . . . . Moldova / leu
Mex$ . . . . México / peso
MGF★ . . . . Madagascar / franc
mk . . . . Finland / markka
MK . . . . Malawi / kwacha
MKD★ . . . . Macedonia / denar
MMK★ . . . . Myanmar / kyat
MNT★ . . . . Mongolia / tugrug
MOP★ . . . . Macao / pataca
MRO★ . . . . Mauritania / ouguiya
M$ . . . . Malaysia / ringgit
Mt . . . . Mozambique / metica
MTL★ . . . . Malta / lira
MTP★ (obsolete) . . . . Malta / lira
MUR★ . . . . Mauritius / rupee
MVR★ . . . . Maldives / rufiyaa
MWK★ . . . . Malawi / kwacha
MXN★ . . . . Mexico / nuevo peso
MXP★ (obsolete) . . . . México / peso
MYR★ . . . . Malaysia / ringgit
MZE★ (obsolete) . Mozambique / escudo
MZM★ . . . . Mozambique / metica

N . . . . Nigeria / naira
NAD★ . . . . Namibia / dollar
NAf . . . . . Netherlands Antilles / guilder
NAfl . . . . . Netherlands Antilles / guilder
NFA . . . . Eritrea / Nakfa
Nfl . . . . Netherlands / guilder
NGN★ . . . . Nigeria / naira
NIC★ (obsolete) . . . Nicaragua / córdoba
NIO★ . . . . . . Nicaragua / córdoba oro
NIS . . . . Israel / new sheqel
NK . . . . Zaïre / new makuta
Nkr . . . . Norway / krone
NKz . . . . . . Angola / new kwanza
NLG★ . . . . . . Netherlands / guilder
NOK★ . . . . Norway / krone
NPR★ . . . . Nepal / rupee
NRs . . . . Nepal / rupee
N$ . . . . México / new peso
N$ . . . . Namibia / dollar

N$ . . . . Uruguay / nuevo peso
NTD . . . . Taiwan (ROC) / yuan
NT$ . . . . Taiwan (ROC) / yuan
Nu . . . . Bhutan / ngultrum
NUr$ . . . . Uruguay / nuevo peso
NZ . . . . New Zaïre / zaïre
NZD★ . . . . New Zealand / dollar
NZ$ . . . . New Zealand / dollar

OMR★ . . . . Oman / rial
Ös . . . . Austria / schilling
Ostmk . . . . German Dem Rep / Mark (obsolete)

P . . . . Botswana / pula
P . . . . Macao / pataca
₱ . . . . Philippines / piso
PAB★ . . . . Panamá / balboa
Pat . . . . Macao / pataca
PEN★ . . . . Perú / nuevo sol
PG . . . . Guinea-Bissau / peso
PGK★ . . . . . Papua New Guinea / kina
PHP★ . . . . Philippines / piso
PKR★ . . . . Pakistan / rupee
PLN★ . . . . Poland / new zloty
PRs . . . . Pakistan / rupees
Ptas . . . . Spain / peseta
PTE★ . . . . Portugal / escudo
Pts . . . . Spain / pesetas
PYG★ . . . . Paraguay / guaraní

Q/ . . . . Guatemala / quetzal
QAR★ . . . . Qatar / riyal
QR . . . . Qatar / riyal

R . . . . Cambodia / riel
R . . . . South Africa / rand
Rbl. . . . Commonwealth of Independent States / ruble
RD$ . . . . Dominican Rep / peso
Re . . . . India / rupee
Re . . . . Nepal / rupee
Re . . . . Pakistan / rupee
RE . . . . Shri Lanka / rupee
Rf . . . . Maldives / rufiyaa
RF . . . . Rwanda / franc
RI . . . . Iran / rial
RM . . . . Malaysia / ringgit
RMB . . . . . . China PR / yuan Renminbi
RO . . . . Oman / rial
ROL★ . . . . Romania / leu
Rp . . . . Indonesia / rupiah
Rs . . . . India / rupees
Rs . . . . Mauritius / rupees
Rs . . . . Nepal / rupees
Rs . . . . Pakistan / rupees
Rs . . . . Arabia / riyals
Rs . . . . Shri Lanka / rupee
R$ . . . . Brazil / real
RUB★ . . . . . . Russia / (new) ruble (1998)
RUR★ . . . . . Russia / ruble (pre-1998)
RWF★ . . . . Rwanda / franc

S . . . . Latvia / santim
S . . . . Austria / schilling
S/ . . . . Ecuador / sucre
S/ . . . . Perú / sol
S$ . . . . Singapore / dollar
SAR★ . . . . Saudi Arabia / riyal
SBD★ . . . . Solomon Islands / dollar
SCR★ . . . . Seychelles / rupee
SDD★ . . . . Sudan / dinar
SDP★ (obsolete) . . . . Sudan / pound
SEK★ . . . . Sweden / krona
Sf . . . . Suriname / guilder
Sfr . . . . Switzerland / franc
SGD★ . . . . Singapore / dollar
Sh . . . . Kenya / shilling
Sh . . . . Tanzania / shilling
Sh . . . . Uganda / shilling
SHP★ . . . . . Saint Helena / pound
SI$ . . . . Solomon Islands / dollar
SIT★ . . . . Slovenia / tolar

Sk . . . . Slovakia / koruna
SKK★ . . . . Slovakia / koruna
SKr . . . . Sweden / krona
SL Rs . . . . Shri Lanka / rupee
SLL★ . . . . Sierra Leone / leone
So Sh . . . . Somalia / shillin
SOS★ . . . . Somalia / shillin
SR . . . . Saudi Arabia / riyals
SR . . . . Seychelles / rupee
SRG★ . . . . Suriname / guilder
SRls . . . . Saudi Arabia / riyals
STD★ . . . . . São Tome & Principe / dobra
SUR★ (obsolete) . . Soviet Union / rouble
SVC★ . . . . El Salvador / colón
SwFr . . . . Switzerland / franc
SYP★ . . . . Syria / pound
SZL★ . . . . Swaziland / lilangeni

T . . . . Mongolia / tugrug
T$ . . . . Tonga / pa'anga
TD . . . . Tunisia / dinar
THB★ . . . . Thailand / baht
TJR★ . . . . Tajikistan / ruble
Tk . . . . Bangladesh / taka
TL . . . . Turkey / lira
TMM★ . . . . . Turkmenistan / manat
TND★ . . . . Tunisia / dinar
TOP★ . . . . Tonga / pa'anga
TRL★ . . . . Turkey / lira
T Sh . . . . Tanzania / shilling
TTD★ . . . . Trinidad and Tobago / dollar
TT$ . . . . . Trinidad and Tobago / dollar
Tug . . . . Mongolia / tugruk
TWD★ . . . . Taiwan (ROC) / yuan
TZS★ . . . . Tanzania / shilling

UAK★ . . . . Ukraine / karbovanets
UGS★ (obsolete) . . . . . Uganda / shilling
UGX★ . . . . Uganda / new shilling
UKS . . . . . . Uzbekistan / sum-currency
UM . . . . Mauritania / ouguiya
USD★ . United States of America / dollar
USh . . . . Uganda / shilling
US$ . . United States of America / dollar
UYU★ . . . . Uruguay / peso uruguayo

VEB★ . . . . Venezuela / bolívar
VND★ . . . . Vietnam / dong
Vt . . . . Vanuatu / vatu
VUV★ . . . . Vanuatu / vatu

W . . . . Korea PR / won
W . . . . Korea, Rep / won
₩ . . . . Korea, Rep / won
Wn . . . . Korea PR / won
WS$ . . . . Samoa / tala
WST★ . . . . Samoa / tala

XAF★ . . . . CFA Central / franc
XCD★ . . . . East Caribbean / dollar
XDR★ . . . . IMF / SDR
XEU★ . . . ECU (European Currency Unit)
XOF★ . . . . CFA West / franc
XPF★ . . . . . French Polynesia / CFA franc

Y . . . . China PR / yuan Renminbi
¥ . . . . Japan / yen
YER★ . . . . Yemen / rial
YR . . . . Yemen / rial
YUM★ . . . . . Yugoslavia / new dinar 1995

Z . . . . Zaïre / zaïre
Z . . . . Zaïre / nouveau zaïre
Z$ . . . . Zimbabwe / dollar
ZAL★ . . . . South Africa / Financial rand
ZAR★ . . South Africa / Commercial rand
ZL . . . . Poland / zloty
ZMK★ . . . . Zambia / kwacha
ZRN★ (obsolete) . . . . . Zaïre / new zaïre
ZRZ★ (obsolete) . . . . Zaïre / zaïre
zt . . . . Poland / zloty
ZWC★ (obsolete) . . Zimbabwe / dollar
ZWD★ . . . . Zimbabwe / dollar

MRI BANKERS' GUIDE TO FOREIGN CURRENCY
P.O.Box 3174 HOUSTON TX 77253 USA

Currency index

Italics represent fractions.

Afghani(s) .... Afghanistan
Agora/agorot .... Israel
Ariary .... Madagascar
Avo(s) .... Macao
Baht .... Thailand
Baisa .... Oman, Pakistan
Balboa(s) .... Panama
Birr .... Ethiopia
Bolivar(es) .... Venezuela
Boliviano(s) .... Bolivia
Butut .... The Gambia
Cedi .... Ghana
Cent(s) .... Aruba, Australia,
The Bahamas, Barbados, Belize,
Bermuda, Canada, Cayman Isl.,
Cook Isl, Cyprus, East Caribbean, EMU,
Eritrea, Ethiopia, Fiji Isl., Hongkong,
Jamaica, Kenya, Liberia, Malta, Mauritius,
The Netherlands, New Zealand,
Seychelles, Singapore, Solomon Isl.,
South Africa, Shri Lanka, Swaziland,
Trinidad and Tobago, U.S.A., Zimbabwe
Centas (centai or centu) .... Lithuania
Centavo(s) .... Argentina, Brazil, Cuba,
Dominican Rep., El Salvador, Guatemala,
Honduras, México, Nicaragua, Peru
Centime(s) ..... Belgium, France, Haïti,
Luxembourg, Morocco, Switzerland
Chetrum .... Bhutan
Colón(es) ..... Costa Rica, El Salvador
Córdoba(s) .... Nicaragua
Cruzeiro(s) Real(Reais) .... Brazil
Dalasi(s) .... The Gambia
Denar(s) .... Macedonia
Deni .... Macedonia
Deutsche Mark .... Germany
Dinar(a) Bosnia-Hercegovina, Yugoslavia
Dinar(s) . Algeria, Bahrain, Iraq, Jordan,
Kuwait, Libya, Sudan, Tunisia
Dirham(s) Morocco, United Arab Emirates
Dirham(s) .... Libya
Dirhem(s) .... Qatar
Dobra(s) ...... São Tomé and Príncipe
Dollar(s) .. Anguilla, Antigua & Barbuda,
Australia, Bahamas, Barbados, Belize,
Bermuda, British Virgin Islands, B,
Canada, Cayman Isl., Cook Isl., Dominica,
Fiji Isl., Grenada, Guyana, Hongkong,
Jamaica, Liberia, Montserrat, Namibia,
New Zealand, St Kitts, St Lucia,
St Vincent, Singapore, Solomon Isl.,
Trinidad and Tobago, U.S.A., Zimbabwe.
Dong .... Vietnam
Drachma(es) .... Greece
Dram .... Armenia
ECU .... European currency unit
Emalangeni .... Swaziland
Escudo(s) ...... Cabo Verde, Portugal
Euro ...... European Monetary Union
Fen ..... People's Republic of China
Fils .... Bahrain, Jordan, Kuwait
United Arab Emirates
Florin .... Aruba
Forint .... Hungary
Franc(s) .... Belgium, Comoro Isl.,
Djibouti, France, Guinea (Conakry),
Liechtenstein, Luxembourg, Monaco,
Switzerland
Franc(s) CFA Central ...... Cameroon,
Central African Rep., Chad, Congo,
Equatorial Guinea, Gabon

Franc(s) CFA West . Benin, Burkina Faso,
Guine Bissau, Ivory Coast, Mali, Niger,
Senegal, Togo, West African States
Franc(s) CFP .... French Polynesia,
New Caledonia
Franc(s) congolaise(s) Dem.Rep. of Congo
Gourde(s) .... Haiti
Grosch(en) .... Austria
Gulden .... The Netherlands,
Netherlands Antilles, Suriname
Halala(s) .... Saudi Arabia
Haler(u) ...... Czech Rep., Slovakia
Halier/haliere/halierov ..... Slovakia
Hryvnia(Hryven) .... Ukraine
Jiao .... China Peoples' Republic
Kapeik .... Belarus
Karbovanetz .... Ukraine
Kina .... Papua New Guinea
Kip .... Lao
Konvertibilna MarkaBosnia & Hercegovina
Korun(a) .... Czech Republic
Koruna/koruny/korún .... Slovakia
Krone(r) ...... Denmark, Norway
Krona(or) .... Sweden
Króna(ur) .... Faroes, Iceland
Kroon(i) .... Estonia
Kuna .... Croatia
Kwacha ...... Malawi, Zambia
Kwanza(s) .... Angola
Kwanza(s) reajustado(s) .... Angola
Kyat .... Myanmar
Laari .... Maldives
Lakh .... India, Sri Lanka
Lari .... Georgia
Lats .... Latvia
Lek(ë) .... Albania
Lempira(s) .... Honduras
Leone(s) .... Sierra Leone
Leu(i) .... Moldova, Romania
Lev(a) .... Bulgaria
Lipa .... Croatia
Lira(e) .... Cyprus, Italy, Malta, Turkey,
San Marino, Vatican City
Lisente .... Lesotho
Litas (litai or litu) .... Lithuania
Livre(s) .... Lebanon
Loti .... Lesotho
Maloti .... Lesotho
Manat .... Azerbaijan, Turkmenistan
Mark .... Germany
Markka(a) .... Finland
Metica/meticais .... Mozambique
Millim .... Tunisia
Naira .... Nigeria
Nakfa .... Eritrea
Nakhar .... Ichkeria (Chechnya)
New Dinar .... Yugoslavia
New Đong .... Vietnam
(New) lev(a) .... Bulgaria
(New) stotinka/stotinki ..... Bulgaria
Ngultrum .... Nepal
Nuevo(s) peso(s) ..... México, Uruguay
Ore . Denmark, Faroes, Norway, Sweden
Ouguiya .... Mauritania
Pa'anga .... Tonga
Paisa/paise .... India, Nepal
Para .... Yugoslavia
Pataca(s) .... Macao
Penni(ä) .... Finland
Penny (pence) .... England,
Falkland/Malvinas Isl., Gibraltar,
Guernsey, Ireland, Isle of Man, Jersey,
Northern Ireland, Scotland, St. Helena
Peseta(s) .... Spain
Peso(s) .... Argentina, Chile, Colombia,
Cuba, Dominican Rep., Guinea-Bissau,
Mexico, Uruguay

Peso uruguayo .... Uruguay
Pfennig Bosnia & Hercegovina, Germany
Piastre(s) .... Egypt, Syria
Piso .... The Philippines
Poisha .... Bangladesh
Pound(s) .... Cyprus, Egypt, England,
Falkland/Malvinas Isl., Gibraltar, Guernsey,
Ireland, Isle of Man, Jersey,
Northern Ireland, Scotland, St Helena,
Sudan, Syria
Pula .... Botswana
Punt .... Ireland
Qirsh .... Jordan
Quetzal(es) .... Guatemala
Rand .... South Africa
Real (reais) .... Brazil
Renminbi .... China Peoples' Republic
Rial(s) .... Oman, Yemen
Riel .... Cambodia
Ringgit .... B, Malaysia
Riyal(s) ...... Qatar, Saudi Arabia
Rubel .... Belarus
Ruble(s) . Russia, Tajikistan, Transnistria
Rufiya(a) .... Maldive Isl.
Rupee(s) ...... India, Mauritius, Nepal,
Pakistan, Seychelles, Shri Lanka
Rupiah .... Indonesia
Satang .... Thailand
Schilling .... Austria
Sen .... Malaysia
Sene .... Samoa
Seniti .... Tonga
Sent(i) .... Estonia
Sente .... Lesotho
Sentimo(s) .... Philippines
Sheqel (sheqalim) .... Israel
Shilin .... Somalia
Shilling(s) .... Kenya, Tanzania, Uganda
Sol(es) .... Peru
Sucre .... Ecuador
Sum Kazakstan, Kyrgyz Rep., Uzbekistan
Super Dinar .... Yugoslavia
Taka .... Bangladesh
Tambala .... Malawi
Tanga .... Kazakstan, Tajikistan
Tetri .... Georgia
Thebe .... Botswana
Toea .... Papua New Guinea
Tolar(jev) .... Slovenia
Toman .... Iran
Tugruk .... Mongolia
Tyyn ...... Kazakstan, Kyrgyzstan
Vatu .... Vanuatu
Won ...... DPR of Korea, Rep. of Korea
Yen .... Japan
Yuan China Peoples' Rep., Taiwan ROC
Zlote (zlotych) .... Poland

Acknowledgments

We thank the following individuals and institutions for their invaluable contribution of data, specimens and pictures, corrections, suggestions to improve the usefulness of this guide, and constructive criticism.

Waldemar **A**lvarez
American Express Travelers Cheques.
Dr Octavio Amiami Castro
Azerbaijan Millie Bankı
Azerbaijani Mission to the United Nations
George Azuma

Bahrain Monetary Agency
Banca d'Italia
Banca Naţională a Moldovei
Banca Nationala a Romaniei
Banco Central da Guiné-Bissau
Banco Central de Bolivia
Banco Central de Chile
Banco Central de Costa Rica
Banco Central de Cuba
Banco Central de Honduras
Banco Central de la República Argentina
Banco Central de la República Dominicana
Banco Central de Nicaragua
Banco Central de Reserva de El Salvador
Banco Central de Reserva del Perú
Banco Central de S.Tomé e Principe
Banco Central de Venezuela
Banco Central del Ecuador
Banco Central del Paraguay
Banco Central del Uruguay
Banco Central do Brasil
Banco da China, Macau
Banco de Cabo Verde
Banco de España
Banco de Guatemala
Banco de la República, Bogotá
Banco de México
Banco de Moçambique
Banco de Portugal
Banco Nacional de Angola
Banco Nacional de Cuba
Banco Nacional Ultramarino, Macao
Bangko Sentral ng Pilipinas
Bangladesh Bank
Bank al-Maghrib
Bank Centrali ta' Malta
Bank Indonesia
Bank Israel
Bank Negara Malaysia
Bank Note Reporter
Bank of Albania
Bank of Botswana
Bank of Canada
Bank of China, Hongkong
Bank of England
Bank of Eritrea
Bank of Ghana
Bank of Greece
Bank of Guyana
Bank of Ireland
Bank of Jamaica
Bank of Japan
The Bank of Korea
Bank of Mauritius
The Bank of Mongolia
Banl of Namibia
Bank of New Zealand
Bank of Papua New Guinea
Bank of Sierra Leone
Bank of Thailand
Bank of Uganda

Bank of Zambia
Bank Rossiya
Bank van de Nederlandse Antillen
Banka Slovenije
Banky Foiben'i Madagasikara
Banque Centrale de la République de Guinée
Banque Centrale des Comores
Banque Centrale des États de l'Afrique de l'Ouest
Banque Centrale de Tunisie
Banque d'Algerie
Banque de France
Banque de la République d'Haïti
Banque des Etats de l'Afrique Centrale
Banque du Liban
Banque du Zaire
Banque Nationale, Djibouti
Banque Nationale du Rwanda
Robert Barber
Barclays Bank, Gibraltar
Yuri & Anna Barshay
Alexander Basok
Robert J. Bauman
Herwig Bayer
Benki Kuu Ya Tanzania
Lauren Benson, Inc.
Bermuda Monetary Authority
Erwin M. Beyer
Milt Blackburn
Board of Commissioners of Currency, Singapore
Christian Bolliot
Ernesto R. Bolmey
British Standards Institute
Colin R. Bruce, II
Brunei Currency Board
Alain Brustel
Robert Buják
Bulgarian National Bank
Bureau for National Development, Rarotonga
Bureau of Engraving and Printing, Washington D.C.

Caisse Centrale de Coopération Economique
Canadian Bank Note Company, Limited
Jaime Caro
Justina Castillo
Cayman Islands Monetary Authority
Central Bank of Barbados
Central Bank of Belize
The Central Bank of China
Central Bank of Cyprus
Central Bank of Egypt
Central Bank of Iraq
Central Bank of Ireland
Central Bank of Jordan
Central Bank of Kenya
Central Bank of Kuwait
Central Bank of Lesotho
Central Bank of Myanmar
Central Bank of Oman
Central Bank of Samoa
Central Bank of Seychelles
Central Bank of Solomon Islands
Central Bank of Sri Lanka
Central Bank of Swaziland
Central Bank of Syria
The Central Bank of the Bahamas
Central Bank of the D. P. R. of Korea
Central Bank of the Gambia
Central Bank of the Islamic Republic of Iran
Central Bank of the Republi of Armenia
Central Bank of the Republic of Uzbekistan
Central Bank of Trinidad and Tobago
Centrale Bank van Aruba
Centrale Bank van Suriname

Centralna Banka a Bosne i Hercegovine
Česká Národní Banka
Simone Chapman
Christlyn Child
Citicorp
Dario Clai
CoinCraft
Coin World
Commissioners of Currency of the Falkland Islands
The Committee of Scottish Clearing Bankers
Consulate of Estonia, New York
Roberto Contreras
Thomas Cook Foreign Currency Services, Inc
Council for Parity Democracy
Ron Cowan
Philip P. Cowitt

Howard A. **D**aniel III
Danmarks Nationalbank
De Nederlandsche Bank
Daniel Denis
Department of State, Washington
Alberto J. Derman
Shamir Desai
Deutsche Bundesbank
Patricio Díaz

Eastern Caribbean Central Bank
Eesti Pank
Fred Eisenberg
Jeffrey Eisenberg
Embassy of Armenia
Embassy of Azerbaijan
Embassy of the Kyrgyz Republic
Embassy of Latvia
Embassy of Lithuania
Brian Etemad
Embassies of the U.S.A.
Steve Eyer

Juan **F**ajardo
Feng's Language Service
Financial Secretary, Roseau, Dominica
First Trust Bank
Vincent Fox
Stan Furman

Francesco **G**iacalone (deceased)
Adrian Glauser
Ashok R. Gohil
Government of Anguilla
Government of the Cook Islands
Government of Gibraltar
Government of St Helena
Government of the British Virgin Islands

William G. **H**enderson
Ruth Hill (Deceased)
Steve Hogan
Hongkong and Shanghai Banking Corporation, Hongkong
Houston Numismatic Exchange, Inc.
Houston Photolab and Imaging
Hrvatska narodna banka

Institut d'Emission d'Outre-Mer
Institut Monétaire Luxembourgeois
International Bank Note Society
Mikhail Istomin

Japan Communication Services
Walt Jellum
Pat Johnson

Jan-Erik **K**leven
Luisa Kluger
Tristan Kolm
Maurice Kolsky
Dimitri Kourbouzo
Krause Publications

Uwe Kunick

L. Lafeuilleé
Joseph Lang
David Laties
Latin American Paper Money Society
Latvijas Banka
Evangelina Laurel
Morris Lawing
Dr. Maria Teresa Leal
Gabriel A. Leichen
Lietuvos Bankas
Mario Livio
Raymond Lloyd
Richard Lobel
Albert Lockhart
Jim Logan
Paul-Henry Longuet

Magyar Nemzeti Bank
Maldives Monetary Authority
Ian Marshall
R. L. Martin
Arthur C. Matz
Renato Maupomé
Michael Maxwell
Ministry of Finance, Rarotonga
Richard L. Miranda
Karen Mitchell
Osvaldo Mitchell
François Morisset
Michael Morris

Narodna Banka Hrvatske
Narodna Banka Jugoslavije
Národna Banka Slovenská
Narodowy Bank Polski
National Bank of Belgium
National Bank of Cambodia
National Bank of Ethiopia
National Bank of Georgia
National Bank of Kazakstan
National Bank of Liberia
National Bank of Macedonia
National Bank of Tajikistan
National Bank of the Republic of Belarus
National Bank of the Republic of Tajikistan
National Bank of Ukraine
National Reserve Bank of Tonga
Paul Nelson

Nepal Rastra Bank
Pamela Nesbit
Paul Nestorowich
Norges Bank
Northern Bank, Northern Ireland
Note Printing Australia
Numis-Phil (S) Pte Ltd., Singapore
Numismatic Museum of the B.E.A.C.

Oesterreichische Nationalbank
Vika Onhvandy
Overseas-Chinese Banking Corp., Ltd.

Panafrican News Agency
Richard Pandolfo
Rebecca Parodi
Antonio Pedraza
People's Bank of China
Philip and Sylvia Phipps
Tony Pisciotta
Rick Post
Miguel Pratt Mayans
Michel Prieur

The Qatar Central Bank

Nazir Rahemtulla
Leo Reich
Jérôme H. Remick
Reserve Bank of Australia
Reserve Bank of Fiji
Reserve Bank of India
Reserve Bank of Malawi
Reserve Bank of New Zealand
Reserve Bank of Vanuatu
Reserve Bank of Zimbabwe
Herman Roif
Anita Rothschild
Royal Monetary Authority of Bhutan
Arnaldo Russo.
John Russo

Karl Sæthre
David M. Salem
Saudi Arabian Monetary Agency
John Savage
Simon Schlee
Dr. Wolfgang Schuster
Secretary of Finance and Economic
    Planning, Republic of Kiribati

Sedlabanki Islands
Neil Shafer
Alex Shapiro
Mike Shibano
Ladislav Šín
Art Smith
Edward Smith
Gary Snover
South African Reserve Bank
Dimas Souza
Standard Chartered Bank, Hongkong
State Bank of Pakistan
State Bank of Vietnam
States Treasurer, States of Jersey
Mel Steinberg
Roneszca Stuur
Suomen Pankki
Sveriges Riksbank
S.W.I.F.T., New York
Swiss Bankers Travellers Cheque Centre
Swiss National Bank

Taiwan Bank
Fran Taurassi
Trans-Dniester Republic Bank
The Treasury, Douglas, Isle of Man
Carmine Turco
Türkiye Cumhuryeti Merkez Bankası
Tuvalu Government

Ulster Bank Ltd
Union Bank of Switzerland
United Arab Emirates Central Bank
Ashok Upadhyaya

Dr Karel Vacek
Dr Hugo van Reijen
Juan C. Vázquez
Felipe M. Villalón
Norbert von Euw

Michael Walker
Chris Whiting
Steve Wiltshire
World Collections News, Genoa

Armen Youssefi

Christof Zellweger

Afghanistan   AFA

Afghani(s) = 100 pul(s).
Minor unit coins are not used.

Currency import-export restrictions:
Local currency in/out: Af 2,000.
Foreign currency in: free, must declare.
Out: up to amount imported and declared.
Travelers are required to exchange a minimum of US$ 26 a day.

Alternative currencies: PKR, USD.

Distinctions are made between notes issued by the anti-Taliban coalition in the North, and the Taliban in the South. Notes of one side do not circulate in the other.

Issuer: "DA AFGHANISTAN BANK."

Dates are in Solar Hegira Calendar (SH).

CURRENT NOTES

Smaller notes not listed because of low value.

5,000 AFGHANIS   166 x 73mm Issued in 1994 **Cat.#62**
  1372 Violet, green, black and multicolor.
  Islamic center and mosque / Blue mosque of Mazar-i-Sharif.

10,000 AFGHANIS   171 x 76mm Issued in 1995 **Cat.#63**
  Blue, olive green, black and multicolor.
  Gate / Arch.
  Varieties: Cat.#63: white background in "Da Afghanistan" in back is continuous.
  Cat.#64: white background in "Da Afghanistan" in back is broken.

Albania   Shqipëri • Albanien • Albanie   ALL

Lek(e) = 100 qindar(ka).
Minor unit coins are not used.

Currency import-export restrictions:
Local currency in/out: free up to 100,000 leke.
Foreign currency in: free, must declare amounts over US$5,000 or equivalent.
Out: up to amount imported and declared.

Alternative currencies: all major.

A BRIEF MONETARY HISTORY
July 1946: 1 (new) franga = 5 franga
July 1947: 9 lekë = 9 Yugoslav dinars = 1 franga
Aug. 1965: 1 "heavy" lek = 10 old leke.
During 1992-93 a lek Valute was worth 50 leke.

Issuer: "BANKA E SHQIPERISE" (Bank of Albania), previously "BANKA E SHTETIT SHQIPTAR" (State Bank of Albania)

CURRENT NOTES

100 LEKE   155 x 72mm **Cat.#55**
  1993-96 Purplish brown and multicolor.
  Man / Eagle and mountains.
  Those dated 1996 have a wider security thread.

100 LEKE   130 x 65mm Issued 14 July 1997 **Cat.#62**
  1996 Violet brown and multicolor.
  Fan S. Noli / Original Parliament Building .

200 LEKE B.e Shqiperise 162 x 78mm Issued 10 Feb 1993 **Cat.#52**
  1992-96 Reddish brown and multicolor.
  Ismail Qemali / Group of people shaped as double headed eagle.
  It commemorates 80 years of independence. Without, or in 1996 with windowed security thread (Cat.#59).

200 LEKE Banka e Shqiperise   162 x 78mm **Cat.#56**
  1994 Reddish brown and multicolor.
  Ismail Qemali / Crowd shaped as a double headed eagle.

200 LEKE   138 x 69mm Issued 14 July 1997 **Cat.#63**
1996 Brown and light blue.
Naim Frasheri / House where he was born and pen.

500 LEKE Banka e Shtetit Shqiptar.   155 x 75mm **Cat.#48**
1991-96 Blue, orange and multicolor.
Woman and sunflowers / Mountains and trees.

500 LEKE B.e Shqiperise 171 x 78mm Issued 10 Feb 1993 **Cat.#53**
1992-96 Green and multicolor.
Naim Frasheri / Candle and mountains shaped like a book.
Without, or in 1996 with windowed security thread (Cat.#60).

500 LEKE B.e Shqiperise 171 x 78mm Issued in late 1994 **Cat.#57**
1994 Dark bluish green and multicolor.
Naim Frasheri / Candle and mountains shaped like a book.

500 LEKE   146 x 69mm Issued 14 July 1997 **Cat.#64**
1996 Blue, brown and light salmon.
Ismail Quemali / Independence House, table, and telegraph.

1,000 LEKE Banka e Shqiperise.   178 x 78mm **Cat.#54**
1992-95 Green and multicolor.
Head of Skenderbeu / Arms and mountain scene.
Without, or in 1995 with windowed security thread (Cat.#61).

1,000 LEKE B.e Shqiperise 178x78mm Issued in late 1994 **Cat.#58**
1994 Green and multicolor.
Head of Skenderbeu / Arms and mountain scene.

1,000 LEKE   153 x 72mm Issued 14 July 1997 **Cat.#65**
1996 Green and multicolor.
Pjeter Bogdani / Church of Vau i Dejes.

5,000 LEKE   160 x 72mm **Cat.#66**
Yellow brown and multicolor.
Skanderbeg / Castle of Kruja.

Algeria

al-Jazair • Algerien • Argelia • Algerie   **DZD**

Dinar(s) = 100 centime(s).

Currency import-export restrictions:
Local currency in/out: forbidden to foreigners, residents limited to 200 dinars.
Foreign currency in: free, **must** declare.
Out: up to amount imported and declared.
Visitors are required to convert hard currency to buy 1,000 dinars. Proof of exchange of hard currency at authorized institutions is required to exit the country.

Alternative currencies: **FRF**, USD.

A BRIEF MONETARY HISTORY
April 1964: dinar = Algerian franc

Issuer: "BANQUE D'ALGERIE", formerly "BANQUE CENTRALE D'ALGERIE".

CURRENT NOTES

100 DINARS Banque Centrale d'Algerie   155 x 71mm **Cat.#131**
1981 Dark and light blue.
Buildings / Man with plants.

100 DINARS Banque Centrale d'Algerie   155 x 71mm **Cat.#134**
1982 Light blue.
Buildings / Man with plants.

100 DINARS B.d'Algerie 131 x 72mm Issued in mid 1996 **Cat.#137**
1992 Blue.
Soldiers charging / Galley.

200 DINARS Banque Centrale d'Algerie   165 x 78mm **Cat.#135**
1983 Brown and multicolor.
Monument / Building with bridge in background, and pottery.

200 DINARS B. d'Algerie 141 x 72mm Issued 2 Oct 1996 **Cat.#138**
1992-05-21 Reddish brown and green.
Koranic school / Mosque, mosaic and branch.

500 DINARS B.d'A.   151 x 72mm Issued in late 1995 **Cat.#139**
21 May 1992 Purple and multicolor.
Battle scene with elephants / Mountains, ruins and elephants.

1,000 DINARS B.d'A.   160 x 72mm Issued in early 1995 **Cat.#140**
21 May 1992 Reddish brown, lilac and orange.
Tassili cave paintings and bull's head / Hoggar cave paintings.

OUTMODED AND REDEEMABLE NOTES

The following notes are redeemable until 31Dec2008.

5 dinars 1964 . . . . Cat.#122
5 dinars 1970 . . . . Cat.#126
10 dinars 1964 . . . . Cat.#123
10 dinars 1970 . . . . Cat.#127
50 dinars 1964 . . . . Cat.#124
50 dinars 1977 . . . . Cat.#130
100 dinars 1964 . . . . Cat.#125
100 dinars 1970 . . . . Cat.#128

Andorra Andorre   **ADP**

Spanish and French currencies are used. Coins denominated in "diners" are minted for collectors.

Although Andorra has no import-export restrictions for currency, travelers should observe those in force in Spain and France.

©MRI Bankers' Guide to Foreign Currency
P.O.Box 3174 Houston TX 77253 USA

Angola   AOR

Kwanza(s) reajustado(s) = 100 lwei.
Minor unit coins are not used.

Currency import-export restrictions:
Local currency in/out: forbidden.
Foreign currency in: free, **must** declare amounts over USD 10,000.
Out: Non-residents may export freely USD 10,000, more only if imported and declared.
Reconversion allowed up to 50% of amount originally exchanged into kwanzas reajustados, with supporting exchange receipts.

Alternative currencies: PTE, ZAR and all major.

A BRIEF MONETARY HISTORY
1958: currency name changed from angolar to escudo
Jan. 1977: currency name changed from escudo to kwanza
Sep. 1990: kwanza changed to novo kwanza, conversion restricted
Jul. 1995: kwanza reajustado equal to 1,000 "novos kwanzas"

Issuer: "Banco Nacional de Angola."

CURRENT NOTES

Smaller notes not listed because of low value.

500,000 KWANZAS REAJUSTADOS   162 x 70mm **Cat.#140**
1 May 1995 Brown, pink, red and light blue.
Dos Santos and Neto / Matala dam.

1,000,000 KWANZAS REAJUSTADOS   162 x 70mm **Cat.#141**
1 May 1995 Green, reddish brown, rose and multicolor.
Dos Santos and Neto / School girl.

5,000,000 KWANZAS REAJUSTADOS   162 x 70mm **Cat.#142**
1 May 1995 Bluish green, lilac brown and orange brown.
Dos Santos and Neto / "Serra da Leba."

Anguilla   XCD

East Caribbean currency is used.

The import and export of local and foreign currencies are free.

United States dollars are widely accepted. Alternative currencies: CAD, DEM, FRF, GBP.

Reconversion of E.C. dollars is subject to a 2 percent tax.

Antigua & Barbuda   XCD

East Caribbean currency is used.

Currency import-export restrictions:
There are no rules about capital movements.

United States dollars are widely accepted. Alternative currencies: CAD, DEM, FRF, GBP.

Gold foil notes of 30 and 100 dollars were issued for collectors. These are never found in general circulation.

Argentina   Argentinien • Argentine   ARS

Peso(s) = 100 centavo(s).

The import and export of all currencies is free.   24AUG1998

U.S. dollar bills circulate widely, but due to the abundance of forgeries some stores will not accept them. Stained, damaged or written dollar bills, however slightly, are not accepted.

Provincial currency

Several provincial governments issue "negotiable certificates" which circulate locally at par with the national currency. These have no market outside the place of issue.

A BRIEF MONETARY HISTORY
Jan. 1970: peso ley 18188 = 100 pesos moneda nacional
Jun. 1983: peso argentino ($a) = 10,000 pesos Ley 18188
Jun. 1985: austral (A) = 1,000 pesos argentinos
Jan. 1992: peso = 10,000 australes

Issuer: "Banco Central de la República Argentina."

CURRENT NOTES

2 PESOS   155 x 65mm Issued 6 Jan 1992 **Cat.#340**
Blue, burgundy and multicolor / Grayish blue and multicolor.
Bartolomé Mitre / "Museo Mitre."

2 PESOS　　　155 x 65mm Issued 1 Dec 1997 **Cat.#346**
Blue, burgundy and multicolor / Grayish blue and multicolor.
Bartolomé Mitre / "Museo Mitre."

5 PESOS　　　155 x 65mm Issued 3 Jan 1992 **Cat.#341**
Olive, orange red and multicolor / Greenish gray and multicolor.
Gen. José de San Martín / Cerro de la Gloria.

5 PESOS　　　155 x 65mm **Cat.#347**
Olive, orange red and multicolor / Greenish gray and multicolor.
Gen. José de San Martín / Cerro de la Gloria.

10 PESOS　　　155 x 65mm Issued 3 Jan 1992 **Cat.#342**
Brown, green and multicolor / Reddish brown and multicolor.
Manuel Belgrano / "Monumento a la Bandera, Rosario."

10 PESOS　　　155 x 65mm Issued 14 Jan 1998 **Cat.#348**
Brown, green and multicolor.
Manuel Belgrano / "Monumento a la Bandera, Rosario."

20 PESOS　　　155 x 65mm Issued 6 Jan 1992 **Cat.#343**
Brownish red, blue, green and multicolor.
Juan Manuel de Rosas / "Combate de la Vuelta de Obligado."

20 PESOS　　　155 x 65mm **Cat.#349**
Brownish red, blue, green and multicolor.
Juan Manuel de Rosas / "Combate de la Vuelta de Obligado."
An improved version is expected to be issued soon.

50 PESOS　　　155 x 65mm Issued 2 Jan 1992 **Cat.#344**
Black, burgundy and green / Black and multicolor.
Domingo Faustino Sarmiento / "Casa de Gobierno."

50 PESOS　　　155 x 65mm **Cat.#350**
Black, burgundy and green / Black and multicolor.
Domingo Faustino Sarmiento / "Casa de Gobierno."
An improved version is expected to be issued in late 1999.

100 PESOS　　　155 x 65mm Issued 6 Jan 1992 **Cat.#345**
Violet, lilac, green and multicolor / Violet and multicolor.
Julio Argentino Roca / "La Conquista del Desierto."
CAUTION: there are many forgeries.

100 PESOS　　　155 x 65mm **Cat.#351**
Violet, lilac, green and multicolor / Violet and multicolor.
Julio Argentino Roca / "La Conquista del Desierto."
An improved version is expected to be issued in 2000.

OUTMODED AND REDEEMABLE NOTES

1 PESO　　　*155 x 65mm* **Cat.#339**
Dark blue, purple brown and multicolor/ Gray and multicolor.
Carlos Pellegrini / "Congreso Nacional."

Armenia Hayastan • Armenien • Arménie AMD

Dram = 100 lumma. (Minor unit coins are not used.)

Currency import/export restrictions:
Local currency: free.
Foreign currency in: free; out: free up to equivalent of USD 10,000.
Larger amounts should be transferred through banks. Jul1998

Alternative currencies: DEM, RUB, USD.

A BRIEF MONETARY HISTORY
November 1993: Dram established.

Issuer: "CENTRAL BANK OF THE REPUBLIC OF ARMENIA"

CURRENT NOTES

Smaller notes not listed because of low value.

50 DRAMS 125 x 62mm Issued 22 Nov 1993 **Cat.#35**
1993 Violet blue and red.
National Museum of History and Art Gallery / Parliament.
Legal tender until 31 Dec 2003, redeemable afterwards without time limit.

50 DRAMS 122 x 65mm **Cat.#41**
1998 Lilac brown and slate.
Aram Khachaturyan / Scene of "Gayane" and Mount Ararat.

100 DRAMS 134 x 65mm Issued 22 Nov 1993 **Cat.#36**
1993 Violet, brown and multicolor.
Mount Ararat and Church of Zvarnots / Opera and Ballet House.
Legal tender until 31 Dec 2003, redeemable afterwards without time limit.

100 DRAMS 122 x 65mm **Cat.#42**
1998 Blue and light pink.
Viktor Hambardzumyan / Observatory of Buragan.

200 DRAMS 136 x 65mm **Cat.#37**
1993 Purple brown, green and red.
Church of St. Hripsime in Echmiadzin / Circular design.

200 DRAMS **Cat.#43**
A new note is planed for future release.

500 DRAMS 136 x 65mm Issued ca. April 1994 **Cat.#38**
1993 Green and orange brown.
Tetradrachm of King Tigran II and Mount Ararat / Book and pen.

500 DRAMS **Cat.#44**
New note expected for future release.

1,000 DRAMS 146 x 68mm Issued in 1994 **Cat.#39**
1994 Brown and multicolor.
Monument to Mesrop Mashtotz and Matenadaran building /
Ruins of monument in Aghut village (7th century).

1,000 DRAMS 136 x 72mm Issued 1 March 1999 **Cat.#45**
1999 Green and rose.
Poet Eghishe Charents / Fiacre.

5,000 DRAMS 146 x 71mm Issued in late 1995 **Cat.#40**
1995 Grayish green and purplish brown.
Pagan temple of Garni / Goddess Anahit.

5,000 DRAMS **Cat.#46**
New note expected for future release.

20,000 DRAMS 136 x 72mm Issued 1 March 1999 **Cat.#48**
1999 Light brown, orange and multicolor.
Painter Martiros Saryan / One of his paintings.

Aruba   AWG

Florin = 100 cent.

Currency import-export restrictions:
Local currency in/out: forbidden.
Foreign currency in: free.   Sep1998
Out: permission needed for amounts exceeding AWG 200,000.

Alternative currencies: USD and all major.

A BRIEF MONETARY HISTORY
Jan. 1986: 0.98 Aruban florin = 1 Netherlands Antillean gulden.

Issuer: "CENTRALE BANK VAN ARUBA."

CURRENT NOTES

10 FLORIN   147 x 66mm **Cat.#7**
1 Jan 1990 Blue.
Snail (Calco Indjian) / Pre-Columbian art.

10 FLORIN   147 x 66mm **Cat.#11**
16 July 1993 Blue.
Snail (Calco Indjian) / Pre-Columbian art.
With "Wettig Betaalmiddel" (Legal tender.)

25 FLORIN   147 x 66mm **Cat.#8**
1 Jan 1990 Brown.
Snake (Cascabel) / Pre-Columbian art.

25 FLORIN   147 x 66mm **Cat.#12**
16 July 1993 Brown.
Snake (Cascabel) / Pre-Columbian art.
With "Wettig betaalmiddel" (Legal tender.)

50 FLORIN   147 x 66mm **Cat.#9**
1 Jan 1990 Reddish brown.
Owl (Shoco) / Pre-Columbian art.

50 FLORIN   147 x 66mm **Cat.#13**
16 July 1993 Reddish brown.
Owl (Shoco) / Pre-Columbian art.
With "Wettig betaalmiddel" (Legal tender.)

100 FLORIN   147 x 66mm **Cat.#10**
1 Jan 1990 Olive green.
Frog (Dori) / Pre-Columbian art.

100 FLORIN   147 x 66mm **Cat.#14**
16 July 1993 Olive green.
Frog (Dori) / Pre-Columbian art.
With "Wettig betaalmiddel" (Legal tender.)

500 FLORIN   147 x 66mm **Cat.#15**
16 July 1993 Blue, green, brown and multicolor.
Fish (Mero) / Pre-Columbian art.

OUTMODED AND REDEEMABLE NOTES

All notes dated 1986 are redeemable until 31 Dec 2021.   rruu20211231

5 FLORIN   *147 x 66mm* **Cat.#6**
1 Jan 1990 Purple.
Turtle / Pre-Columbian art.
                                                      ito

©MRI BANKERS' GUIDE TO FOREIGN CURRENCY
P.O.Box 3174 HOUSTON TX 77253 USA

Australia   Australien • Australie   AUD

Dollar(s) = 100 cent(s).

Currency import-export restrictions:
The import and export of local and foreign currencies are free. Amounts over AUD 10,000 must be reported to the Australian Transaction Reports and Analysis Centre (Austrac), formerly the Cash Transaction Report Agency. Austrac disseminates the reported information to law enforcement agencies and to the Australian Tax Office. Forms are available from Customs.

Alternative currencies: all major.

A BRIEF MONETARY HISTORY
Feb. 1966: dollar = 0.50 Australian pound

Issuer: "RESERVE BANK OF AUSTRALIA."

Australian currency is used in:
Australian Antarctic Territory, Christmas Islands, Cocos (Keeling) Islands, Heard and McDonald Islands, Kiribati, Nauru, Norfolk Island, Territory of Ashmore and Cartier Islands, Territory of Coral Sea Islands and Tuvalu.

CURRENT NOTES

5 DOLLARS   130 x 65mm 24 April 1995 **Cat.#51**
Violet, orange and black.
Elizabeth II / Parliament House.
Printed on polymer, with a gumflower in a "window".

5 DOLLARS   **Cat.#56**
A new note without Elizabeth II will be issued soon.

10 DOLLARS   137 x 65mm Issued 1 Nov 1993 **Cat.#52**
Blue, yellow brown and multicolor.
A.B. "Banjo" Paterson, and horseman / Dame Mary Gilmore.
Printed on polymer, with a windmill in a "window."

20 DOLLARS   144 x 65mm Issued 31 Oct 1994 **Cat.#53**
Orange red and black.
Mary Reibey, ship and building / John Flynn.
Printed on polymer, with a compass in a "window".

50 DOLLARS   151 x 65mm Issued 4 Oct 1995 **Cat.#54**
Gold, violet, gray and multicolor.
David Unaipon / Edith Cowan .
Printed on polymer, with the Southern Cross in a "window".

100 DOLLARS   158 x 65mm Issued 15 May 1996 **Cat.#55**
Green, orange and multicolor.
Dame Nellie Melba / Sir John Monash and military scenes.
Printed on polymer, with a bird in a "window".

OUTMODED AND REDEEMABLE NOTES

All notes of the Commonwealth Bank and the Reserve Bank are redeemable. A pound equals 2 dollars and 10 shillings make 1 dollar. Notes above 10 pounds are very rare, and command high premiums.

Austria   Oesterreich • Autriche   ATS

Euro = 13.7603 schilling   Schilling = 100 groschen.

The import and export of all currencies is free.   Jul1998

Alternative currencies: all major.

A BRIEF MONETARY HISTORY
1945: "military" schilling established.
Dec 1945: schilling replaces "Military" schilling and reichsmark, subject to limits.
1947: new schilling = 3 (old) schillings, subject to limits.
1 Jan 1999: Euro adopted at 13.7603 schilling.

Issuer: "OESTERREICHISCHE NATIONALBANK." After 2002 "EUROPEAN CENTRAL BANK."

CURRENT NOTES

20 SCHILLING   123 x 62mm Issued in Oct 1988 **Cat.#148**
1 Oct 1986 Brown.
Moritz M. Daffinger / Albertina.

50 SCHILLING   134 x 65mm **Cat.#149**
2 Jan 1986 Purple and multicolor.
Sigmund Freud / Josephinum.

100 SCHILLING   137 x 69mm **Cat.#150**
2 Jan 1984 Green, brown and multicolor.
E. Böhm v. Bawerk / Akademie der Wissenschaften.

500 SCHILLING   148 x 72mm Issued 20 Oct 1997 **Cat.#154**
1 Jan 1997 Orange brown and lilac brown.
Poet Rosa Mayreder / Rosa and Karl Mayreder.

1,000 SCHILLING   154 x 72mm Issued 20 Oct 1997 **Cat.#155**
1 Jan 1997 Blue and purple.
Physician Karl Landsteiner / Karl Landsteiner at his lab.

5,000 SCHILLING   160 x 80mm **Cat.#153**
4 Jan 1988 Purple and light brown.
Wolfgang Amadeus Mozart / Staatsoper.
With a "kinegram" showing Mozart's head looking both ways.

OUTMODED AND REDEEMABLE NOTES

20 SCHILLING   132 x 65mm *Cat.#142*
2 July 1967 Brown, olive and lilac.
C. Ritter von Ghega / Alpine scene.   rruu20091230

50 SCHILLING   140 x 70mm *Cat.#143*
2 Jan 1970 Purple and multicolor.
Ferdinand Raimund / Theater.   rruu20080831

100 SCHILLING   150 x 75mm *Cat.#145*
2 Jan 1969 Green and multicolor.
Angelika Kauffman / Farmhouse.   rruu20061128

500 SCHILLING   155 x 80mm *Cat.#139*
  1 July 1965 Reddish brown and multicolor.
  J Ressel / Ship.   rruu20070831

500 SCHILLING   144 x 72mm *Cat.#151*
  1 July 1985 Reddish brown.
  Otto Wagner / "Postsparkassengebäude."   rruu20180420

1,000 SCHILLING   159 x 84mm *Cat.#147*
  1 July 1966 Blue violet.
  Bertha von Suttner / Palace.   rruu20050830

1,000 SCHILLING   152 x 76mm *Cat.#152*
  3 Jan 1983 Dark blue and multicolor.
  E. Schrödinger / Universität-Wien.   rruu20180420

Azerbaijan
Aserbaidschan • Azerbaïdjan   **AZM**

Manat = 100 qepıq.
Minor unit coins are not used.

Currency import-export restrictions:
Local currency in/out: forbidden.
Foreign currency in: free.
Out: up to amount imported and declared. Russian rubles may only be exported to Russia or other countries of the Commonwealth of Independent States.

Alternative currencies: DEM, RUB, USD. U.S. dollars are required in some hotels, and preferred in many restaurants.

A BRIEF MONETARY HISTORY
End 1992: manat = 10 Soviet rubles.
January 1994: rubles cease to be legal tender.

Issuer: "AZƏRBAYCAN MİLLİ BANKI" (National Bank of Azerbaijan).

CURRENT NOTES

Smaller notes not listed because of low value.

250 MANAT   125 x 63mm **Cat.#13**
  Rose and multicolor.
  Maiden Tower / Bank name.

500 MANAT   125 x 63mm **Cat.#19**
  Brown, yellow, blue, pink and multicolor.
  Nızamı Gəncevı / Value.

1,000 MANAT   125 x 63mm **Cat.#20**
  Bluish black, blue, brown and multicolor.
  M. ə. Rəsulzadə / Value.

10,000 MANAT   130 x 65mm **Cat.#21a**
  1994 Brown, yellow and light purple.
  Shirvanshas Palace / Value.
  Without, and with windowed security thread (Cat.#21b).

50,000 MANAT   132 x 66mm Issued in 1996 **Cat.#22**
  1995 Green, light brown and multicolor / Green and multicolor.
  Mausoleum in Nachziban / Value.

The Bahamas   BSD

Dollar(s) = 100 cent(s)
Parity: 1 US dollar.

Currency import-export restrictions:
Local currency in/out: B$200.
The import and export of foreign currencies by visitors is free.

U.S. dollars are accepted everywhere.

A BRIEF MONETARY HISTORY
May 1966: 2.86 Bahamian dollars = 1 Bahamian pound

Issuer: "THE CENTRAL BANK OF THE BAHAMAS."

CURRENT NOTES

50 CENTS   156 x 67mm **Cat.#42**
Law of 1974 Green and multicolor.
Elizabeth II and baskets / Sister Sarah in Nassau Market.

1 DOLLAR   156 x 67mm **Cat.#43**
Law of 1974 Green and multicolor.
Elizabeth II and fish / Royal Bahamas Police Force Band.
Cat.#43a with horizontal serial numbers and solid metal gray security thread;
Cat.#43b same, with "cleartext" security thread
Cat.#51 with vertical serial numbers and added security features.

1 DOLLAR   156 x 67mm **Cat.#50**
1992 Violet and multicolor / Blue, green, rose and multicolor.
Christopher Columbus / Map, fauna and Columbus' ships.
Commemorates "Bahamas First Landfall 1492 Quincentennial."

1 DOLLAR   156 x 67mm Issued in May 1996 **Cat.#57**
1996 Green and multicolor.
Elizabeth II and fish / Royal Bahamas Police Force Band.

3 DOLLARS   156 x 67mm **Cat.#44**
Law of 1974 Red violet and multicolor.
Elizabeth II and Paradise Beach / Family Island Regatta.

5 DOLLARS   156 x 67mm **Cat.#45**
Law of 1974 Orange and multicolor.
Elizabeth II and statue of Columbus / Junkanoo group.

5 DOLLARS   156 x 67mm Issued in June 1995 **Cat.#52**
Law of 1974 Brown and orange brown.
Sir Cecil Wallace-Whitfield and statue of Columbus / "Junkanoo".
Without, and with ascending serial numbers (Cat.#63).

10 DOLLARS   156 x 67mm **Cat.#46**
Law of 1974 Blue and multicolor.
Elizabeth II and flamingos / Lighthouse and Abaco settlement.
Without, and with vertical serial numbers and added security features (Cat.#53).

10 DOLLARS   156 x 67mm Issued in Nov. 1996 **Cat.#59**
Series 1996 Green and multicolor.
Elizabeth II and flamingos / Lighthouse and Abaco settlement.

20 DOLLARS   156 x 67mm **Cat.#47**
Law of 1974 Red, black and multicolor.
Elizabeth II and horse drawn surrey / Nassau's harbor.

20 DOLLARS   156 x 67mm Issued in Dec. 1993 **Cat.#54**
Law of 1974 Red, black and multicolor.
Sir Milo B. Butler and horse drawn surrey / Nassau's harbor.

20 DOLLARS   156 x 67mm Issued in 1997 **Cat.#64**
Series 1997 Red, black and multicolor.
Sir Milo B. Butler and horse drawn surrey / Nassau's harbor.
Like Cat.#54, with a gold seal and ascending serial numbers.

50 DOLLARS   156 x 67mm **Cat.#48**
Law of 1974 Brown and multicolor.
Elizabeth II and lighthouse / Central Bank.
Without, and with vertical serial numbers and added security features (Cat.#55).

50 DOLLARS   156 x 67mm Issued in Nov. 1996 **Cat.#61**
Series 1996 Reddish brown, green and multicolor.
Elizabeth II and lighthouse / Central Bank.

100 DOLLARS   156 x 67mm **Cat.#49**
Law of 1974 Blue, violet and carmine.
Elizabeth II and sailboat / Fish.
Without, and with vertical serial numbers and added security features.

100 DOLLARS   156 x 67mm Issued in August 1996 **Cat.#62**
1996 Blue, violet and carmine.
Elizabeth II and sailboat / Fish.

OUTMODED AND REDEEMABLE NOTES

All pound/shilling notes are redeemable at the rate of 2.86 Bahamian dollars per pound or 0.143 per shilling.

Older dollar notes issued by The Bahamas Government, Bahamas Monetary Authority and Central Bank of the Bahamas are outmoded, but remain legal tender.

Bahrain   BHD

Dinar(s) = 1,000 fils.

The import and export of local and foreign currencies are free.

Alternative currencies: all major.

A BRIEF MONETARY HISTORY
Oct 1965: dinar = 10 Gulf rupees

Issuer: "BAHRAIN MONETARY AGENCY"

CURRENT NOTES

½ DINAR   142 x 72mm Issued in March 1993 **Cat.#12**
Law of 1973 Brown, reddish brown and multicolor.
Traditional weaver / "Aluminum Bahrain" plant.

½ DINAR   142 x 72mm Issued in 1997 **Cat.#17**
Law of 1973 Light brown, reddish brown and multicolor.
Traditional weaver / "Aluminum Bahrain" plant.
Colors changed to avoid confusion with the old 20 dinars note.

1 DINAR   142 x 72mm Issued in March 1993 **Cat.#13**
Law of 1973 Rose red. green and multicolor.
Dilmun seal / Bahrain Monetary Agency building.

5 DINARS   142 x 72mm Issued in March 1993 **Cat.#14**
Law of 1973 Blue and multicolor.
Riffa Fort / Bahrain International Airport.

5 DINARS   142 x 72mm Issued 1 June 1998 **Cat.#17**
Law of 1973 Bluish green and multicolor.
Riffa Fort / Bahrain International Airport.
With a hologram in the lower left corner.

10 DINARS   142 x 72mm Issued in March 1993 **Cat.#15**
Law of 1973 Green and multicolor.
Dhow / King Fahad Causeway.

10 DINARS   142 x 72mm Issued 1 June 1998 **Cat.#18**
Law of 1973 Green, brown and multicolor.
Dhow / King Fahad Causeway.
With a hologram in the lower left corner.

20 DINARS   142 x 72mm Issued 1 Aug 1998 **Cat.#20**
Orange, olive and multicolor.
Gate "Bab al Bahrain" / Ahmed al Fateh Islamic centre.

Bangladesh Bangladesch   **BDT**

Taka = 100 poisha.

Currency import-export restrictions:
Local currency in/out: 500 taka.
Foreign currency in: free, must declare on form "FMJ" amounts exceeding USD 5,000 or its equivalent.
Out: free to USD 5,000 or its equivalent, more if declared on arrival. Tk 6,000 may be reconverted on departure.

Alternative currencies: AED, AUD, CAD, CHF, DEM, FRF, GBP, HKD, ITL, JPY, KWD, NLG, SAR, SGD, USD.

A BRIEF MONETARY HISTORY
Jan. 1972: taka established at par with Pakistani rupee

Issuer: "BANGLADESH BANK"

CURRENT NOTES

Smaller notes not listed because of low value.

5 TAKA   119 x 65mm **Cat.#15**
Light brown.
Star Mosque / Industrial landscape with a river with two sailing boats in foreground.

5 TAKA   119 x 65mm **Cat.#20**
Light brown and multicolor.
"Kushumba" mosque / Industrial landscape, with two sailing boats.

5 TAKA   199 x 65mm **Cat.#25**
Light brown and multicolor.
"Kushumba" mosque / Industrial landscape, with two sailing boats.

10 TAKA   140 x 69mm **Cat.#16**
Maroon.
Atiya Jam-e mosque in Tangail / Paddy harvesting.

©MRI BANKERS' GUIDE TO FOREIGN CURRENCY
P.O.Box 3174 HOUSTON TX 77253 USA

10 TAKA　　140 x 69mm　**Cat.#21**
Maroon.
Star mosque / Paddy harvesting.

10 TAKA　　140 x 69mm　**Cat.#26**
Lilac·on green.
Atiya Jam-e mosque in Tangail / Spillway of Kaptai dam.
There are two varieties, with or without a line of text on top of the mosque.

10 TAKA　140 x 69mm　Issued in early December 1997　**Cat.#34**
Blue, brown and multicolor.
Mujibur Rahman / Building (Mazar.)

20 TAKA　　146 x 69mm　**Cat.#22**
Olive green.
Chote Sona mosque / Four men washing jute in water beside a paddy field.

20 TAKA　　146 x 69mm　**Cat.#27**
Olive green.
Chote Sona mosque / Four men washing jute in water beside a paddy field.

50 TAKA　　153 x 69mm　**Cat.#17**
Dark orange.
Star mosque / Typical tea garden.

50 TAKA　　153 x 69mm　**Cat.#23**
Dark orange.
Sat Gumbuj Mosque / Typical tea garden.

50 TAKA　　153 x 69mm　**Cat.#28**
Black, red, green and multicolor.
National Monument in Savar / National Assembly Building.

100 TAKA　　160 x 69mm　**Cat.#18**
Blue violet and multicolor.
Star mosque / River scape of rural Bangladesh.

100 TAKA　　160 x 69mm　**Cat.#24**
Blue violet, brown and multicolor.
Star Mosque in Dhaka / Lalbagh Fort.
Without, and with windowed security thread (Cat.#32).

500 TAKA　　170 x 69mm　**Cat.#19**
Blue and lilac.
Star Mosque / Supreme Court Building, Dhaka.

500 TAKA　　170 x 69mm　**Cat.#30a**
Gray, blue, violet and multicolor.
Star Mosque / High Court Building, Dhaka.
Without, and with windowed security thread (Cat.#30b).

500 TAKA　　170 x 69mm　Issued in mid 1998　**Cat.#35**
Brown, green, olive green and red.
National Monument in Savar / High Court building, Dhaka.

Barbados Barbades   BBD

Dollar(s) = 100 cent(s).

Currency import-export restrictions:
Local currency in: free; out: BD$ 500.
Foreign currency in: free.
Out: up to USD 1,000 or equivalent, or amount imported and declared. It is advisable to keep exchange receipts in case reconversion is desired.   Aug1998

U.S. dollars are widely accepted. Alternative currencies: CAD, DEM, FRF and GBP.

A BRIEF MONETARY HISTORY
Dec. 1973: dollar = East Caribbean dollar

Issuer: "CENTRAL BANK OF BARBADOS."

CURRENT NOTES

2 DOLLARS   150 x 65mm **Cat.#35**
Blue.
John Redman Bovell / Trafalgar Square, Bridgetown.

2 DOLLARS   150 x 65mm Issued 23 Oct 1995 **Cat.#41**
Violet blue and multicolor.
John Redman Bovell / Trafalgar Square, Bridgetown.

2 DOLLARS   150 x 65mm Issued in 1999 **Cat.#48**
Violet blue and multicolor.
John Redman Bovell / Trafalgar Square, Bridgetown.

5 DOLLARS   150 x 65mm **Cat.#36**
Green.
Sir Frank Worrell / Trafalgar Square, Bridgetown.

5 DOLLARS   150 x 65mm Issued 23 Oct 1995 **Cat.#42**
Green, light brown and multicolor / Green and blue.
Sir Frank Worrell / Trafalgar Square, Bridgetown.

5 DOLLARS   **Cat.#49**
A new upgraded note will be issued in late 1999 or early 2000.

10 DOLLARS   150 x 65mm **Cat.#31**
Brown.
Charles Duncan O'Neal / Trafalgar Square, Bridgetown.

10 DOLLARS   150 x 65mm **Cat.#37**
Brown and green.
Charles Duncan O'Neal / Trafalgar Square, Bridgetown.
Without, and with ascending serial numbers, and brighter colors on back (Cat.#43).

10 DOLLARS   **Cat.#50**
A new upgraded note will be issued in late 1999 or early 2000.

20 DOLLARS   150 x 65mm **Cat.#32**
Purple.
Samuel Jackman Prescod / Trafalgar Square, Bridgetown.

20 DOLLARS   150 x 65mm **Cat.#38**
Purple and multicolor.
Samuel Jackman Prescod / Trafalgar Square, Bridgetown.
Enhanced version of Cat.#32.

20 DOLLARS   150 x 65mm Issued in late 1996 **Cat.#44**
Purple, gold and multicolor.
Samuel Jackman Prescod / Trafalgar Square, Bridgetown.

20 DOLLARS   150 x 65mm Issued in early 1998 **Cat.#47**
Purple, orange, blue and multicolor.
Samuel Jackman Prescod / Trafalgar Square, Bridgetown.

©MRI BANKERS' GUIDE TO FOREIGN CURRENCY
P.O.Box 3174 HOUSTON TX 77253 USA

50 DOLLARS   150 x 65mm **Cat.#39**
Orange, blue and gray.
Errol Barrow / Trafalgar Square, Bridgetown.

50 DOLLARS   150 x 65mm **Cat.#45**
Orange, blue and gray.
Errol Barrow / Trafalgar Square, Bridgetown.

100 DOLLARS   150 x 65mm **Cat.#40**
Gray blue, brown and purple / Multicolor.
Sir Grantley Adams / Trafalgar Square, Bridgetown.
Current notes have serial numbers E3,200,000 or higher, treetops on back are
green and have a vertical white rectangle in front. Older notes must be
exchanged at the Central Bank.

100 DOLLARS   150 x 65mm **Cat.#46**
Gray blue, brown and purple / Multicolor.
Sir Grantley Adams / Trafalgar Square, Bridgetown.
Commemorative of the 25th anniversary of the Central Bank of Barbados.

OUTMODED AND REDEEMABLE NOTES

1 DOLLAR   150 x 65mm *Cat.#29*
Red.
Samuel Jackman Prescod / Trafalgar Square, Bridgetown.

5 DOLLARS   150 x 65mm *Cat.#30*
Green.
Samuel Jackman Prescod / Trafalgar Square, Bridgetown.

100 DOLLARS   150 x 65mm *Cat.#33*
Gray blue and multicolor / Gray blue.
Sir Grantley Adams / Trafalgar Square, Bridgetown.
*Redeemable at the Central Bank. It differs from current notes because serial
number is E3,200,000 or lower, treetops on back are grayish blue and it lacks a
white vertical rectangle on the left front side.*

Belarus   BYB

Rubel(rubliei) = 100 kapeik.
Minor unit coins are not used.

Currency import/export restrictions:
Foreign currency in: free.
Out: free up to USD 500. Larger amounts with proof of previous
import or exchange receipt for an authorized bank.

Alternative currencies: RUB, USD, DEM and all major.

A BRIEF MONETARY HISTORY
25 May 1992: rubel = 10 Soviet rubles
10 November 1992: Russian rubles cease to be legal tender, later its
legal tender status is restored. On 8 Nov 1994 they cease to be legal
tender.

Issuer: "Нацыянальны Банк Рэспублікі Беларусь" (National
Bank of the Republic of Belarus).

CURRENT NOTES

Smaller notes not listed because of low value.

20,000 RUBLIEI   151 x 64mm **Cat.#13**
1994 Brown and multicolor.
National Bank building / "Pagonya" (Emblem of Belarus).

50,000 RUBLIEI   151 x 69mm Issued in April 1996 **Cat.#14**
1995 Reddish brown, yellow and light green / Brown and light
green.
Brest's Tower, Holmsky gate / Brest's Tower, entrance to the
Memorial.

100,000 RUBLIEI   151 x 69mm Issued 17 Oct 1996 **Cat.#15**
1996 Brown, blue and multicolor.
Bolshoi Opera and Ballet Theater of the Republic of Belarus /
Scene of the Glebov's ballet "Izbrannitsa".

500,000 RUBLIEI   150 x 71mm Issued 1 Dec. 1998 **Cat.#18**
1998 Red and green.
Palace of Culture / Fragment of the façade of the palace.

1,000,000 RUBLIEI   150 x 71mm Issued in 30 April 1999 **Cat.#19**
1999 Green.
National Museum of Art of the Republic of Belarus / Fragment of
"Wife's portrait with flowers and fruits."

Belgium
Belgien/België/Belgique • Bélgica   **BEF**

Euro = 40.3399 francs Franc(s) = 100 centime(s).

The import and export of all currencies is free.   Jul1998

Alternative currencies: all major. Luxembourg francs are widely
accepted.

A BRIEF MONETARY HISTORY
1 Jan 1999: Euro adopted at BEF 40.3399.

Issuer: "BANQUE NATIONALE DE BELGIQUE-NATIONALE BANK VAN
BELGIE-BELGISCHE NATIONALBANK." After 2002 "EUROPEAN CENTRAL
BANK."

CURRENT NOTES

100 FRANCS   139 x 76mm **Cat.#147**
Purplish red, dark blue and multicolor.
James Ensor and masks / Scene with several pregnant women.

200 FRANCS   144 x 76mm Issued in late 1995 **Cat.#148**
Yellowish orange, brown, green and multicolor.
Adolphe Sax and saxophone / Saxophone players .

500 FRANCS   150 x 76mm Issued 16 Apr 1998 **Cat.#149**
Blue, green, violet blue and multicolor.
René Magritte and tree / Eight men in bowlers and chair with
tail.

1,000 FRANCS   154 x 76mm Issued 24 April 1997 **Cat.#150**
Brown.
Constant Permeke and sailboat / "Sleeping farmer."

2,000 FRANCS   159 x 76mm **Cat.#151**
Mauve and multicolor.
Victor Horta and "Art Nouveau" designs / "Art Nouveau" design.

10,000 FRANCS   169 x 76mm Issued 19 June 1997 **Cat.#152**
Purplish gray and multicolor.
Albert II and Paola, and the Parliamentary chamber / Green-
houses at Lacken royal residence.

OUTMODED AND REDEEMABLE NOTES

100 FRANCS = 20 BELGAS 150 x 85mm Cat.#53
1.2.1943 Red and green.
Albert and Elisabeth, and female allegory / Allegories of the
Escaut and Meuse rivers.

100 FRANCS = 20 BELGAS 179 x 108mm Cat.#38
1944 Orange red.
Albert and Elisabeth, and female allegory / Allegories of the
Escaut and Meuse rivers.
Similar grayish notes dated 1943 and before are worthless.

100 FRANCS 160 x 85mm Cat.#56
1945-50 Yellow, vermilion and green.
Leopold I and Place Royale / Painting of the arrival of Leopold I.

100 FRANCS 147 x 75mm Cat.#57
1952-59 Black on brown / Beige.
Leopold I / Head of Frère-Orban.

100 FRANCS 138 x 69mm Cat.#134
1962-75 Lilac brown and multicolor.
Lombard / Statue of Orpheus.

100 FRANCS 142 x 76mm Issued 5 April 1978 Cat.#140
Red lilac and multicolor.
Hendrik Beyaert and façade of National Bank in Antwerp /
Architectural design.

500 FRANCS = 100 BELGAS 150 x 85mm Cat.#54
1.2.1943 Blue on violet and green.
Lion and allegories of the Escaut and Meuse Rivers /
"Abundance."

500 FRANCS 170 x 90mm Cat.#59
1944-47 Brown and yellow.
Leopold II / Landscape of Congo.

500 FRANCS 160 x 80mm Cat.#60
1952-58 Brown and yellow.
Leopold II / "Four Blacks" by Rubens.

500 FRANCS 147 x 74mm Cat.#135
1961-75 Blue and multicolor.
Van Orley / Margaret of Austria, palace.

500 FRANCS　　　　147 x 76mm Issued 4 April 1979 **Cat.#143**
Blue and multicolor.
Constantin Meunier / Five spheres representing different sources
of power.

1,000 FRANCS = 200 BELGAS　　223 x 135mm **Cat.#55**
1.2.1943 Brown, violet and brown.
Female allegory, and Albert and Elisabeth / Allegories of the
Escaut and Meuse rivers.

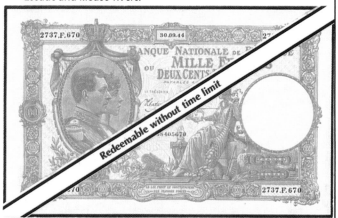

1,000 FRANCS = 200 BELGAS　　223 x 135mm **Cat.#44**
1944 Red.
Albert and Elisabeth and seated woman / Lace maker at work.
Earlier green notes are worthless.

1,000 FRANCS　　　　180 x 95mm **Cat.#62**
1944-48 Olive green and gray.
Albert I with helmet / City view.

1,000 FRANCS　　　　170 x 85mm **Cat.#63**
1950-58 Blue and multicolor.
Albert I / Geeraert and lock scene.

1,000 FRANCS　　　　157 x 79mm **Cat.#136**
1961-75 Brown and blue.
Kremer and Globe / Atlas.

1,000 FRANCS　　　　154 x 76mm Issued 3 Dec 1980 **Cat.#144**
Brown and multicolor.
André Grétry and string instrument / Tuning forks and internal
view of ear.　　　　　　　　　　　　　　　　rwtl

5,000 FRANCS　　　　167 x 84mm Issued 1 Feb 1971 **Cat.#137**
1971-77 Green and multicolor.
André Vésale and statue of St Michael / Statue of Æsculapius
with view of a temple in Epidaurus.

5,000 FRANCS　　　　160 x 76mm Issued 15 Sep 1982 **Cat.#145**
Green and multicolor.
Guido Gezelle / Dragonfly and leaf.

10,000 FRANCS　　　　166 x 76mm Issued 11 Dec 1992 **Cat.#146**
Purplish gray and multicolor.
Baudouin and Fabiola / Greenhouses at Lacken royal residence.
The "10000" in back is printed in optical variable ink.　　　rwtl

Belize   BZD

Dollar(s) = 100 cent(s).
Parity: US$ 0.50

Currency import-export restrictions:
Local currency in/out: BZ$100.
Foreign currency in: free.
Out: equivalent of BZD 500.00 or up to amount imported and declared.

U.S. dollars are widely accepted. Alternative currencies: GBP, MXN.

Issuer: "Central Bank of Belize."

CURRENT NOTES

2 DOLLARS   158 x 69mm **Cat.#52**
1990-91 Violet, deep mauve and blue / Violet and carmine.
Elizabeth II and stela from Nim Li Punit / Three Mayan sites.

2 DOLLARS   140 x 70mm Issued 1 June 1999 **Cat.#64**
1 Jan 1999 Violet, deep mauve and blue / Violet and carmine.
Elizabeth II and stela from Nim Li Punit / Three Mayan sites.

5 DOLLARS   158 x 69mm **Cat.#53**
1990-96 Red, carmine and orange / Red and carmine.
Elizabeth II and medallion portrait of Thomas Potts / Scenes from St. George's Caye.
Without, and since 1996 with windowed security thread and ascending serial numbers (Cat.#58).

5 DOLLARS   140 x 70mm Issued 1 June 1999 **Cat.#65**
1 Jan 1999 Red, carmine and orange / Red and carmine.
Elizabeth II and medallion portrait of Thomas Potts / Scenes from St. George's Caye.

10 DOLLARS   158 x 69mm **Cat.#54**
1990-96 Black, green and ochre / Black and red.
Elizabeth II and Clock Tower of the Belize City Court House (ca. 1910) / Three historical buildings of Belize.
Without, and since 1996 with windowed security thread and ascending serial numbers (Cat.#59).

10 DOLLARS   140 x 70mm **Cat.#60**
1997 Black, green and ochre / Black and red.
Elizabeth II and Clock Tower of the Belize City Court House (ca. 1910) / Three historical buildings of Belize.

20 DOLLARS   158 x 69mm **Cat.#55**
1990 Brown, chestnut and orange / Brown and orange.
Elizabeth II and jaguar / Belizean fauna.

20 DOLLARS   140 x 70mm **Cat.#61**
1997 Brown, chestnut and orange / Brown and orange.
Elizabeth II and jaguar / Belizean fauna.

50 DOLLARS   158 x 69mm **Cat.#56**
1990-91 Burgundy, pink and olive green / Burgundy and pink.
Elizabeth II and swing bridge / Bridges of Belize.

50 DOLLARS   150 x 75mm **Cat.#62**
1997 Burgundy, pink and olive green / Burgundy and pink.
Elizabeth II and swing bridge / Bridges of Belize.
With green fish at left, windowed security thread and ascending serial numbers.

100 DOLLARS   158 x 69mm **Cat.#57**
1990-94 Blue, purple and red / Blue and red.
Elizabeth II and yellow chest keel billed toucan / Birds of Belize.

100 DOLLARS   150 x 75mm **Cat.#63**
1997 Blue, purple and red / Blue and red.
Elizabeth II and yellow chest keel billed toucan / Birds of Belize.
With silver birds at left, windowed security thread and ascending serial numbers.

OUTMODED AND REDEEMABLE NOTES

*All regular older notes issued by Government of British Honduras,
Government of Belize, Monetary Authority of Belize and Central Bank
of Belize are redeemable without time limit. Gold foil notes are no
longer redeemable.*

Benin   XOF

It uses notes issued by "BANQUE CENTRALE DES ETATS DE L'AFRIQUE
DE L'OUEST."

For description of notes and currency import-export restrictions see
WEST AFRICAN STATES.

Alternative currencies: **FRF**, USD.

Bermuda   BMD

Dollar(s) = 100 cent(s).
Parity: US$ 1.00

United States dollars are widely accepted.

Currency import-export restrictions:
Local currency in: free.
Local currency out: BMD250. Export of larger amounts requires
specific permission.
Foreign currency in: free, must declare if export of a large amount
is intended.
Out: Visitors and non-residents: banknotes which they brought in
with them or which are otherwise beneficially owned by them.
Residents: BMD 3,000 equivalent. Export of larger amounts requires
specific permission.
There are no limits on the import or export of coin.   Jul1998

A BRIEF MONETARY HISTORY
Feb. 1970: 2.40 dollars = 1 Bermudian pound

Issuer: "BERMUDA MONETARY AUTHORITY."

CURRENT NOTES

2 DOLLARS   140 x 68mm Issued 23 Nov 1988 **Cat.#34**
1988- Blue green and multicolor
Elizabeth II and seahorse / Clocktower Building.

5 DOLLARS   140 x 68mm **Cat.#35**
1989- Red and violet.
Elizabeth II and conch shell / St. David's Lighthouse and view of
the town of St. George.

10 DOLLARS   140 x 68mm **Cat.#36**
1989- Purple, blue and ochre.
Oleander flower and Elizabeth II / Cahow, Flatts bridge and the
Bermuda Aquarium, Museum and Zoo.

20 DOLLARS   140 x 68mm **Cat.#37**
1989- Green and red.
Elizabeth II and Hibiscus flower / Somerset bridge and view of
Ely's Harbour.

20 DOLLARS   140 x 68mm Issued 17 Jan 1997 **Cat.#47**
17 Jan 1997 Green and red.
Elizabeth II and Burnaby House / Somerset bridge and view of
Ely's Harbour.
To commemorate the opening of / "Burnaby House" / by the / Bermuda
Monetary / Authority."

©MRI BANKERS' GUIDE TO FOREIGN CURRENCY
P.O.Box 3174 HOUSTON TX 77253 USA

50 DOLLARS   150 x 68mm **Cat.#38**
1989 Brown, olive and multicolor.
Elizabeth II and Easter lilies / Gibb's Hill Lighthouse and map.

50 DOLLARS   150 x 68mm **Cat.#44**
1992- Green, red, light brown and multicolor.
Elizabeth II and "Commissioner's House" / Divers.

50 DOLLARS   140 x 68 mm **Cat.#40**
12 Oct 1992 Green, red, light brown and multicolor.
Elizabeth II and "Commissioner's House" / Divers.
Overprinted: "Christopher Columbus / Quincentenary / 1492-1992"

50 DOLLARS   140 x 68mm **Issued in 1997 Cat.#48**
6 June 1997 Green, red, light brown and multicolor.
Elizabeth II and "Commissioner's House" / Underwater diving.
Similar to Cat.#44, with windowed security thread.

100 DOLLARS   140 x 68mm **Cat.#39**
1989- Orange, brown and multicolor.
Elizabeth II and Bermudiana / House of Assembly.

100 DOLLARS   140 x 68mm **Cat.#46**
20 Feb 1994 Orange, brown and multicolor.
Elizabeth II and Bermudiana / House of Assembly.
Commemorates the "25th Anniversary of the / Bermuda Monetary Authority /
1969-1994."

OUTMODED AND REDEEMABLE NOTES

*Old notes of 1 dollar are redeemable until 30 April 2000. Older style
notes in dollars are outmoded, and can be redeemed.*

Bhutan Druk-yul   BTN

Ngultrum = 100 chetrum.
Parity: 1 ngultrum = 1 Indian rupee.

Currency import-export restrictions:
The import and export of local and foreign currencies are free,
except that non-Indians are not allowed to bring in Indian currency.
Visitors must exchange only at authorized places, and keep the
exchange receipt. Within 90 days visitors may reconvert on
departure 30% of amount exchanged.

Indian rupees circulate widely. Alternative currency: USD.

Notes issued now by "ROYAL MONETARY AUTHORITY OF BHUTAN."

CURRENT NOTES

5 NGULTRUM   130 x 62mm **Cat.#14**
Orange brown and multicolor.
Royal Government seal and mythical birds / Paro Dzong.

10 NGULTRUM   139 x 69mm **Cat.#15**
Blue violet and multicolor.
King Jigme Singye Wangchuk / Paro Dzong.

20 NGULTRUM   152 x 69mm **Cat.#16**
Olive and multicolor / Olive and reddish brown.
King Jigme Dorji Wangchuk / Punakha Dzong.

50 NGULTRUM   154 x 70mm **Cat.#17**
Purple and multicolor.
King Jigme Dorji Wangchuk / Tongsa Dzong.

50 NGULTRUM   154 x 70mm **Cat.#19**
Purple and multicolor.
King Jigme Dorji Wangchuk / Tongsa Dzong.
Changed underprint, security devices added.

100 NGULTRUM   160 x 70mm **Cat.#18**
Green and multicolor / Green and reddish brown.
King Jigme Singye Wangchuk / Tashichho Dzong.

100 NGULTRUM   160 x 70mm **Cat.#20**
Green and multicolor / Green and reddish brown.
King Jigme Singye Wangchuk / Tashichho Dzong.
Changed underprint, security devices added.

500 NGULTRUM   160 x 70mm Issued 17 Dec 1994 **Cat.#21**
Orange red, light brown and light green
Portrait / Punakha dzong.
Commemorates the National Day.

OUTMODED AND REDEEMABLE NOTES

All older notes issued by The Royal Government of Bhutan may be exchanged at the Bank of Bhutan.

Bolivia   Bolivien • Bolivie   BOB

Boliviano(s) = 100 centavo(s).

The import and export of all currencies is free.   Jul1998

Alternative currencies: ARS, BRL and all major.

A BRIEF MONETARY HISTORY
Jan. 1963: peso boliviano = 1,000 bolivianos
Jan. 1987: boliviano = 1,000,000 pesos bolivianos

Issuer: "BANCO CENTRAL DE BOLIVIA."

CURRENT NOTES

5 BOLIVIANOS   140 x 69mm **Cat.#203**
1986 Olive green and multicolor.
Adela Zamudio / Virgen del Socavón.
There are several printers, with variations in the security features.

10 BOLIVIANOS   140 x 69 mm **Cat.#204**
1986 Blue black and multicolor.
Cecilio Guzmán de Rojas / Monumento de la Coronilla, "Heroinas de la Coronilla."
There are several printers, with variations in the security features.

20 BOLIVIANOS   140 x 69mm **Cat.#205**
1986 Orange and multicolor.
Pantaleón Dalence / Casa Dorada, Tarija.
There are several printers, with variations in the security features.

50 BOLIVIANOS   140 x 69mm **Cat.#206**
1986 Purple and multicolor.
Melchor Pérez de Holguín / Torre de la Compañía.
There are several printers, with variations in the security features.

©MRI BANKERS' GUIDE TO FOREIGN CURRENCY
P.O.Box 3174   HOUSTON TX 77253   USA

100 BOLIVIANOS   140 x 69 mm   **Cat.#207**
1986 Red and multicolor.
Gabriel René Moreno / Universidad San Francisco Xavier, Chuquisaca.
There are several printers, with variations in the security features.

200 BOLIVIANOS   140 x 69mm   **Cat.#208**
1986 Brown and multicolor.
Franz Tamayo / Cultura Tiahuanacota.
There are several printers, with variations in the security features.

OUTMODED AND REDEEMABLE NOTES

2 BOLIVIANOS   140 x 69mm   Cat.#202
1986 Black and multicolor.
Antonio Vaca Diez / Palm trees.   Ito

Bosnia-Hercegovina   BAK

Konvertibilna(nih) marka(maraka) = 100 pfenig(a).
Parity: 1 konvertibilna marka = 1 Deutschemark.

The import and export of all currencies is free.   Jul1998

German marks are widely used.

Issuer: "CENTRALNA BANKA A BOSNE I HERCEGOVINE"

CURRENT NOTES

50 KONVERTIBILNIH PFENIGA
                    120 x 60mm Issued in June 1998 **Cat.#47**
Grayish blue.
Skender Kulenovic / "Stećak Zgośća" fragment.
Bosnian-Croat Federation Version.

50 KONVERTIBILNIH PFENIGA
                    120 x 60mm Issued in June 1998 **Cat.#47A**
Grayish blue.
Branko Ćopić / Cabin and book.
Serbian version.

1 KONVERTIBILNA MARKA
                    120 x 60mm Issued in June 1998 **Cat.#48**
Green.
Ivan Franjo Jukić / "Stećak Stolac" fragment.
Bosnian-Croat Federation Version.

1 KONVERTIBILNA MARKA
                    120 x 60mm Issued in June 1998 **Cat.#48A**
Green.
Ivo Andrić / Bridge.
Serbian version.

5 KONVERTIBILNIH MARAKA
                    123 x 62mm Issued in June 1998 **Cat.#49**
Lilac brown.
Meša Selimović / Trees.
Bosnian-Croat Federation Version.

5 KONVERTIBILNIH MARAKA
                    123 x 62mm Issued in June 1998 **Cat.#49A**
Mesa Selimović / Trees.
Serbian version.

10 KONVERTIBILNIH MARAKA
                    130 x 65mm Issued in June 1998 **Cat.#50**
Orange and light slate.
Mehmedalija Mak Dizdar / "Stećak Radimlja" fragment.
Bosnian-Croat Federation Version.

10 KONVERTIBILNIH MARAKA

130 x 65mm Issued in June 1998 **Cat.#50A**

Orange and light slate.
Alexsa Šantić / Loaf of bread.
Serbian version.

20 KONVERTIBILNIH MARAKA

138 x 68mm Issued in June 1998 **Cat.#51**

Brown.
Antun Branko Šimić / Stećak Radimilja fragment.
Bosnian-Croat Federation version.

20 KONVERTIBILNIH MARAKA

138 x 68mm Issued in June 1998 **Cat.#51A**

Brown.
Filip Višnjić / Gusle (musical instrument.)
Serbian version.

50 KONVERTIBILNIH MARAKA

146 x 71mm Issued in June 1998 **Cat.#52**

Lilac red and lilac brown.
Musa Ćazim Ćatić / Stone relief.
Bosnian-Croat Federation version.

50 KONVERTIBILNIH MARAKA

146 x 71mm Issued in June 1998 **Cat.#52A**

Lilac red and lilac brown.
Iovan Dučić / Pen, glasses and book.
Serbian version.

100 KONVERTIBILNIH MARAKA

154 x 74mm Issued in June 1998 **Cat.#53**

Brown.
Nikola Šop / Stećak Sgošća fragment.
Bosnian-Croat Federation version.

100 KONVERTIBILNIH MARAKA

154 x 74mm Issued in June 1998 **Cat.#53A**

Brown.
Petar Kočić / Pen, glasses and book.
Serbian version.

Botswana Botsuana BWP

Pula = 100 thebe.

Currency import-export restrictions:
The import and export of local or foreign currencies up to BOP 10,000 or its equivalent is free.
Larger amounts must be declared on entry; and may be exported if legally imported and evidence of declaration (Form J) to customs is produced. Jul1998

Alternative currencies: CHF, DEM, GBP, USD, ZAR.

A BRIEF MONETARY HISTORY
Aug. 1976: pula = 1 South African rand

Issuer: "BANK OF BOTSWANA."

CURRENT NOTES

5 PULA 132 x 66mm **Cat.#8**

Purple and multicolor.
Pres Q.K.G. Masire / Longhorns.

10 PULA 138 x 69mm **Cat.#9**

Green and multicolor.
Pres Q.K.G. Masire / Building.

20 PULA   144 x 72mm **Cat.#10**
   Red, violet blue and multicolor.
   Pres Q.K.G. Masire / Mining installation.

50 PULA   150 x 75mm **Cat.#14**
   Brown, green and multicolor.
   Pres Q.K.G. Masire / Man in canoe and bird with fish.

100 PULA   156 x 78mm Issued in August 1993 **Cat.#15**
   Purplish blue, light brown and multicolor.
   Pres. Q.K.G. Masire, diamond and eagle / Worker sorting rough
   diamonds.

OUTMODED AND REDEEMABLE NOTES

All older notes issued by the Bank of Botswana are redeemable.

Brazil   Brasil • Brasilien • Brésil   **BRL**

Real (reais) = 100 centavo(s).

Currency import-export restrictions:
The import and export of local and foreign currencies is free,
amounts over 10,000 reais or equivalent must be declared.
It was reported that some travelers were robbed outside the
airport, presumably as a result of the declaration.
Reconversion limited to amounts originally exchanged, with
supporting receipts.   Jul1998

Alternative currencies: All major.

A BRIEF MONETARY HISTORY
Feb. 1967: cruzeiro novo = 1,000 cruzeiros
May 1970: cruzeiro = 1,000 cruzeiros novos
Feb. 1986: cruzado = 1,000 cruzeiros
Jan. 1989: cruzado novo = 1,000 cruzados
Mar. 1990: cruzeiro = 1 cruzado novo
Aug. 1993: cruzeiro Real = 1,000 cruzeiros.
July 1. 1994: real = 2,750 cruzeiros reais

Issuer: "BANCO CENTRAL DO BRASIL."

CURRENT NOTES

1 REAL   140 x 65mm Issued 1 July 1994 **Cat.#243**
   Green and light brown.
   Allegory of the Republic / Hummingbird.
   With watermark Republic's head (Cat.#243) or, since 1997, watermark flag
   (Cat.#248).

5 REAIS   140 x 65mm Issued 1 July 1994 **Cat.#244**
   Violet and blue.
   Allegory of the Republic / Crane.
   With watermark Republic's head (Cat.#244) or, since 1997, watermark flag
   (Cat.#244d).

10 REAIS   140 x 65mm Issued 1 July 1994 **Cat.#245**
   Carmine and dark brown.
   Allegory of the Republic / "Arara" bird.
   With watermark Republic's head (Cat.#245) or, since 1997, watermark flag
   (Cat.#245d).

50 REAIS   140 x 65mm Issued 1 July 1994 **Cat.#246**
Brown, and reddish brown.
Allegory of the Republic / "Onça pintada."
BEWARE!!! There are forgeries printed on washed 1 or 5 reais notes.

100 REAIS   140 x 65mm Issued 1 July 1994 **Cat.#247**
Bluish green and dark gray.
Allegory of the Republic / "Garoupa."
Beware!!! There are forgeries printed on washed 1 and 5 reais notes.

British Virgin Islands
**Britische Jungferninseln • Îles Vierges Anglaises •
Islas Vírgenes Británicas**   **USD**

United States currency is used.

There are no restrictions to the import and export of currencies.

British West Africa
**Britische Westafrika • Africa Occidental Británica •
Afrique Anglaise de l'Ouest**

Pound = 20 shilling(s).
Shilling = 12 penny(pence).

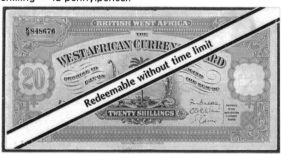

*All notes issued by "West African Currency Board", are redeemable
at the Bank of England at the ratio of 1 pound for every 20 shilling.
Their numismatic value is far higher. There are many counterfeits.*

Brunei   BND

Dollar(s) = 100 cent.
Parity: SGD 1.00

The import and export of all currencies is free.   Jul1998

Singaporean dollars are current. Alternative currencies: CHF, DEM,
GBP, JPY, USD.

A BRIEF MONETARY HISTORY
12 June 1967: dollar established at par with Malayan dollar.

Issuer: "BRUNEI CURRENCY BOARD."

CURRENT NOTES

1 RINGGIT   125 x 62mm **Cat.#13**
1989-94 Purple and multicolor / Violet blue.
Hassanal Bolkiah I / Aerial view.

1 RINGGIT   141 x 69mm **Cat.#22**
Blue, green, yellow and multicolor.
Hassanal Bolkiah I and flower / Rainforest waterfall.
Printed on polymer, with a clear window.

5 RINGGIT   133 x 65mm **Cat.#14**
1989-93 Green and multicolor.
Hassanal Bolkiah I / Houses and boats.

5 RINGGIT   141 x 69mm **Cat.#23**
Black, green and yellow.
Hassanal Bolkiah I and Pitcher plant / Rainforest floor.
Printed on polymer, with a clear window.

©MRI BANKERS' GUIDE TO FOREIGN CURRENCY
P.O.BOX 3174   HOUSTON TX 77253   USA

10 RINGGIT   141 x 69mm   **Cat.#15**
1989-92 Purple, red orange and multicolor.
Hassanal Bolkiah I / Houses and mosque.

10 RINGGIT   141 x 69mm   **Cat.#24**
Brown, red and yellow.
Hassanal Bolkiah I and Purple leafed forest yam / Rain forest
canopy.
Printed on polymer, with a clear window.

25 RINGGIT   150 x 72mm   **Cat.#21**
1992   Brown, yellow brown, lilac, green, dark violet and
multicolor.
Hassan Bolkiah I, and Royal Procession / Coronation scene.
Commemorates the 25th anniversary of accession to the throne.

50 RINGGIT   158 x 75 mm   **Cat.#16**
1989-92 Orange and multicolor.
Hassanal Bolkiah I / People on boat.

50 RINGGIT   157 x 75mm Issued in 1996 **Cat.#25**
Brown and green / Green, red and brown.
Hassanal Bolkiah I and ship / Marine installation.

100 RINGGIT   158 x 75mm   **Cat.#17**
1989-94 Purple, blue and multicolor.
Hassanal Bolkiah I / River scene.

100 RINGGIT   158 x 75mm   **Cat.#26**
Brown and multicolor.
Hassanal Bolkiah I / Airport.

500 RINGGIT   174 x 81mm   **Cat.#18**
1989- Orange, yellow brown, violet blue and multicolor.
Hassanal Bolkiah I and houses / Boat.

500 RINGGIT   **Cat.#27**
A new note will be issued in the future.

1,000 RINGGIT   183 x 84mm   **Cat.#19**
1989- Lilac brown, yellow brown, green and multicolor.
Hassanal Bolkiah I and boat / Buildings by river.

1,000 RINGGIT   **Cat.#28**
A new note will be issued in the future.

10,000 RINGGIT   203 x 132mm   **Cat.#20**
1989 Green and multicolor.
Hassanal Bolkiah I / Aerial view of Bandar Seri Begawan.

10,000 RINGGIT   **Cat.#29**
A new note will be issued in the future.

OUTMODED AND REDEEMABLE NOTES

All older notes of all denominations are redeemable.

Bulgaria   Bulgarien • Bulgarie   **BGN**

New Lev(a) = 100 stotinka(i).

Currency import-export restrictions:
Local currency in/out: free up to 10 (new) leva. Larger amounts require permission from the BNB.
Foreign currency in: free, must declare if amount exceeds USD1,000 or equivalent. Out: up to amount imported and declared. (Different rules apply to Bulgarian residents.)   Jul 1998

Alternative currencies: all major.

A BRIEF MONETARY HISTORY
May 1952: new lev exchanged at between 25 to 200 (old) leva.
Jan 1962: "heavy" lev = 10 (old) leva.
1 July 1999: (new) lev = 1,000 (old) leva.
A new lev equal to 1,000 current leva will be introduced 1 July 1999.

Issuer: "Българска Народна Банка" (Bulgarian National Bank).

CURRENT NOTES

Smaller notes not listed because of low value.

{200 LEVA} = **0.20 [NEW] LEV**
                    137 x 67mm Issued 1 Nov 1992 **Cat.#103**
1992 Brown, reddish brown, yellow and multicolor.
Ivan Vazov / Lyre and laurel wreath.
Remains legal tender until 31 Dec 1999. Redeemable afterwards.

WARNING
Notes dated 1997 and before are expressed in OLD leva.
One NEW lev equals 1,000 OLD leva.

{500 LEVA} = **0.50 [NEW] LEV**
                    143 x 71mm Issued 1 Nov 1993 **Cat.#104**
1993 Green and light brown.
Dobri Hristov / Opera house in Varna and sea gulls.
Remains legal tender until 31 Dec 1999. Redeemable afterwards.

{1,000 LEVA} = **1 [NEW] LEV**
                    149 x 74mm Issued 1 Nov 1994 **Cat.#105**
1994-96 Green and olive.
Vasil Levski and allegory of "Liberated Bulgaria" / His monument.
Plain (Cat.#105), or, since 1996, with holographic band at left (Cat.#110).
Remains legal tender until 31 Dec 1999. Redeemable afterwards.

1 [NEW] LEV   112 x 60mm Issued 5 July 1999 **Cat.#115**
1999 Red.
Icon of St. John of Rila / Rila monastery.

{2,000 LEVA} = **2 [NEW] LEVA**
                    155 x 77mm Issued 21 Dec 1994 **Cat.#106**
1994-96 Gray and multicolor.
Master builder Nicola Fichev / Holy Trinity church in Svishtov and bridge over the Yantra river.
With "holographic" stripe at left.
Remains legal tender until 31 Dec 1999. Redeemable afterwards.

©MRI BANKERS' GUIDE TO FOREIGN CURRENCY
P.O.Box 3174 HOUSTON TX 77253 USA

2 [NEW] LEVA   116 x 64mm Issued 5 July 1999 **Cat.#116**
1999 Violet.
Paisii Hilendarski / Heraldic lion.

{5,000 LEVA} = **5 [NEW] LEVA**
                161 x 79mm Issued 17 June 1996 **Cat.#108**
1996 Lilac red and multicolor.
Zachari Stoyanov / Monument and "Proclamation to the Bulgarian People" of 1885.
With holographic band at left (Cat.#108), or, since 1997 without (Cat.112).
Remains legal tender until 31 Dec 1999. Redeemable afterwards.

5 [NEW] LEVA   121 x 67mm Issued 5 July 1999 **Cat.#117**
1999 Red, brown, green and multicolor.
Painter Ivan Milev / Fragments of his paintings.

{10,000 LEVA} = **10 [NEW] LEVA**
                167 x 80mm Issued 9 Dec 1996 **Cat.#109**
1996 Brown, lilac, purple and multicolor.
Vladimir Dimitrov and National Academy of Arts / "Bulgarian Madonna".
Remains legal tender until 31 Dec 1999. Redeemable afterwards.

{10,000 LEVA} = **10 [NEW] LEVA**
                112 x 62mm Issued 27 Oct. 1997 **Cat.#113**
1997 Green and ochre on beige paper.
Dr Peter Beron and his book "Riben Bookvari" / Sketches of his studies of astronomy and his telescope.
Remains legal tender until 31 Dec 1999. Redeemable afterwards.

10 [NEW] LEVA   126 x 70mm Issued 5 July 1999 **Cat.#118**
1999 Green and ochre.
Dr Peter Beron and his book "Riben Bookvari" / Sketches of his studies of astronomy and his telescope.

20 [NEW] LEVA   131 x 72mm Issued 5 July 1999 **Cat.#119**
1999 Blue and multicolor.
Statesman Stefan Stambolov / National Assembly and fragments of Eagles' and Lions' bridges in Sofia.
It has a holographic stripe at left.

{50,000 LEVA} = **50 [NEW] LEVA**
                120 x 66mm Issued 8 May 1997 **Cat.#114**
1997 Grey, violet, green and yellow.
Sts. Cyril and Methodius / Architectural monuments of the ancient Bulgarian capitals Pliska and Preslav.
Remains legal tender until 31 Dec 1999. Redeemable afterwards.

50 [NEW] LEVA   136 x 76mm Issued 5 July 1999 **Cat.#119**
1999 Brown, yellow and multicolor.
Poet Pencho Slaveykov / Illustrations to his poetry books.

Burkina Faso   XOF

It uses notes issued by "BANQUE CENTRALE DES ETATS DE L'AFRIQUE DE L'OUEST."

For description of notes and currency import-export restrictions See WEST AFRICAN STATES.

Alternative currencies: **FRF**, USD.

Burundi   BIF

Franc(s) = 100 centime(s).
Minor unit coins are not used.

Currency import-export restrictions:
Local currency in/out: Fbu 5,000.
Foreign currency in: free for currencies quoted by the Banque de
la République de Burundi.
Out: up to amount imported and declared.
Visitors must settle hotel bills by selling foreign currency, or by
credit card.

Alternative currencies: BEF, **USD**.

A BRIEF MONETARY HISTORY
May 1964: Burundian franc established at par with franc of Rwanda-
Burundi.

Issuer: "BANQUE DE LA RÉPUBLIQUE DU BURUNDI."

CURRENT NOTES

Smaller notes not listed because of low value.

100 FRANCS   150 x 69mm **Cat.#29**
1977-90 Purple.
Prince Rwagasore / "Unité-Ubumbwe ..." and arms.

100 FRANCS   150 x 69mm Issued in late 1994 **Cat.#37**
1993 Violet brown and multicolor.
Prince Rwagasore and arches / House building.

500 FRANCS   160 x 73mm **Cat.#30**
1977-88 Blue and multicolor.
Building / "Unité - Ubumbwe ..." and arms.

500 FRANCS   160 x 73mm **Cat.#34**
1979-80 Violet, brown, green and multicolor.
Building / "Unité - Ubumbwe ..." and arms.

500 FRANCS   160 x 73mm Issued in 1997 **Cat.#38**
01-05-97 Brown, gray and greenish blue/ Light blue.
Women / Modern building.

1,000 FRANCS   170 x 76mm **Cat.#31**
1977-89 Green and multicolor.
Bird and flowers / Cattle.

1,000 FRANCS   170 x 76mm Issued in late 1994 **Cat.#39**
1994 Green and multicolor.
Cattle / Monument and flags.
Beware of forgeries!!!

5,000 FRANCS   179 x 79mm **Cat.#32**
1978-95 Purple and multicolor.
Building / Port scene.
Beware of forgeries!!!

5,000 FRANCS   179 x 79mm Issued in 1997 **Cat.#40**
05-02-97 Green, olive and light red.
Building / Port scene.

OUTMODED AND REDEEMABLE NOTES

Older notes dated since 1968 are valid, but seldom seen.

©MRI BANKERS' GUIDE TO FOREIGN CURRENCY
P.O.Box 3174 HOUSTON TX 77253 USA

Cambodia
Kampuchea •
Kambodscha • Camboya • Cambodge   **KHR**

Riel = 100 su.
Minor unit coins are not used.

Currency import-export restrictions:
Local currency in/out: free up to 100,000 riel.
Foreign currency in: free, must declare.
Out: up to amount imported and declared.

U.S. dollars are used extensively. Thai baht are also accepted.

A BRIEF MONETARY HISTORY
Oct. 1955: riel established at par with piastre.
Sep. 1975: currency abolished.
March 1980: riel reëstablished.

Issuer: "NATIONAL BANK OF CAMBODIA", formerly "BANQUE NATIONALE DU CAMBODGE."

CURRENT NOTES

Smaller notes not listed because of low value.

500 RIEL   149 x 70mm Issued 21 Oct 1992 **Cat.#38**
1991 Red, purple, brown and multicolor.
National emblem and Angkor Wat temple / Tractor.

500 RIEL   133 x 62mm **Cat.#43**
Lilac red and lilac brown.
Angkor Wat / Rice paddy.

1,000 RIEL   128 x 67mm Issued 25 March 1995 **Cat.#44**
Green and yellow.
Bayon Temple tower with four faces of Avalokitesvara Bohdisattva / "Prasat Chan Chaya" square.

2,000 RIEL   128 x 67mm Issued 25 March 1995 **Cat.#45**
Reddish brown and green.
Fishing in the great lake "Tonle Sap" / Rear view of Angkor Vat.

5,000 RIEL   138 x 67mm Issued 25 March 1995 **Cat.#46**
Violet blue, light orange brown and multicolor / Light violet, brown and blue.
King Norodom Sihanouk Varman and Banteai Srei temple. / New Market in Phnom Penh.

10,000 RIEL   138 x 67mm Issued 25 March 1995 **Cat.#47**
N.d., 1998 Violet blue, green and multicolor / Grayish violet and green.
King Norodom Sihanouk Varman and Bayon statue / Scene of the water festival.

20,000 RIEL   147 x 67mm Issued 25 March 1995 **Cat.#48**
Bright red and violet brown / Red and gray.
King Norodom Sihanouk Varman and Phnom Penh river port / Throne Room in the National Palace.

50,000 RIEL   147 x 67mm Issued 25 March 1995 **Cat.#49**
Dark brown, green and light brown.
King Norodom Sihanouk Varman and Preah Vihear Temple / Road leading to Preah Vihear Temple.

100,000 RIEL   156 x 67mm Issued 25 March 1995 **Cat.#50**
Green and gray.
King Norodom Sihanouk Varman and Queen Monineath Sihanouk / The King and Queen receiving the homage of the people.

Notes of 1,000 and 2,000 riel dated 1992 are spurious. These look quite real, but have never been released into circulation, and their origin is unknown. In any event they are worthless.

Cameroon
Cameroun • Kamerun • Camerón   XAF

Franc(s) CFA Central = 100 centime(s).
Parity: FFR 0.01.

Two types of notes run concurrently, old with names of the six Central African countries, and new of common design.
See CENTRAL AFRICAN STATES for current and outmoded notes, restrictions and other details.

Canada   Kanada • Canadá   CAD

Dollar(s) = 100 cent(s).

The import and export of local and foreign currencies is free.Jul1998

Alternative currencies: all major.

Issuer: "BANK OF CANADA / BANQUE DU CANADA"

CURRENT NOTES

5 DOLLARS   152 x 69mm Issued 28 April 1986 **Cat.#95**
1986 Blue and multicolor.
Sir W. Laurier and arms / Bird (Belted kingfisher).

5 DOLLARS   **Cat.#101**
A new note is being planned for issue in 2000.

10 DOLLARS   152 x 69mm Issued 27 June 1989 **Cat.#96**
1989 Purple and multicolor.
Sir J.A. MacDonald and arms / Bird (Osprey).

10 DOLLARS   **Cat.#102**
A new note is being planned for issue in 2000.

20 DOLLARS   152 x 69mm Issued 30 June 1993 **Cat.#97**
1991 Green and multicolor.
Elizabeth II / Birds (Common loons).
With a square which when tilted under light changes from gold to green.

20 DOLLARS   **Cat.#103**
A new note is being planned for issue in 2000.

50 DOLLARS   152 x 69mm Issued 1 Dec 1989 **Cat.#98**
1988 Red and multicolor.
W. L. MacKenzie King and arms / Bird (Snowy owl).
With a square which when tilted under light, changes from gold to green.

50 DOLLARS   **Cat.#104**
A new note is being planned for issue in 2000.

100 DOLLARS   152 x 69mm Issued 3 Dec 1990 **Cat.#99**
1988 Brown and multicolor.
Borden / Canada goose.
With a square which when tilted under light changes from gold to green.

100 DOLLARS   **Cat.#105**
A new note is being planned for issue in 2000.

1,000 DOLLARS   152 x 69mm **Cat.#83**
1954 Black and rose.
Elizabeth II / Central Canadian landscape.
Beware of forgeries.

1,000 DOLLARS   152 x 69mm Issued 4 May 1992 **Cat.#100**
1988 Reddish purple and multicolor.
Elizabeth II and Parliament / Two pine grosbeak birds.
With a square which when tilted under light changes from gold to green.

©MRI BANKERS' GUIDE TO FOREIGN CURRENCY
P.O.Box 3174 HOUSTON TX 77253 USA

OUTMODED AND REDEEMABLE NOTES

All older notes of all denominations issued by the Bank of Canada, Dominion of Canada and Chartered banks are redeemable.

Notes of 20, 50 and 100 dollars dated 1954 were counterfeited extensively. Fakes lack "planchettes" (little colored paper dots) embedded in the paper. In genuine notes these can be easily flaked-off with a pin.

Notes of the following chartered banks are still redeemable. Their collector's value exceeds by far face value.

Bank of British North America,
Bank of Hamilton,
Bank of Montreal,
Bank of Nova Scotia,
Bank of Ottawa,
Bank of Toronto,
Banque Canadienne Nationale,
Banque d'Hochelaga,
La Banque Nationale,

La Banque Provinciale du Canada,
Banque de St. Jean,
Barclays Bank (Canada),
Canadian Bank of Commerce,
The Dominion Bank,
Home Bank of Canada,
Imperial Bank of Canada,
Merchants Bank of Canada,
The Metropolitan Bank,
The Molsons Bank,
The Northern Crown Bank,
The Quebec Bank,
Royal Bank of Canada,
The Standard Bank of Canada,
The Sterling Bank of Canada,
Union Bank of Canada.

Cape Verde
Cabo Verde • Kap Verde • Cap-Vert   **CVE**

Escudo(s) = 100 centavo(s).

Currency import-export restrictions:
Local currency in/out: forbidden.
Foreign currency in: free, must declare.
Out: equivalent of CVE 20,000, or amount imported and declared.

Alternative currencies: all major.

Issuer: "BANCO DE CABO VERDE."

CURRENT NOTES

100 ESCUDOS   121 x 67mm **Cat.#57**
　　20.1.1989 Red, brown and multicolor.
　　Amilcar Cabral / Festival.

200 ESCUDOS   129 x 67mm **Cat.#58**
　　20.1.1989 Green,black and multicolor.
　　Amilcar Cabral / Airport design.

200 ESCUDOS   129 x 67mm **Cat.#63**
　　8 Aug 1992 Green, brown and multicolor.
　　Packet-boat "Ernestina" / Airport.

©MRI BANKERS' GUIDE TO FOREIGN CURRENCY
P.O.Box 3174 HOUSTON TX 77253 USA

500 ESCUDOS 135 x 67mm **Cat.#59**
20.1.1989 Blue and multicolor.
Amilcar Cabral / Shipyard.

500 ESCUDOS 135 x 67mm **Cat.#64**
23 April 1992 Violet blue, brown and multicolor.
Dr Baltasar Lopes da Silva / Shipyard.

1,000 ESCUDOS 144 x 67mm **Cat.#60**
20.1.1989 Brown, reddish brown and multicolor.
Amilcar Cabral / Insects.

1,000 ESCUDOS 144 x 67mm **Cat.#65**
5 June 1992 Brown, red orange and multicolor.
Bird (Acrocephalus Brevipennis Keulemans) / Grasshopper
(Schistocerca Gregaria).

2,500 ESCUDOS 150 x 67mm **Cat.#61**
20.1.1989 Violet and multicolor.
Amilcar Cabral / National Assembly palace.

Cayman Islands
Kaimaninseln • Islas Caimanes • Îles Caïmanes **KYD**

Dollar(s) = 100 cent(s).

The import and export of all currencies is free. Aug1998

Alternative currencies: CAD, GBP, **USD**.

A BRIEF MONETARY HISTORY
1971: dollar = 1 Jamaican dollar

Issuer: "CAYMAN ISLANDS MONETARY AUTHORITY.", previously "CAYMAN ISLANDS CURRENCY BOARD"

CURRENT NOTES

1 DOLLAR Series B CICB
156 x 66mm Issued in June 1996 **Cat.#16**
1996 Blue, violet, orange and multicolor.
Elizabeth II / Fish and coral.

1 DOLLAR CIMA 156 x 66mm Issued in July 1998 **Cat.#21**
1998 Blue, violet, orange and multicolor.
Elizabeth II / Fish and coral.

5 DOLLARS Series B CICB 156 x 66mm **Cat.#12**
1991 Dark green, olive green and multicolor.
Elizabeth II / A Cayman schooner.

5 DOLLARS Series C CICB156 x 66mm Issued in June 1996 **Cat.#17**
1996 Dark green, olive green and multicolor.
Elizabeth II / A Cayman schooner.

©MRI BANKERS' GUIDE TO FOREIGN CURRENCY
P.O.Box 3174 HOUSTON TX 77253 USA

5 DOLLARS CIMA   156 x 66mm Issued in July 1998 **Cat.#22**
1998 Dark green, olive green and multicolor.
Elizabeth II / A Cayman schooner.

10 DOLLARS Series B CICB   156 x 66mm **Cat.#13**
1991 Red, violet and multicolor.
Elizabeth II / Seven Mile Beach.

10 DOLLARS CICB   156 x 66mm Issued in June 1996 **Cat.#18**
1996 Upgraded version of the 1991 note.
Elizabeth II / Seven Mile Beach.

10 DOLLARS CIMA   156 x 66mm Issued in July 1998 **Cat.#23**
1998 Upgraded version of the 1991 note.
Elizabeth II / Seven Mile Beach.

25 DOLLARS Series B CICB   156 x 66mm **Cat.#14**
1991 Brown, orange, light brown and multicolor.
Elizabeth II / Map of the Cayman Islands.

25 DOLLARS CICB   156 x 66mm Issued in June 1996 **Cat.#19**
1996 Red, purple, olive green and multicolor.
Elizabeth II / Map of Cayman Islands.

25 DOLLARS CIMA   156 x 66mm Issued in June 1999 **Cat.#24**
Red, purple, olive green and multicolor.
Elizabeth II / Map of Cayman Islands.

50 DOLLARS Series A CICB   156 x 66mm **Cat.#10**
1974 Blue and multicolor.
Elizabeth II / Old Caymanian house.

100 DOLLARS Series B CICB   156 x 66mm **Cat.#15**
1991 Orange, brown and multicolor
Elizabeth II / George Town Harbor.

100 DOLLARS CICB   156 x 66mm Issued in June 1996 **Cat.#20**
1996 Orange, brown and multicolor.
Elizabeth II / George Town Harbor.

100 DOLLARS CIMA   156 x 66mm Issued in June 1999 **Cat.#25**
Orange, brown and multicolor.
Elizabeth II / George Town Harbor.

OUTMODED AND REDEEMABLE NOTES

Notes dated 1971 and 1974 are redeemable without time limit.

Central African Republic
République Centrafricaine • Zentralafrikanische Republic • República Centroafricana. **XAF**

Franc(s) CFA Central = 100 centime(s).
Parity: FFR 0.01

Two types of notes run concurrently, old with the names of the six Central African countries, and new of common design.

See CENTRAL AFRICAN STATES for current and outmoded notes, restrictions and other details

Central African States
États de l'Afrique Centrale • Zentralafrikanische Staaten • Estados del Africa Central **XAF**

Franc(s) CFA Central = 100 centime(s).
Minor unit coins are not used.
Parity: FRF 0.01.

It is the common currency of the six members of the Central African Monetary Zone, Cameroon, Central African Republic, Chad, Congo, Equatorial Guinea and Gabon.

Currency import-export restrictions:
Local currency in/out: forbidden, except between countries of the Central African group.
Foreign currency in: free. Must declare amounts over equivalent to CFAf 250,000 if reëxport is intended.
Out: up to equivalent of CFAF 250,000, or more if imported and declared.

Two types of notes run concurrently, old with the names of the six Central African countries, which circulate in all countries, without regard to the name that appears on the note; and, since 1992, new of common design. Old style notes with "République Populaire du Congo" are worthless.

Since 1992 the first two digits of serial number indicate year of issue. Black letters at upper right and lower left corners indicate country of issue, as follows:
- E: Cameroon
- F: Central African Republic
- C: Congo
- L: Gabon
- N: Equatorial Guinea
- P: Chad

Alternative currency: **FRF**, USD.

Issuer: "BANQUE DES ÉTATS DE L'AFRIQUE CENTRALE"

CURRENT NOTES

500 FRANCS 140 x 75mm **Cat.#1**
1992- Brown, light blue and multicolor.
Shepherd, cattle and map of Central Africa / Baobab, antelopes and kota mask.

WARNING

Notes of 5,000 and 10,000 francs of the "République Populaire du Congo" are worthless

1,000 FRANCS 146 x 75mm **Cat.#2**
1993- Brown, green and multicolor.
Young man's head, coffee picking and map of Central Africa / Forest exploitation and transportation of wood on an Okoume raft, and Bakele wood mask.

2,000 FRANCS 154 x 75mm **Cat.#3**
1993- Brown, red, green and multicolor.
Woman's head, tropical fruits and map of Central Africa / Port scene.

5,000 FRANCS 161 x 86mm **Cat.#99**
Green, brown and multicolor.
Woman carrying bundle, and mask / Musical instrument, plowing and mine ore conveyor.
Common design for Cameroon, Central African Republic, Chad, Equatorial Guinea and Gabon.
Caution: Notes of the "République Populaire du Congo" are worthless.

5,000 FRANCS 160 x 80mm Issued 20 Dec 1994 **Cat.#4**
1994 Multicolor.
Oil industry / Cotton picking.
First two digits of serial number indicate date of issue.

10,000 FRANCS   169 x 92mm **Cat.#100**
Green, brown and multicolor.
Woman / Truck.
Common design for Cameroon, Central African Rep., Chad, Congo and Gabon.
Caution: Notes of the "République Populaire du Congo" are worthless.

10,000 FRANCS   164 x 85mm Issued 20 Dec 1994 **Cat.#5**
1994 Multicolor.
Young Bororo woman and BEAC building / Fishermen and
"Capitaine" fish.
First two digits of serial number indicate year of issue.

OUTMODED AND REDEEMABLE NOTES

*Older notes of Cameroon, Central African Republic, Chad, Equatorial
Guinea and Gabon issued by "Banque Centrale des États de l'Afrique
Equatoriale et du Cameroun", "Banque Centrale des États de l'Afrique
Equatoriale" and "Banque des États de l'Afrique Centrale" are
redeemable, except those of 5,000 and 10,000 francs of Chad with
portrait of Pres. Tombalbaye, and those of the "République Populaire
du Congo", which are worthless. Their numismatic value is high.*

*The redemption of Cameroonian notes of 5,000 and 10,000 francs
with the portrait of Ahidjo is restricted, and very difficult, if not
impossible for non-residents.*

CFA francs

Common currency of several African nations. Its parity is FFR 0.01

"Central" CFA francs issued by "Banque des Etats de l'Afrique
Centrale" are used in Cameroon, Central African Republic, Chad,
Congo, Equatorial Guinea and Gabon.
Notes bearing the name of one nation are current in every other.
See "CENTRAL AFRICAN STATES" for banknote descriptions.

"West" CFA francs are issued by "Banque Centrale des Etats de
l'Afrique de l'Ouest" and are of uniform design.
These are used in Benin, Burkina Faso, Guinea-Bissau, Ivory Coast,
Mali, Niger, Senegal and Togo.
See "WEST AFRICAN STATES" for banknote descriptions.

French currency is accepted widely in urban areas at the ratio of
CFA fr 100 per French franc.

Recent rules restrict the movement of banknotes in CFA francs.

CFP francs   XPF

Franc(s) CFP (Change franc Pacifique) = 100 centime(s).

Currency import-export restrictions:
No restrictions, except that reporting required for amounts above
CFPF 909,090 or FF 50,000.

CFP francs are the common currency of French Polynesia, New
Caledonia, and Wallis and Futuna.

Notes with "PAPEETE" or "NOUMEA" are valid. Those with "NOUVELLES
HÉBRIDES" must be exchanged in Vanuatu.

Alternative currencies: AUD, CAD, CHF, DEM, **FRF**, GBP, NZD, USD.

A BRIEF MONETARY HISTORY
25 Dec 1945: franc CFP established at 49.60 to the U.S. dollar.
1 Jan 1960: parity established at FRF .055 per CFP F.

Issuer: "INSTITUT D'EMISSION D'OUTRE-MER"

CURRENT NOTES

500 FRANCS   150 x 80mm Issued in 1970 **Cat.#1a**
Blue and multicolor.
Fisherman / Man.
CAUTION: Notes with "NOUVELLES HÉBRIDES" are exchangeable in Vanuatu.

500 FRANCS   Issued in late 1995 **Cat.#1b**
Blue and multicolor.
Fisherman / Man.
Like Cat.#1a, with security thread and new penal clause on back.

1,000 FRANCS   160 x 86mm Issued in 1969 **Cat.#2a**
Reddish brown and multicolor.
Hut under palm trees and girl / Hut, deer and bird.
CAUTION: Notes with "NOUVELLES HÉBRIDES" are exchangeable in Vanuatu.

1,000 FRANCS   Issued in late 1995 **Cat.#2b**
Reddish brown and multicolor.
Hut under palm trees and girl / Hut, deer and bird.
Like Cat.#2a, with security thread and new penal clause on back.

5,000 FRANCS   170 x 90mm Issued in 1971 **Cat.#3**
Yellow, green and multicolor.
Bougainville and ships / Portrait and boat.

5,000 FRANCS   Issued in late 1995 **Cat.#7**
Like Cat.#3, with security thread and new penal clause on back.

10,000 FRANCS   172 x 92mm Issued in 1986 **Cat.#4**
Multicolor.
Girl, bungalows and palm trees / Girl and fish.

OUTMODED AND REDEEMABLE NOTES

20 FRANCS   128 x 70 Cat.#15
Multicolor.
Young man and flute player / Woman and fruit bowl.
With "NOUMÉA" or "PAPEETE", redeemable in France, French Polynesia and New Caledonia. With "NOUVELLES HÉBRIDES", see Vanuatu.

100 FRANCS   205 x 120mm Cat.#17
Multicolor.
Woman / Statue from Angkor Wat.
With "NOUMÉA" or "PAPEETE", redeemable in France, French Polynesia and New Caledonia. With "NOUVELLES HÉBRIDES", see Vanuatu.

100 FRANCS   139 x 75mm Cat.#24
Brown and multicolor.
Young woman playing guitar, totem-like statue and view of islands / Girl and view of islands.
Issued in 1969. With "NOUMÉA" or "PAPEETE", redeemable in France, French Polynesia or New Caledonia. With "NOUVELLES HÉBRIDES", see Vanuatu.

All "Papeete" and "Nouméa" notes may be redeemed at the Institut d'Emission d'Outre-Mer or at the Banque de France. The Central Bank of Vanuatu redeems those marked "Nouvelles Hébrides."

Chad Tchad • Tschad   XAF

Franc(s) CFA Central = 100 centime(s).

Two types of notes run concurrently, old with the names of the six Central African countries, and new of common design.
See Central African States for current and outmoded notes, restrictions and other details.

Chile Chili   CLP

Peso(s) = 100 centavo(s).
Minor unit coins are not used.

The import and export of all and currencies is free.   Aug 1998

Alternative currencies: ARS, BRL, PYG, UYU and all major.

A BRIEF MONETARY HISTORY
Jan. 1960: escudo = 1,000 pesos
Sep. 1975: peso = 1,000 escudos

Issuer: "BANCO CENTRAL DE CHILE"

CURRENT NOTES

500 PESOS   145 x 70mm **Cat.#153**
1977- Lilac and brown.
Pedro de Valdivia / Founding of Santiago.
The issue of a coin to replace it is under study.

1,000 PESOS   145 x 70mm **Cat.#154**
1978- Green and multicolor.
Carrera Pinto / Monument "Chile a sus Héroes."

2,000 PESOS   145 x 70mm **Cat.#157**
1997 Lilac brown and multicolor.
Manuel Rodríguez E. and his statue / Iglesia de los Dominicos.

©MRI BANKERS' GUIDE TO FOREIGN CURRENCY
P.O.Box 3174 HOUSTON TX 77253 USA

5,000 PESOS 145 x 70mm **Cat.#155**
1981- Red and multicolor.
Gabriela Mistral / "Premio Nobel."
Without, and since 1994 with windowed security thread (Cat.#155e).

10,000 PESOS 145 x 70mm **Cat.#156**
1989- Blue, brown and multicolor.
Capt. A. Prat / "Hacienda San Agustín de Puñual"
Without, and since 1994 with windowed security thread (Cat.#156b).

20,000 PESOS 145 x 70mm Issued 2 Dec 1998 **Cat.#158**
1998 Lilac brown, green and multicolor.
Don Andrés Bello L. / Casa Central Universidad de Chile.

OUTMODED AND REDEEMABLE NOTES

Notes issued before 1975 are redeemable at the rate of 1,000 escudos = 1 peso. Those not listed are of minimal value.

50 PESOS 145 x 70mm **Cat.#151**
1975-81 Blue and multicolor.
Capt. A. Prat / "Escuadra Nacional."

100 PESOS 145 x 70mm **Cat.#152**
1976-81 Purple and multicolor.
Portales / "Reunión de notables."

China   Zhonghuo Renmin Gonghe Guo   CNY

Yuan = 10 jiao = 100 fen.

Currency import-export restrictions:
Local currency in/out: 6,000 yuan.
Foreign currency in: free. Must declare amounts over USD 5,000 or equivalent, including permitted amounts of local currency.
Out: up to amount imported and declared.

Alternative currencies: HKD and all major.

A BRIEF MONETARY HISTORY
1948: peoples' yuan (jen min piao) created.
Mar. 1955: (new) yuan = 10,000 (old) yuan
1969: renminbi = 1 yuan

Issuer: "PEOPLE'S BANK OF CHINA."

CURRENT NOTES

Caution!!!
This note
is worth only
0.10 yuan

{1 JIAO} = **0.10 YUAN**   112 x 51mm **Cat.#881**
1980 Brown and multicolor.
Two men / Arms.

Caution!!!
This note
is worth only
0.20 yuan

{2 JIAO} = **0.20 YUAN**   119 x 55mm **Cat.#882**
1980 Gray olive and multicolor.
Two youths / Arms.

Caution!!!
This note
is worth only
0.50 yuan

{5 JIAO} = **0.50 YUAN**   125 x 58mm **Cat.#883**
1980 Purple, red violet and blue.
Two children / Arms.

1 YUAN 140 x 63mm **Cat.#884a**
1980- Brown violet and multicolor.
Two youths / Great Wall.
With engraved back (1980), offset back (1990) and offset front and back (1996).

2 YUAN 144 x 64mm **Cat.#885a**
1980- Olive green and multicolor.
Two youths / Rocky shoreline.
With engraved back, and since 1990 (Cat.#885b) offset back.

5 YUAN 150 x 71mm **Cat.#886**
1980 Brown and multicolor.
Two people / River between mountains.

10 YUAN 154 x 70mm **Cat.#887**
1980 Black, blue and multicolor.
Two people / Mountains.

50 YUAN 159 x 77mm **Cat.#888a**
1980- Black, green and multicolor.
Three people / Waterfalls.
Without, or since 1990 with security thread (Cat.#888b).

100 YUAN 166 x 78mm **Cat.#889a**
1980 Black and multicolor.
Four Great Leaders / Mountains.
Without, or since 1990 with security thread (Cat.#889a).

OUTMODED AND REDEEMABLE NOTES

Old Renminbi notes dated between 1953 and 1972 are legal tender, but seldom found in circulation.

Colombia Kolumbien • Colombie COP

Peso(s) = 100 centavo(s).
Minor unit coins are not used.

Currency import-export restrictions:
Local currency in/out: COP 2,546,227.57
Foreign currency in: USD 7,000.00. Larger amounts require a Customs
Declaration. 27AUG1998
Out: up to amount imported and declared.

The exchange of foreign currency into Colombian pesos is subject
to a 3% withholding, which does not apply to foreign visitors
staying less than 90 days.

A BRIEF MONETARY HISTORY
1 Jan 1993: Peso replaces Peso Oro.

Alternative currencies: **USD**, VEB or any major.

Issuer: "BANCO DE LA REPÚBLICA"

CURRENT NOTES

2,000 PESOS 140 x 70mm Issued 2 April 1996 **Cat.#445**
1996- Blue, red and multicolor.
General Francisco de Paula Santander / Casa de Moneda de
Santafé de Bogotá.

5,000 PESOS 140 x 70mm **Cat.#441**
1995- Brown, green, blue and multicolor.
Poet José Asunción Silva / Art Nouveau flower design, woman in
garden and column with poem.

10,000 PESOS 140 x 70mm Issued 30 Nov 1995 **Cat.#444**
1 July 1995 Reddish brown, green and multicolor.
Policarpa Salavarrieta, "La Pola" / Town of Guaduas around 1846.
Commemorates 200 years of her birth.

©MRI BANKERS' GUIDE TO FOREIGN CURRENCY
P.O.BOX 3174 HOUSTON TX 77253 USA

20,000 PESOS   140 x 70 **Cat.#447**
   23 July 1996 Black, blue and green / Blue, yellow brown and multicolor.
   Astronomer and mathematician Julio Garavito A. and view of the moon / Satellite view of earth and geometrical figures.

OUTMODED AND REDEEMABLE NOTES

All older notes issued by Banco de la República are redeemable. The following notes are worthless because of a big robbery:

2,000 pesos "Julio 1, 1993" *43,150,001/43,500,000*
. . . . 53,450,001/54,200,000   61,000,001/61,600

5,000 pesos "Enero 3, 1994" *28,100,001/28,200,000*
48,300,001/48,900,000 63,200,001/64,100,000 79,200,001/79,800,000

10,000 pesos "1993"   68,200,001/68,600,000   75,000,001/75,600,000

Comoros   Comores • Komoren   **KMF**

Franc(s)
Minor unit coins are not used.
Parity: KMF 1.00 = FRF .0133 (Since 12 Jan 1994).

Currency import-export restrictions:
Local currency in: free, out: CF500,000.
Foreign currency in: free.
Out: equivalent to CF 500,000; or more if declared on entry.

Alternative currencies: **FRF** or USD.

A BRIEF MONETARY HISTORY
1972: Comorian franc established at par with Malagasy franc.

Issuer: "BANQUE CENTRALE DES COMORES"

CURRENT NOTES

500 FRANCS   140 x 75mm **Cat.#10**
   Yellow, red and multicolor.
   Building and woman / Two women.

1,000 FRANCS   150 x 80mm **Cat.#11**
   Green, blue and multicolor.
   Woman / Women and palm trees.

2,500 FRANCS   150 x 85mm Issued in mid 1997 **Cat.#13**
   Multicolor.
   Woman with colorful scarf / Sea turtle.

5,000 FRANCS   160 x 85mm **Cat.#12**
   Green and multicolor.
   Couple, building and boats / Pres. Djohr.

10,000 FRANCS   170 x 85mm **Cat.#14**
   Yellow, orange and brown / Yellow, brown and blue.
   Al-Habib Seyyid Omar bin Sumeit and mosque / Two women making baskets.

OUTMODED AND REDEEMABLE NOTES

Similar notes issued by "Institut d'Émission des Comores" are still valid, but seldom seen in circulation.

©MRI BANKERS' GUIDE TO FOREIGN CURRENCY
P.O.Box 3174 HOUSTON TX 77253 USA

Congo (Brazzaville)   **XAF**

Franc(s) CFA Central = 100 centime(s).

Two types of notes run concurrently, old with the names of the Central African countries, and new of common design.
See CENTRAL AFRICAN STATES for current and outmoded notes, restrictions and other details.
Please note that banknotes with "République Populaire du Congo" are worthless.

Dem. Rep. of Congo (ex Zaïre)
République Democratique du Congo • DR Kongo •
Rep. Dem. del Congo   **CDF**

Franc(s) congolaise(s) = 100 centime(s)

In the two Kasai regions the old zaire circulates at 14 million for 100,000 new zaires or one Congolese franc. (Panafrican News Agency, 28 July 1998.)

Currency import-export restrictions:
Local currency in/out: USD 100 or equivalent.
Foreign currency in/out: free.

Due to the volatility of the zaïre, U.S. dollars are used widely.

In the Kasai area only old zaïres are accepted. Notes of 500,000 and 1,000,000 nouveaux zaïres are reported to circulate in some areas, but are not accepted in Kinshasa.

U.S. notes which are damaged or dirty and 50's and 100's dated 1988 or before may be hard to exchange. Even small new dollar notes may be hard to exchange, as it has been reported that there is a shortage of local notes.

A BRIEF MONETARY HISTORY
1967: 1 zaïre = 1,000 Congolese francs.
1993: 1 nouveau zaïre = 3,000,000 zaïres.
1998: 1 franc congolaise = 100,000 nouveaux zaïres.

Issuer: "BANQUE CENTRALE DU CONGO", formerly "BANQUE DU ZAÏRE."

CURRENT NOTES

Smaller notes not listed because of low value.

Caution!!!
This note
is worth only
0.50 franc

{50,000 NOUVEAUX ZAÏRES} = **0.50 FRANC CONGOLAISE**
159 x 74mm Issued 29 Jan 1996 **Cat.#74**
30.1.1996 Blue and lilac.
Pres. Mobutu / Value.

50 CENTIMES = 0.50 FR. CONGOLAISE
120 x 70mm Issued 30 June 1998 **Cat.#82**
01.11.1997 Brown.
Okapi / Okapi family.

Caution!!!
This note
is worth only
1 franc

{100,000 NOUVEAUX ZAÏRES} = **1 FRANC CONGOLAISE**
159 x 74mm Issued in Dec 1996 **Cat.#76**
30.6.1996 Orange and green.
Pres. Mobutu / Value.
FORGERIES ABOUND!!! There are notes of other colors which seem to be of irregular issue.

1 FRANC CONGOLAISE   150 x 70mm Issued 30 June 1998 **Cat.#83**
Violet blue, dark blue and multicolor.
Mining installations - Gecamines / Lumumba and his companions.

5 FRANCS CONGOLAISES 150 x 70mm Issued 30 June 1998 **Cat.#84**
1 Nov. 1997 Dark lilac and multicolor.
White rhinoceros / Kamwanga waterfalls.

10 FRANCS CONGOLAISES
150 x 70mm Issued 30 June 1998 **Cat.#85**
1 Nov 1997 Green, brown and multicolor.
Statuette of two people / Wood statuette.

20 FRANCS CONGOLAISES
150 x 70mm Issued 30 June 1998 **Cat.#86**
1 Nov 1997 Orange brown and multicolor.
Lions' head / Family of lions.
FORGERIES ABOUND!!!

50 FRANCS CONGOLAISES
150 x 70mm Issued 30 June 1998 **Cat.#87**
In circulation, details not available.
Head / Village.

100 FRANCS CONGOLAISES
150 x 70mm Issued 30 June 1998 **Cat.#88**
In circulation, details not available.
Elephant / Dam.

Cook Islands
Cookinseln • Islas Cook • Îles Cook

NZD

Dollar(s) = 100 cent(s).
Parity NZD 1.00

The import and export of local and foreign currencies are free.

New Zealand dollars are current. Alternative currencies: AUD, USD.

Issuer: "MINISTRY OF FINANCE"

CURRENT NOTES

3 DOLLARS
148 x 75mm Issued in 1992 **Cat.#7**
Mauve, green and multicolor / Mauve, violet brown and multicolor.
Group of people walking by building / Scenes from Aitutaki.

OUTMODED AND REDEEMABLE NOTES

All notes of all denominations can be redeemed without time limit.

Costa Rica   CRC

Colón (colones) = 100 céntimo(s).
Minor unit coins are not used.

Currency import-export restrictions:
Local currency in: free. Out: forbidden.
Foreign currency: free. In practice persons carrying large amounts may be questioned.   29JUL1998

It is advisable not to bring USD 100.00 bills, as many banks will not accept them. Stick to lower denominations of the new style. Avoid bringing dirty or torn notes.

Alternative currencies: all major.

Issuer: "Banco Central de Costa Rica."

CURRENT NOTES

Smaller notes not listed because of low value.

50 COLONES   146 x 67mm **Cat.#242**
1978-93 Green and multicolor.
G. Ortuño y Ors / Bank building.
Coins are replacing this note.

100 COLONES   146 x 67mm **Cat.#241**
1977- Black and multicolor.
R. Jiménez / Supreme Court building.
Coins are replacing this note.

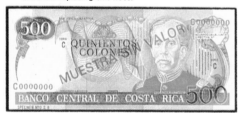

500 COLONES   146 x 67mm **Cat.#238A**
1987-89 Orange, brown and multicolor.
Manuel María Gutiérrez / Teatro Nacional de Costa Rica.

500 COLONES   146 x 67mm **Cat.#262**
1994- Orange and multicolor.
Manuel María Gutiérrez / Teatro Nacional de Costa Rica.

1,000 COLONES   146 x 67mm **Cat.#233**
1975- Red and multicolor.
T Soley Güell / National Insurance Institute building.
Without (1975-1994 Cat.#23), or with windowed security thread and ascending serial numbers (1997- Cat.#26).

2,000 COLONES   146 x 67mm Issued 1 Dec 1998 **Cat.#265**
1997- Orange brown, light green and brown.
Clodomiro Picado and Isla del Coco / Dolphin and hammershark.

5,000 COLONES   146 x 67mm **Cat.#257**
1991-95 Blue, brown, green and multicolor / Blue, brown, red and multicolor.
Pre-Columbian gold figure / Jaguar, stone ball and toucan.

5,000 COLONES   146 x 67mm Issued in Nov. 1997 **Cat.#266**
1996 Blue, brown, green and multicolor / Blue, brown, red and multicolor.
Pre-Columbian gold figure / Jaguar, stone ball and toucan.
With improved security features.

10,000 COLONES   146 x 67mm Issued 1 Dec 1998 **Cat.#267**
1997 Blue and multicolor / Blue, brown and multicolor.
Emma Gamboa A. and four volcanoes / Puma and jaguar.

OUTMODED AND REDEEMABLE NOTES

All older notes issued by the Banco Central de Costa Rica are redeemable.

©MRI BANKERS' GUIDE TO FOREIGN CURRENCY
P.O.Box 3174 HOUSTON TX 77253 USA

Croatia
Hrvatska • Kroatien • Croacia • Croatie   **HRK**

Kuna = 100 lipa.

Currency import/export restrictions:
Foreign currency in/out: free to visitors. Declaration required for amounts above equivalent of HRK 40,000.
Local in/out: 2,000 kuna.
Reconversion requires presentation of proof of prior exchange.

Jul1998

A BRIEF MONETARY HISTORY
30 May 1994: kuna = 1,000 Croatian dinara.

Issuer (since Dec 1997): "HRVATSKA NARODNA BANKA."

CURRENT NOTES

5 KUNA   122 x 61mm Issued 30 May 1994 **Cat.#28**
1993 Green and multicolor.
Fran Krsto Frankopan and Petar Zrinski / Old fortress in Varaždin.

10 KUNA   126 x 63mm Issued 30 May 1994 **Cat.#29**
1993 Purple and multicolor.
Juraj Dobrila / Amphitheater in Pula.

10 KUNA   126 x 63mm Issued 30 June 1995 **Cat.#36**
15 Jan 1995 Brown, gray and green.
Juraj Dobrila / Amphitheater in Pula.
Colors changed because 1993 notes were confused with German 10 marks.

20 KUNA   130 x 65mm Issued 30 May 1994 **Cat.#30**
1993 Red and brown.
Josip Jelačić / Castle of Count Eltz in Vukovar, and pottery dove.

50 KUNA   134 x 67mm Issued 30 May 1994 **Cat.#31**
1993 Blue and dark blue.
Ivan Gundulić / Old City of Dubrovnik.

100 KUNA   138 x 69mm Issued 30 May 1994 **Cat.#32**
1993 Orange brown and yellow brown.
Ivan Mažuranić / Church of St. Vitus in Rijeka.

200 KUNA   142 x 71mm Issued 30 May 1994 **Cat.#33**
1993 Reddish brown and multicolor.
Stjepan Radić / Building of Town Command in Osijek.

500 KUNA   146 x 73mm Issued 30 May 1994 **Cat.#34**
1993 Olive green and multicolor.
Marko Marulić / Palace of Diocletian in Split.

1,000 KUNA   150 x 75mm Issued 30 May 1994 **Cat.#35**
1993 Gray, blue and pink.
Ante Starčević / Monument to first Croatian king Tomislav, and front of the Cathedral of Zagreb.

Cuba Kuba   CUP

Peso(s) = 100 centavo(s).

Currency import-export restrictions:
Local currency in/out: forbidden.
Foreign currency in: free, must declare.
Out: up to amount imported and declared.

Alternative currencies: **USD** or all major. Travellers cheques in U.S. dollars issued by American banks are not accepted.

Issuers: "BANCO CENTRAL DE CUBA", formerly "BANCO NACIONAL DE CUBA."

CURRENT NOTES

Smaller notes not listed because of low value.

1 PESO Banco Nacional de Cuba   150 x 70mm **Cat.#112**
   1995 Olive green, light orange and blue.
   José Martí / "Entrada a La Habana 8 de enero de 1959."

3 PESOS Banco Nacional de Cuba   150 x 70mm **Cat.#107**
   1983-89 Red and multicolor.
   Ernesto "Ché" Guevara / "Ché" Guevara cutting sugarcane.
   These notes are being replaced by coins.

3 PESOS BNC   150 x 70mm Issued in Oct 1997 **Cat.#113**
   1995 Reddish brown, green and blue.
   Ernesto "Ché" Guevara / "Ché" Guevara cutting sugarcane.
   Issued to commemorate the 29th anniversary of Guevara's death. These notes
   are being replaced by coins.

5 PESOS Banco Nacional de Cuba   150 x 70mm **Cat.#95**
   1961-65 Green on pink.
   A. Maceo / Invasion of 1958.

5 PESOS Banco Nacional de Cuba   150 x 70mm **Cat.#103**
   1967-90 Green on pink.
   A. Maceo / Invasion of 1958.

5 PESOS Banco Nacional de Cuba   150 x 70mm **Cat.#108**
   1991 Green and blue on multicolor.
   A.Maceo / Two groups of patriots. "Cuba será un eterno Baraguá."

5 PESOS Banco Central de Cuba   150 x 70mm **Cat.#116**
   1997 Green.
   Antonio Maceo / Two groups of patriots. "Cuba será un eterno Baraguá."

10 PESOS Banco Nacional de Cuba   150 x 70mm **Cat.#96**
   1961-65 Brown on yellow.
   Máximo Gómez / Castro speaking.

10 PESOS Banco Nacional de Cuba   150 x 70mm **Cat.#104**
   1967-89 Brown on yellow.
   Máximo Gómez / Castro speaking.

10 PESOS Banco Nacional de Cuba   150 x 70mm **Cat.#109**
   1991 Reddish brown and multicolor / Light brown.
   Máximo Gómez / "Guerra de todo el Pueblo", hands holding
   weapons.

10 PESOS BCC   150 x 70mm Issued in March 1998 **Cat/#117**
1997 Brown and yellow.
Máximo Gómez / Machine guns and flags.

20 PESOS Banco Nacional de Cuba   150 x 70mm **Cat.#97**
1961-65 Blue on pink.
Camilo Cienfuegos / Rebels disembarking from the "Granma."

20 PESOS Banco Nacional de Cuba   **150 x 70mm Cat.#105**
1971-90 Blue on pink.
Camilo Cienfuegos / Rebels disembarking from the "Granma."

20 PESOS Banco Nacional de Cuba   150 x 70mm **Cat.#110**
1991 Blue green, brown and multicolor.
Camilo Cienfuegos / Banana harvest.

20 PESOS Banco Central de Cuba   150 x 70mm **Cat.#118**
A new note is in circulation. Details not available.

50 PESOS Banco Nacional de Cuba   150 x 70mm **Cat.#111**
1990 Red, violet and multicolor.
Calixto Garcia Iniguez / Centro de Ingeniería Genética y
Biotecnología.

50 PESOS Banco Central de Cuba   150 x 70mm **Cat.#119**
A new note was issued. Details not available.
xxx

"PESOS CONVERTIBLES"

Issued to visitors in exchange for hard currency, may be
reconverted on departure.

1 PESO CONVERTIBLE BNC   150 x 70mm **Cat.#FX24**
1994 Brown, orange and multicolor / Orange red, green and
multicolor.
Monumento a José Martí / Arms.

3 PESOS CONVERTIBLES BNC   150 x 70mm **Cat.#FX25**
1994 Orange red, green and multicolor.
Monumento a Ernesto "Ché" Guevara / Arms.

5 PESOS CONVERTIBLES BNC   150 x 70mm **Cat.#FX26**
1994 Green, orange and multicolor.
Monumento a Antonio Maceo / Arms.

10 PESOS CONVERTIBLES BNC   150 x 70mm **Cat.#FX27**
1994 Brown, green and multicolor / Orange red, green and
multicolor.
Monumento a Máximo Gómez / Arms.

20 PESOS CONVERTIBLES BNC   150 x 70mm **Cat.#FX28**
  1994 Red, blue, brown and multicolor / Orange red, green and multicolor.
  Monumento a Camilo Cienfuegos / Arms.

50 PESOS CONVERTIBLES BNC   150 x 70mm **Cat.#FX29**
  1994 Dark brown, orange and multicolor / Orange red, green and multicolor.
  Monumento a Calixto García / Arms.

100 PESOS CONVERTIBLES BNC   150 x 70mm **Cat.#FX30**
  1994 Red orange and multicolor / Orange red, green and multicolor.
  Monumento a Carlos Manuel de Céspedes / Arms.

Cyprus
Kyproy/Kıbrıs • Zypern • Chipre • Chypre   **CYP**

Pound(s) = 100 cent(s).

Currency import-export restrictions:
Local currency in: free, out CYP 100.
Foreign currency in: declaration required if reëxport of USD 1,000 or equivalent is intended.
Out: up to USD 1,000 or equivalent (including up to CYP 100); more if declared on arrival.   Aug 1998

Alternative currencies: AUD, CAD, CHF, DEM, FRF, GBP, GRD and **USD.**

Issuer: "CENTRAL BANK OF CYPRUS"

In the area of the Republic of Cyprus invaded by Turkey, Turkish currency is used, although Cypriot pounds are widely accepted.

CURRENT NOTES

1 POUND   141 x 71mm **Cat.#46**
  1979-93 Brown and multicolor.
  Mosaic of nymph Acme / Bellapais Abbey.

1 POUND   140 x 68mm Issued 6 May 1997 **Cat.#57**
  1 Feb 1997 Brown and multicolor.
  Cypriot girl dressed in traditional costume / Pottery and handicraft laces with the Kato Drys village in background.

1 POUND   140 x 68mm Issued 4 March 1998 **Cat.#57**
  1 Oct 1997 Brown and multicolor.
  Cypriot girl dressed in traditional costume / Pottery and handicraft laces with the Kato Drys village in background.
  Colors slightly changed.

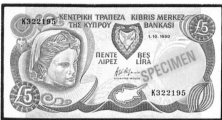

5 POUNDS   149 x 74mm **Cat.#47**
  1979-90 Purple and multicolor.
  Limestone head / Theatre at Salamis.
  Those issued in 1990 have enhanced security features.

5 POUNDS   148 x 72mm Issued 6 May 1997 **Cat.#58**
  1 Feb 1997 Lilac brown, reddish brown, grayish green and multicolor.
  Limestone head of a young man / Peristerona church and Turkish mosque in background.

10 POUNDS   160 x 77mm **Cat.#48**
  1977-85 Green and multicolor.
  Archaic head / Two birds.

10 POUNDS   160 x 77mm **Cat.#51**
1987-92 Green and multicolor.
Archaic head / Two birds.
With enhanced security features.

10 POUNDS   156 x 76mm Issued 6 May 1997 **Cat.#59**
1 Feb 1997 Green and multicolor.
Bust of Aphrodite / Bird, turtle, butterfly, moufflon and flowers.

20 POUNDS   165 x 80mm **Cat.#56**
1992 Blue and multicolor.
Bust of Aphrodite / Kyrenia boat.
There are two varieties, with "YIRMI" or "YİRMİ"

20 POUNDS   164 x 80mm Issued 4 March 1998 **Cat.#60**
1 Oct 1997 Blue and multicolor.
Bust of Aphrodite / Kyrenia boat.

OUTMODED AND REDEEMABLE NOTES

Warning!!!
This note
is worth only
¼ pound

{250 MILS} = **0.25 POUND** Republic of Cyprus 125 x 74mm **Cat.#37**
1961 Blue and multicolor.
Fruit and arms / Mine.

Warning!!!
This note
is worth only
¼ pound

{250 MILS} = **0.25 POUND** Central Bank of Cyprus 125 x 74mm **Cat.#41**
1964-82 Blue and multicolor.
Fruit and arms / Mine.

Warning!!!
This note
is worth only
½ pound

{500 MILS} = **0.50 POUND** Republic of Cyprus 141 x 82mm **Cat.#38**
1961 Green and multicolor.
Geometric design / Mountain road.

Warning!!!
This note
is worth only
½ pound

{500 MILS} = **0.50 POUND** C.B. of Cyprus   141 x 82mm **Cat.#42**
1964-79 Green and multicolor.
Geometric design / Mountain road.

Warning!!!
This note
is worth only
½ pound

{500 MILS} = **0.50 POUND**   133 x 68mm **Cat.#45**
1.6.1982 Light brown and multicolor.
Cypriot girl / Yermasoyia dam.

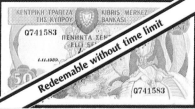

50 CENTS   133 x 68mm **Cat.#49**
1983-89 Light brown and multicolor.
Cypriot girl / Yermasoyia dam.

©MRI BANKERS' GUIDE TO FOREIGN CURRENCY
P.O.Box 3174 HOUSTON TX 77253 USA

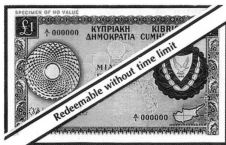

1 POUND Republic of Cyprus.   149 x 89mm **Cat.#39**
1961 Brown and multicolor.
Geometric design / Viaduct and pillars.

1 POUND Central Bank of Cyprus   149 x 89mm **Cat.#43**
1966-78 Brown and multicolor.
Geometric design / Viaduct and pillars.

5 POUNDS Republic of Cyprus   166 x 93mm **Cat.#40**
1961 Dark green and multicolor.
Geometric design / Ornamental design.

5 POUNDS Central Bank of Cyprus.   166 x 93mm **Cat.#44**
1966-76 Blue and multicolor.
Geometric design / Ornamental design.

Czech Republic
Ceská Republika • Tschechische Republik •
República Checa • République Tchèque   **CZK**

Koruna (korun) = 100 haler(u).

Currency import-export restrictions:

Local and/or foreign currency in/out: Declaration required for amounts in excess of 200,000 korun or equivalent.

Alternative currencies: all major.

A BRIEF MONETARY HISTORY
May 1945: Prewar notes are declared legal tender.
Oct. 1945: (new) Czechoslovakian koruna replaces all previous currencies.
June 1953: (new) koruna issued at variable rates (5 to 50) depending of circumstances.
Feb. 1993: Czech koruna replaces Czechoslovakian koruna.

Issuer: "ČESKA NARODNI BANKA."

CURRENT NOTES

20 KORUN   128 x 64mm Issued 20 April 1994 **Cat.#10**
1994 Blue.
King Přemysl Otakar I and his seal / Royal crown, Golden Bull seal of Sicily and arms.

50 KORUN   133 x 64mm Issued 6 Oct 1993 **Cat.#4**
1993- Rose, brown and multicolor.
Sv. Anežka Česka (St. Agnes of Bohemia) / "A" and arms.
There are slightly different versions dated 1994 and 1997.

100 KORUN   140 x 68mm Issued 30 June 1993 **Cat.#5**
1993- Green and wine red.
Karel IV / Seal of Charles University.
There are slightly different versions dated 1995 and 1997.

200 KORUN   146 x 69mm Issued 8 Feb 1993 **Cat.#6**
1993- Yellow orange, brown and green.
J.A. Komensky / Orbis Pictus.
There are slightly different versions dated 1996 and 1998.

©MRI BANKERS' GUIDE TO FOREIGN CURRENCY
P.O.Box 3174 HOUSTON TX 77253 USA

500 KORUN   152 x 69mm Issued 21 July 1993 **Cat.#7**
1993- Brown and orange / Brown.
Božena Němcová and rose / Woman's head.
There are slightly different versions dated 1995 and 1997.

1,000 KORUN   158 x 73mm Issued 12 May 1993 **Cat.#8**
1993- Purple, lilac and multicolor.
František Palacký / Arms, eagle and Kroměříž Castle.
There is a slightly different version dated 1996.

2,000 KORUN   164 x 74mm Issued 1 October 1996 **Cat.#16**
1996 Green, gray and multicolor.
Ema Destinnová / Euterpe and musical motifs.

5,000 KORUN   170 x 74mm Issued 15 Dec 1993 **Cat.#9**
1993 Gray and pink.
Tomáš Garrigue Masaryk / Montage of cathedrals and historical
buildings of Prague.

Denmark
Danmark • Dänemark • Danemark • Dinamarca   **DKK**

Krone(r) = 100 øre.

The import and export of all currencies is free.   Jul1998

Alternative currencies: all major.

Issuer: "DANMARKS NATIONALBANK."

CURRENT NOTES

50 KRONER   139 x 71mm Issued 21 Jan 1975 **Cat.#50**
Series 1972 Blue green and black.
Mrs. Ryberg's portrait / Fish.

50 KRONER   125 x 72mm Issued 7 May 1999 **Cat.#55**
Series 1997
Writer Karen Blixen / Centaur from Landet Church, Tåsinge.

100 KRONER   150 x 77mm Issued 22 Oct 1974 **Cat.#51**
Series 1972 Red, black and multicolor.
Jens Juel's self-portrait / Butterfly.

100 KRONER   150 x 77mm Issued 16 Oct 1995 **Cat.#54**
Series 1972A Red, black and multicolor.
Jens Juel's self-portrait / Butterfly.

100 KRONER   **Cat.#56**
Series 1997
Musician Carl Nielsen / Basilisk from Tømmerby Church.
Expected to be issued in late 1999.

200 KRONER   145 x 72mm Issued 10 March 1997 **Cat.#57**
Series 1997 Green and gray / Green and orange.
Actress Johanne Luise Heiberg / Lion from the apse of Viborg
Cathedral.

500 KRONER   164 x 85mm Issued 18 April 1974 **Cat.#52**
Series 1972 Green, black and multicolor.
"Unknown lady" / Lizard.

500 KRONER   155 x 72mm Issued 12 Sep 1997 **Cat.#58**
Series 1997 Blue, orange and multicolor.
Niels Bohr / Motif from the Lihme Church in Salling.

1,000 KRONER   176 x 94mm Issued 11 March 1975 **Cat.#53**
Series 1972 Black, green and red / Brown, green and red.
Thomasine Heiberg's portrait / Squirrel.

1,000 KRONER   165 x 72mm Issued 18 September 1998. **Cat.#59**
Series 1997 Orange red, black and dark brown.
Painters Anna and Michael Ancher / Tournament scene from
Bislev Church.

OUTMODED AND REDEEMABLE NOTES

*The two center digits of the six character string indicates date of
issue. For instance C3518D means 1951.*

The "1936" date in some notes refers to the year of the law of issue.

5 KRONER   129 x 72mm Issued 23 July 1945 **Cat.#35**
1945-53 Blue.
Value / Arms.   red

5 KRONER   124 x 65mm Issued 14 Oct 1952 **Cat.#42**
1950-61 Blue green.
Bertel Thorvaldsen and Three Graces / Town and church of
Kalundborg.   red

10 KRONER   130 x 79mm Issued 23 July 1945 **Cat.#36**
1944-45 Brown.
Value / Arms.   red

10 KRONER   133 x 79mm Issued 22 May 1947 **Cat.#37**
1947-53 Green / Green and gray.
Value / Arms.
Caution: *earlier brown notes are worthless.*   red

10 KRONER   124 x 65mm Issued 14 Oct 1952 **Cat.#43**
1950-53 Black and ochre / Ochre and olive green.
Hans Christian Andersen and bird nest / Windmill.   red

10 KRONER   124 x 70mm Issued 15 March 1954 **Cat.#44**
1950-74 Black and brown.
Hans Christian Andersen and bird nest / Windmill.   red

10 KRONER Series 1972   125 x 67mm Issued 8 April 1975 **Cat.#48**
Black on brown and multicolor / Olive brown and black.
C.S. Kirchhoff / Duck.   red

20 KRONER Series 1972 125 x 71mm Issued 11 March 1980 *Cat.#49*
Black on reddish brown and multicolor.
"Mrs. Tutein" / Two birds.
red

50 KRONER 157 x 101mm Issued 23 July 1945 *Cat.#38*
1944-57 Purple brown on pale olive.
Fishermen / Arms.
Caution: earlier blue green notes are worthless.
red

50 KRONER 155 x 79mm Issued 21 May 1957 *Cat.#45*
1950-70 Black blue on grayish green / Grayish blue.
Ole Rømer and tower / Dolmens.
red

100 KRONER 157 x 101mm Issued 23 July 1945 *Cat.#39*
1945-62 Green / Green and black.
Ornamental designs / Arms.
Caution: earlier brown notes are worthless.
red

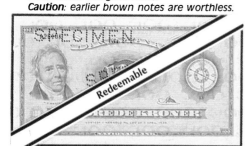

100 KRONER 154 x 84mm Issued 3 May 1962 *Cat.#46*
1961-67 Red / Brown.
Ørsted and compass / Church.
red

500 KRONER 176 x 107mm Issued 23 July 1945 *Cat.#41*
1945-64 Red / Brown.
Farmer plowing / Arms.
Caution: earlier grayish blue notes are worthless.
red

500 KRONER 175 x 90mm Issued 4 June 1964 *Cat.#47*
1963-74 Green and black.
Chr. D.F. Reventlow and farmer plowing / Church.
red

Djibouti   Dschibuti • Jibuti   DJF

Franc = 100 centime(s).
Minor unit coins are not used.

The import and export of local and foreign currencies are free.

A BRIEF MONETARY HISTORY
March 1949: Djiboutian franc established, linked to the U.S. Dollar at
the rate of 1 USD = 214,3920 DJF.
1971: rate changed to 1 USD = 197.466 DJF.
1973: rate changed to 1 USD = 177.721 DJF

Alternative currencies: FRF, **USD.**

Issuer: "BANQUE NATIONALE."

CURRENT NOTES

1,000 FRANCS 150 x 80mm **Cat.#37**
Multicolor.
Woman and train / Dromedaries and driver.

©MRI BANKERS' GUIDE TO FOREIGN CURRENCY
P.O.Box 3174 HOUSTON TX 77253 USA

2,000 FRANCS   170 x 80mm Issued in June 1997 **Cat.#40**
Blue, yellow and multicolor.
Young woman and camel caravan / Statue and palace.
Issued to commemorate the 20th Anniversary of Independence.

5,000 FRANCS   160 x 85mm **Cat.#38**
Multicolor.
Man and trees / Aerial view of city.

10,000 FRANCS   172 x 92mm **Cat.#39**
Brown, red and green on multicolor.
Woman with child / Seven fish and man-made harbor.

OUTMODED AND REDEEMABLE NOTES

Notes of 500, 1,000 and 5,000 francs of the "Côte Française des Somalis" are redeemable at the Banque Nationale.

Type 1973 notes issued by "Territoire Française des Afars et des Issas" and 500 francs notes issued by the Banque Nationale are legal tender, but outmoded.

Dominica Dominique   **XCD**

East Caribbean currency is used.

The import and export of all currencies is free. Authorization is required for the export of XCD 250,000 or equivalent (USD 92,500.)

United States dollars are widely accepted. Alternative currencies: CAD, DEM, FRF, GBP.

Dominican Republic   Rep. Dominicana •
Dominikanische Rep. • Rép. Dominicaine   **DOP**

Peso(s) oro = 100 centavo(s).

Currency import-export restrictions:
Local currency in/out RD$ 20,000 in notes, and RD$100 in coin (Effective 19 Dec 1991).
Foreign currency in: free. Amounts over US$10,000 or its equivalent should be declared if reëxport is intended.
Out: free to US$ 10,000 or equivalent. Larger amounts require authorization from the Central Bank.   Jul1998

Alternative currencies: CAD, CHF, DEM, ESP, FRF, GBP, **USD.**

Issuer: "BANCO CENTRAL DE LA REPÚBLICA DOMINICANA."

CURRENT NOTES

5 PESOS   156 x 67mm **Cat.#118**
1978- Brownish red and multicolor.
Sánchez / Hydroelectric dam.
There are small variations between notes produced by different printers.

10 PESOS   156 x 67mm **Cat.#119**
1978- Green and multicolor.
Mella / Mining.
There are small variations between notes produced by different printers.

20 PESOS   156 x 67mm **Cat.#120**
1978- Brown and multicolor.
Altar de la Patria / Puerta del Conde.
There are small variations between notes produced by different printers.

20 PESOS   156 x 67mm **Cat.#139**
Serie 1992
"B A Banknote" note overprinted "1492-1992 / V CENTENARIO / DEL DESCUBRIMIENTO / Y EVANGELIZACIÓN / DE AMÉRICA."

50 PESOS   156 x 67mm **Cat.#121**
1978- Purple and multicolor.
"Basílica de N. S. de la Altagracia" / Cathedral.
These notes are produced by different printers with different security features.

100 PESOS   156 x 67mm **Cat.#122**
1977- Orange and multicolor.
Casa de Moneda / Central Bank.
These notes are produced by different printers with different security features.

500 PESOS   156 x 67mm **Cat.#123**
1978- Greenish blue and multicolor.
Teatro Nacional / Fortaleza San Felipe .
These notes are produced by different printers with different security features.

500 PESOS   156 x 67mm **Cat.#141**
Regular note overprinted: "1492-1992 / V CENTENARIO / DEL
DESCUBRIMIENTO / Y EVANGELIZACION / DE AMERICA"

500 PESOS   156 x 67mm **Cat.#140**
Serie 1992. Brown, blue, orange red and multicolor.
Columbus and his three ships / "Faro a Colón".
Commemorative of the 5th Centennial of the Discovery and Colonization of the
Americas. **Caution:** forgeries were reported.

1,000 PESOS   156 x 67mm **Cat.#124**
1978- Red and multicolor.
Palacio Nacional / Alcázar de Colón.
These notes are produced by different printers with different security features.

WARNING

**Low serial numbered notes stamped
"SPECIMEN" are worthless.**

1,000 PESOS   156 x 67mm **Cat.#142**
Regular note overprinted "1492-1992 / V CENTENARIO / DEL
DESCUBRIMIENTO / Y EVANGELIZACION / DE AMERICA."

Eastern Caribbean Ostkaribischer
Staaten • Caribe Oriental • Caraïbes Orientales **XCD**

Dollar(s) = 100 cent(s).

It is the common currency of Anguilla, Antigua, Dominica, Grenada,
Montserrat, St Kitts and Nevis, St Lucia and St Vincent.

Currency import-export restrictions:
See under each island heading.

The serial suffix letter in notes of the Central Bank is a territorial
code for the island for which they were issued. These are:

    A   Antigua.
    D   Dominica.
    G   Grenada.
    K   St Christopher
    L   St Lucia.
    M   Montserrat.
    U   Anguilla.
    V   St Vincent.

All may be used in any island.

Issuer: "EASTERN CARIBBEAN CENTRAL BANK."

CURRENT NOTES

5 DOLLARS   145 x 69mm Issued in October 1993 **Cat.#26**
Green and brownish red.
Elizabeth II, turtle and bird / Admiral's House, Antigua and
Barbuda; and Trafalgar Falls, Dominica.

5 DOLLARS   145 x 69mm   Issued 12 Dec 1994   **Cat.#31**
Green and brownish red.
Elizabeth II, turtle and bird / Admiral's House, Antigua and
Barbuda; and Trafalgar Falls, Dominica.
Design modified for easier readability.

10 DOLLARS   145 x 69mm   Issued in October 1993   **Cat.#27**
Grayish blue, olive, olive brown, orange red and multicolor.
Elizabeth II, turtle and bird / Admiralty Bay, St. Vincent and the
Grenadines; The Warspite, Anguilla.

10 DOLLARS   145 x 69mm   Issued 12 Dec 1994   **Cat.#32**
Grayish blue, olive, olive brown, orange red and multicolor.
Elizabeth II, turtle and bird / Admiralty Bay, St. Vincent and the
Grenadines; The Warspite, Anguilla.
Design modified for easier readability.

20 DOLLARS   145 x 69mm   Issued in October 1993   **Cat.#28**
Reddish brown, green and orange red.
Elizabeth II, turtle and bird / Government House, Montserrat;
Nutmeg, Grenada.

20 DOLLARS   145 x 69mm   Issued 12 Dec 1994   **Cat.#33**
Reddish brown, green and orange red.
Elizabeth II, turtle and bird / Government House, Montserrat;
Nutmeg, Grenada.
Design modified for easier readability.

50 DOLLARS   145 x 69mm   Issued in October 1993   **Cat.#29**
Purple, olive green and red.
Elizabeth II, turtle and bird / Brimstone Hill, St. Kitts; Les Pitons,
St. Lucia.

50 DOLLARS   145 x 69mm   Issued 12 Dec 1994   **Cat.#34**
Yellow brown, orange and green.
Elizabeth II, turtle and bird / Brimstone Hill, St. Kitts; Les Pitons,
St. Lucia.
Modified in color and design for easier readability.

100 DOLLARS   145 x 69mm   Issued in October 1993   **Cat.#30**
Brown and green
Elizabeth II, turtle and bird / Sir Arthur Lewis and ECCB building.

100 DOLLARS   145 x 69mm   Issued 12 Dec 1994   **Cat.#35**
Brown and green.
Elizabeth II, turtle and bird / Sir Arthur Lewis and ECCB building.
Design modified for easier readability.

100 DOLLARS   145 x 69mm Issued in February 1998 **Cat.#36**
Brown and green.
Elizabeth II, turtle and bird / Sir Arthur Lewis and ECCB building.
With additional security features, including a gold flower added to the front.

OUTMODED AND REDEEMABLE NOTES

All older notes issued by the British Caribbean Territories, East Caribbean Currency Authority and Eastern Caribbean Central Bank are redeemable.

ECU European Currency Unit XEU

The ECU was a unit made of a basket of several currencies. Effective 1 Jan 1999 it was replaced by the "Euro."

There are travelers checks in ECUS.

Ecuador   Equateur   ECS

Sucre(s) = 100 centavo(s).
Minor unit coins are not used.

The import and export of local and foreign currency are free.

Alternative currencies: CAD, CHF, COP, DEM, ESP, FRF, GBP, ITL, **USD**.

Issuer: "BANCO CENTRAL DEL ECUADOR."

CURRENT NOTES

Smaller notes not listed because of low value.

1,000 SUCRES   156 x 67mm **Cat.#125**
1976-88 Green, olive, reddish brown and multicolor / Green.
Rumiñaui / Arms.
It is being replaced by a coin.

5,000 SUCRES   156 x 67mm **Cat.#126**
1987- Purple and multicolor.
J Montalvo / Birds and sea tortoise.

10,000 SUCRES   156 x 67mm **Cat.#128**
30.7.1988 Brown and multicolor.
Vicente Rocafuerte / Monumento a la Independencia, Quito.

20,000 SUCRES   156 x 67mm Issued Nov. 1995 **Cat.#129**
31.1.1995 Black, brown and blue.
Dr. Gabriel García Moreno / Arms.

50,000 SUCRES   156 x 67mm Issued in 1996 **Cat.#130**
31 Jan 1995 Slate, reddish brown and multicolor.
Eloy Alfaro / Arms and value.

100,000 SUCRES   **Cat.#131**
It may possibly be issued in the future.

©MRI BANKERS' GUIDE TO FOREIGN CURRENCY
P.O.Box 3174 HOUSTON TX 77253 USA

Egypt   Misr • Ägypten • Egipto • Egypte   EGP

Pound(s) = 100 piastre(s).

Currency Import-export restrictions:
Local currency in/out: LE 1,000.
Foreign currency in/out: free.

Aug1998

Alternative currencies: any major.

Issuer: "CENTRAL BANK OF EGYPT"

CURRENT NOTES

Several notes of 5 and 10 piastres (= 0.05 and 0.10 pounds) were issued recently. These are not listed because of their low value.

Caution!!!
This note
is worth only
¼ pound

{25 PIASTRES} = **0.25 POUND**   130 x 70mm **Cat.#49**
1979 Gray on light brown and blue.
As-sayida Aisha mosque / Eagle, cotton, maize and wheat.

Caution!!!
This note
is worth only
¼ pound

{25 PIASTRES} = **0.25 POUND**   130 x 70mm **Cat.#54**
1980-84 Dark green on green and multicolor.
As-sayida Aisha mosque / Eagle, cotton, maize and wheat.

Caution!!!
This note
is worth only
¼ pound

{25 PIASTRES} = **0.25 POUND**   130 x 70mm **Cat.#57**
1985-91 Blue and multicolor.
As-sayida Aisha mosque / Eagle, cotton, maize and wheat.

Caution!!!
This note
is worth only
½ pound

{50 PIASTRES} = **0.50 POUND**   135 x 70mm **Cat.#51**
1981-83 Green, brown and multicolor.
Al Azhar mosque / Ramses II.

Caution!!!
This note
is worth only
½ pound

{50 PIASTRES} = **0.50 POUND**   135 x 70mm **Cat.#58**
1985-95 Brown, gray and multicolor.
Mosque / Ramses II.

Caution!!!
This note
is worth only
½ pound

{50 PIASTRES} = **0.50 POUND**   135 x 70mm Issued 15 July 1996 **Cat.#62**
Olive green / Brown, yellow and green.
Mosque / Ramses II.

1 POUND   140 x 70mm **Cat.#50**
1978- Brown.
Qaitbay mosque / Part of the façade of Abu Simbel temple.

5 POUNDS   145 x 70mm **Cat.#56**
Blue, green and red.
Ibn Touloun mosque / Engraving representing the Nile offering its bounties to the Valley.

10 POUNDS   150 x 70mm **Cat.#51**
1978- Brown and brown violet.
Interior of Al-Rifai mosque / Statue of Chephren and Pyramids.

20 POUNDS   175 x 70mm **Cat.#52**
1979- Green, violet and multicolor.
Mohammed Ali mosque / Relief in the Chapel of Sesostris I at Karnak.

©MRI BANKERS' GUIDE TO FOREIGN CURRENCY
P.O.BOX 3174 HOUSTON TX 77253 USA

50 POUNDS 160 x 70mm **Cat.#60**
1993 Blackish purple, deep violet and orange brown on multicolor / Brown, olive brown and deep violet.
Mosque / Colonnade.

100 POUNDS 165 x 70mm **Cat.#53**
1978-92 Blue and multicolor.
As-sayida Zainab mosque / Mask of Tutankhamon.

100 POUNDS 165 x 70mm Issued 15 Nov 1994 **Cat.#61**
Brown, green and multicolor.
Sultan Hassan mosque / Sphinx.

OUTMODED AND REDEEMABLE NOTES

Older notes of 25 piastres up to 20 pounds issued by the National Bank of Egypt or the Central Bank of Egypt are still legal tender, but seldom found in circulation.

El Salvador   SVC

Colón (colones) = 100 centavo(s).

The import and export of local and foreign currencies are free.

Alternative currencies: GTQ, HNL, MXN, **USD.**

Issuer: "BANCO CENTRAL DE RESERVA DE EL SALVADOR."

CURRENT NOTES

5 COLONES 155 x 67mm **Cat.#106**
1956-93 Black and green / Green.
"Delgado acompañado ... / Columbus.

5 COLONES 155 x 67mm **Cat.#145**
18 April 1997 Green, brown and multicolor / Green.
Edificio del Palacio Nacional / Columbus.

10 COLONES 155 x 67mm **Cat.#141**
1995-96 Black and multicolor / Black.
Manuel José Arce / Columbus.

10 COLONES 155 x 67mm **Cat.#146**
18 April 1997 Bluish violet and multicolor / Bluish violet and green.
Volcán de Izalco / Columbus.

25 COLONES 155 x 67mm **Cat.#142**
1995 Black, blue and yellow / Blue.
Puerto de Acajutla / Columbus.

25 COLONES 155 x 67mm Issued in early Dec 1997 **Cat.#147**
18 April 1997 Blue and multicolor.
Pirámide de San Andrés / Columbus.

50 COLONES 155 x 67mm **Cat.#143**
1995-96 Purple and multicolor.
Capitán General Gerardo Barrios and National Palace / Columbus and his ships.
With windowed security thread and ascending serial numbers.

©MRI BANKERS' GUIDE TO FOREIGN CURRENCY
P.O.Box 3174 HOUSTON TX 77253 USA

50 COLONES   155 x 67mm Issued in early Dec 1997 **Cat.#148**
18 April 1997 Purple, blue and multicolor.
Lago de Coatepeque / Columbus.

100 COLONES   155 x 67mm **Cat.#140**
1993-96 Rose, blue and green / Bluish green and light olive green.
Pirámide del Tazumal / Columbus.
With ascending serial number and windowed security thread.

100 COLONES   155 x 67mm Issued in early Dec 1997 **Cat.#149**
18 April 1997 Green / Green and light orange red.
Pirámide del Tazumal / Columbus.

200 COLONES   155 x 67mm Issued in early Dec 1997 **Cat.#150**
18 April 1997 Brown, blue, green and multicolor.
Monumento El Salvador del Mundo / Columbus.

500 COLONES   **Cat.#151**
Planned for future issue.

OUTMODED AND REDEEMABLE NOTES

All older notes issued by the Banco Central de Reserva de El Salvador are valid, and can be used or redeemed.

England Inglaterra • Angleterre   GBP

Pound(s) = 100 penny (pence).

The import and export of all currencies is free. Customs officers may question anyone carrying more than £10,000 or its equivalent.

Alternative currencies: all major. Scottish and Northern Irish pounds are accepted in most large cities.

Issuer: "BANK OF ENGLAND."

CURRENT NOTES

5 POUNDS Series E   135 x 70mm Issued in June 1990 **Cat.#382**
Turquoise, brown violet and multicolor.
Elizabeth II / George Stephenson.

5 POUNDS Series E   135 x 70mm Issued in 1993 **Cat.#385**
Turquoise, brown violet and multicolor.
Elizabeth II / George Stephenson.
Modified version.

10 POUNDS Series E   142 x 75mm Issued 29 April 1992 **Cat.#383**
Dark violet, orange brown and multicolor / Brown and blue.
Elizabeth II / Charles Dickens and cricket match.

10 POUNDS Series E   142 x 75mm Issued in 1993 **Cat.#386**
Dark violet, orange brown and multicolor / Brown and blue.
Elizabeth II / Charles Dickens and cricket match.
Modified version.

WARNING

In most forgeries background lines are made out of dots instead of solid lines.

The windowed security thread must appear as a solid line when seen through the light.

20 POUNDS Series E   150 x 80mm Issued in June 1991 **Cat.#384**
Lilac, violet brown and multicolor / Lilac and multicolor.
Elizabeth II / Michael Faraday and his lecture in 1826.

20 POUNDS Series E   150 x 80mm Issued in 1993 **Cat.#387**
Lilac, violet brown and multicolor / Lilac and multicolor.
Elizabeth II / Michael Faraday and his lecture in 1826.
Modified version.

20 POUNDS   150 x 80mm Issued 22 June 1999 **Cat.#387**
Lilac, violet brown and multicolor / Lilac and multicolor.
Elizabeth II / Sir Edward Elgar.

50 POUNDS Series E   156 x 85mm **Cat.#388**
©1994 Orange red, violet gray and silver.
Elizabeth II / The bank gatekeeper, Sir John Houblon, and his house on Threadneedle street.

OUTMODED AND REDEEMABLE NOTES

All notes issued by the Bank of England since 1694 are redeemable.

Those dated 1943 and before must be verified, because vast quantities were forged by Germany during World War II.

Caution!!!
This note is worth only ½ pound

{10 SHILLINGS} = *0.50 POUND*   137 x 79mm **Cat.#126**
Brown.
Britannia / Value.

Caution!!!
This note is worth only ½ pound

{10 SHILLINGS} = *0.50 POUND*   137 x 79mm **Cat.#123**
Violet.
Britannia / Value.

Caution!!!
This note is worth only ½ pound

{10 SHILLINGS} = *0.50 POUND*
             140 x 67mm Issued 12 Oct 1961 **Cat.#373**
Brown and multicolor.
Elizabeth II / Britannia.

1 POUND   150 x 83mm **Cat.#127**
Green.
Britannia / Value.

1 POUND 150 x 83mm Cat.#124
  Blue.
  Britannia / Value.

1 POUND 150 x 72mm Issued 17 March 1960 Cat.#374
  Green.
  Elizabeth II / Britannia.

1 POUND 135 x 67mm Issued 9 Feb 1978 Cat.#377
  Green and multicolor.
  Elizabeth II / Sir Isaac Newton.

5 POUNDS 159 x 88mm Cat.#371
  Blue and multicolor.
  Britannia / Value.

5 POUNDS 140 x 85mm Issued 21 Feb 1963 Cat.#375
  Blue.
  Elizabeth II / Britannia.

5 POUNDS Series D 145 x 77mm Issued 11 Nov 1971 Cat.#378
  Blue and multicolor.
  Elizabeth II / Duke of Wellington.

10 POUNDS 151 x 93mm Issued 21 Feb 1964 Cat.#376
  Brown.
  Elizabeth II / Lion.

10 POUNDS Series D 150 x 85mm Issued 20 Feb 1975 Cat.#379
  Brown and multicolor.
  Elizabeth II / Florence Nightingale.
  With or without windowed security thread.

20 POUNDS Series D 160 x 90mm Issued 9 Jul 1970 Cat.#380
  Purple lilac and multicolor.
  Elizabeth II / Statue of Shakespeare.
  With or without windowed security thread.

50 POUNDS Series D 169 x 95mm Issued 20 March 1981 Cat.#381
  Olive green and multicolor.
  Elizabeth II / Sir Christopher Wren, view and plan of St. Paul's
  Cathedral.
  With or without windowed security thread.

Equatorial Guinea
Guinea Ecuatorial •
Äquatorialguinea • Guinée Equatoriale   **XAF**

Franc(s) CFA Central = 100 centime(s).
Parity: FFR 0.01

Two types of notes run concurrently, old with the names of the six Central African countries, and new of common design.

A BRIEF MONETARY HISTORY
1969: Guinean peseta established at par with Spanish peseta
1975: named changed to ekuele
1979: spelling changed to epkwele (plural bipkwele)
1985: CFA (Central) franc = 4 bipkwele

See CENTRAL AFRICAN STATES for current and outmoded notes, restrictions and other details.

Eritrea   Érythrée   **ERN**

Nakfa = 100 cents

The import and export of all currencies is free.   Jul1998
Visitors are expected to pay hotel bills and airline tickets with dollars or hard currencies.

A BRIEF MONETARY HISTORY:
8 Nov 1997: Nakfa introduced at par with Ethiopian birr.

Alternative currencies: any major currency.

Issuer: "BANK OF ERITREA"

CURRENT NOTES

1 NAKFA   140 x 70mm Issued 8 November 1997 **Cat.#1**
24.5.1997 Brown and green / Green.
Three heads and "Fighters" with Eritrean flag / "Bush" school.

5 NAKFA   140 x 70mm Issued 8 November 1997 **Cat.#2**
24.5.1997 Brown and green / Green.
Three heads and "Fighters" with Eritrean flag / Jacaranda tree.
With a holographic band at front left.

10 NAKFA   140 x 70mm Issued 8 November 1997 **Cat.#3**
24.5.1997 Brown and green / Green.
Three heads and "Fighters" with Eritrean flag / Restored railway crossing the bridge on the Dogali river.
With a holographic band at front left.

20 NAKFA   140 x 70mm Issued 8 November 1997 **Cat.#4**
24.5.1997 Brown and green / Green.
Three heads and "Fighters" with Eritrean flag / Agricultural scenes.
With a holographic band at front left.

50 NAKFA   140 x 70mm Issued 8 November 1997 **Cat.#5**
24.5.1997 Brown and green / Green.
Three heads and "Fighters" with Eritrean flag / Port of Masawa.
With a holographic band at front left.

100 NAKFA   140 x 70mm Issued 8 November 1997 **Cat.#6**
24.5.1997 Brown and green / Green.
Three heads and "Fighters" with Eritrean flag / Farmer plowing a field.
With a holographic band at front left.

Estonia   Eesti Vabariik • Estland • Estonie   **EEK**

Kroon(i) = 100 sent(i).

A BRIEF MONETARY HISTORY
20 June 1992: kroon = 10 rubles or 0.125 DM.

Currency import-export restrictions:
Local and foreign currency in or out: free up to EEK 80,000 or equivalent. Declaration required for larger amounts. Documentation of source of funds required on EEK 200,000 or more.

Alternative currencies: CAD, CHF, **DEM**, FIM, FRF, GBP, SEK, USD.

Issuer: "EESTI PANK."

CURRENT NOTES

1 KROON   140 x 70mm Issued 20 June 1992 **Cat.#69**
1992 Brown and gray.
Kristjan Raud / Ancient stronghold Toompea in Tallinn.

2 KROONI   140 x 70mm Issued 20 June 1992 **Cat.#70**
1992 Gray and bluish gray.
Karl Ernest von Baer / Tartu University.

5 KROONI   140 x 70mm Issued 20 June 1992 **Cat.#71**
1991-92 Orange brown and bluish gray / Brown and multicolor.
Paul Keres / View of Teutonic Order stronghold, Narva river and fortified stronghold of Jaanilinn.

5 KROONI   140 x 70mm Issued 1 July 1997 **Cat.#76**
1994 Orange brown and bluish gray.
Karl Ernest von Baer / Tartu University.

10 KROONI   140 x 70mm Issued 20 June 1992 **Cat.#72**
1991-92 Lilac red and violet brown / Violet brown and multicolor.
Jakob Hurt / Tamme-Lauri oak tree at Urvaste.

10 KROONI   140 x 70mm Issued 1 July 1997 **Cat.#77**
1994 Red / Violet brown and multicolor.
Jakob Hurt / Tamme-Lauri oak tree at Urvaste.

25 KROONI   140 x 70mm Issued 20 June 1992 **Cat.#73**
1991-92 Green and multicolor.
Anton Hansen-Tammsaare / View of Vargamäe.

50 KROONI   **140 x 70mm** Issued 10 Oct 1994 **Cat.#78**
1994 Green, blue and multicolor.
Rudolf Tobias / Estonia Opera House in Tallinn.

100 KROONI   140 x 70mm Issued 20 June 1992 **Cat.#74**
1991-92 Dark blue and multicolor.
Lydia Koidula and nightingale / Estonian North coast.

100 KROONI   140 x 70mm Issued 13 Oct 1994 **Cat.#79**
1994 Dark blue and multicolor.
Lydia Koidula and nightingale / Estonian North coast.
With variable image gray seal in front.

100 KROONI 140 x 70mm Issued 30 May 1999 **Cat.#82**
1999 Dark blue and multicolor.
Lydia Koidula and nightingale / Estonian North coast.
With a holographic stripe at left front.

500 KROONI 140 x 70mm Issued 20 June 1992 **Cat.#75**
1991 Violet brown, violet, light blue and multicolor / Lilac, dark blue, green, yellow and multicolor.
C. R. Jakobson / Bird (Barn swallow).

500 KROONI 140 x 70mm Issued 3 Jan 1995 **Cat.#80**
1994 Violet brown, violet, light blue and multicolor / Lilac, dark blue, green, yellow and multicolor.
C.R. Jakobson / Bird (Barn swallow).

500 KROONI 140 x 70mm Issued 2 Jan 1997 **Cat.#81**
1996 Violet brown, violet, light blue and multicolor / Lilac, dark blue, green, yellow and multicolor.
C.R. Jakobson / Bird (Barn swallow).
It has a hologram in front, and additional security devices.

Ethiopia Äthiopien • Etiopía • Éthiopie **ETB**

Birr = 100 cent(s).

Currency import-export restrictions:
Local currency in/out: 100 birr.
Foreign currency in: free, must declare.
Out: up to amount imported and declared. The currency declaration may be needed when applying for an exit visa.
Visitors must pay hotel and car rental charges with hard currency.
Reconversion requires proof of exchange, but it is difficult.

Alternative currencies: all major.

A BRIEF MONETARY HISTORY
July 1945: dollar established = .6667 talari = 2 East African shillings
14 Oct 1976: birr created. Small Ethiopian dollar notes exchanged at par, those of 50 and up subject to a "wealth" tax of 10 to 20%.

Issuer: "NATIONAL BANK OF ETHIOPIA."

WARNING
Check colors!! Older notes are worthless.

CURRENT NOTES

1 BIRR 135 x 60mm **Cat.#30**
1889/1997 Grayish violet and multicolor.
Young man / Birds and waterfalls.

5 BIRR 140 x 65mm **Cat.#31**
1889/1997 Blue and multicolor.
Man harvesting coffee / Kudu and leopard.

10 BIRR 142 x 67mm **Cat.#32**
1889/1997 Brown, red, green and multicolor.
Woman / Tractor.

50 BIRR 145 x 70mm **Cat.#33**
1889/1997 Yellowish orange and multicolor.
Farmer plowing / Castle of Gondar.

1999

100 BIRR 147 x 72mm **Cat.#34**
1889/1997 Deep green and multicolor.
Farmer plowing / Man with microscope.

Euro   EUR

It is the currency of the European Monetary Union since 1999. Banknotes denominated in euros will be issued in 2002 for circulation in Austria, Belgium, Finland, France, Germany, Ireland, Italy, Luxembourg, Netherlands, Portugal and Spain.

Models provided by the European Monetary Institute. Actual issued notes may be different.

5 EURO   **Cat.#1**
   Purple brown and olive.
   Window / Bridge.

10 EURO   **Cat.#2**
   Red and multicolor.
   Window / Bridge.

20 EURO   **Cat.#3**
   Purple and multicolor.
   Window / Bridge.

50 EURO   **Cat.#4**
   Orange, black and multicolor.
   Window / Bridge.

100 EURO   **Cat.#5**
   Green and multicolor.
   Window / Bridge.

200 EURO   **Cat.#6**
   Yellow, purple brown and multicolor.
   Window / Bridge.

500 EURO   **Cat.#7**
   Pink and multicolor.
   Windows / Bridge.

Falkland Isl. / Islas Malvinas   FKP

Pound(s) = 100 penny (pence).
Parity: GBP 1.00

The import and export of all currencies is free.   Jul1998

Alternative currencies: **GBP**, USD.

Issuer: "THE GOVERNMENT OF THE FALKLAND ISLANDS."

CURRENT NOTES

5 POUNDS   145 x 75mm **Cat.#12**
   1983 Red and multicolor.
   Elizabeth II / Three houses.

10 POUNDS   145 x 75mm **Cat.#14**
   1986 Gray green and multicolor.
   Elizabeth II / Three houses.

20 POUNDS 145 x 75mm **Cat.#15**
1984 Brown and multicolor.
Elizabeth II / Three houses.

50 POUNDS 145 x 75mm **Cat.#16**
1990 Violet blue, green, lilac brown and multicolor.
Elizabeth II / Three houses.

Faroes Føroyar DKK

Krona (krónur) = 100 ore.
Parity: DEK 1.00.

Currency import-export restrictions: oct98
The import and export of local and foreign currency is free.

Danish currency is readily accepted.

Issuer: "Føroyar Landstýri."

The two center digits of the six character string indicate the date of issue. For instance A0**83**2D means the date is 1983.

CURRENT NOTES

50 KRÓNUR Series 1974 139 x 71mm Issued 15 Nov 1982 **Cat.#20**
1982- Blue and black / Light olive and dark green.
Nólsoyar Páll / Sketch of homes and church.

100 KRÓNUR Series 1974 150 x 77mm Issued 30 Oct 1978 **Cat.#21**
1978- Light ochre and black / Ochre, black and green.
V.U. Hammershaimb / Sketch of house and mountains.

500 KRÓNUR Series 1974 175 x 90mm Issued 22 Oct 1980 **Cat.#22**
1980- Grayish green, black and purple / Green and black.
Fisherman / Sketch of fishermen at sea.

1,000 KRÓNUR Series 1974 175x93mm Issued 22 Oct 1980 **Cat.#23**
1980- Purple brown and blue / Brown, dark brown and blue.
J.H.O. Djurhuus / Sketch of houses.

OUTMODED AND REDEEMABLE NOTES

5 KRÓNUR 124 x 65mm Issued in 1951 **Cat.#13**
Law of 1949 Black on green / Green.
Coin / Fishermen at sea.

10 KRÓNUR 124 x 71mm Issued in 1954 **Cat.#14**
Law of 1949 Black on orange red / Orange red.
Shield with sheep / Houses in mountain background.

10 KRÓNUR Series 1974 124 x 66mm Issued 24 Feb 1978 **Cat.#16**
1978 Green and black / Dark green.
Shield with sheep / Houses in mountain background.

©MRI Bankers' Guide to Foreign Currency
P.O.Box 3174 Houston TX 77253 USA

20 KRÓNUR   *125 x 72mm Issued 2 Jan 1987 Cat.#19*
1986-88 Purple brown / Reddish brown, black and light slate.
Fisherman / Sketches of sheep.

50 KRÓNUR   *155 x 79mm Issued in 1967 Cat.#17*
Law of 1949 Black on blue green / Blue green.
Nólsoyar Páll / Sketch of homes and church.

100 KRÓNUR   *157 x 101mm Cat.#15*
Law of 1949 Blue green.
Writings / Porpoises.

100 KRÓNUR   *155 x 84mm Issued in 1964 Cat.#18*
Law of 1949 Black on pink / Black on ochre.
V.U. Hammershaimb / Sketch of house and mountains.

Fiji Fidschi • Fidji   FJD

Dollar(s) = 100 cent(s).

Currency import-export restrictions:
Local currency in: free; out FJD 500.
Foreign currency in: free. Declaration required if reëxport of amounts above limit is intended.
Out: up to FJD 5,000 in foreign currency, inclusive of a maximum of FJD 500 in local currency; more if imported and declared. There are no limits for travelers checks and drafts.

Alternative currencies: AUD, CHF, DEM, FRF, GBP, JPY, NZD, USD.

A BRIEF MONETARY HISTORY
Jan. 1969: Dollar = 0.50 Fijian pound

Issuer: "RESERVE BANK OF FIJI."

CURRENT NOTES

2 DOLLARS   *156 x 67mm* **Cat.#88**
Green, blue and multicolor.
Elizabeth II / Group of five people.

5 DOLLARS   *156 x 67mm Issued in mid-1995* **Cat.#89**
Orange brown and multicolor.
Elizabeth II / Nadi International Airport.

5 DOLLARS   *156 x 67mm Issued in 1998* **Cat.#89A**
Brown, orange and multicolor.
Elizabeth II / Nadi International Airport.
Color changed to avoid confusion with 50 dollars note.

10 DOLLARS   *156 x 67mm* **Cat.#90**
Purple, brown and multicolor.
Elizabeth II / Raft and children bathing.

20 DOLLARS   156 x 67mm Issued in mid-December 1996 **Cat.#91**
Blue, dark blue and violet / Blue, dark blue, green and yellow
brown.
Elizabeth II / Reserve Bank and Parliament House.

50 DOLLARS   156 x 67mm **Cat.#92**
Orange and grayish brown.
Elizabeth II and Kacau bird / Flag raising ceremony, Signing of
deed of Cession and Cession stone.

OUTMODED AND REDEEMABLE NOTES

*All older notes issued by Commissioners of Currency, Government of
Fiji, Currency Board and Central Monetary Authority are redeemable.
One pound equals 2 dollars; 10 shillings equal 1 dollar.*

Finland
Suomi • Finnland • Finlandia • Finlande   **FIM**

Euro = 5.94573 markkaa Markka(a) = 100 penni(ä).

The import and export of local and foreign currencies are free.

Alternative currencies: CAD, CHF, DEM, DKK, FRF, GBP, JPY, NOK, SEK,
USD.

A BRIEF MONETARY HISTORY
1963: (new) markka = 100 (Old) markkaa
1 Jan 1999: Euro adopted at 5.94573 markkaa.

Issuer: "SUOMEN PANKKI-FINLANDS BANK", after 2000 "EUROPEAN
CENTRAL BANK."

CURRENT NOTES

20 MARKKAA   142 x 69mm **Cat.#123**
1993 Dark blue, dark green and gray / Light yellow to bluish
green.
Väinö Linna / Industrial scene surrounding the river Tammerkoski
at Tampere.
A similar note, without the hologram, is legal tender, outmoded.

50 MARKKAA   142 x 69mm **Cat.#114**
1986 Brown and multicolor.
Alvar Aalto / Finlandia Hall.
Beware of notes with an extra "0" added, to pass them as 500 Markkaa.

50 MARKKAA   142 x 69mm **Cat.#119**
1991 Litt.A Brown and multicolor.
Alvar Aalto / Finlandia Hall.
It features a latent image.

100 MARKKAA   142 x 69mm **Cat.#115**
1986 Black on green and multicolor.
Jan Sibelius / Four white swans.
Beware of notes with an added "0", to pass them as 1,000 Markkaa.

100 MARKKAA   142 x 69mm **Cat.#120**
1991 Litt.A
Black on green and multicolor.
Jan Sibelius / Four white swans.
It features a latent image.

500 MARKKAA   142 x 69mm **Cat.#116**
1986 Black on red and multicolor.
Elias Lönnrot / Punkuharju esker.

500 MARKKAA   142 x 69mm **Cat.#121**
1991 Litt.A Black on red and multicolor.
Elias Lönnrot / Punkuharju esker.
It features a variable optical device.

1,000 MARKKAA　　142 x 69mm **Cat.#117**
　1986 Purple and dark blue.
　Anders Chydenius and clipper / King's gate.

1,000 MARKKAA　　142 x 69mm **Cat.#122**
　1991 Litt.A Purple and dark blue.
　Anders Chydenius and clipper / King's gate.
　It features a variable optical device.

OUTMODED AND REDEEMABLE NOTES

Ten markkaa notes dated 1986 (Cat.#113) are legal tender, but seldom seen in circulation, as these were replaced by coins.

The following notes may be redeemed until 31 Dec 2003.

{5 MARKKAA} = 0.05 MARKKA 1945 . . . . Cat.#76
{10 MARKKAA} = 0.10 MARKKA 1945 . . . . Cat.#77
{20 MARKKAA} = 0.20 MARKKA 1945 . . . . Cat.#78
{50 MARKKAA} = 0.50 MARKKA 1945 . . . . Cat.#79

{100 MARKKAA} = 1 MARKKA 1945 . . . . Cat.#80
{100 MARKKAA} = 1 MARKKA 1955 . . . . Cat.#91
{100 MARKKAA} = 1 MARKKA 1957 . . . . Cat.#97
1 MARKKA 1963 . . . . Cat.#98

{500 MARKKAA} = 5 MARKKAA 1945 . . . . Cat.#81
{500 MARKKAA} = 5 MARKKAA 1955 . . . . Cat.#92
{500 MARKKAA} = 5 MARKKAA 1956 . . . . Cat.#96
5 MARKKAA 1963 . . . . Cat.#99

{1,000 MARKKAA} = 10 MARKKAA 1945 . . . . Cat.#82
{1,000 MARKKAA} = 10 MARKKAA 1955 . . . . Cat.#93
10 MARKKAA 1963 . . . . Cat.#100
10 MARKKAA 1980 . . . . Cat.#111

{5,000 MARKKAA} = 50 MARKKAA 1945 . . . . Cat.#83
{5,000 MARKKAA} = 50 MARKKAA 1955 . . . . Cat.#94
50 MARKKAA 1963 . . . . Cat.#105
50 MARKKAA 1977 . . . . Cat.#110

{10,000 MARKKAA} = 100 MARKKAA 1955 . . . . Cat.#95
100 MARKKAA 1963 . . . . Cat.#106
100 MARKKAA 1976 . . . . Cat.#109
500 MARKKAA 1975 . . . . Cat.#108

France　　Frankreich • Francia　　FRF

Euro = 5.55957 francs Franc(s) = 100 centime(s).

Currency import-export restrictions:
The import and export of local and foreign currencies are free. Amounts near or over FF50,000 or its equivalent must be declared to Customs on arrival or departure. The import or export by mail of FF 10,000 or more, or its equivalent in foreign currency, must be declared to Customs.

Alternative currencies: all major.

A BRIEF MONETARY HISTORY
1960: nouveau franc = 100 francs
1962: franc = nouveau franc
1 Jan 1999: Euro adopted at 6.55957 francs.

Issuer: "BANQUE DE FRANCE", after 2002 "EUROPEAN CENTRAL BANK."

French currency is legal tender in France and its departments and overseas territories of Guadeloupe, Guyane, Martinique, Mayotte, St Martin, St Pierre and Miquelon, and Wallis and Futuna.

CURRENT NOTES

20 FRANCS　　140 x 75mm **Cat.#151**
　1980- Violet, brown and multicolor.
　Claude Debussy and La Mer (The Sea) / Debussy and scene from his opera "Pelléas et Mélisande."
　With security thread since 1990.

50 FRANCS　　123 x 80mm **Cat.#157**
　1993- Deep blue and multicolor.
　Antoine de Saint-Exupèry and "The Little Prince" / Airplane and "The Little Prince."
　There are varieties in the spelling of Éxupéry and the titles of signers.

100 FRANCS　　133 x 80mm Issued 15 Dec 1997 **Cat.#158**
　1997 Orange brown and green.
　Paul Cézanne / "Pommes et biscuits."

©MRI BANKERS' GUIDE TO FOREIGN CURRENCY
P.O.Box 3174 HOUSTON TX 77253 USA

Caution!!!
This note
is worth only
50 francs

{5,000 FRANCS} = **50 FRANCS**   162 x 86mm **Cat.#66**
1957-59 Multicolor.
Henri IV and Pont Neuf / Henri IV, castle of Pau and view of
the Pyrenees.   rruu20031231

50 {NOUVEAUX} FRANCS   Red overprint on 5,000 Francs.
                                        162 x 86mm **Cat.#71**
1958-59 Multicolor.
Henri IV and Pont Neuf / Henri IV, castle of Pau and view of
the Pyrenees.   rruu20031231

50 NOUVEAUX FRANCS   162 x 86mm **Cat.#143**
1959-62 Multicolor.
Henri IV and Pont Neuf / Henri IV, castle of Pau and view of
the Pyrenees.   rruu20031231

50 FRANCS   162 x 86mm **Cat.#148**
1962-76 Multicolor.
Racine and view of the abbey of Port Royal des Champs /
Racine and view of La Ferte-Millon.   rruu20031231

50 FRANCS   150 x 80mm **Cat.#152**
1976-93 Gray blue and multicolor.
M Quentin de la Tour and Versailles palace / Quentin de la
Tour and City Hall at St Quentin.   rruu20051130

Caution!!!
This note
is worth only
100 francs

{10,000 FRANCS} = **100 FRANCS**   221 x 119mm **Cat.#67**
1945-56 Multicolor.
Young woman with book and globe / Young man with
capital of column, representing Architecture.   rruu20031231

Caution!!!
This note
is worth only
100 francs

{10,000 FRANCS} = **100 FRANCS**   173 x 92mm **Cat.#68**
1955-58 Multicolor.
Napoleon Bonaparte and Arc du Triomphe / Napoleon
Bonaparte and The Invalides.   rruu20031231

100 {NOUVEAUX} FRANCS   Red overprint on 10,000 Francs.
                                        173 x 92mm **Cat.#72**
1958 Multicolor.
Napoleon Bonaparte and Arc du Triomphe / Napoleon
Bonaparte and The Invalides.   rruu20031231

100 {NOUVEAUX} FRANCS   173 x 92mm **Cat.#144**
1959-64 Multicolor.
Napoleon Bonaparte and Arc du Triomphe / Napoleon
Bonaparte and The Invalides.   rruu20031231

100 FRANCS   173 x 92mm *Cat.#149*
1964-79 Multicolor.
Corneille / Corneille and view of Rouen, his birthplace and
the Courthouse.   rruu20031231

100 FRANCS   160 x 85mm *Cat.#153*
1978-96 Brown, yellow and multicolor.
Eugene Delacroix and detail from "Liberty guiding the
People" / Delacroix and Furstenberg square.
There are two slightly different varieties.   ru20090201

200 FRANCS   173 x 92mm *Cat.#155*
1981-94 Blue green, yellow and multicolor.
Baron de Montesquieu and allegory of Justice and Science /
Montesquieu, Palace of Brede and statue of Sylla.   rruu20080331

500 {NOUVEAUX} FRANCS   181 x 97mm *Cat.#145*
1959-66 Multicolor.
Molière with theater boxes in background / Molière and scene of
"The Imaginary Invalid."   rruu20031231

500 FRANCS   181 x 97mm *Cat.#16*
Yellow brown and dark brown.
1968-94 Blaise Pascal and tower of St Jacques church / Pascal
and abbey of Port Royal.   rruu20070301

French Equatorial Africa
**Afrique Equatoriale Française • Französische
Äquatorialafrika • Africa Ecuatorial Francesa**

Franc(s) CFA = 100 centime(s).

*Notes of the "Caisse Centrale de la France Libre"; "Caisse Centrale de
la France d'Outre-Mer" and "Institut d'Emission de l'Afrique
Equatoriale Française et du Cameroun" are redeemable at the
Banque des Etats de l'Afrique Centrale. All have high numismatic
value.*

French Guyana Guyane Française •   **FRF**
Französische Guyana • Guayana Francesa

*French currency is used now. All older notes issued by the Caisse
Centrale de la France Libre, Caisse Centrale de la France d'Outre-Mer
and Caisse Centrale de la France are redeemable only in Cayenne.
Each "nouveau franc" is worth 100 old francs. All these notes have
high numismatic value.*

French Overseas Territories
**Départements d'Outre-mer • Französische Überseeische
Länder • Departamentos Franceses de Ultramar**

*Notes issued by the "INSTITUT D'ÉMISSION DES DEPARTEMENTS
D'OUTRE-MER." for use in French Guyana, Guadeloupe, and Martinique. Since 1975 those of the Banque de France are used. A "nouveau
franc" is worth 100 old francs. These notes have high numismatic
value, and may be redeemed only at the Institut d'Émission d'Outre-
mer in the French Guyana, Guadeloupe or Martinique.*

French Polynesia   **XPF**

See C.F.P. Francs.

Gabon Gabun **XAF**

Franc(s) CFA Central = 100 centime(s).
Parity: FFR 0.01

Two types of notes run concurrently, old with names of the six Central African countries, and new of common design.

See CENTRAL AFRICAN STATES for current and outmoded notes, restrictions and other details.

The Gambia **GMD**

Dalasi(s) = 100 butut(s).

The import and export of local and foreign currencies are free.

Alternative currencies: USD, DEM, GBP.

A BRIEF MONETARY HISTORY
May 1964: Gambian pounds created at par with West African pound.
July 1971: dalasi = 0.50 Gambian pound

Issuer: "CENTRAL BANK OF THE GAMBIA."

CURRENT NOTES

5 DALASIS 132 x 69mm **Cat.#12**
Red and multicolor.
Sir Dawda Kairaba Jawara and bird / Agricultural scene.

5 DALASIS 132 x 69mm **Cat.#16**
Red and multicolor.
Young girl and bird (Giant kingfisher) / Agricultural scene.

10 DALASIS 138 x 72mm **Cat.#13**
Green and multicolor.
Sir Dawda Kairaba Jabara and bird / Abuko Earth satellite station.

10 DALASIS 138 x 72mm **Cat.#17**
Green and multicolor.
Young boy and bird (Sacred ibis) / Abuko Earth satellite station.

25 DALASIS 144 x 75mm **Cat.#14**
Dark blue and multicolor.
Sir Dawda Kairaba Jabara and bird / State House.

25 DALASIS 144 x 75mm **Cat.#18**
Greenish blue and multicolor.
Man and bird (Carmine bee eater) / State House.

50 DALASIS 154 x 78mm **Cat.#15**
Violet blue and multicolor.
Sir Dawda Kairaba Jawara and two birds / Stone circles at Wassu.

50 DALASIS 154 x 78mm **Cat.#19**
Violet blue and multicolor.
Woman and two birds / Stone circles at Wassu.

OUTMODED AND REDEEMABLE NOTES

Old notes in dalasis are legal tender but seldom seen in use, and are exchangeable at the Central Bank.

Georgia   Sakartvelo • Georgien • Georgie   **GEL**

Lari = 100 tetri.

Currency import/export restrictions:
Local currency in: limited. Out: limited to four notes of each denomination.   27OCT1998
The import and export of foreign currency is free. Declaration is required for statistical purposes.   Aug1998

A BRIEF MONETARY HISTORY
5 April 1993: 1 kuponi = 1 Russian ruble
11 June 1993: Russian ruble ceases to be legal tender.
25 Sep 1995: 1 lari = 1,000,000 kuponi

Alternative currencies: DEM, RUB, USD.

A BRIEF MONETARY HISTORY
April 1993: "kuponi" = Russian ruble.
25 Sep 1995: lari = 1,000,000 "kuponi."

Issuer: "GEORGIAN GOVERNMENT BANK".

CURRENT NOTES

1 LARI   115 x 61mm Issued 25 Sep 1995 **Cat.#53**
1995 Light violet blue.
Painter Niko Pirosmani / Deer and view of Tbilisi.

2 LARI   115 x 61mm Issued 25 Sep 1995 **Cat.#54**
1995 Green and orange.
Musician Zacharia Paliashvili / Opera House in Tbilisi.

5 LARI   115 x 61mm Issued 25 Sep 1995 **Cat.#55**
1995 Brown and light blue.
Ivane Javakhishvili / Map of Georgia, and Tbilisi State University.

10 LARI   125 x 63mm Issued 25 Sep 1995 **Cat.#56**
1995 Violet blue.
Poet and patriot Akaki Tseriteli / Woman weaving.

20 LARI   130 x 65mm Issued 25 Sep 1995 **Cat.#57**
1995 Brown.
Ilia Chavchavadze / King Vachtan Gorgosal, founder of Tbilisi.
With a vertical color shifting band in front.

50 LARI   135 x 66mm Issued 25 Sep 1995 **Cat.#58**
1995 Brown and green.
Princess Tamara / Mythical creature.
It has a vertical golden band in front.

100 LARI   140 x 67mm Issued 25 Sep 1995 **Cat.#59**
1995 Brown and green.
Classical Georgian writer Schota Rustaveli / Frieze.
It has a vertical pearl essence bar in front.

Germany
Deutschland • Alemania • Allemagne   **DEM**

Euro = 1.95583 DEM Deutsche mark = 100 pfennig.

The import and export of all currencies is free.   Jul1998

Alternative currencies: any major.

A BRIEF MONETARY HISTORY
Nov. 1923: rentenmark = 1,000,000,000,000 mark
1924: 1 reichsmark = 1 rentenmark
20 June 1948: Deutsche Mark = 10 Reichsmark. Each person is issued DM40. All older notes as well as those issued by the Allied Military Authorities were called in and became worthless.
1 Jan 1999: Euro adopted at 1.95583 Deutsche mark.

Issuer: "DEUTSCHE BUNDESBANK", after 2002 "EUROPEAN CENTRAL BANK."

10 POUNDS   142 x 75mm Issued in Dec. 1995 **Cat.#26**
1 July 1995 Orange brown and multicolor.
Elizabeth II / Gral. Eliott and "The Great Siege, 1779-83."

20 POUNDS   150 x 80mm Issued in Dec. 1995 **Cat. #27**
1 July 1995 Purple and multicolor / Blue and violet brown.
Elizabeth II / Admiral Nelson and "HMS Victory returning to Gibraltar, 1805."

50 POUNDS   157 x 85mm Issued in Dec. 1995 **Cat.#28**
1 July 1995 Red and multicolor.
Elizabeth II / Winston Churchill and "Spitfires at the North Front, 1942."

OUTMODED AND REDEEMABLE NOTES

All older notes issued by the Government of Gibraltar are redeemable. Ten shillings equal half pound.

Greece
Ellas • Griechenland • Grecia • Grèce   **GRD**

Drachme(s) = 100 lepton (lepta).
Minor unit coins are not used.

Currency import-export restrictions:
The import and export of all currencies is free. Declaration required for the import of local or foreign currencies exceeding ECU 10,000; and export if currency and personal checks exceeds ECU 2,000. Visitors are advised to keep exchange receipts.   Jul1998
Reconversion limited to equivalent of ECU 2,000.

Alternative currencies: any major.

A BRIEF MONETARY HISTORY
May 1954: drachma = 1,000 (old) drachmai

Issuer: "ΤΡΑΠΕΖΑ ΤΗΣ ΕΛΛΑΔΟΣ" (Bank of Greece).

CURRENT NOTES

100 DRACHMAI   158 x 67mm Issued 18 May 1981 **Cat.#200**
8 Dec 1978 Reddish brown and violet.
Athena Promachos and Athens University / Adamantios Koraes and church of the Arkadi Monastery in Crete.
It is being gradually replaced by a coin.

200 DRACHMES   129 x 65mm Issued 4 Nov 1996 **Cat.#204**
2 Sep 1996 Orange brown and multicolor.
Rigas Velestinlis-Fereos / "The Secret School".

500 DRACHMES   158 x 72mm Issued 28 Feb 1984 **Cat.#201**
1 Feb 1983 Green and multicolor.
Ioannis Capodistrias / The Citadel of Corfu.

500 DRACHMES   **Cat.#207**
A new note may be issued.

1,000 DRACHMES   158 x 77mm Issued 1 Aug 1988 **Cat.#202**
1 July 1987 Brown and multicolor.
Apollo and ancient silver stater / Discus thrower and ruins of the Temple of Hera at Olympia.

1,000 DRACHMES   **Cat.#208**
A new note may be issued.

5,000 DRACHMES   163 x 81mm Issued 30 Aug 1984 **Cat.#203**
23 March 1984 Gray blue and multicolor.
Theodoros Kolokotronis / View of Carytaina.

©MRI BANKERS' GUIDE TO FOREIGN CURRENCY
P.O.Box 3174 HOUSTON TX 77253 USA

5,000 DRACHMES   147 x 74mm Issued 1 July 1998 **Cat.#206**
1 June 1997 Gray blue and multicolor.
Theodoros Kolokotronis and church of the Holy Apostles at
Calamata / View of Karytaina.

10,000 DRACHMES   153 x 77mm Issued 7 March 1995 **Cat.#205**
16 Jan 1995 Lilac brown and multicolor.
Dr Georgios Papanikolaou / Æsculapius.

OUTMODED AND REDEEMABLE NOTES

50 DRACHMAI   *143 x 64mm* *Cat.#199*
8 Dec 1978 Blue and multicolor.
Poseidon / Man and woman, and sailing ship.
rruu20070530

1,000 DRACHMAI   *158 x 81mm* *Cat.#198*
1 Nov 1970 Brown and multicolor.
Zeus / Woman and view of city.
rruu20000630

Greenland   Grønland/Kalaallit Nunaat •
Grønland • Croenlandia • Groenland   DKK

A self governing overseas administrative division of the Danish
kingdom, it uses Danish currency.

Grenada   XCD

East Caribbean dollars are used.

The import of local and foreign currencies is free. A declaration is
required for the export of XCD 250,000 or its equivalent (USD92,500.)
Aug1998

United States Dollars are widely accepted. Alternative currencies:
CAD, DEM, FRF, GBP.

Guadeloupe   FRF

French francs are used now.
Older notes issued by Caisse Centrale de la France d'Outre-Mer and
Caisse Centrale de la France are redeemable only in Pointe-à-Pitre.
A "nouveau" franc is worth 100 old francs. These notes have high
numismatic value.

Guatemala   GTQ

Quetzal(es) = 100 centavo(s).

The import and export of all currencies is free.   Jul1998

Alternative currencies: MXN, USD.

Issuer: "BANCO DE GUATEMALA."

CURRENT NOTES

½ QUETZAL   156 x 68mm **Cat.#79**
1992- Brown and multicolor.
Tecún Umán / Tikal temple.
These notes will soon be replaced by coins.

1 QUETZAL   156 x 68mm **Cat.#80**
1992- Green and multicolor.
Quetzal and Gen. José M. Orellana / Banco de Guatemala building.
These notes will soon be replaced by coins.

©MRI Bankers' Guide to Foreign Currency
P.O.Box 3174 Houston TX 77253 USA

5 QUETZALES   156 x 68mm **Cat.#81**
  1992- Purple and multicolor.
  Quetzal bird and Rufino Barrios / Classroom.

10 QUETZALES   156 x 68mm **Cat.#82**
  1992- Red and multicolor.
  Quetzal and Gen. M. García Granados / National Assembly of 1872.

20 QUETZALES   156 x 68mm **Cat.#83**
  1992- Blue and multicolor.
  Quetzal and Dr. Mariano Gálvez / Declaration of Independence.

50 QUETZALES   156 x 68mm **Cat.#84**
  1992- Orange and multicolor.
  Quetzal bird and Gen. Carlos O. Zachrisson / Coffee picking.

100 QUETZALES   156 x 68mm **Cat.#85**
  1992- Brown and multicolor.
  Quetzal and Francisco Marroquín / Universidad de San Carlos.

200 QUETZALES   **Cat.#96**
  New note planned for 1999.

500 QUETZALES   **Cat.#97**
  New note planned for 1999.

OUTMODED AND REDEEMABLE NOTES

*All notes of the Banco de Guatemala are legal tender, and those
from the Banco Central de Guatemala are redeemable.*

Guernsey   GBP

Pound(s) = 100 penny (pence).
Parity: GBP 1.00

The import and export of local and foreign currency are free.

English notes are legal tender. Alternative currencies: any major.

Issuer: "THE STATES OF GUERNSEY."

CURRENT NOTES

1 POUND   129 x 65mm Issued 25 July 1991 **Cat.#52**
  Green and multicolor.
  Value, seal and group of people / Daniel de Lisle Brock and Royal
  Court.
  Larger notes of same design are redeemable without time limit.

5 POUNDS   135 x 70mm Issued 28 March 1996 **Cat.#56**
  Purple brown and multicolor.
  Elizabeth II and Town Church, St. Peter Port / Fort Grey and
  Hanois Lighthouse.

10 POUNDS   142 x 75mm Issued 9 March 1995 **Cat.#57**
  1995 Violet blue, purplish brown and multicolor.
  Elizabeth II, Elizabeth College / Saumarez Park, Les Niaux
  Watermill and Le Trepied Dolmen.

20 POUNDS   148 x 79mm Issued 2 May 1996 **Cat.#58**
  Lilac red, violet brown and multicolor.
  Elizabeth II and St. James Concert Hall / Vale Castle, St.
  Sampsons's Church and two sailboats.

50 POUNDS   156 x 85mm Issued 12 July 1994 **Cat.#59**
Brown, greenish blue and multicolor.
Elizabeth II and Royal Court House / St. Andrew's church, Point
de la Moye, la Gran'mere and Letter of Marque.

OUTMODED AND REDEEMABLE NOTES

All older notes are redeemable without time limit.

*Those dated 1914 or before are redeemable for 20/21 of their face
value. Their numismatic value is far higher.*

Guinea-Bissau   Guiné-Bissau   XOF

It uses notes issued by "BANQUE CENTRALE DES ETATS DE L'AFRIQUE
DE L'OUEST".

For description of notes and currency import-export restrictions see
WEST AFRICAN STATES.

A BRIEF MONETARY HISTORY
Feb. 1976: peso = 1 Guinean escudo
2 May 1997: franc CFA West = 65 pesos

Alternative currencies: **FRF**, PTE, USD.

Guinea (Conakry)   Guinée   GNF

Franc(s) = 100 centime(s).
Minor unit coins are not used.

Currency import-export restrictions:
Local currency in/out: GF 5,000.
Foreign currency in: free, must declare.   Aug1998
Out: up to amount imported and declared.
It is advisable to keep an exact record of amounts exchanged on the
currency declaration, to avoid problems on departure.

Alternative currencies: **FRF**, USD.

A BRIEF MONETARY HISTORY
March 1960: franc = 1 CFA franc
1971: syli = 10 francs
1985: franc guinéen = 1 syli

Issuer: "BANQUE CENTRALE DE LA RÉPUBLIQUE DE GUINÉE."

CURRENT NOTES

Smaller notes not listed because of low value.

100 FRANCS   130 x 65mm **Cat.#30**
1985 Purple and multicolor.
Young woman / Banana harvest.

500 FRANCS   140 x 73mm **Cat.#31**
1985 Green and multicolor.
Woman / Mine.

1,000 FRANCS   150 x 80mm **Cat.#32**
1985 Yellow brown and multicolor.
Girl and drum / Ore loading.

5,000 FRANCS   156 x 86mm **Cat.#33**
1985 Blue, brown and multicolor.
Woman and sculpture / Dam and mask.

Guyana Guyane   GYD

Dollar(s) = 100 cent(s).
Minor unit coins are not used.

Currency import-export restrictions:
Local currency in/out: free.
Foreign currency in: free, must declare USD 10,000 or more.
Out: free.
Exchange receipt needed for reconversion.

Alternative currencies: GBP, **USD.**

A BRIEF MONETARY HISTORY
Nov. 1965: 1 Guyanese dollar = 1 British East Caribbean dollar.

Issuer: "BANK OF GUYANA."

CURRENT NOTES

20 DOLLARS   156 x 65mm **Cat.#24**
  Purple and multicolor.
  Kaieteur Falls / Shipbuilding.

20 DOLLARS   156 x 65mm **Cat.#27**
  Purple and multicolor.
  Kaieteur Falls / Shipbuilding.
  Without (Cat.#27), and since 1996 (Cat.#30) with ascending serial numbers.

100 DOLLARS   156 x 65mm **Cat.#28**
  Blue and multicolor.
  Map / Cathedral of St George.
  Without (Cat.#28), and since 1998 with windowed security thread and ascending
  serial numbers (Cat.#31.)

500 DOLLARS   156 x 65mm **Cat.#29**
  Lilac brown, purple and multicolor.
  Map of Guyana and bank's seal / "Public buildings" in
  Georgetown.
  Without (Cat.#29) and, since 1996 (Cat.#32), with windowed security thread and
  ascending serial numbers.

1,000 DOLLARS   156 x 65mm Issued 23 Dec 1996 **Cat.#33**
  Olive, red and multicolor.
  Map of Guyana and bank's seal / Bank of Guyana.

Haïti Haití   HTG

Gourde(s) = 100 centime(s).

The import and export of local and foreign currencies are free. The
import of amounts exceeding HTG 100,000 or its equivalent must be
declared.   Jul1988

Alternative currencies: CAD, FRF, **USD.**

Issuer: "BANQUE DE LA RÉPUBLIQUE D'HAÏTI", formerly "BANQUE
NATIONALE DE LA RÉPUBLIQUE D'HAÏTI."

CURRENT NOTES

Smaller notes not listed because of low value.

5 GOURDES   162 x 70mm **Cat.#246**
  1987- Orange, brown and multicolor.
  Monument to the Combat of Vertiéres / Arms.
  With or without dollar parity clause. These notes are being replaced by coins.

10 GOURDES   162 x 70mm **Cat.#247**
  1988 Green, red and blue.
  Catherine Flon Arcahaie sewing flag / Arms.

10 GOURDES   162 x 70mm **Cat.#256**
  1991 Green, red and multicolor / Green.
  Catherine Flon Arcahaie sewing flag / Arms.

25 GOURDES   162 x 70mm **Cat.#248**
1988 Purple, blue and multicolor.
Palace of Justice / Arms.

50 GOURDES   162 x 70mm **Cat.#249**
No date-1986 Gray olive and multicolor.
Lysius Félicité Salomon Jeune / Arms.
Some are printed on plastic. With or without dollar parity clause.

50 GOURDES   162 x 70mm **Cat.#257**
1991 Gray olive and multicolor.
Lysius Féucité (sic) Salomon Jeune / Arms.

100 GOURDES   162 x 70mm **Cat.#236**
Purple and multicolor
Henri Christophe / Arms

100 GOURDES   162 x 70mm **Cat.#250**
1986 Purple and multicolor
Henri Christophe / Arms

100 GOURDES   162 x 70mm **Cat.#258**
1991- Purple and multicolor
Henri Christophe / Arms.
With or without dollar parity clause.

250 GOURDES   156 x 67mm **Cat.#251**
No date-1988 Yellow green and multicolor.
Jean-Jacques Dessalines / Arms.

250 GOURDES   162 x 70mm **Cat.#262**
1994 Olive brown and multicolor.
Jean-Jacques Dessalines / Arms.

500 GOURDES   156 x 65mm **Cat.#252**
1988 Red and multicolor.
Alexandre Pétion / Arms.

500 GOURDES   162 x 70mm **Cat.#263**
1993 Brownish red and multicolor.
Alexandre Pétion / Arms.
Misspelling "Cinq Cent Gourdes" instead of "Cinq Cents Gourdes."

OUTMODED AND REDEEMABLE NOTES

All older notes issued by the Banque Nationale de la République d'Haïti and the Banque de la République d'Haïti are valid.

Honduras   HNL

Lempira(s) = 100 centavo(s).

Currency import-export restrictions:
The import and export of local and foreign currencies are free, but visitors carrying large amounts of lempiras may be questioned by Customs or police.

Alternative currency: USD.

Issuer: "BANCO CENTRAL DE HONDURAS."

CURRENT NOTES

1 LEMPIRA   156 x 67mm **Cat.#68**
1980- Red and multicolor.
Indian chief Lempira / Ruinas de Copán.

2 LEMPIRAS   156 x 67mm **Cat.#61**
1976- Purple and multicolor.
Marco Aurelio Soto / "Isla del Tigre ...."
With regular serial numbers (Cat.#61), and with ascending serial numbers (Cat.#72).

5 LEMPIRAS   156 x 67mm **Cat.#63**
1978- Black, blue and multicolor.
Morazán and arms / "Batalla de la Trinidad."
With regular serial numbers (Cat.#63), and since 1993 (Cat.#63c), with ascending serial numbers.

10 LEMPIRAS   156 x 67mm **Cat.#64**
1976-89 Brown and multicolor.
Cabañas and arms / Ciudad Universitaria.

10 LEMPIRAS   156 x 67mm **Cat.#70**
21 Sep 1989 Brown, red and rose.
Cabañas and arms / Ciudad Universitaria.

20 LEMPIRAS   156 x 67mm **Cat.#65**
1978-93 Green and multicolor.
Dionisio de Herrera / Puerto Cortés.

20 LEMPIRAS   156 x 67mm Issued in September 1994 **Cat.#73**
1993- Green, brown and multicolor.
Dionisio de Herrera / Casa Presidencial.

50 LEMPIRAS   156 x 67mm **Cat.#66**
1976-93 Blue and multicolor.
Juan Manuel Gálvez D. / Banco Nacional de Fomento.

50 LEMPIRAS   156 x 67mm Issued in September 1994 **Cat.#74**
1993- Green, brown an multicolor.
Juan Manuel Gálvez D. / Anexo Banco Central de Honduras.

100 LEMPIRAS   156 x 67mm **Cat.#69**
1981-94 Yellow brown.
Valle / "Escuela Nacional de Ciencias Forestales - Siguatepeque."
Without (Cat.#69) and with ascending serial numbers (Cat.#75).

100 LEMPIRAS   156 x 67mm **Cat.#78**
Orange brown, green and multicolor.
José Cecilio del Valle and bridge over the Choluteca river. / His ancestral house.

500 LEMPIRAS   156 x 67mm Issued 14 Jan 1998 **Cat.#76**
16 Nov 1995 Magenta, gray and multicolor.
Ramón Rosa, "Antiguo Paraninfo" and mailbox / Mina del Rosario de Sanjuancito.

OUTMODED AND REDEEMABLE NOTES

All older notes from the "Banco Central de Honduras" are legal tender, but outmoded.

Hongkong   HKD

Dollar(s) = 100 cent(s).

The import and export of all currencies is free.   Jul1998

Alternative currencies: any major.

Issuers: BANK OF CHINA, THE HONGKONG AND SHANGHAI BANKING CORPORATION LIMITED AND STANDARD CHARTERED BANK.

CURRENT NOTES

20 DOLLARS Bank of China   144 x 72mm **Cat.#329**
1994- Blue and multicolor.
Bank logo, Bank of China Tower and Narcissus flower / Buildings in Central and Wanchai districts of Hongkong.

20 DOLLARS HKSBC   144 x 72mm **Cat.#201**
1993- Gray, orange and multicolor.
Lion's head / Two lions, bank building, old Kowloon Railway Station Clock Tower and Cultural Centre.

20 DOLLARS Standard Chartered Bank   144 x 72mm **Cat.#279**
1985-92 Blue gray, lilac and multicolor.
Mythological tortoise / Building.

20 DOLLARS Standard Chartered Bank   144 x 72mm **Cat.#285**
1993- Blue gray, lilac and multicolor.
Mythological tortoise / Bank building and Bahuinia flower.

50 DOLLARS Bank of China   148 x 74mm **Cat.#330**
1994- Purple and multicolor.
Bank logo and to Tower and flower / Cross-harbor tunnel.

50 DOLLARS HKSBC   148 x 74mm **Cat.#202**
1993- Violet blue, lilac red and multicolor.
Lion's head / Two lions, bank building, and a dragon boat race.

50 DOLLARS Standard Chartered Bank   148 x 74mm **Cat.#280**
1985-92 Violet and multicolor.
Mythological lion / Bank building.

50 DOLLARS Standard Chartered Bank   144 x 74mm **Cat.#286**
1993- Violet and multicolor.
Mythological lion / Bank building and Bahuinia flower.

100 DOLLARS Bank of China   154 x 77mm **Cat.#331**
1994- Red and multicolor.
Bank logo, Bank of China Tower and Lotus flower / Kowloon Peninsula.

100 DOLLARS HKSBC   154 x 77mm **Cat.#203**
1993- Red and multicolor.
Lion's head / Two lions, bank building and Ten Thousand Buddha Pagoda at Shatin.

100 DOLLARS Standard Chartered Bank 154 x 77mm **Cat.#281**
1985-92 Red and multicolor.
Unicorn / Bank building.

100 DOLLARS Standard Chartered Bank 154 x 77mm **Cat.#287**
1993- Red and multicolor.
Unicorn / Bank building and Bauhinia flower.

500 DOLLARS Bank of China 158 x 79mm **Cat.#332**
1994- Brown and multicolor.
Bank logo and Tower, and Peony flower / Container terminal in
Kwai Chung.

500 DOLLARS HKSBC 158 x 79mm **Cat.#204**
1993- Brown and red orange on multicolor.
Lion's head / Two lions, bank building and aerial view of the
Government House.

500 DOLLARS Standard Chartered Bank 158 x 79mm **Cat.#288**
1993- Brown and multicolor.
Phoenix / Bank building and Bahuinia flower.

1,000 DOLLARS Bank of China 164 x 82mm **Cat.#333**
1994- Golden orange and multicolor.
Bank logo, Bank of China Tower and Bahuinia flower / Central
Hongkong district.

1,000 DOLLARS HKSBC 164 x 82mm **Cat.#205**
1993- Orange and multicolor.
Lion's head / Two lions, bank building and Legislative Council
Building.
CAUTION: good quality counterfeits exist.

1,000 DOLLARS Standard Chartered Bank 164 x 82mm **Cat.#283**
1985-92 Gold and multicolor.
Dragon / Building.

500 DOLLARS Standard Chartered Bank 158 x 79mm **Cat.#282**
1988-92 Reddish brown and multicolor.
Phoenix / Building.

1,000 DOLLARS Standard Chartered Bank 164 x 82mm **Cat.#289**
1993- Gold and multicolor.
Dragon / Bank building and Bahuinia flower.
BEWARE OF FORGERIES!

OUTMODED AND REDEEMABLE NOTES

Older notes from Chartered Bank of India, Australia and China; Chartered Bank; Government of Hong Kong; Hong Kong and Shanghai Banking Co. Ltd.; The Hongkong and Shanghai Banking Corp. and Mercantile Bank of India are redeemable.

Hungary
Köztársaság • Ungarn • Hungría • Hongrie
Magyar HUF

Forint.
Minor coins are not used.

Currency import-export restrictions:
Local currency in/out: free up to Ft. 350,000. Larger amounts require permission from the National Bank.
Foreign currency in: free, must declare.
Out: up to equivalent of Ft. 100,000 or larger amount imported and declared. Larger amount require permission from the National Bank.

International travel tickets must be paid with hard currency.

Alternative currencies: any major.

A BRIEF MONETARY HISTORY
Jul 1946: adó-pengoe = 2 quadrillion pengoe
Aug 1946: forint = 400,000 quadrillion pengoe

Issuer: "MAGYAR NEMZETI BANK"

CURRENT NOTES

200 FORINT   154 x 70mm Issued 1 May 1998 **Cat.#179**
1998 Green, brown and multicolor.
King Róbert Károly and arms / View of Diósgyőri Vár.

500 FORINT   176 x 80mm **Cat.#172**
1969-90 Purple.
Endre Ady / Landscape of Budapest with Elisabeth Bridge.
Legal tender until 21 Dec 2000, redeemable until 1 Dec 2002.

500 FORINT   154 x 70mm Issued 1 Dec 1998 **Cat.#180**
1998 Brown, orange brown and multicolor.
Ferenc Rákóczi II / Sárospatak Castle.

1,000 FORINT   176 x 80mm **Cat.173**
1983-96 Green, yellow and multicolor.
Béla Bartók / "Mother with her child."
Legal tender until 30 Aug 2000, redeemable until 1 Sep 2002.   rruu20000830

1,000 FORINT   154 x 70mm Issued 1 Sep 1998 **Cat.#181**
1998 Blue, light yellow brown and multicolor.
King Mátyás Corvinus / Fountain in the palace at Visegrád.

2,000 FORINT   154 x 70mm Issued 1 Feb 1998 **Cat.#182**
1998 Olive brown and multicolor.
Gábor Bethlen and arms / The Prince among his scientists.

5,000 FORINT   176 x 80mm **Cat.#177**
1990-95 Reddish brown, gray and orange.
Count István Széchenyi / Hungarian Academy of Science.
Legal tender until 31 March 2000, and redeemable until 1 April 2002.

5,000 FORINT   154 x 70mm **Cat.#183**
1999 Violet brown and grayish blue on green and multicolor.
Count István Széchenyi / His mansion at Nagycenk.

10,000 FORINT   154 x 70mm **Cat.#184**
1997- Brown, purple and multicolor.
Szent István Király (St. Stephen King) and coat of arms / View of Esztergom.
Those dated 1998 have a UV imprint in the front, in the watermark area.

OUTMODED AND REDEEMABLE NOTES

100 FORINT   154 x 70mm **Cat.#163**
1947-92 Brown violet.
Lajos Kossuth / "Flight from impending storm."
There are several varieties in the coat of arms.   ru31dec2000

Iceland   Island • Islandia • Islande   ISK

Króna (krónur) = 100 eyrir (aurar).

The import and export of local and foreign currencies is free.Jul1998

Alternative currencies: any major.

A BRIEF MONETARY HISTORY
Jan. 1981: króna = 100 (old) krónur

Issuer: "SEÐLABANKI ÍSLANDS."

CURRENT NOTES

500 KRÓNUR   145 x 70mm **Cat.#51**
Laws of 1961 or 1986 Red and multicolor.
Jon Sigurðsson / Sigurðsson at his writing desk.

1,000 KRÓNUR   150 x 70mm **Cat.#52**
Laws of 1961 or 1986 Purple and multicolor.
Bishop Brynjolfur Sveinsson / Old church at Skálholt.

2,000 KRÓNUR   150 x 70mm **Cat.#57**
Lilac brown, green and multicolor.
Painter Johannes Sveinsson Kjarval and painting "Uti og Inni"
(Inside and Outside) / Painting "Leda and the Swan."

5,000 KRÓNUR   155 x 70mm **Cat.#53**
Laws of 1961 or 1986 Blue and multicolor.
Ragnbeiður Jónsdóttir / Ragnbeiður Jónsdóttir teaching two
girls embroidery.

10,000 KRÓNUR   **Cat.#59**
Issue plans are in early stages, and it will not be released soon.

OUTMODED AND REDEEMABLE NOTES

10 KRÓNUR   **Cat.#48**
Law of 1961 Blue and multicolor.
Arngrímur Jónsson lærði / Old household scene.

50 KRÓNUR   **Cat.#49**
Law of 1961 Brown and multicolor.
Bishop Guðbrandur Porláksson / Early printers at work.

100 KRÓNUR   **Cat.#50**
Laws of 1961 or 1986 Green and multicolor.
Prof. Árni Magnússon / Monk working on manuscript.

Ichkeria (Chechnya Republic)

It is reported that banknotes of 1 to 1,000 "nakhar" are ready to be
issued, once a reserve to back them is arranged.

Issuer: "NATIONAL BANK OF THE REPUBLIC OF ICHKERIA"

India   Indien • Indie   **INR**

Rupee(s) = 100 paisa (paise).
Lakh = 100,000 rupees, written 1.00.000.
Crore = 10 Million rupees, written 1.00.00.000.

Currency import-export restrictions:
Local currency in/out: forbidden, except to or from Bhutan or Nepal.
Foreign currency in: free, must declare on Currency Declaration Form (CDF) amounts over US$ 10,000 in foreign currency travellers cheques and foreign currency notes, and amounts over USD 2,500 or its equivalent in foreign currency notes.
Out: up to amount imported and declared, less amounts sold to authorized dealers.

Alternative currencies: any major.

All, except 1 rupee notes, issued by "RESERVE BANK OF INDIA."

CURRENT NOTES

Smaller notes not listed because of low value.

5 RUPEES   117 x 63mm   **Cat.#80**
　　Green and multicolor.
　　Ashoka column / Tractor.

10 RUPEES   137 x 63mm   **Cat.#57**
　　Brown and multicolor.
　　Ashoka column / Sailing boat.
　　There are several design varieties.

10 RUPEES   137 x 63mm   **Cat.#81**
　　Lilac, brown and multicolor.
　　Ashoka column / Two peacocks on a branch, deer, horses, bird and lotus.
　　There are several design varieties.

10 RUPEES   137 x 63mm   **Cat.#88**
　　Yellow brown, blue green and multicolor.
　　Ashoka column / Shalimar Garden, Kashmir.

10 RUPEES   137 x 63mm Issued 13 June 1996   **Cat.#89**
　　Mauve, brown orange and pink.
　　M.K. Gandhi / Hippopotamus, tiger and elephant.
　　With "M.K. Gandhi" (Cat.#89); and later "Mahatma Ghandi" (Cat.#94.)

20 RUPEES   147 x 63mm   **Cat.#82**
　　Orange and multicolor.
　　Ashoka column / Chariot wheel, or Konarak Sun temple.

50 RUPEES   147 x 73mm   **Cat.#83**
　　Lilac and multicolor.
　　Ashoka column / Parliament House.

50 RUPEES   147 x 73mm   **Cat.#84**
　　Purple, orange and multicolor.
　　Ashoka column / Parliament House.

50 RUPEES   147 x 73mm Issued in January 1997   **Cat.#90**
　　Lilac, purple, yellow and multicolor.
　　M.K. Gandhi / Parliament House.
　　With "M.K. Gandhi" (Cat.#90); and later "Mahatma Ghandi" (Cat.#95.)

100 RUPEES   157 x 63mm   **Cat.#70**
　　Blue and multicolor.
　　Ashoka column / Dam.
　　There are several design varieties.

100 RUPEES   157 x 63mm **Cat.#85**
Blue, brown and multicolor.
Ashoka column / Agricultural work.
There are several varieties of background colors.

100 RUPEES   157 x 63mm Issued ca. July 1996 **Cat.#91**
Violet, violet blue, green and olive.
M.K. Gandhi / Kanchanjunga range.
With "M.K. Gandhi" (Cat.#91); and later "Mahatma Ghandi" (Cat.#96.)

500 RUPEES   167 x 73mm **Cat.#87**
Brown, blue and multicolor.
M.K. Gandhi / Gandhi leading a group of people.

500 RUPEES   167 x 63mm **Cat.#91**
Olive on green, mauve and blue.
M.K. Gandhi / Gandhi leading a group of people.

1,000 RUPEES   **Cat.#92**
New note with portrait of Mahatma Gandhi to be issued in 1999.

OUTMODED AND REDEEMABLE NOTES

All older large and small size notes up to 100 rupees issued by the Reserve Bank of India are legal tender, although seldom found in circulation. Notes of 1,000 rupees with the Ashoka column, as well as all bills with portraits of British kings, are worthless. However their numismatic value is high.

Red large size notes of 1, 5 and 10 rupees were issued for use in the Gulf. These are redeemable.

Indonesia   Indonesien • Indonésie   **IDR**

Rupiah = 100 sen.
Minor unit coins are not used.

Currency import-export restrictions:
Local currency in/out: Rp. 10,000,000.
Foreign currency in/out: free.   oct98

Alternative currencies: any major.

Issuer: "BANK INDONESIA."

CURRENT NOTES

Smaller notes not listed because of low value.

1,000 RUPIAH   144 x 68mm **Cat.#129**
1992- Blue and yellow.
Lake Toba / Stone jumping from Nias island.

5,000 RUPIAH   144 x 72mm **Cat.#130**
1992- Brown, light red, green and multicolor / Brown, green, red and multicolor.
Traditional musical instrument "Sasando" from Rote / Kelimutu Lakes.

5,000 RUPIAH   **Cat.#136**
A new note will be issued soon.

10,000 RUPIAH   148 x 72mm **Cat.#131**
1992 Violet, rose red, green and multicolor.
Sri Sultan Hamengku Buwono XX / "Candi Temple Borobodur."

10,000 RUPIAH   148 x 72mm Issued 18 Feb 1998 **Cat.#137**
1998 Brown, light green and green.
Tjut Njak Dhien / Segara Anak lake.

20,000 RUPIAH   153 x 72mm **Cat.#131**
1992-95 Dark brown, reddish brown and red on gray and greenish gray.
Red Paradise bird / Clove flower stalk with clover tree.
Without (Cat.#131) and, since 1995, with windowed security thread (Cat.#134).

20,000 RUPIAH   153 x 72mm Issued in early 1998 **Cat.#138**
1998 Grayish green and purple brown.
Ki Hadjar Dewantara / Taman Siswa School Center.

50,000 RUPIAH   152 x 76mm Issued 1 March 1993 **Cat.#133**
1993-95 Blue, dark green and multicolor.
Pres. Soeharto / Airplane and view of Soekarno-Hatta international airport.
Printed on paper or polymer, without windowed security thread (Cat.#133); and since 1995 (Cat.#135), with windowed security thread.

50,000 RUPIAH   152 x 76mm Issued in early June 1999 **Cat.#139**
1999 Grayish blue, light purple and light green, on cream paper.
Wage Rudolf Soepratman / Flag hoisting.

100,000 RUPIAH   **Cat.#140**
A new note is planned for future issue.

OUTMODED AND REDEEMABLE NOTES

Some smaller redeemable notes are omitted because of low value.

1,000 RUPIAH 1968 Cat.#110 . . . . . *Redeemable until 30 Dec 2007.*
1,000 RUPIAH 1975 Cat.#113 . . . . . *Redeemable until 31 Dec 2020.*
1,000 RUPIAH 1980 Cat.#119 . . . . . *Redeemable until 30 Apr 2025.*
1,000 RUPIAH 1987 Cat.#124 . . . . *Redeemable until 24 Sep 2028.*

5,000 RUPIAH 1968 Cat.#111 . . . . . *Redeemable until 30 Dec 2007.*
5,000 RUPIAH 1975 Cat.#114 . . . . . *Redeemable until 31 Dec 2020.*
5,000 RUPIAH 1980 Cat.#120 . . . . . *Redeemable until 30 Apr 2025.*
5,000 RUPIAH 1986 Cat.#125 . . . . *Redeemable until 24 Sep 2028.*

10,000 RUPIAH 1968 Cat.#112 . . . *Redeemable until 30 Dec 2007.*
10,000 RUPIAH 1975 Cat.#115 . . . . *Redeemable until 31 Dec 2011.*
10,000 RUPIAH 1979 Cat.#118 . . . *Redeemable until 30 Apr 2025.*
10,000 RUPIAH 1985 Cat.#126 . . . *Redeemable until 24 Sep 2028.*

Iran   IRR

Rial(s) = 100 dinar(s).
Toman = 10 rials (Unofficial popular usage)
Minor unit coins are not used.

Currency import-export restrictions:
Local currency in/out: Rls 200,000.
Foreign currency in: free, except Afghani, Iraqi and Lebanese currencies which are forbidden. Declaration required if reëxport is intended.
Out: Up to amount imported and declared.
Reconversion limited to USD500. Foreigners must exchange their foreign currencies through the banking system at the Export rate, and keep receipts in order to submit them to Customs officials on departure.

Alternative currencies: any major.

Issuer: "CENTRAL BANK OF THE ISLAMIC REPUBLIC OF IRAN."

CURRENT NOTES

Smaller notes not listed because of low value.

1,000 RIALS   148 x 73mm Issued 11 Feb 1982 **Cat.#138**
Red, brown and green.
Feizieh school in Ghom / A mosque in Jerusalem.
There are two different watermarks.

1,000 RIALS   148 x 73mm Issued 24 Oct 1992 **Cat.#143**
Green, yellow and brown.
Imam Khomeini / A mosque in Jerusalem.

2,000 RIALS   148 x 73mm Issued 5 Aug 1986 **Cat.#141**
Purple and olive green.
Liberation of the town of Khorramshahr / Kaaba in Mecca.

5,000 RIALS   154 x 75mm Issued 6 June 1981 **Cat.#133**
Purple red.
Islamic demonstration / Shrine of Hazrat Masoumeh.
There are two similar varieties.

©MRI BANKERS' GUIDE TO FOREIGN CURRENCY
P.O.Box 3174 HOUSTON TX 77253 USA

5,000 RIALS   154 x 75mm Issued 6 Oct 1993 **Cat.#145**
Brown, reddish brown, green and multicolor.
Imam Khomeini / Bird and flowers.

10,000 RIALS   160 x 77mm Issued 20 Dec 1981 **Cat.#134**
Blue and yellow.
Islamic Demonstration / Shrine of Imam Reza.

10,000 RIALS   160 x 77 Issued 24 Oct 1992 **Cat.#146**
Green, blue, brown and multicolor.
Imam Khomeini / Damavand Mountain.

OUTMODED AND REDEEMABLE NOTES

Smaller notes not listed because of low value.

1,000 RIALS   153 x 74mm Issued 10 June 1980 **Cat.#129**
Light brown and multicolor.
Shrine of Imam Reza / Tomb of Hafez.

5,000 RIALS   166 x 78mm Issued 10 June 1980 **Cat.#130**
Purple blue and multicolor.
Shrine of Imam Reza / Tehran refinery.   *rruu20070520*

10,000 RIALS   174 x 81mm Issued 6 May 1980 **Cat.#131**
Green and brown.   *rruu20070520*
Shrine of Imam Reza / Former National Assembly building.

Iraq   Irak   IQD

Dinar(s) = 1,000 fils.
Minor unit coins are not used.

Currency import-export restrictions:
Local currency in: ID 1,000; out ID 5.
Foreign currency in: free, must declare if reëxport is intended. It is forbidden to import Israeli currency.
Out: up to the amount imported and declared.
Visitors are required to exchange USD 5.00 in the official market for each day of stay.

Alternative currencies: DEM, GBP, JOD, USD.

Issuer: "CENTRAL BANK OF IRAQ."

CURRENT NOTES

Smaller notes not listed because of low value.

100 DINARS   175 x 85mm **Cat.#84**
1994 Dark blue, light blue and light ochre.
Saddam Hussein and Al-Ukhyder castle / Baghdad Clock.
Lithographed on paper of poor quality.

250 DINARS   175 x 85mm **Cat.#85**
1995 Purple.
Saddam Hussein and Al-Qadisia dam / Frieze from Al Tahrir square in Baghdad.
Lithographed on paper of poor quality.

Republic of Ireland
Poblacht na Héireann • Irland • Irlanda • Irlande IEP

Euro = .787564 pounds Pound(s) = 100 penny (pence).

The import or export of all currencies is free.   Jul1998

Alternative currencies: any major.

A BRIEF MONETARY HISTORY:
1 Jan 1999: Euro adopted at .787564

Issuer: "CENTRAL BANK OF IRELAND", after 2002 "EUROPEAN CENTRAL BANK."

CURRENT NOTES

5 POUNDS   120 x 64mm Issued 18 April 1994 **Cat.#75**
1993- Brown, grayish violet and orange brown.
Catherine McAuley and "Mater Misericordiæ" Hospital in Dublin / Classroom with three children.

10 POUNDS   128 x 68mm Issued 20 September 1993 **Cat.#76**
1993- Green, brown, blue and multicolor.
James Joyce and panoramic view of Dublin and environs / Sculpted head.

20 POUNDS   136 x 72mm Issued 9 November 1992 **Cat.#77**
1992- Brown violet, yellow brown and grayish blue / Brown violet and multicolor.
Daniel O'Connell and Derrynane Abbey / Writings and building.

50 POUNDS   144 x 76mm Issued 6 November 1995 **Cat.#78**
1995- Blue, green and lilac.
Douglas Hyde and "Áras an Uachtaráin" / Piper and crest of Conradh na Gaeilge.

> Notes of Allied Irish Banks, Bank Of Ireland, First Trust Bank, Northern Bank, and Ulster Bank are in Sterling currency; see Northern Ireland.

100 POUNDS   152 x 80mm Issued 16 September 1996 **Cat.#79**
1996- Lilac brown, light orange brown and slate / Purple brown, green and lilac brown.
Charles Stewart Parnell and Avondale House and gardens, Rathdrum, Co Wicklow / Parnell monument.

OUTMODED AND REDEEMABLE NOTES

Older issues of the Central Bank of Ireland are redeemable without time limit. Ten shillings equal half pound.

©MRI BANKERS' GUIDE TO FOREIGN CURRENCY
P.O.BOX 3174 HOUSTON TX 77253 USA

200 NEW SHEQALIM   138 x 76mm Issued 16 Feb 1992 **Cat.#57**
1991- Red, purple, blue green and multicolor.
Zalman Shazar and DNA shaped candelabrum / Schoolgirl.
Legal tender until 30 June 2000, redeemable until 31 Dec 2005.

200 NEW SHEQALIM   71 x 138mm To be issued in 1999 **Cat.#62**
Orange red and multicolor.
Zalman Shazar / Alley in Safed and Abuhav synagogue in Safed..

500 NEW SHEQALIM   **Cat.#63**
Planned for future issue. It will honor Yitzhak Rabin.

OUTMODED AND REDEEMABLE NOTES

1 NEW SHEQEL   138 x 76mm Issued 8 May 1986 **Cat.#51A**
1986 Green and multicolor.
Maimonides / View of Tiberias.
Legal tender (outmoded) until 30 June 2000, redeemable until 31 Dec 2005.

5 NEW SHEQALIM   138 x 76mm Issued 4 Sep 1985 **Cat.#52**
1985-87 Blue and multicolor.
Levy Eshkol and old city / Water pipe.
Legal tender (outmoded) until 30 June 2000, redeemable until 31 Dec 2005.

10 NEW SHEQALIM   138 x 76mm Issued 4 Sep 1985 **Cat.#53**
1985-92 Orange, gold and multicolor.
Golda Meir and tree / Golda Meir among crowd at
Moscow synagogue.
Legal tender (outmoded) until 30 June 2000, redeemable until 31 Dec 2005.

Italy   Italia • Italien • Italie   **ITL**

Euro = 1,936.27 lire Lira(e)

Currency import-export restrictions:
Local or foreign currency in: Lit 20 million or equivalent. Larger
amounts require filing a customs declaration.
Local or Foreign currency out: free to ITL 20 million or to amount
declared on entry.

Alternative currencies: any major.

A BRIEF MONETARY HISTORY:
1 Jan 1999: Euro adopted at 1,936.27 lire.

Issuer: "BANCA D'ITALIA", after 2002 "EUROPEAN CENTRAL BANK."

CURRENT NOTES

1,000 LIRE   113 x 61mm Issued 27 December 1990 **Cat.#114**
1990 Violet and multicolor
M. Montessori / Two children.
It will be replaced by a coin.

2,000 LIRE   119 x 61mm Issued 8 July 1991 **Cat.#115**
1990 Brown and multicolor.
G. Marconi / Ocean liner "Elettra", antennae and wireless
telegraph receiver.

5,000 LIRE   126 x 70mm **Cat.#111**
1985 Green and multicolor.
Vincenzo Bellini / Rosa Ponselle as "Norma."

10,000 LIRE   133 x 70mm **Cat.#112**
1984 Blue and multicolor.
A. Volta and his original battery / Temple of Volta in Como.

50,000 LIRE   149 x 70mm Issued 7 Dec 1992 **Cat.#116**
1992 Lilac brown, green and multicolor.
Gian Lorenzo Bernini and detail from Triton fountain /
Equestrian statue of Constantine.
Older notes with value in lilac brown at top left are redeemable.

100,000 LIRE   157 x 70mm **Cat.#110**
1983 Brown and multicolor.
Caravaggio and "The fortune teller" / "Canestro di Frutta" (Fruit
basket) by Caravaggio.

100,000 LIRE   157 x 70mm Issued 12 Dec 1994 **Cat.#117**
1994 Green, dark brown and orange brown.
Caravaggio and "The fortune teller" / "Canestro di Frutta" (Fruit
basket) by Caravaggio.

500,000 LIRE   163 x 78mm Issued in mid-1997 **Cat.#118**
1997 Black, blue and yellow.
Raphael and "The triumph of Galatea" / "The School of Athene."

OUTMODED AND REDEEMABLE NOTES

500 LIRE   109 x 55mm Issued in 1966 **Cat.#93**
1966-75 Gray blue and brown.
Eagle with snake, and Arethusa / Value.   rruu20020406

500 LIRE   115 x 58mm Issued in 1974 **Cat.#94**
1974-79 Green blue and multicolor / Purplish brown.
Mercury / Sculpture of man and horse.   rruu20020406

1,000 LIRE   157 x 76mm **Cat.#88**
1947-61 Purple and brown.
Woman's head / Value.
There are two seal varieties.   rruu20020406

1,000 LIRE   125 x 62mm Issued in 1963 **Cat.#96**
1962-68 Blue, red and brown.
G. Verdi / Value.   rruu20020406

1,000 LIRE   125 x 62mm Issued in 1969 **Cat.#101**
1969-81 Blue and lilac.
G. Verdi / La Scala in Milano.   rruu20020406

1,000 LIRE   112 x 61mm **Cat.#109**
Decree of 1982 Gray and multicolor.
Marco Polo / Doge's Palace in Venice.   rruu20050630

2,000 LIRE   134 x 65mm Issued in 1975 Cat.#103
  1973-76 Brown and green.
  Galileo / Zodiac signs and telescope.   rruu20031115

5,000 LIRE   208 x 125mm Issued in 1951 Cat.#85
  1947-63 Green and brown.
  Two seated women (Venice and Genoa) / Dante.

5,000 LIRE   142 x 70mm Issued in 1964 Cat.#98
  1964-70 Green and pink.
  C. Colombo / Sailing ship.   rruu20020406

5,000 LIRE   142 x 70mm Issued in 1972 Cat.#102
  1971-77 Olive.
  Cristoforo Colombo / Columbus' Three Caravels.   rruu20020406

5,000 LIRE   125 x 60mm Issued in 1979 Cat.#105
  1979-83 Brown and green.
  Antonello di Messina / Building.   rruu20020406

10,000 LIRE   234 x 125mm Issued in 1951 Cat.#89
  1948-62 Brown and orange.
  Two women seated representing Venice and Genoa / Dante
  Alighieri.   rruu20020406

10,000 LIRE   158 x 78mm Issued in 1963 Cat.#97
  1962-73 Brown, violet and lilac.
  Michelangelo / Piazza with three buildings.   rruu20020406

10,000 LIRE   133 x 70mm Issued in 1977 Cat.#106
  1976-84 Black and multicolor.
  Machiavelli / Architectural design.   rruu20020406

20,000 LIRE   160 x 80mm Issued in 1976 Cat.#104
  1974 Brown.
  Tiziano / Painting.   rruu20020406

50,000 LIRE   166 x 82mm Issued in 1967 Cat.#99
  1967-74 Brown and green.
  Leonardo / Old city view.   rruu20020406

50,000 LIRE 149 x 70mm Issued in 1977 Cat.#107
1977-82 Blue, red and multicolor.
Woman / Buildings.
rruu20020406

50,000 LIRE 149 x 70mm Cat.#113
1984-90 Red violet and multicolor.
Gian Lorenzo Bernini and detail from Triton fountain / Equestrian
statue of Constantine.
rruu20060205

100,000 LIRE 176 x 86mm Issued in 1967 Cat.#100
1967-74 Brown and multicolor.
A. Manzoni / Village and mountains.
rruu20020406

100,000 LIRE 157 x 70mm Issued in 1978 Cat.#108
1978-82 Red and multicolor.
Young woman / Arches.
rruu20020406

Ivory Coast
Côte d'Ivoire Costa de Marfil   XOF

Franc(s) CFA West

It uses notes issued by "BANQUE CENTRALE DES ETATS DE L'AFRIQUE
DE L'OUEST."

For description of notes and currency import/export restrictions see
WEST AFRICAN STATES.

Travelers who cannot find or do not wish to bring in CFA West
francs, may carry French francs, which are easily exchanged or
accepted. U.S. notes which are damaged or dirty and 50's or 100's
dated 1988 or before may be hard to exchange.

Jamaica Jamaika • Jamaïque   JMD

Dollar(s) = 100 cent(s).

The import and export of local and foreign currencies are free.

Alternative currencies: CAD, GBP, **USD.**

A BRIEF MONETARY HISTORY:
Sep. 1969: Dollar = 0.50 Jamaican pound

Issuer: "BANK OF JAMAICA."

CURRENT NOTES

10 DOLLARS 145 x 68mm **Cat.#71**
1985- Bluish purple and multicolor.
George William Gordon / "The Bauxite industry."
These notes are being replaced by coins.

20 DOLLARS 145 x 68mm **Cat.#72**
1985- Red orange and multicolor.
Noel N. Nethersole / Bank of Jamaica.
Larger notes dated 1978-83 seldom found in use, but still valid.
CAUTION: Maroon notes are worthless.

50 DOLLARS 145 x 68mm **Cat.#73**
1988- Purple, brown, and multicolor.
Samuel Sharpe / Doctor's Cave Beach.

100 DOLLARS 145 x 68mm **Cat.#74**
1986-87 Black, green and multicolor.
Sir Donald Sangster / Dunn's River Falls.

©MRI BANKERS' GUIDE TO FOREIGN CURRENCY
P.O.BOX 3174 HOUSTON TX 77253 USA

100 DOLLARS   145 x 68mm **Cat.#75**
1991- Black, green and multicolor.
Sir Donald Sangster / Dunn's River Falls.
Without (Cat.#75), since 1994 (Cat.#76) with ascending serial numbers, and since
1996 (Cat.#76), with windowed security thread.

500 DOLLARS   145 x 68mm **Cat.#77**
1.5.94 Purplish brown, brown, orange brown, green and
multicolor.
"Nanny of the Maroons" / Port Royal.
With light gold clubs on left.

1,000 DOLLARS   **Cat.#78**
New note planned for issue in the near future.

OUTMODED AND REDEEMABLE NOTES

*Notes of 1; 2 and 5 dollars were replaced by coins, and may be
redeemed at the Bank of Jamaica without time limit.*

10 DOLLARS   *153 x 72mm* *Cat.#67*
1978-81 Bluish purple and multicolor.
George William Gordon / "The Bauxite Industry"
CAUTION: Blue notes with brown arms are worthless.

20 DOLLARS   *156 x 76mm* *Cat.#68*
1978-83 Red orange and multicolor.
Noel N. Nethersole / Bank of Jamaica.
CAUTION: Maroon notes are worthless.

Japan Nihon Koku • Japón • Japon **JPY**

Yen.

Currency import-export restrictions:
Local and foreign currency in/out: free. Declaration required for
amounts over ¥ 1 million or equivalent in foreign currency.   Jul1998

Alternative currencies: any major.

Issuer: "NIPPON GINKO."

CURRENT NOTES

1,000 YEN   150 x 76mm Issued 1 Nov 1984 **Cat.#97**
Blue and multicolor.
Natsume Soseki / Two cranes.
With black serial numbers (Cat.#97), since 1 Dec 1993 with reddish brown serial
numbers, microlettering and other anti-counterfeit devices (Cat.#100.)

5,000 YEN   155 x 76mm Issued 1 Nov 1984 **Cat.#98**
Violet, yellow and multicolor.
Nitobe Inazo and globe / Lake and Mount Fuji.
With black serial numbers (Cat.#98), since 1 Dec 1993 with reddish brown serial
numbers, microlettering and other anti-counterfeit devices (Cat.#101.)

10,000 YEN   160 x 76mm Issued 1 Nov 1984 **Cat.#99**
Brown and multicolor.
Fukuzawa Yukichi / Two pheasants.
With black serial numbers (Cat.#99), since 1 Dec 1993 with reddish brown serial
numbers, microlettering and other anti-counterfeit devices (Cat.#102.)

OUTMODED AND REDEEMABLE NOTES

Smaller notes not listed because of low value.

50 YEN   *143 x 68mm* *Cat.#88*
Black, yellow and olive / Brown.
Takahashi Korekiyo / Bank of Japan.

100 YEN　　　　　165 x 93mm Cat.#89
Black on brown or lilac / Lilac or blue.
Prince Shotoku / Horyuji Temple.

100 YEN　　　　　148 x 76mm Cat.#90
Brown violet on green.
Itagaki Taisuke / Diet Building.

500 YEN　　　　　156 x 76mm Cat.#91
Blue.
Iwakura Tomomi / Mount Fuji.

500 YEN　　　　　160 x 72mm Cat.#95
Blue.
Iwakura Tomomi / Mount Fuji.

1,000 YEN　　　　165 x 76mm Cat.#92
Black on green / Brown and blue.
Prince Shotoku / "Dream Hall" of Horyuji Temple.

1,000 YEN　　　　164 x 76mm Cat.#96
Green, brown and multicolor.
Ito Hirobumi / Bank of Japan.

5,000 YEN　　　　160 x 80mm Cat.#93
Green and multicolor.
Prince Shotoku / Bank of Japan.

10,000 YEN　　　174 x 84mm Cat.#94
Brown and green / Brown.
Prince Shotoku / Two phoenixes.

Jersey　　　　　　　　　　　　　GBP

Pound(s) = 100 penny (pence).
Parity: GBP 1.00

The import and export of local and foreign currencies are free.

English pounds are current. Alternative currencies: any major.

Issuer: "THE STATES OF JERSEY."

CURRENT NOTES

1 POUND　　　　　128 x 65mm Cat.#15
Green and multicolor.
Elizabeth II / Church of St Helier.
With outlined numeral in top right corner (Cat.# 15), or with solid numeral in top right corner, to aid the partially sighted (Cat.#20.)

1 POUND　　　　128 x 65mm Issued in May 1995 Cat.#25
Series LJ 9 May 1995 Green and multicolor.
Elizabeth II / Vraic (seaweed) collection and reproduction of a German Occupation 1 pound note.
Commemorative of the 50th anniversary of the Liberation of Jersey.

©MRI BANKERS' GUIDE TO FOREIGN CURRENCY
P.O.BOX 3174 HOUSTON TX 77253 USA

5 POUNDS   135 x 70mm **Cat.#21**
Rose and multicolor.
Elizabeth II / Lighthouse of La Corbière.

10 POUNDS   142 x 75mm **Cat.#22**
Orange brown and multicolor.
Elizabeth II / Battle of Jersey.
Without or with solid numeral in top right corner to aid the partially sighted.

20 POUNDS   150 x 80mm **Cat.#23**
Blue and multicolor.
Elizabeth II / St Ouen's manor.

50 POUNDS   156 x 86mm **Cat.#24**
Dark gray and multicolor.
Elizabeth II / Government House.

OUTMODED AND REDEEMABLE NOTES

Older notes with portrait of Elizabeth II are redeemable without time limit. Ten shillings equal half pound.

Jordan   Jordanien • Jordania • Jordanie   **JOD**

Dinar(s) = 100 piaster(s) or qirsh.

Currency import-export restrictions:
Local currency in: free; out JD 5,000.
Foreign currency in/out: free for nonresidents.

Alternative currencies: any major.

A BRIEF MONETARY HISTORY:
1949: Dinar established at par with Palestine Currency Board pound.

Issuer: "CENTRAL BANK OF JORDAN."

CURRENT NOTES

½ DINAR   131 x 62mm **Cat.#23**
1992-93 Lilac brown on orange brown and multicolor.
Hussein / Qusayr Amra.

½ DINAR   131 x 62mm Issued 12 Feb 1996 **Cat.#28**
Lilac brown on orange brown and multicolor.
Hussein / Qusayr Amra.
Updated version with "Hashemite Kingdom of Jordan."

1 DINAR   137 x 66mm **Cat.#24**
1992-93 Green, olive and multicolor.
Hussein / Ruins of Jerash.

1 DINAR   137 x 66mm Issued 26 August 1995 **Cat.#29**
1995 Green, olive and multicolor.
Hussein / Ruins of Jerash.
Updated version, with "Hashemite Kingdom of Jordan."

5 DINARS   143 x 71mm **Cat.#25**
1992 Red, violet brown and multicolor.
Hussein / The Treasury at Petra.

5 DINARS   143 x 71mm Issued 12 Feb 1996 **Cat.#30**
Red, violet brown and multicolor.
Hussein / The Treasury at Petra.
Updated version with "Hashemite Kingdom of Jordan."

10 DINARS   150 x 75mm **Cat.#26**
1992 Blue, gray violet, green and multicolor.
Hussein / Al-Rabadh Castle.

10 DINARS   150 x 75mm Issued 17 Sep 1996 **Cat.#31**
Blue, gray violet, green and multicolor.
Hussein / Ajloun Castle.
Updated version with "Hashemite Kingdom of Jordan".

20 DINARS   155 x 78mm **Cat.#27**
1992 Olive, orange red, blue and multicolor / Brown, blue,
orange red and multicolor.
Hussein / Al Aqsa Mosque.

20 DINARS   155 x 78mm Issued 9 Dec 1995 **Cat.#32**
Olive, orange red, blue and multicolor / Brown, blue, orange red
and multicolor.
Hussein / Dome of the Rock.
Updated version with "Hashemite Kingdom of Jordan."

OUTMODED AND REDEEMABLE NOTES

{500 FILS = 0.50 DINAR   140 x 70mm **Cat.#9**
Brown.
Hussein looking to right / Columns semicircle.   rwtl

½ DINAR   140 x 70mm **Cat.#13**
Brown and multicolor.
Hussein looking to right / Columns semicircle.   rwtl

½ DINAR   136 x 68mm **Cat.#17**
Brown and multicolor.
Hussein / Columns in Jerash.   outm

1 DINAR   152 x 76mm **Cat.#10**
Green and multicolor.
Hussein looking to right / Al Aqsa Mosque.   rwtl

1 DINAR   144 x 72mm **Cat.#18**
Green and multicolor.
Hussein / Dome of The Rock.   outm

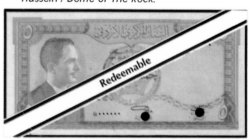

5 DINARS   164 x 82mm **Cat.#11**
Reddish brown and multicolor.
Hussein looking to right / Treasury of Pharaoh at Petra.   rwtl

5 DINARS   152 x 76mm **Cat.#19**
Red and multicolor.
Hussein / Ruins in Petra.   outm

10 DINARS   176 x 88mm **Cat.#12**
Blue gray and multicolor.
Hussein looking to right / Small building at riverside.   rwtl

10 DINARS   160 x 80mm **Cat.#20**
Blue and multicolor.
Hussein / Palace and amphitheater.   outm

20 DINARS   168 x 84mm **Cat.#21**
1977-88 Brown and multicolor.
Hussein / Electric power station.   rwtl

20 DINARS   168 x 84mm Issued in 1991 **Cat.#22**
1977-82 Blue, brown and multicolor.
Hussein / Electric power station.   rwtl

Kazakstan Kasachstan • Kazakhstan **KZT**

Tenge = 100 tiyin.

Currency import/export restrictions:
Foreign currency in: free, declaration necessary for reëxport.
Out: free up to amount imported and declared. Otherwise proof of
origin of funds and authorization is required.

A BRIEF MONETARY HISTORY:
15 Nov. 1993: "Tenge" established.

Alternative currencies: DEM, RUB, USD.

Issuer: "Казахстан Улттык Банкі." (National Bank of
Kazakstan.)

CURRENT NOTES

Smaller notes not listed because of low value.

10 TENGE   144 x 69mm **Cat.#10**
1993 Green and yellow.
Writer Chockan / Lake and mountain.

20 TENGE   144 x 69mm **Cat.#11**
1993 Brown and yellow.
Writer Abay / Knight with eagle.

50 TENGE   144 x 69mm **Cat.#12**
1993 Brownish red and multicolor.
Abulkhair Khan / Horse and human paintings.

100 TENGE   144 x 69mm **Cat.#13**
1993 Blue and rose.
Ablay Khan / Dome.

©MRI BANKERS' GUIDE TO FOREIGN CURRENCY
P.O.BOX 3174 HOUSTON TX 77253 USA

200 TENGE   144 x 69mm **Cat.#14**
1993 Red, brown and green.
Al-Farabi / Ruins.

500 TENGE   144 x 69mm Issued 27 July 1994 **Cat.#15**
1994 Black blue, violet and multicolor.
Al-Farabi / Ruins.

1,000 TENGE   144 x 69mm **Cat.#16**
1994 Green, red and multicolor.
Al-Farabi / Ruins.
Beware of forgeries!!!

2,000 TENGE   144 x 69mm Issued in end 1996 **Cat.#17**
1996 Green and violet.
Al-Farabi / Mausoleum of Khodka Akhmed Yassavi.
Beware of forgeries!!!

Kenya   Kenia   KES

Shilling(s) = 100 cent(s).

Currency import-export restrictions:
Local currency in/out: 100,000 shillings.
Foreign currency in: free for currencies whose export is not restricted. Amounts of or equivalent to USD 5,000 must be declared.
Out: amounts of or equivalent to USD 5,000 must be declared.

Visitors must settle hotel bills in foreign currency or against an external account

Alternative currencies: any major.

A BRIEF MONETARY HISTORY:
Sep 1967: Kenyan shilling established at par with East African shillings.

Issuer: "CENTRAL BANK OF KENYA."

10 SHILLINGS   140 x 72mm **Cat.#20**
1981-88 Green and multicolor.
Pres. Daniel arap Moi / Children and cows.
It is being gradually replaced by a coin.

10 SHILLINGS   140 x 72mm **Cat.#24**
1989-94 Green and multicolor.
Pres. Daniel arap Moi / University.
It is being gradually replaced by a coin.

20 SHILLINGS   146 x 76mm **Cat.#21**
1981-87 Blue and multicolor.
Pres. Daniel arap Moi / Women reading newspaper.
It is being gradually replaced by a coin.

20 SHILLINGS   146 x 76mm **Cat.#25**
1988-92 Blue and multicolor.
Pres. Daniel arap Moi / Stadium.
It is being gradually replaced by a coin.

20 SHILLINGS   146 x 76mm **Cat.#31**
1993-94 Blue and multicolor.
Pres. Daniel arap Moi / Stadium and runner.
It is being gradually replaced by a coin.

20 SHILLINGS   135 x 70mm Issued in late 1995 **Cat.#32**
1995- Blue and multicolor.
Pres. Daniel arap Moi / Kasarani Sports Complex and runner.
Without (Cat.#32) or, since 1996 (Cat.#38), with windowed security thread.
It is being gradually replaced by a coin.

50 SHILLINGS   152 x 79mm **Cat.#22**
1980-88 Red and multicolor / Olive.
Pres. Daniel arap Moi / Jet over airport.

50 SHILLINGS   152 x 79mm **Cat.#26**
1990-92 Reddish brown, brown, green and multicolor / Olive,
reddish brown and multicolor.
Pres. Daniel arap Moi / Modern buildings.

50 SHILLINGS   138 x 72mm **Cat.#33**
1996- Purple brown and multicolor.
Pres. Daniel arap Moi / Scene in Mombasa.

100 SHILLINGS   158 x 82mm **Cat.#23**
1980-88 Purple and multicolor.
Pres. Daniel arap Moi / Statue of Jomo Kenyatta and Kenyatta
Conference Center.

100 SHILLINGS   158 x 82mm **Cat.#27**
1989-94 Purple, green and multicolor.
Pres. Daniel arap Moi / Nyayo monument.

100 SHILLINGS   142 x 74mm **Cat.#34**
1 July 1996 Purple, orange, green and multicolor.
Pres. Daniel Toroitich arap Moi / Nyayo monument.

200 SHILLINGS   162 x 84mm **Cat.#28**
1986-94 Brown and multicolor.
Pres. Daniel arap Moi / Uhuru monument.
With horizontal serial numbers (Cat.#28), and since 1989 (Cat.#29), with vertical
serial numbers.

200 SHILLINGS   144 x 76mm **Cat.#35**
1 July 1996 Brown, green and multicolor.
Pres. Daniel Toroitich arap Moi / Uhuru monument.

500 SHILLINGS   164 x 86mm **Cat.#30**
1988-95 Black and multicolor.
Pres. Daniel arap Moi / National Assembly building.

500 SHILLINGS　　　　148 x 78mm　**Cat.#36**
1995- Black and multicolor.
Pres. Daniel arap Moi / National Assembly building.
Without (Cat.#36), or, since 1998 with windowed security thread (Cat.#39.)

1,000 SHILLINGS　　　　150 x 80mm　**Cat.#37**
1994- Brown and light green.
Pres. Daniel arap Moi / Elephants and other animals.
Without (Cat.#37), or, since 1998 with windowed security thread (Cat.#40.)

OUTMODED AND REDEEMABLE NOTES

Notes with Kenyatta are valid, except the 100 shillings dated 1966 to 1972, which are demonetized.

5 SHILLINGS　　　　133 x 70mm　Cat.#19
1981-84 Brown and multicolor.
Pres Moi / Rams and giraffes.

Kiribati　　　　　　　　　　AUD

Australian currency is used.

The import and export of local and foreign currencies are free.

D.P.R. of Korea
Chosun Minchu-chui Inmin Konghwa-guk •
Korea DVR • RDP de Corea • RDP de Corée　　KPW

Won = 100 chon.

Currency import-export restrictions:
Local currency in/out: forbidden.
Foreign currency in: free, must declare.
Out: up to amount imported and declared.
Reconversion requires presentation of proof of exchange of hard currency.

Alternative currencies: any major.

In addition to regular currency, there are several types of coupons issued to visitors for use in "Hard currency shops." North Koreans are not allowed to own them.

A BRIEF MONETARY HISTORY:
Feb. 1959: New won = 100 old won

Issuer: "CENTRAL BANK OF THE DEMOCRATIC PEOPLE'S REPUBLIC OF KOREA."

CURRENT NOTES

1 WON　　　　115 x 55mm　Issued 14 July 1992　**Cat.#39**
1992 Olive and multicolor.
"A Flower Girl" / Fairy playing a flute, descending from the Three Fairy Rock, against Mt. Kumgang.

5 WON　　　　125 x 60mm　Issued 14 July 1992　**Cat.#40**
1992- Dark grayish blue and multicolor.
University student, with group of people in background, Kim Il Sung University and Mangyongdae School children's palace / Grand People's Study House.

10 WON　　　　135 x 65mm　Issued 14 July 1992　**Cat.#41**
1992- Orange brown and multicolor.
Remote control operator, statue of Chollima / West Sea Dam.

50 WON　　　　145 x 70mm　Issued 14 July 1992　**Cat.#42**
1992 Dark brown and multicolor.
Three people and Tower of the Juche Idea / Mount Paektu.

100 WON   156 x 74mm Issued 14 July 1992 **Cat.#43**
1992 Brown, pink and multicolor.
Kim Il Sung / His native home in Mangyengdae.

500 WON   154 x 74mm Issued in late 1998 **Cat.#44**
1998 Dark grayish green and light purple.
Building / Bridge.

Republic of Korea
Daehan Min-kuk • Corea • Corée   **KRW**

Won = 100 chon.
Minor unit coins are not used.

Currency import-export restrictions:
Local currency in/out: 8,000,000 won. Larger amounts require authorization.
Foreign currency in/out: free, must declare if it exceeds US$ 10,000 or equivalent. Reconversion on departure requires proof of prior exchange.   Jul1998

Alternative currencies: any major.

A BRIEF MONETARY HISTORY
1962: Won = 10 hwan

Issuer: "THE BANK OF KOREA."

CURRENT NOTES

1,000 WON   151 x 76mm Issued 11 June 1983 **Cat.#47**
(1983) Purple and multicolor.
Scholar Yi Hwang / Tosansŏwon Academy.
It will be replaced by a coin.

5,000 WON   156 x 76mm Issued 11 June 1983 **Cat.#48**
(1983) Brown and multicolor.
Scholar Yi I / Ojukŏn, birthplace of Yi I.

10,000 WON   161 x 76mm Issued 8 Oct 1983 **Cat.#49**
(1983) Green and multicolor.
King Sejong the Great / Kyŏnghoeru Pavilion.

10,000 WON   161 x 76mm Issued 20 Jan 1994 **Cat.#50**
(1994) Green and multicolor.
King Sejong the Great / Kyŏnghoeru Pavilion.
With windowed security thread, microlettering and intaglio latent image added.

OUTMODED AND REDEEMABLE NOTES

Smaller notes not listed because of low value.

500 WON   155 x 65mm **Cat.#37**
1962-67 Blue, lilac and green.
Namdaemun, South gate of Seoul / Sacred fire.

500 WON   165 x 73mm **Cat.#39**
1966-75 Gray and multicolor.
Namdaemun, South gate of Seoul / Tortoise warship.

500 WON   160 x 70mm **Cat.#43**
(1973-93) Blue and multicolor.
Adm. Yi Sun-shin / Hyŏnchungsa, shrine of Adm. Yi Sun-shin.

©MRI BANKERS' GUIDE TO FOREIGN CURRENCY
P.O.Box 3174 HOUSTON TX 77253 USA

1,000 WON   163 x 73mm Cat.#44
  (1975-1993) Purple and multicolor.
  Scholar Yi Hwang / Tosansŏwon, Academy.

5,000 WON   167 x 77mm Cat.#41
  1972-80 Brown, green and multicolor.
  Scholar Yi I / Bank of Korea's main office.

5,000 WON   167 x 77mm Cat.#45
  (1977-93) Brown, green and multicolor.
  Scholar Yi I / Ojukŏn, his birthplace.

10,000 WON   171 x 81mm Cat.#42
  (1973-81) Dark grayish brown and multicolor.
  King Sejong the Great / Gŭnjŏng-jŏn in Kyŏngbokkung,
  pavilion.

10,000 WON   171 x 81mm Cat.#46
  (1979-1993) Black, green and multicolor.
  King Sejong the Great and water clock / Kyŏnghoeru Pavilion.

Kurdistan

U.S. dollars, Iraqi dinars and Turkish lira are used widely. Old 1; 5 and 10 Iraqi dinars notes are reported to be current, at a rate of about 15 to the U.S. dollar. (April 1999.)

Kuwait   Koweit   KWD

Dinar(s) = 1,000 fils.

The import and export of local and foreign currencies are free.

Alternative currencies: any major.

A BRIEF MONETARY HISTORY:
Apr. 1961: Dinar established at par with British pound.

Issuer: "CENTRAL BANK OF KUWAIT."

CURRENT NOTES

¼ DINAR 5th Issue   110 x 67mm **Cat.#23**
  (1994) Law of 1968 Brown, orange, greenish blue and multicolor.
  Arms, dhow and chest / Group of girls playing traditional game.

½ DINAR 5th Issue   120 x 67mm **Cat.#24**
  (1994) Law of 1968 Green, violet brown, and orange.
  Arms, money changers stalls and coffee pot / Boys playing marbles.

1 DINAR 5th Issue   130 x 67mm **Cat.#25**
  (1994) Law of 1968 Green, violet brown and blue.
  Arms, Kuwait towers and oil lamp / Mina Al-Shuwaikh and water storage vessel.

5 DINARS 5th Issue   140 x 67mm **Cat.#26**
(1994) Law of 1968 Red, orange, green and multicolor.
Arms and Telecom tower and grinding stone / Oil refinery,
A'Zour power station, Kuwait water tanks and electricity pylons.

10 DINARS 5th Issue   150 x 67mm **Cat.#27**
(1994) Law of 1968 Violet brown, purple blue and multicolor.
Arms, Great State Mosque and traditional water vessel /
Traditional door, pearl diving and incense burner.

20 DINARS 5th Issue   160 x 67mm **Cat.#28**
(1994) Law of 1968 Olive brown, orange and multicolor.
Arms, Red Fort at Jahra and cannon / Central Bank gateway in
the Old Wall at Kuwait City.

OUTMODED AND REDEEMABLE NOTES

¼ DINAR 4th Issue   115 x 68mm Cat.#17
Law of 1968 Light lilac red, olive brown and multicolor.
Oil rig and arms / Oil refinery.
CAUTION: Brown notes are worthless.

½ DINAR 4th Issue   126 x 68mm Cat.#18
Law of 1968 Blue
Tower and arms / Harbor scene.   rruu20040816
CAUTION: Brownish purple notes are worthless.

WARNING

The first, second and third Kuwaiti dinar bank notes issued prior to 2 Aug 1990 have become worthless.

1 DINAR 4th Issue   137 x 68mm Cat.#19
Law of 1968 Green, light pink and multicolor.
Modern building and arms / Fortress.   rruu20040816
CAUTION: Reddish purple notes are worthless.

5 DINARS 4th Issue   148 x 68mm Cat.#20
Law of 1968 Olive brown, pink, green and multicolor.
Minaret and arms / Building.   rruu20040816
CAUTION: Blue notes are worthless.

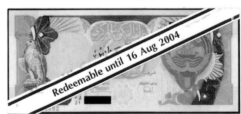

10 DINARS 4th Issue   160 x 68mm Cat.#21
Law of 1968 Orange red, brown olive and multicolor.
Falcon and arms / Sailing boat.   rruu20040816
CAUTION: Green notes are worthless.

20 DINARS 4th Issue   165 x 68mm Cat.#22
Law of 1968 Violet brown and multicolor.
Building and arms / Modern building.   rruu20040816
CAUTION: Olive brown notes are worthless.

Kyrgyzstan   Kirgisistan • Kirguistán   **KGS**

Som = 100 tyiyn.

The import and export of local and foreign currencies are free.

22JUL1998

Alternative currencies: DEM, RUB, USD.

A BRIEF MONETARY HISTORY:
10 May 1993: 1 som = 200 rubles

Issuer: "КЫРГЫЗ БАНКЫ" (Kyrgyz Bank).

CURRENT NOTES

Smaller notes not listed because of low value.

5 SOM   140 x 70mm **Cat.#5**
Green and multicolor.
Equestrian statue of Manas the Noble / His mausoleum.

5 SOM   135 x 65mm Issued 25 April 1994 **Cat.#8**
Blue, yellow and multicolor.
Ballerina Bibisara Beishenalieva / National Opera Theater.

5 SOM   135 x 65mm Issued in 17 Dec 1997 **Cat.#13**
Violet blue and multicolor.
Ballerina Bibisara Beishenalieva / National Opera Theater.

10 SOM   135 x 65mm **Cat.#9**
Green, brown and multicolor.
Kassim / Mountains.

10 SOM   135 x 65mm Issued 17 Dec 1997 **Cat.#14**
Green, red and multicolor.
Kassim / Mountains.

20 SOM   140 x 70mm **Cat.#6**
Violet blue and multicolor.
Equestrian statue of Manas the Noble / His mausoleum.

20 SOM   135 x 65mm Issued 25 April 1994 **Cat.10**
Orange red.
Folk poet and singer Togolak Moldo / Mausoleum of Manas the
Great.

50 SOM   135 x 65mm Issued 29 Aug 1994 **Cat.11**
Reddish brown and multicolor.
Kurmanjan Datka / Uzgen Architectural Ensemble.

100 SOM   135 x 65mm **Cat.#12**
Brown, pink and yellow brown.
Toktogul / Toktogul Hydroelectric Power Station.

Lao PDR   Laos   **LAK**

Kip = 100 att.
Minor unit coins are not used.

The import and export of local and foreign currencies are free.

U.S. dollars and Thai baht circulate extensively.

A BRIEF MONETARY HISTORY
5 May 1955: kip created to replace Indochinese piastre.
Jun. 1976: 1 Lao liberation kip = 20 old kip
Dec. 1979: 1 new kip = 100 liberation kip

Issuer: "BANK OF THE LAO PDR."

©MRI BANKERS' GUIDE TO FOREIGN CURRENCY
P.O.BOX 3174 HOUSTON TX 77253 USA

CURRENT NOTES

Smaller notes not listed because of low value.

1,000 KIP   152 x 68mm **Cat.#32**
1992-96 Blue black, greenish black, green and multicolor.
Three women and temple / Cattle.
Notes dated 1994 and 1996 have a security thread.

1,000 KIP   152 x 68mm **Cat.#32**
1998 Blue black, greenish black, green and multicolor.
Three women and temple / Cattle.

2,000 KIP   152 x 68mm Issued 1 June 1998 **Cat.#33**
1997 Dark blue, violet brown and multicolor.
Kaysone Phomvihane / Cement factory.

5,000 KIP   152 x 68mm Issued 1 June 1998 **Cat.#34**
1997 Lilac brown, violet gray and multicolor.
Kaysone Phomvihane / Hydroelectric complex.

Latvia
Latvija • Lettland • Letonia • Lettonie   **LVL**

Monetary unit: Lats (lati) = 100 santims (santimi).

The import or export of all currencies is free.   Jul1998

Alternative currencies: CAD, CHF, DEM, DKK, FIM, GBP, NOK, SEK, USD.

A BRIEF MONETARY HISTORY
1992: rublis = Soviet ruble.
1 March 1993: lats = 200 rublu.

Issuer: "LATVIJAS BANKA."

CURRENT NOTES

5 LATI   130 x 65mm Issued 5 March 1993 **Cat.#43**
1992- Green and dark green.
Tree / Six petals flower.
With regular security thread (Cat.#43), and since 1996 (Cat.#49) with a thin
holographic band.

10 LATI   130 x 65mm Issued 28 June 1993 **Cat.#44**
1992 Violet.
Daugava river / National bow brooch.

10 LATI   **Cat.#49**
A new note will be issued in the future.

20 LATI   130 x 65mm Issued 28 June 1993 **Cat.#45**
1992 Brown.
Country house / Ornamented woven linen.

50 LATI   130 x 65mm Issued 2 May 1994 **Cat.#46**
1992 Blue.
Sailing ship / Two crossed keys and cross.

100 LATI   130 x 65mm Issued 2 May 1994 **Cat.#47**
1992 Red.
Krišjānis Barons / Ornaments of the woven national belt.

500 LATI   130 x 65mm Issued 20 July 1998 **Cat.#48**
1992 Purple.
Young woman's head / Ornamental little brass crowns.

Lebanon   Liban • Libanon • Líbano   **LBP**

Livre = 100 piastre(s).
Minor unit coins are not used.

The import and export of local and foreign currencies are free.

Alternative currencies: any major.

Issuer: "BANQUE DU LIBAN."

CURRENT NOTES

Smaller notes not listed because of low value.

250 LIVRES   165 x 98mm **Cat.#67**
1978-88 Green, blue and multicolor.
Temple of Tyre / Columns of Douris.
It is being gradually replaced by a coin.

500 LIVRES   157 x 67mm **Cat.#68**
1988 Brown, green and multicolor.
View of Beirut / Frieze and columns.
It is being gradually replaced by a coin.

1,000 LIVRES   157 x 67mm **Cat.#69**
1988-92 Blue and multicolor.
Map of Lebanon / Ruins of Baalbek and Bank of Lebanon.

5,000 LIVRES   157 x 67mm **Cat.#71**
1994-95 Black, green, violet, red and orange.
Value, cedar and geometrical designs / Geometrical design.
It commemorates the 30th anniversary of the Bank's foundation.

10,000 LIVRES   155 x 67mm Issued 26 June 1993 **Cat.#70**
Purple, brown, blue and multicolor.
Ruins of Tyre and Baalbeck / Fortress of Byblos.

10,000 LIVRES   145 x 73mm Issued in late 1998 **Cat.#75**
Green, orange and green / Green, orange, yellow and brown.
Value / Monument and cedars.

20,000 LIVRES   150 x 80mm **Cat.#72**
1994-95 Reddish brown, brown, orange and pale olive green.
Value / "LIBAN."
It commemorates the 30th anniversary of the Bank's foundation.

50,000 LIVRES   155 x 85mm **Cat.#73**
1994-95 Dark blue, light blue, brownish red and yellow.
Value and two little boats / Rhombus (diamond) with initials
"BDL".
It commemorates the 30th anniversary of the Bank's foundation.

100,000 LIVRES   160 x 90mm **Cat.#74**
1994-95 Green, yellow and blue.
Bunch of grapes / Value and geometrical designs.
It commemorates the 30th anniversary of the Bank's foundation.

500,000 LIVRES   **Cat.#76**
Reported to be ready for issue at a later date.

Lesotho   LSL

Loti (maloti) = 100 sente (lisente).
Parity: ZAR 1.00

Currency import/export restrictions:
Local currency and rands in/out: M 2,000.
Unlimited from/to South Africa or Swaziland.
Foreign currency in: free. Must be declared.
Out: up to amount imported and declared.   Jul1998
Reconversion requires proof of prior exchange.

South African rands are current. Alternative currencies: GBP, USD.

A BRIEF MONETARY HISTORY
Jan. 1980: loti = South African rand

Issuer: "CENTRAL BANK OF LESOTHO."

CURRENT NOTES

10 MALOTI   133 x 70mm **Cat.#11**
1989-90 Red and multicolor.
King Moshoeshoe II / Horseman and mountains.

20 MALOTI   135 x 70mm **Cat.#15**
1994 Green, olive and blue.
King Moshoeshoe the First / Herdsman and cows.

50 MALOTI   138 x 70mm **Cat.#16**
1994 Violet, green and multicolor.
King Moshoeshoe the First / Man on horseback, ass and stone formation.

100 MALOTI   141 x 70mm **Cat.#17**
1994 Olive green, orange brown and multicolor.
King Moshoeshoe the First / Rams.

200 MALOTI   144 x 70mm **Cat.#18**
1994 Purple brown, brown, orange and multicolor.
King Moshoeshoe the First / Herdsmen and sheep.

OUTMODED AND REDEEMABLE NOTES

All older notes issued by the Lesotho Monetary Authority and the Central Bank of Lesotho are redeemable.

Liberia   LRD

Dollar(s) = 100 cent(s).

United States dollars are current in theory. In practice they are worth much more than local currency. Both types of local 5 dollar notes are in circulation at different rates.

Currency import-export restrictions:
There is a export limit of $1,000 in cash.

Issuer: "NATIONAL BANK OF LIBERIA."

CURRENT NOTES

5 DOLLARS   155 x 67mm Issued in Aug 1989 **Cat.#19**
12 April 1989 Black and green
J.J. Roberts / National Bank building.
Nicknamed "JJ", these circulated in areas controlled by Charles Taylor.

5 DOLLARS   155 x 67mm **Cat.#20**
6 April 1991 Black and green.
Coat of arms and man by rubber tree / National Bank building.
Nicknamed "Liberty", these circulated in areas controlled by ECOMOG.

20 DOLLARS   **Cat.#21**
Reported to be printed and ready to be issued.

50 DOLLARS   **Cat.#22**
Reported to be printed and ready to be issued.

100 DOLLARS   **Cat.#23**
Reported to be printed and ready to be issued.

Libya   Libia • Libye   **LYD**

Dinar(s) = 1,000 dirham(s).

Currency import-export restrictions:
Local currency in/out: forbidden.
Foreign currency in: free, must declare.
Out: up to amount imported and declared.
Reconversion permitted with proof of exchange, deducting $50 per day of stay. Many tourist services must be paid with hard currency, or else proof of official market exchange must be furnished.

Alternative currencies: any major.

A BRIEF MONETARY HISTORY
Mar. 1952: Libyan pound = 1 Egyptian pound
Sep. 1971: Dinar = Libyan pound

Issuer: "CENTRAL BANK OF LIBYA."

CURRENT NOTES

Smaller notes not listed because of low value.

½ **DINAR** Series 2   152 x 76mm **Cat.#43**
Green and multicolor.
Oil refinery at left / Irrigation system.

½ **DINAR** Series 3   152 s 76mm **Cat.#48**
Olive brown and multicolor.
Oil refinery at left / Irrigation system.

½ **DINAR** Series 4, first type   152 x 76mm **Cat.#53**
Dark olive brown, blue green and multicolor / Purple.
Oil refinery at center left / Irrigation system.
White top and bottom at front, English text on back.

½ **DINAR** Series 4, second type   152 x 76mm **Cat.#58**
Dark olive brown, blue green and multicolor / Purple.
Oil refinery at center left / Irrigation system.
Colored background from top to bottom at front, Arabic text on back.

1 **DINAR** Series 2   162 x 81mm **Cat.#44**
Green and multicolor.
Mosque / Interior of a mosque.

1 **DINAR** Series 3   162 x 81mm **Cat.#49**
Green, violet blue and multicolor.
Mosque / Interior of a mosque.

1 **DINAR** Series 4, first type   162 x 81mm **Cat.#54**
Blue and multicolor.
Muammar Qadhafy / Mosque.
White top and bottom at front, Arabic text on back.

1 **DINAR** Series 4, second type   162 x 81mm **Cat.#59**
Blue, green and multicolor.
Muammar Qadhafy / Mosque.
Colored background from top to bottom at front, Arabic text on back.

5 DINARS Series 2   172 x 86mm **Cat.#45**
Green and multicolor.
Dromedaries at left / Monument and crowd.

5 DINARS Series 3   172 x 86mm **Cat.#50**
Green, brown and multicolor.
Dromedaries at left / Monument and crowd.

5 DINARS Series 4, first type   172 x 86mm **Cat.#55**
Olive brown, lilac brown, green and multicolor.
Dromedaries at center left / Monument and crowd.
White edge at top and bottom of front, English text on back.

5 DINARS Series 4, second type   172 x 86mm **Cat.#60**
Olive brown, lilac brown, green and multicolor.
Dromedaries at center left / Monument and crowd.
Colored background from top to bottom of front, Arabic text on back.

10 DINARS Series 2   182 x 91mm **Cat.#46**
Green, rose and multicolor.
Omar el-Mukhtar / Hilltop fortress and crowd.

10 DINARS Series 3   182 x 91mm **Cat.#51**
Dark green and multicolor.
Omar el-Mukhtar / Hilltop fortress and crowd.

10 DINARS Series 4, first type   182 x 91mm **Cat.#56**
Green and multicolor.
Omar el-Mukhtar / Fortress and crowd.
White top and bottom edges in front and white background on octagon on
back, Arabic text on back.

10 DINARS Series 4, second type 182 x 91mm **Cat.#61**
Green and multicolor.
Omar el-Mukhtar at center left / Fortress and crowd.
Colored background from top to bottom in front, colored background on
octagon and Arabic text on back.

OUTMODED AND REDEEMABLE NOTES

¼ DINAR   140 x 70mm **Cat.#33**
Orange brown and multicolor.
Arms / Doorway.

½ DINAR   160 x 80mm **Cat.#34**
Purple and multicolor.
Arms / Oil refinery.

1 DINAR   170 x 85mm Cat.#35
Blue and multicolor.
Minaret / Fort.

Military Authority in Tripolitania

Issued during the occupation of Tripolitania, in World War II, by the British "Military Authority in Tripolitania", are redeemable at the Bank of England in London at the ratio of 1 Sterling pound for every 480 lire. Their numismatic value is far higher than face.

Smaller notes not listed because of low value.

{50 LIRE} = 0.1042 POUND   113 x 72mm Cat.#M5
Brown.
Lion over crown / Value.

{100 LIRE} = 0.2083 POUND   113 x 72mm Cat.#M6
Red orange on blue.
Lion over crown / Value.

{500 LIRE} = 1.04167 POUNDS   140 x 77mm Cat.#M7
Green on blue.
Lion over crown / Value.

{1,000 LIRE} = 2.0833 POUNDS   151 x 83mm Cat.#M8
Blue on brown.
Lion over crown / Value.

Liechtenstein   CHF

Swiss currency is used.

The import and export of Swiss and foreign currencies are free.

Alternative currencies: any major.

Lithuania   LTL
Lietuva • Litauen • Lituania • Lituanie

Litas (litų) = 100 centas (centų).

Currency import-export restrictions:
Local or foreign currency in/out: LTL 500,000 or equivalent of USD 125,000.
Declaration required for the import or export of local or foreign currency in the amount of LTL 10,000 or equivalent (USD 2,500.00.)

Alternative currencies: CAD, CHF, DEM, DKK, FIM, GBP, NOK, SEK, USD.

A BRIEF MONETARY HISTORY
1991: Talonas = Soviet ruble
June 1993: 1 litas = 100 talonų

Issuer: "LIETUVOS BANKAS."

CURRENT NOTES

1 LITAS   135 x 65mm Issued 1 March 1994 **Cat.#53**
1994 Brown and multicolor.
J. Žemaitė / Old wooden house.

2 LITAI   135 x 65mm Issued 25 Jan 1994 **Cat.#54**
1993 Green and gray.
M. Valančius / Island castle of Trakai.

5 LITAI   135 x 65mm Issued 10 Dec 1993 **Cat.#55**
1993 Violet, greenish blue and multicolor.
J. Jablonskis / Wooden sculpture "Lithuanian school."

10 LITŲ   135 x 65mm Issued 1 March 1994 **Cat.#56**
1993 Bluish gray.
Aviators Steponas Darius and Stasys Girėnas / Airplane "Lituanica."

10 LITŲ   135 x 65mm Issued 22 Dec 1997 **Cat.#59**
1997 Blue, yellow, light orange and green / Violet blue and green.
Aviators Steponas Darius and Stasys Girėnas / Airplane "Lituanica."

20 LITŲ   135 x 65mm Issued 25 Jan 1994 **Cat.#57**
1993 Light purple and green / Reddish brown.
Poet and theologician Maironis / War Museum and statue of Freedom.

20 LITŲ   135 x 65mm Issued 22 Dec 1997 **Cat.#60**
1997 Light purple, green and pink / Brown and green.
Poet Maironis / War Museum and statue of Freedom.

50 LITŲ   135 x 65mm Issued 10 Dec 1993 **Cat.#58**
1993 Brown, orange brown and yellow.
Dr Jonas Basanavičius / Cathedral of Vilnius and the Belfry.

50 LITŲ   135 x 65mm Issued 14 Dec 1998 **Cat.#62**
1998 Brown, orange brown and green.
Dr Jonas Basanavičius / Cathedral of Vilnius and the Belfry.

100 LITŲ   135 x 65mm Issued 25 June 1993 **Cat.#50**
1991 Light green.
Simonas Daukantas and "Vytis", emblem of Lithuania / Aerial view of the University of Vilnius and Old City.

200 LITŲ   135 x 65mm Issued 24 Nov 1997 **Cat.#61**
1997 Blue, violet and green / Blue, yellow and brown.
Vydūnas (Vilhelmas Storosta) / Klaipéda lighthouse.

Notes of 500 and 1,000 litų dated 1991 were printed, but not issued.

OUTMODED AND REDEEMABLE NOTES

10 LITŲ   *135 x 65mm Issued in June 1993 Cat.#47*
1991 Grayish brown.
Aviators Steponas Darius and Stasys Girėnas / Airplane "Lituanica."

20 LITŲ   *135 x 65mm Cat.#48*
1991 Light purple.
Poet and theologician Maironis / War Museum and statue of Freedom.

50 LITŲ   *135 x 65mm Cat.#49*
1991 Gold.
Dr Jonas Basanavičius / Cathedral of Vilnius and the Belfry.

Luxembourg
Letzeburg • Luxemburg • Luxemburgo   **LUF**

Euro = 40.3399 francs Franc(s) = 100 centime(s).
Parity: BEF 1.00

The import and export of local and foreign currencies are free.

Belgian notes are current. Alternative currencies: any major.

A BRIEF MONETARY HISTORY:
1 Jan 1999: Euro adopted at 40.3399 francs.

Issuers: "BANQUE CENTRALE DU LUXEMBOURG", formerly "INSTITUT MONÉTAIRE LUXEMBOURGEOIS", and "BANQUE INTERNATIONALE A LUXEMBOURG", after 2002 "EUROPEAN CENTRAL BANK."

CURRENT NOTES

100 FRANCS Inst. Mon. Luxembourgeois.   142 x 76mm **Cat.#58**
Multicolor.
Grand Duke Jean and Palace / City of Luxembourg.

1,000 FRANCS Inst. Mon. Luxembourgeois.   153 x 76mm **Cat.#59**
Brown and multicolor.
Grand Duke Jean and Castle of Vianden / City of Echternach.

5,000 FRANCS Inst. Mon. Luxembourgeois.   160 x 76mm **Cat.#60**
April 1993 Green, brown and orange.
Grand Duke Jean and castle of Clervaux / Buildings from the European Center of Luxembourg-Kirchberg.

OUTMODED AND REDEEMABLE NOTES

All notes issued by the Caisse Générale de l'Etat since 1953 are redeemable. Notes of 100 francs of the Banque Internationale with two portraits are redeemable until 28 February 2002. Their older notes are worthless.

Macao Macau   **MOP**

Pataca(s) = 100 avo(s).

The import and export of local and foreign currencies are free.

Alternative currencies: any major.

Issuers: "BANCO DA CHINA" AND "BANCO NACIONAL ULTRAMARINO."

CURRENT NOTES

20 PATACAS B. da China   143 x 72mm Issued 1 Sep 1996 **Cat.#91**
1 Sep 1996 Purple and multicolor.
Temple of Barra / Banco da China building.

20 PATACAS B.N.U.   143 x 72mm Issued 1 Sep 1996 **Cat.#66**
1 Sep 1996 Purple and multicolor.
Building / View of Macao.

50 PATACAS B. da China   149 x 75mm **Cat.#92**
16 Oct 1995 Grayish blue and multicolor.
University of Macao / Bank's building and lotus flowers.

50 PATACAS B.N.U.   149 x 75mm **Cat.#67**
13 July 1992 Olive brown and multicolor.
Chinese New Year dragon / City view.

100 PATACAS B. da China   154 x 77mm **Cat.#93**
16 Oct 1995 Blue and multicolor.
New terminal of Porto Exterior / Bank building and lotus flowers.

100 PATACAS B.N.U. 154 x 77mm **Cat.#68**
1992 Black and multicolor.
Junk / Skyline.

500 PATACAS B. da China 158 x 80mm **Cat.#94**
16 Oct 1995 Green and multicolor.
Friendship bridge / Bank's building and lotus flowers.

500 PATACAS B.N.U. 160 x 80mm **Cat.#69**
3 Sep 1990 Olive and multicolor.
Chinese building / Bridge and view of city.

1,000 PATACAS B. da China 164 x 82mm **Cat.#95**
16 Oct 1995 Golden orange and multicolor.
Praia Oeste / Bank's building and lotus flowers.

1,000 PATACAS B.N.U. 163 x 81mm **Cat.#63**
1988- Orange, brown and multicolor.
Dragon / View of Macao.

OUTMODED AND REDEEMABLE NOTES

Redeemable until 31 Dec 2003

10 PATACAS B. da China 138 x 69mm **Cat.#90**
16 Oct 1995 Brown and multicolor. rruu20031231
Lighthouse in Guia / Bank's building and lotus flowers.

Redeemable until 31 Dec 2003

10 PATACAS B.N.U. 138 x 69mm **Cat.#65**
8 July 1991 Brown, olive and multicolor.
Building / Tall buildings and bridge. rruu20031231

Macedonia
Makedonija • Mazedonien • Macédoine **MKD**

(New) denari = 100 deni.

Currency import-export restrictions:
Local in or out: 5,000 denari in notes of 100 or below.
Foreign currency in: free, must declare amounts exceeding DEM 300
or its equivalent. Aug1998
Out: free to DEM 300 or equivalent, or more if declared on entry.

Alternative currencies: DEM, USD.

A BRIEF MONETARY HISTORY
1992: Macedonian denar = Yugoslavian dinar.
May 1993: "new" denar = 100 old denari

Currency notes issued by "НАРОДНЕ БАНКА НА РЕПУБЛИКА
МАКЕДОНИЈА" (National Bank of the Republic of Macedonia).

CURRENT NOTES

10 DENARI 140 x 70mm Issued 8 September 1996 **Cat.#14**
8 Sep 1996 Multicolor.
Statue of goddess Isida from III Century BC., in Ohrid / Mosaic
with peacock from the Episcopal Basilica in Stobi (V-VI century.)
Commemorative of the 5th Anniversary of Independence.

50 DENARI   143 x 70mm Issued 8 September 1996 **Cat.#15**
8 Sep 1996 Multicolor.
Copper follis and arch from the church of St. Panteleimon in
Gorno Nerezi / Archangel Gabriel from the church of St. George
in Kurbinovo.
Commemorative of the 5th Anniversary of Independence.

100 DENARI   145 x 70mm Issued 8 September 1996 **Cat.#16**
8 Sep 1996 Violet, lilac, yellow, brown and multicolor.
Ceiling rosette in an Albanian town house in Debar / View of
Skopje by Jacopus Harevin (1594) with an Albanian window
superimposed.
Commemorative of the 5th Anniversary of Independence.

500 DENARI   149 x 70mm Issued 8 September 1996 **Cat.#17**
8 Sep 1996 Orange, Green, blue and multicolor / Deep red and
multicolor.
Golden mask / Poppy.
Commemorative of the 5th Anniversary of Independence.

1,000 DENARI   152 x 70mm Issued 8 September 1996 **Cat.#18**
8 Sep 1996 Dark orange, violet brown and multicolor / Violet
brown on light brown and multicolor.
Icon of Madonna Episkepsis from the church of St. Vrachi-Mali in
Ohrid (Early XIV Century) / Detail from the church of St. Sophia
in Ohrid.
Commemorative of the 5th Anniversary of Independence.

5,000 DENARI   155 x 70mm Issued 8 September 1996 **Cat.#19**
8 Sep 1996 Green, orange and multicolor / Green, yellow, orange
mauve and multicolor.
Bronze figurine from Tetovo (VI century B.C.) / Mosaic depicting
Cerberus tied to a fig tree, from the Great Basilica in Heraklea.
Commemorative of the 5th Anniversary of Independence.

OUTMODED AND REDEEMABLE NOTES

10 (NEW) DENARI   150 x 73mm **Cat.#9**
1993 Blue and multicolor.
"Ilinden" monument in Krushevo / View of Krushevo.   *RWTL*

20 (NEW) DENARI   150 x 73mm **Cat.#10**
1993 Wine red, blue and multicolor.   *RWTL*
Daut-Pasha Bath in Skopje / XVII century clock tower in Skopje.

50 (NEW) DENARI   150 x 73mm **Cat.#11**
1993 Orange red and multicolor.
Monastery of St. Pantaleimon, Skopje / Old building of the
National Bank of Macedonia, in Skopje.   *RWTL*

100 (NEW) DENARI   150 x 73mm **Cat.#12**
1993 Brown and multicolor.
St. Sophia church in Ohrid / National Museum in Ohrid.   *RWTL*

500 (NEW) DENARI   150 x 73mm **Cat.#13**
1993 Olive, orange and multicolor.
St. Jovan Caneo monastery in Ohrid / Fortress of Samuil and old
part of Ohrid.   *RWTL*

Madagascar Madagaskar MGF

Franc(s) = 100 centime(s).
Ariary = 5 francs.
Minor unit coins are not used.

Currency import-export restrictions:
Local currency in/out: FMG 25,000.
Foreign currency in: free, **must** declare.
Out: up to the amount imported and declared.
Exchange controls are strict.

Alternative currencies: DEM, FRF, GBP, USD.

Issuer: "Banky Foiben'i Madagasikara."

CURRENT NOTES

Smaller denominations not listed because of low value.

1,000 FRANCS　　137 x 76mm Issued 19 Sep 1994 **Cat.#76**
Blue, brown and orange.
Young man and piraguas / Young woman and fishermen working net.

2,500 FRANCS = 500 ARIARY　　147 x 80mm **Cat.#77**
Red, brown, green, and multicolor.
Portrait of a woman / Flora and fauna.

2,500 FRANCS　　146 x 76mm Issued in mid-1998 **Cat.#81**
Orange and multicolor.
Queen's Palace at Manjakiamadana and old woman / Two women, loom and handicrafts.

5,000 FRANCS　　155 x 76mm Issued 8 May 1995 **Cat.#78**
Lilac violet and multicolor.
Young man's head, oxen driven cart and cane cutting scene / Lemurs, butterflies, birds and sea shells.

10,000 FRANCS　　165 x 76mm Issued 8 May 1995 **Cat.79**
Brown and multicolor.
Statuette, traditional musical instruments and an "Alolao" / Three artisans at work.

25,000 FRANCS = 5,000 ARIARY　　178 x 92mm **Cat.#80**
Olive and multicolor
Old man / Traditional bullfighting scene.

25,000 FRANCS　　173 x 76mm Issued in mid-1998 **Cat.#82**
Lilac rose and multicolor.
Woman carrying child and cocoa and papaya trees and coffee bushes / Two women harvesting Ylang-ylang and fruits.

Malaŵi   MWK

Kwacha = 100 tambala.

Currency import-export restrictions:
Local currency in/out: MK 3,000. (Effective 28 May 1997.)
Foreign currency in: free, must declare.
Out: up to the amount imported and declared.

Alternative currencies: GBP, USD.

A BRIEF MONETARY HISTORY
Jul 1964: Malaŵi pound = 1 Rhodesian pound
Feb 1971: kwacha = 0.50 pound

Issuer: "RESERVE BANK OF MALAŴI."

CURRENT NOTES

5 KWACHA   141 x 73mm **Cat.#24**
1990-94 Light red and green.
Pres. Banda / University of Malaŵi.

5 KWACHA   125 x 63mm Issued 22 April 1996 **Cat.#30**
1 June 1995 Orange red and olive green.
Pres. Muluzi and Lake Malaŵi / Zebras, "Malaŵi wildlife."

5 KWACHA   125 x 63mm Issued in mid-1997 **Cat.#36**
1 July 1997 Green.
John Chilembwe / Woman pounding maize.

10 KWACHA   147 x 76mm **Cat.#25**
1990-94 Gray green and brown.
Pres. Banda / Capital City-Lilongwe.

10 KWACHA   132 x 66mm Issued 22 April 1996 **Cat.#31**
1 June 1995 Green and brown.
Pres. Muluzi and Lake Malaŵi / "Capital city Lilongwe."

10 KWACHA   132 x 66mm **Cat.#37**
1 July 1997 Reddish brown and violet brown.
John Chilembwe / Three young girls reading under a baobab.

20 KWACHA   151 x 80mm **Cat.#26**
1990-93 Green and orange.
Pres. Banda / Kamuzu International Airport.
Those dated 1993 have a different airplane on the back.

20 KWACHA   138 x 70mm Issued 22 April 1996 **Cat.#33**
1 June 1995 Green and brown.
Pres. Muluzi and Lake Malaŵi / "Tea picking - Mulanje."

20 KWACHA   138 x 70mm **Cat.#38**
1 July 1997 Purple.
Julius Chilembwe / Two farmers picking tea in a plantation at the
foot of the Mulanje mountain.

50 KWACHA   157 x 80mm **Cat.#28**
1990-94 Purple and multicolor.
Pres. Banda / Independence Arch.

50 KWACHA   144 x 72mm Issued 22 April 1996 **Cat.#33**
1 June 1995 Purplish brown and green.
Pres. Muluzi and Lake Malaŵi / "Independence Arch."

50 KWACHA   144 x 72mm **Cat.#39**
1 July 1997 Green.
Julius Chilembwe / Independence Arch at Chichiri in Blantyre.

100 KWACHA   160 x 85mm **Cat.#29**
1993-94 Grayish violet, rose, green and multicolor / Violet, green and multicolor.

100 KWACHA   150 x 75mm Issued 22 April 1996 **Cat.#34**
1 June 1995 Green and brown.
Pres. Muluzi and Lake Malaŵi / "Maize silos."

100 KWACHA   150 x 75mm **Cat.#40**
1 July 1997 Red and purple brown.
Julius Chilembwe / Government offices at Capital Hill, Lilongwe.

200 KWACHA   156 x 78mm Issued 10 July 1995 **Cat.#35**
1 June 1995 Lilac brown, olive green, silver and multicolor.
Pres. Muluzi and Lake Malaŵi at sunrise / Elephants.

200 KWACHA   156 x 78mm **Cat.#41**
1 July 1997 Bluish green and black.
Julius Chilembwe / Reserve Bank of Malaŵi.

500 KWACHA   **Cat.#42**
It may be issued in the near future.

OUTMODED AND REDEEMABLE NOTES

All older notes are legal tender, but seldom seen in use.

Malaysia Malaisie   MYR

Ringgit = 100 sen.

Currency import-export regulations:
Local in/out: 1,000 ringgit.
Foreign: in free; out limited to the equivalent of 10,000 ringgit, more if declared on entry; except for Israeli and Yugoslavian, which require permission of the Controller of Foreign Exchange.
Permission is needed for the import or export of Malaysian notes by post and for the export of foreign notes by any other means.

Alternative currencies: any major.   Sep1998

A BRIEF MONETARY HISTORY
Jun. 1967: Malaysian ringgit established at par with Malayan dollar.

Issuer: "BANK NEGARA MALAYSIA."

CURRENT NOTES

2 RINGGIT   130 x 65mm   Issued in February 1996 **Cat.#39**
Purplish blue, red, ochre and multicolor.
Tuanku Abdul Rahman / K.L. tower and satellite.

5 RINGGIT   126 x 68mm **Cat.#20**
Green and multicolor.
Tuanku Abdul Rahman / Palace (Istana Negara).
Cat.#20: With horizontal serial numbers.
Cat.#28a: With vertical serial numbers.
Cat.#28c: Windowed security thread added.

5 RINGGIT   **Cat.#40**
A new style note is planned.

10 RINGGIT   132 x 71mm **Cat.#21**
Red and multicolor.
Tuanku Abdul Rahman / Railway station.
Without or with windowed security thread and ascending vertical serial numbers.

10 RINGGIT   140 x 65mm Issued in January 1998 **Cat.#41**
Red and multicolor.
Tuanku Abdul Rahman / Train, ship and airplane.

20 RINGGIT   138 x 74mm **Cat.#22**
Brown and multicolor.
Tuanku Abdul Rahman / Central Bank building.
Without or with windowed security thread and ascending vertical serial numbers.

50 RINGGIT   144 x 78mm **Cat.#23**
Blue and multicolor.
Tuanku Abdul Rahman / Building (Muzium Negara).
Without or with windowed security thread and ascending vertical serial numbers.

50 RINGGIT   152 x 76mm Issued 1 June 1998 **Cat.#47**
Blue, orange brown and yellow.
Tuanku Abdul Rahman and buildings in Kuala Lumpur / Stadium Utama Bukit Jalil and logo of the 98-XVI Commonwealth Games.
With two clear windows, one with a gold colored optically variable device.

50 RINGGIT   145 x 69mm Issued 20 July 1998 **Cat.#43**
Bluish green and multicolor.
Tuanku Abdul Rahman / Central oil drilling platform.

100 RINGGIT   150 x 83mm **Cat.#24**
Purple and multicolor.
Tuanku Abdul Rahman / National Mosque.
Without or with windowed security thread and ascending vertical serial numbers.

100 RINGGIT   150 x 69mm Issued 26 Oct 1998 **Cat.#44**
Purple, brown and multicolor.
Tuanku Abdul Rahman / Car production themes.

OUTMODED AND REDEEMABLE NOTES

All older notes of 1 to 100 ringgit issued by Bank Negara Malaysia are redeemable. All notes of 500 and 1,000 ringgit are worthless.

©MRI BANKERS' GUIDE TO FOREIGN CURRENCY
P.O.BOX 3174 HOUSTON TX 77253 USA

Maldives Malediven • Maldivas   **MVR**

Rufiyaa = 100 laari.

The import and export of local and foreign currencies are free.

Alternative currencies: ATS, AUD, BEF, CAD, CHF, DEM, DKK, FIM, FRF, GBP, HKD, INR, ITL, JPY, LKR, NLG, NOK, SGD, SAR, SEK, THB, **USD**.

A BRIEF MONETARY HISTORY
1960: Maldivian rupee created at par with Ceylonese Rupee.

Issuer: "MALDIVES MONETARY AUTHORITY"

CURRENT NOTES

5 RUFIYAA   150 x 70mm **Cat.#10**
   1983-90 Violet and multicolor.
   Coconuts and boat / Fishing.

5 RUFIYAA   150 x 70mm Issued 29 September 1998 **Cat.#16**
   1998 Violet, green and multicolor.
   Coconuts and boat / Fishing.

10 RUFIYAA   150 x 70mm **Cat.#11**
   1983 Brown violet and multicolor.
   Coconuts and boat / Life in the islands.

20 RUFIYAA   150 x 70mm **Cat.#12**
   1983-87 Indigo and multicolor.
   Coconuts and boat / Inner harbor, Male'.

50 RUFIYAA   150 x 70mm **Cat.#13**
   1983-87 Violet and multicolor.
   Coconuts and boat / Male' Market.

100 RUFIYAA   150 x 70mm **Cat.#14**
   1983-87 Green and multicolor.
   Coconuts and boat / Tomb of Abul Barakaath Yoosuf-al-Barubary-
   Medhuziyaaraiy.

100 RUFIYAA   150 x 70mm **Cat.#18**
   1995 Green, light brown and multicolor.
   Coconuts and boat / Tomb of Abul Barakaath Yoosuf-al-Barubary-
   Medhuziyaaraiy.

500 RUFIYAA   150 x 70mm **Cat.#17**
   1990 Red, green, blue and multicolor.
   Coconuts and boat / Grand Friday Mosque and Islamic Center.

500 RUFIYAA   150 x 70mm **Cat.#19**
   1996 Red, green, blue and multicolor.
   Coconuts and boat / Grand Friday Mosque and Islamic Center.
   With added security devices.

OUTMODED AND REDEEMABLE NOTES

2 RUFIYAA   150 x 70mm **Cat.#9**
   1983-90 Olive green and multicolor.
   Coconuts and boat / Beach of an inhabited island.   Ito

©MRI Bankers' Guide to Foreign Currency
P.O.Box 3174   Houston TX 77253   USA

Mali   XOF

It uses notes issued by "BANQUE CENTRALE DES ETATS DE L'AFRIQUE DE L'OUEST."

For description of notes and currency import-export restrictions see WEST AFRICAN STATES.

Alternative currencies: FRF, USD. Pre-1997 notes of FRF 100 are not accepted.

A BRIEF MONETARY HISTORY
1984: franc CFA West = 2 Mali francs

WARNING

Notes issued by the Central Bank of Mali are worthless.

Malta   Malte   MTL

Lira (liri) = 100 cent(s).

Currency import-export restrictions:
Local currency: in £M 50; out £M 25.
Foreign currency in: free, may declare. Out: free.
It is recommended to keep exchange receipts to facilitate reconversion.   Jul1998

Alternative currencies: any major.

Issuer: "BANK CENTRALI TA'MALTA."

CURRENT NOTES

2 LIRI   138 x 69mm **Cat.#41**
Burgundy red and multicolor.
Melita holding rudder / Two buildings. (Seats of Municipal institutions).

2 LIRI   138 x 69mm Issued in June 1994 **Cat.#45**
Burgundy red and multicolor.
Melita holding rudder / Two buildings. (Seats of Municipal institutions).
With additional security devices.

5 LIRI   145 x 69mm **Cat.#42**
Blue and multicolor.
Melita holding rudder / Torri ta' I-Istandard.

5 LIRI   145 x 69mm Issued in June 1994 **Cat.#46**
Blue and multicolor.
Melita holding rudder / Torri ta' I-Istandard.
With added security devices.

10 LIRI   159 x 73mm **Cat.#43**
Green and multicolor.
Melita holding rudder / Wounded of June 7, 1919 and Monument.

10 LIRI   152 x 73mm Issued in June 1994 **Cat.#47**
Green and multicolor.
Melita holding rudder / Wounded of June 7, 1919 and Monument.
With added security devices.

20 LIRA   179 x 76mm **Cat.#44**
Brown and multicolor.
Melita holding rudder / Dr Giorgio Borg Olivier and tablet commemorating Independence.

20 LIRA   159 x 76mm Issued in June 1994 **Cat.#48**
Brown and multicolor.
Melita holding rudder / Dr Giorgio Borg Olivier and tablet commemorating Independence.
With added security devices.

OUTMODED AND REDEEMABLE NOTES

1 LIRA　　　　　　　　137 x 69mm　**Cat.#34**
　Brown and multicolor.
　Watch tower "Gardjola" / New University.　　rruu20030430

2 LIRI　　　　　　　　138 x 67mm　**Cat.#37**
　Red and multicolor.
　Agatha Barbara / Crane and harbor.　　rruu20080615

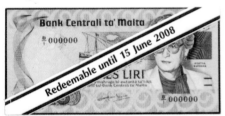

5 LIRI　　　　　　　　145 x 69mm　**Cat.#38**
　Blue and multicolor.
　Agatha Barbara / Mellieha Bay, lace maker and fisherman making
　fishing pots.　　rruu20080615

10 LIRI　　　　　　　152 x 80mm　**Cat.#36**
　Gray, pink and multicolor.
　Statue of "Justice" / Malta Drydocks.　　rruu19991215

10 LIRI　　　　　　　152 x 73mm　**Cat.#39**
　Green and multicolor.
　Agatha Barbara / Welder, ship and view of Grand Harbor.　　Ito

20 LIRA　　　　　　　159 x 76mm　**Cat.#40**
　Brown and multicolor.　　rruu20021130
　Agatha Barbara / Auberge de Castille and Workers monument.

Rep of the Marshall Islands　　USD

United States currency is used.
So-called "coins" are issued for collectors. Redemption is limited to
$10 per day, or a single coin if larger, is subject to a 10% fee, and
must be done in person.

Martinique　Martinika • Martinica　FRF

French currency is used now. Older notes issued by the Caisse
Centrale de la France d'Outre-Mer and Caisse Central de la France are
redeemable only in Fort de France. All have high numismatic
premium. Each 100 old francs equal one new franc.

Mauritania　Mauritanie • Mauretanien　MRO

Ouguiya

Currency import-export restrictions:
Local currency in/out: forbidden.
Foreign currency in: free, must declare.
Out: up to the amount imported and declared.

Alternative currencies: FRF, USD.

A BRIEF MONETARY HISTORY
June 1979: ouguiya = 5 CFA francs West

Issuer: "BANQUE CENTRALE DE MAURITANIA."

CURRENT NOTES

100 OUGUIYA　　　　　145 x 70mm　**Cat.#4**
　1974-　Violet and brown lilac.
　Text / Musical instruments, cow and tower.

©MRI BANKERS' GUIDE TO FOREIGN CURRENCY
P.O.Box 3174 HOUSTON TX 77253 USA

200 OUGUIYA   156 x 80mm **Cat.#5**
1974- Brown, green and blue.
Text / Bowl, canoe and palm tree.

500 OUGUIYA   161 x 86mm **Cat.#6**
1979- Green, brown and multicolor.
Text / Field workers and factory.

1,000 OUGUIYA   165 x 90mm **Cat.#7**
1974- Blue and multicolor.
Text / Bowl of fish, camel, hut and tower.

Mauritius   Mauricio • Maurice   **MUR**

Rupee(s) = 100 cent(s).

The import and export of local and foreign currencies are free.

Alternative currencies: any major.

Issuer: "BANK OF MAURITIUS."

CURRENT NOTES

10 RUPEES   132 x 64mm Issued 20 Dec 1985 **Cat.#35**
Green and multicolor.
Government House / Hesketh Bell Bridge.
After being declared out of circulation by end February 1999, the legal tender
status of this note has been restored.

25 RUPEES   135 x 67mm Issued in late 1998 **Cat.#42**
1998 Lilac brown, brown, green and multicolor.
Sir Moilin Jean Ah-Chuen / Fisherman and 1873 building.
To be replaced in 1999 to reflect a new order of languages in front.

25 RUPEES   **Cat.#49**
A new note to be issued in mid-1999 will replace Cat.#42.

50 RUPEES   155 x 67mm **Cat.#37**
Blue and multicolor.
Government House / Butterfly, deer and various plants.
After being declared out of circulation by end February 1999, the legal tender
status of this note has been restored.

50 RUPEES   140 x 68mm Issued in late 1988 **Cat.#43**
1998 Violet, blue, black and multicolor.
Joseph Maurice Paturau / Building.
To be replaced in 1999 to reflect a new order of languages in front.

50 RUPEES   **Cat.#50**
A new note to be issued in mid-1999 will replace Cat.#43.

100 RUPEES   160 x 70mm Issued 10 Nov 1986 **Cat.#38**
Government House / Colored earth at Chamarel, and Moka
mountains.
After being declared out of circulation by end February 1999, the legal tender
status of this note has been restored.

100 RUPEES   145 x 70mm Issued in late 1998 **Cat.#44**
1998 Green, yellow, black and multicolor.
Renganden Seeneevassen / Building.
To be replaced in 1999 to reflect a new order of languages in front.

100 RUPEES   **Cat.#51**
A new note to be issued in mid-1999 will replace Cat.#44.

200 RUPEES   165 x 73mm Issued 18 Sep 1985 **Cat.#39**
Turquoise and multicolor.
Sir Seewoosagur Ramgoolam / Le Reduit compound.
After being declared out of circulation by end February 1999, the legal tender status of this note has been restored.

200 RUPEES   150 x 72mm Issued in late 1998 **Cat.#45**
1998 Green, orange, lilac and multicolor.
Abdool Razack Mohamed / Market scene.
To be replaced in 1999 to reflect a new order of languages in front.

200 RUPEES   **Cat.#52**
A new note to be issued in mid-1999 will replace Cat.#45.

500 RUPEES   170 x 76mm Issued in Nov. 1988 **Cat.#40**
Brown, orange and multicolor.
Sir Anerood Jugnauth / Sugar cane harvest.
After being declared out of circulation by end February 1999, the legal tender status of this note has been restored.

500 RUPEES   155 x 75mm Issued in late 1998 **Cat.#46**
1998 Reddish brown, black, violet and multicolor.
Sookdeo Bissoondoyal / University of Mauritius.
To be replaced in 1999 to reflect a new order of languages in front.

500 RUPEES   **Cat.#53**
A new note to be issued in mid-1999 will replace Cat.#46.

1,000 RUPEES   175 x 78mm Issued 8 Sep 1990 **Cat.#41**
Blue and multicolor.
Sir Veerasamy Ringadoo / Port Louis Harbour
After being declared out of circulation by end February 1999, the legal tender status of this note has been restored.

1,000 RUPEES   160 x 76mm Issued in late 1998 **Cat.#47**
1998 Blue violet, black, orange, red and multicolor.
Sir Charles Gaëtan Ducal, QC / Group of women.
To be replaced in 1999 to reflect a new order of languages in front.

1,000 RUPEES   **Cat.#54**
A new note to be issued in mid-1999 will replace Cat.#46.

2,000 RUPEES   165 x 79mm Issued in late 1998 **Cat.#48**
1998 Rose, orange, black, yellow brown and multicolor.
Seewoosagur Ramgoolam / Oxcart.
To be replaced in 1999 to reflect a new order of languages in front.

2,000 RUPEES   **Cat.#55**
A new note to be issued in mid-1999 will replace Cat.#48.

OUTMODED AND REDEEMABLE NOTES

All notes with portrait of Elizabeth II and all previous notes of the Bank of Mauritius are redeemable.

México • Mexiko • Mexique　　**MXN**

Peso(s) = 100 centavo(s).

Currency import-export restrictions:
Local or foreign currency in: free, must declare to customs amounts over USD10,000 or equivalent in cash or checks.
Out: free.

Alternative currencies: any major.

A BRIEF MONETARY HISTORY
Jan. 1993: nuevo peso = 1,000 pesos
Jan. 1996: peso = nuevo peso

Issuer: "BANCO DE MÉXICO."

CURRENT NOTES

10 NUEVOS PESOS = **10 PESOS**
　　　　　　　130 x 66mm Issued in Sep 1994 **Cat.#99**
10 Dec 1992 Bluish green, orange brown and yellow.
Emiliano Zapata and ears of corn / Monument to Zapata in Cuautla, Morelos and sugar mill.

10 PESOS　　　　　130 x 66mm Issued in Jan 1996 **Cat.#105**
6 May 1994 Bluish green, orange brown and yellow.
Emiliano Zapata and ears of corn / Monument to Zapata in Cuautla, Morelos and sugar mill.

20 NUEVOS PESOS = **20 PESOS**
　　　　　　　130 x 66mm Issued in Sep. 1994 **Cat.#100**
10 Dec 1992 Violet blue and lilac.
Benito Juárez and eagle / "Hemiciclo a Juárez."

20 PESOS　　　　　130 x 66mm Issued in Jan 1996 **Cat.#106**
6 May 1994 Violet blue and lilac.
Benito Juárez and eagle / "Hemiciclo a Juárez."

50 NUEVOS PESOS = **50 PESOS**
　　　　　　　130 x 66mm Issued in Sep. 1994 **Cat.#101**
10 Dec 1992 Lilac red and violet.
José María Morelos and his flag and emblems / Fishermen and butterflies.

50 PESOS　　　　　130 x 66mm Issued in Jan. 1996 **Cat.#107**
6 May 1994 Lilac red and violet.
José María Morelos and his flag and emblems / Fishermen and butterflies.

100 NUEVOS PESOS = **100 PESOS**
　　　　　　　155 x 66mm Issued in Sep. 1994 **Cat.#102**
10 Dec 1992 Rose red and yellow.
Nezahualcoyotl and glyph / Xochipilli.

100 PESOS　　　　　155 x 66mm Issued in Jan. 1996 **Cat.#108**
6 May 1994 Rose red and yellow.
Nezahualcoyotl and glyph / Xochipilli.

200 NUEVOS PESOS = **200 PESOS**
　　　　　　　155 x 66mm Issued in Sep. 1994 **Cat.#103**
10 Dec 1992 Olive and brown.
Juana de Asbaje and books / "Templo de San Jerónimo."

200 PESOS　　　　　155 x 66mm Issued in Jan. 1996 **Cat.#109**
7 Feb 1995 Olive and brown.
Juana de Asbaje and books / "Templo de San Jerónimo."

©MRI BANKERS' GUIDE TO FOREIGN CURRENCY
P.O.Box 3174 HOUSTON TX 77253 USA

500 NUEVOS PESOS = 500 PESOS
155 x 66mm Issued in Sep. 1994 **Cat.#104**
10 Dec 1992 Rose brown and black.
Ignacio Zaragoza and Battle of Puebla / "Catedral de Puebla".

500 PESOS 155 x 66mm Issued in Jan. 1996 **Cat.#110**
7 Feb 1995 Rose brown and black.
Ignacio Zaragoza and Battle of Puebla / "Catedral de Puebla".

OUTMODED AND REDEEMABLE NOTES

Smaller notes not listed because of low value.

Caution!!!
This note
is worth only
1 peso

{1,000 PESOS} = 1 (NEW) PESO 155 x 66mm Cat.#52
Black and multicolor / Brown.
Cuauhtémoc / El Castillo, Chichen Itza.

Caution!!!
This note
is worth only
1 peso

{1,000 PESOS} = 1 (NEW) PESO 155 x 66mm Cat.#70
1978-85 Brown and multicolor.
Juana de Asbaje / Santo Domingo plaza.

Caution!!!
This note
is worth only
2 pesos

{2,000 PESOS} = 2 (NEW) PESOS 155 x 66mm Cat.#82
1983-92 Green, brown and multicolor.
Justo Sierra and Central Library of the National University /
Courtyard of the old University building.

Caution!!!
This note
is worth only
5 pesos

{5,000 PESOS} = 5 (NEW) PESOS 155 x 66mm Cat.#77
1980-83 Red and multicolor on blue paper.
"Niños héroes" and flag of the "Batallón activo de San Blas" /
Chapultepec castle.

Caution!!!
This note
is worth only
5 pesos

{5,000 PESOS} = 5 (NEW) PESOS 155 x 66mm Cat.#88
1985-92 Brown orange and multicolor.
"Niños héroes" and flag of the "Batallón activo de San Blas" /
Chapultepec castle.

Caution!!!
This note
is worth only
10 pesos

{10,000 PESOS} = 10 (NEW) PESOS 155 x 66mm Cat.#72
1943-78 Purple and multicolor.
Matías Romero / National Palace.

Caution!!!
This note
is worth only
10 pesos

{10,000 PESOS} = 10 (NEW) PESOS 155 x 66mm Cat.#78
1981-85 Blue, brown and multicolor on green paper.
Lázaro Cárdenas and oil industry / Findings of Templo Mayor:
Coyolxauhqui and sea shell.

Caution!!!
This note
is worth only
10 pesos

{10,000 PESOS} = 10 (NEW) PESOS 155 x 66mm Cat.#90
1987-92 Blue, green and brown.
Lázaro Cárdenas and oil industry / Findings of Templo Mayor:
Coyolxauhqui and sea shell.

{10 NUEVOS PESOS} = 10 PESOS 155 x 66mm Cat.#95
31 July 1992 Blue, green and brown.
Lázaro Cárdenas and oil industry / Findings of Templo Mayor:
Coyolxauhqui and sea shell.

Caution!!!
This note
is worth only
20 pesos

{20,000 PESOS} = 20 (NEW) PESOS   155 x 66mm Cat.#92
   1985 Blue and multicolor.
   Tulum and Andrés Quintana Roo / "Mural de Bonampak" and
   "Dintel de Yaxchilan."

Caution!!!
This note
is worth only
20 pesos

{20,000 PESOS} = 20 (NEW) PESOS   155 x 66mm Cat.#91
   1988-92 Blue and multicolor.
   Tulum and Andrés Quintana Roo / "Mural de Bonampak" and
   "Dintel de Yaxchilan."

{20 NUEVOS PESOS} = 20 PESOS   155 x 66mm Cat.#95
   31 July 1992 Blue and multicolor.
   Tulum and Andrés Quintana Roo / "Mural de Bonampak" and
   "Dintel de Yaxchilan."

Caution!!!
This note
is worth only
50 pesos

{50,000 PESOS} = 50 (NEW) PESOS   155 x 66mm Cat.#93
   1986-92 Violet and multicolor.
   Cuauhtémoc / Mural "Fusion of two cultures" by Jorge González
   Camarena.

{50 NUEVOS PESOS} = 50 PESOS   155 x 66mm Cat.#97
   31 July 1992 Violet and multicolor.
   Cuauhtémoc / Mural "Fusion of two cultures" by Jorge González
   Camarena.

Caution!!!
This note
is worth only
100 pesos

{100,000 PESOS} = 100 (NEW) PESOS   155 x 66mm Cat.#94
   1988-92 Black and maroon.
   Plutarco Elías Calles and Banco de México / Deer, cactus, lake and
   mountain.

100 NUEVOS PESOS = 100 PESOS   155 x 66mm Cat.#98
   31 July 1992 Black and maroon.
   Plutarco Elías Calles and Banco de México / Deer, cactus, lake and
   mountain.

Fed. States of Micronesia   USD

United States currency is used.

Moldova   Moldau • Moldavie   MDL

Leu(i) = 100 Ban(i).

Currency import-export restrictions:
Local currency in/out: forbidden, except that Rumanians are allowed
to bring in or out 2,500 Moldovan lei.
Out: Residents 500 lei, or 2,500 lei if leaving to Romania.
Foreign currency in: free, must declare.
Foreign currency out: limited to the amount imported and
declared. Amounts over USD 50,000 must be transferred by bank
transfer.   Jul1998
All foreign exchange transactions must be certified.

Alternative currencies: DEM, USD.

A BRIEF MONETARY HISTORY
1992: (ruble) coupon = Soviet ruble
1993: lei (coupon) = 1,000 (ruble) coupons
29 November 1993: lei = lei coupon.

Issuer: "BANCA NAȚIONALA A MOLDOVEI."

CURRENT NOTES

1 LEU   120 x 61mm Cat.#8
   1994- Lilac brown on pale yellow green.
   King Ștefan cel Mare / "Mînăstirea Căpriana."

5 LEI   120 x 61mm Cat.#9
   1994- Bluish green and violet / Bluish green.
   King Ștefan cel Mare / "Biserica sf. Dumitru din Orhei."

©MRI Bankers' Guide to Foreign Currency
P.O.Box 3174 Houston TX 77253 USA

10 LEI   120 x 61mm **Cat.#10**
1994- Reddish brown on pale violet and yellow underprint / Reddish brown.
King Ştefan cel Mare / "Mînăstirea Hîrjăuca."

20 LEI   120 x 61mm **Cat.#13**
1992- Green and yellow.
King Ştefan cel Mare / "Cetatea Soroca."

50 LEI   120 x 61mm **Cat.#14**
1992- Red and violet.
King Ştefan cel Mare / "Mînăstire Hîrboveţ."

100 LEI   121 x 61mm Issued 15 Sep 1995 **Cat.#15**
1992- Brown, orange red, yellow and lilac / Brown and yellow brown.
King Ştefan cel Mare / "Cetatea Thighina."

200 LEI   133 x 66mm Issued 15 Sep 1995 **Cat.#16**
1992 Violet brown, orange, pink and brownish yellow / Violet brown and rose.
King Ştefan cel Mare / "Primăria Municipiului Chişinău."

Monaco   **FRF**

French coins and currency, as well as Monegasque coins are used.

French currency import-export regulations apply.

Mongolia   **MNT**
Mongol Uls • Mongolien • Mongolie

Tugruk = 100 mongo.
Minor unit coins are not used.

Currency import-export restrictions:
Local currency in/out: forbidden.
Foreign currency in: free, must declare.
Out: up to the amount imported and declared.
Reconversion permitted with proof of prior exchange.

Alternative currencies: USD.

Notes issued now by "МонголБанк." (Mongol Bank).

CURRENT NOTES

Smaller notes are not listed because of low value.

100 TUGRUK   140 x 68mm **Cat.#57**
ND, 1994 Violet brown and multicolor.
D. Sukhbataar / Horses.

500 TUGRUK   145 x 70mm Issued 6 June 1993 **Cat.#58**
Olive green and olive brown.
Genghis Khan / Yurt (tent) being moved by oxen.
Without and with windowed security thread.

1,000 TUGRUK   150 x 72mm **Cat.#59**
Green, brown and multicolor.
Genghis Khan / Yurt (tent) being moved by oxen.
Without and with windowed security thread.

5,000 TUGRUK   150 x 72mm **Cat.#60**
1994 Lilac brown, red, violet and multicolor.
Genghis Khan / Building with fountain.

10,000 TUGRUK   150 x 72mm   Issued in early 1996   **Cat.#61**
1995 Green and orange.
Genghis Khan / Scene with large old building, large tree and groups of people.

OUTMODED AND REDEEMABLE NOTES

Old style notes issued since 1966 are redeemable.

Montenegro   Czerna Gora   YUM

Part of former Yugoslavia, along with Serbia, it contemplates creating its own national currency to free itself from the volatility of the Yugoslavian currency caused by Serbia.

Montserrat   XCD

East Caribbean currency is used.

Currency import-export restrictions:
The import of all currencies is free. Amounts above XCD 250,000 or equivalent require permission from the Ministry of Finance.   Jul1998
Export up to the amount declared on entry.

United States dollars are widely accepted. Alternative currencies: CAD, GBP, USD.

Morocco
Maghrib • Marokko • Marruecos • Maroc   **MAD**

Dirham(s) = 100 centime(s).

Currency import-export restrictions:
Local currency in/out: forbidden.
Foreign currency in/out: free.
Exchange receipts should be kept to facilitate reconversion.   Jul1998

Alternative currencies: any major.

A BRIEF MONETARY HISTORY
Oct. 1959: dirham = 100 francs

Issuer: "BANK AL-MAGHRIB."

CURRENT NOTES

10 DIRHAMS   142 x 70mm   **Cat.#60**
1987 Reddish brown, red and multicolor.
Hassan II and section of Qaraouiyne Mosque / Lute and column.
These notes are gradually being replaced by coins.

10 DIRHAMS   142 x 70mm   **Cat.#63**
1987 Violet blue, violet brown and multicolor.
Hassan II and section of Qaraouiyne Mosque / Lute and column.
These notes are gradually being replaced by coins.

20 DIRHAMS   130 x 68mm   Issued ca. August 1996   **Cat.#67**
1996 Reddish brown, olive brown and blue.
Hassan II and mosque Hassan II in Casablanca / Wall fountain in the mosque.

50 DIRHAMS   148 x 70mm   **Cat.#61**
1987 Green and multicolor.
Hassan II and fortified village / Cavalry charge scene.

©MRI BANKERS' GUIDE TO FOREIGN CURRENCY
P.O.Box 3174 HOUSTON TX 77253 USA

50 DIRHAMS   148 x 70mm *Cat.#64*
1987 Green and multicolor.
Hassan II and fortified village / Cavalry charge scene.

100 DIRHAMS   153 x 75mm *Cat.#62*
1987 Brown and multicolor.
Hassan II and minaret / Demonstration.

100 DIRHAMS   153 x 75mm *Cat.#65*
1987 Brown and multicolor.
Hassan II and minaret / Demonstration.

200 DIRHAMS   158 x 75mm *Cat.#66*
1987 Violet blue, blue and multicolor.
Hassan II and mausoleum of Muhammad V / Sailboat, shell and coral.

OUTMODED AND REDEEMABLE NOTES

5 DIRHAMS   140 x 75mm *Cat.#53*
ND, 1965-69 Multicolor.
Muhammad V and view of Fes / Harvest scene.   rruu20021231

5 DIRHAMS   140 x 70mm *Cat.#56*
1970 Purple.
Hassan II and Casbah / Sugar factory.   rruu20021231

10 DIRHAMS   150 x 80mm *Cat.#54*
ND, 1965-69 Multicolor.
Muhammad V and Hassan Tower / Orange harvest.   rruu20021231

10 DIRHAMS   145 x 72mm *Cat.#57*
1970-85 Brown lilac.
Hassan II and Oudaïas Garden / Orange packing station.rruu20021231

50 DIRHAMS   160 x 85mm *Cat.#55*
1965-69 Multicolor.
Hassan II / Phosphate mining.   rruu2002123

50 DIRHAMS   150 x 75mm *Cat.#58*
1970-85 Green.
Hassan II and city of Chaouen / Dam.   rruu2002123

100 DIRHAMS   155 x 77mm *Cat.#59*
1970-85 Brown and green.   rruu2002123
Hassan II and Bank al-Maghrib building / Chemical complex at Safi.

Mozambique
Moçambique • Mosambik   **MZM**

Metical (meticais) = 100 centavo(s).
Minor unit coins are not used.

Currency import-export restrictions:
Local currency in/out: MZM 500,000. Must declare export.
Foreign currency in: free, must declare if amount exceeds USD5,000
or equivalent.   Jul1998
Out: up to the amount imported and declared.

Alternative currencies: GBP, PTE, USD, ZAR.

A BRIEF MONETARY HISTORY
16 June 1980 1 Metical = 1 Escudo

Issuer: "BANCO DE MOÇAMBIQUE."

CURRENT NOTES

Smaller notes not listed because of low value.

5,000 METICAIS   142 x 68mm **Cat.#133**
   1988-89 Lilac and brown.
   Sculpture and paintings / Musicians and dancers.
   It is being replaced by a coin.

5,000 METICAIS   143 x 69mm **Cat.#136**
   16 June 1991 Purple, red and violet brown.
   Samora Moisés Machel and monument to the 3rd Congress of
   Frelimo / Workmen in foundry.
   It is being replaced by a coin.

10,000 METICAIS   150 x 69mm **Cat.#137**
   16 June 1991 Green, orange and brown.
   Joaquim Alberto Chissano and power line / Plowing scene.

50,000 METICAIS   157 x 69mm Issued 25 May 1994 **Cat.#138**
   16 June 1993 Reddish brown and multicolor.
   Banco de Moçambique building / Cabora Bassa hydroelectric dam.

100,000 METICAIS   165 x 69mm Issued 1 March 1995 **Cat.#139**
   16 June 1993 Orange and multicolor.
   Banco de Moçambique building/Cabora Bassa hydroelectric dam.

Myanmar
Birmanien • Burma • Birmania • Birmanie   **MMK**

Kyat(s) = 100 pya(s).

Currency import-export restrictions:
Local currency in/out: forbidden.
Foreign currency in: free, must declare amounts over USD2,000 or
equivalent.
Visitors must exchange US$300 or its equivalent into "Foreign
Exchange Certificates" which can be used for hotel, restaurant and
travel expenses, but are not reconvertible. Unused FEC's above the
300 unit limit may be reconverted upon departure.
Visitors are allowed to convert hard currency into FEC, and then
those into kyat at the free market rate.
Visitors staying 6 months or longer must exchange all foreign
currency into kyats, or open a foreign currency account.
Out: up to the amount imported and declared.
Reconversion requires supporting receipts.

Alternative currencies: THB, USD.

A BRIEF MONETARY HISTORY
1 July 1952: kyat introduced at par with Burmese rupee.

Notes issued now by "CENTRAL BANK OF MYANMAR."

CURRENT NOTES

Smaller notes not listed because of low value.

20 KYATS C.B.M.   146 x 70mm Issued 27 Mar 1994 **Cat.#72**
   Green, brown and multicolor.
   King Lion / Water fountain with elephants, and esplanade.

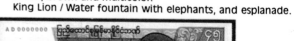

45 KYATS U.B.B.   158 x 76mm Issued 22 Sep 1987 **Cat.#64**
   Blue gray and multicolor.
   Soldier (Po Hla Gyi) / Two workers with oil field.

50 KYATS C.B.M.　　146 x 70mm Issued 27 Mar 1994 **Cat.#73**
Yellowish brown, reddish brown and green.
King Lion / Coppersmith.

90 KYATS U.B.B.　　167 x 80mm Issued 22 Sep 1987 **Cat.#66**
Brown, green and multicolor.
Portrait (Seya San) / Farming.

100 KYATS C.B.M.　　146 x 70mm Issued 27 Mar 1994 **Cat.#74**
Purplish blue, lilac brown, green and multicolor.
King Lion / Masons at work.

200 KYATS C.B.M.　　167 x 80mm **Cat.#75**
Green blue and multicolor.
King Lion / Elephant.

500 KYATS C.B.M.　　167 x 80mm Issued 27 Mar 1994 **Cat.#76**
Purplish brown and multicolor.
King Lion / Statue makers.

1,000 KYATS C.B.M.　　177 x 80mm Issued 25 Nov 1998 **Cat.#79**
Purplish brown, green and multicolor.
King lion / Modern building.

Foreign Exchange Certificates

Visitors must exchange US$300 into these so certificates, which can be used to pay hotel bills or exchanged in the parallel market.

1 DOLLAR　　152 x 65mm **Cat.#FX1**
Green and blue.
Statue / Text.

5 DOLLARS　　152 x 65mm **Cat.#FX2**
Orange.
Statue / Text.

10 DOLLARS　　152 x 65mm **Cat.#FX3**
Brown, and blue green.
Statue / Text.

20 DOLLARS　　152 x 65mm **Cat.#FX4**
Red, brown and multicolor.
Statue / Text.

Namibia   Namibie   NAD

Dollar = 100 cent(s).
Parity: 1 dollar = 1 South African rand.

Currency import/export restrictions:
Local currency in/out: NAD 2,000.
Foreign currency in: unlimited.
Out: Limited to unspent remainder of amount imported.   Jul1998

South African rands are current. Alternative currencies: DEM, GBP, USD.

Issuer: "BANK OF NAMIBIA."

CURRENT NOTES

10 NAMIBIA DOLLARS   129 x 70mm Issued 14 Sep 1993 **Cat.#1**
Black blue and multicolor.
Kaptein Hendrik Witbooi with Parliament in background / Namibian National flag and springbok.

20 NAMIBIA DOLLARS   133 x 70mm Issued 2 Dec 1996 **Cat.#8**
Orange brown and multicolor.
Kaptein Hendrik Witbooi with Parliament in background / Red hartebeest.

50 NAMIBIA DOLLARS   140 x 70mm Issued 14 Sep 1993 **Cat.#2**
Green and multicolor.
Kaptein Hendrik Witbooi with Parliament in background / Namibian National flag and kudu.

50 NAMIBIA DOLLARS   Issued in May 1999 **Cat.#10**
An enhanced version was issued. Details not yet available.

100 NAMIBIA DOLLARS   146 x 70mm Issued 14 Sep 1993 **Cat.#3**
Red and multicolor.
Kaptein Hendrik Witbooi with Parliament in background / Namibian National flag and oryx.

100 NAMIBIA DOLLARS   **Cat.#11**
An enhanced version will be issued soon.

200 NAMIBIA DOLLARS   152 x 70mm Issued 2 Dec 1996 **Cat.#9**
Brown, violet and multicolor.
Kaptein Hendrik Witbooi with Parliament in background / Roan antelope.

Nauru   AUD

Australian currency is used.

The import and export of local and foreign currencies are free.

Nepal   NPR

Rupee(s) = 100 paisa.

Currency import-export restrictions:
Local and Indian currency in: free only to Indians or Nepalese nationals.
Local and Indian currency out: free only to Indians traveling to India.
Foreign currency in: free, except for Indian rupees. Must declare if amount exceeds equivalent to US$ 2,000.
Out: up to the amount imported and declared.
Tourists may only exchange their foreign money with authorized dealers, and must keep the "Foreign Exchange Encashment Receipts" until they leave. Visitors are required to exchange a minimum of US$20 per day of stay.
Up to 15% of amount exchanged may be reconverted at departure.

Alternative currencies: GBP, HKD, SGD, USD.

Issuer: "NEPAL RASTRA BANK" (Central Bank of Nepal).

CURRENT NOTES

Smaller notes not listed because of low value.

10 RUPEES   133 x 70mm **Cat.#31**
Brown, orange lilac and multicolor.
King Birendra Bir Bikram Shah with coronation crown, and idol / Three black bucks.

©MRI BANKERS' GUIDE TO FOREIGN CURRENCY
P.O.Box 3174 HOUSTON TX 77253 USA

20 RUPEES   138 x 70mm **Cat.#32**
  Orange and multicolor.
  King Birendra Bir Bikram Shah with coronation crown, and
  temple / Stag.
  Without (Cat.#32), and with windowed security thread (Cat.#32b).

25 RUPEES   140 x 70mm Issued in 1997 **Cat.#41**
  Olive brown and light green / Olive brown and red.
  King Birendra Bir Bikram Shah / Cow.

50 RUPEES   142 x 70mm **Cat.#33**
  Blue and multicolor.
  King Birendra Bir Bikram Shah with coronation crown, and
  palace / Himalayan Thar.
  Without (Cat.#33), and with windowed security thread (Cat.#33c).

100 RUPEES   145 x 70mm **Cat.#34**
  Green, purple and brown / Green.
  King Birendra Bir Bikram Shah with coronation crown, and
  temple / Rhinoceros.
  Without (Cat.#34), and with windowed security thread (Cat.#34c).

250 RUPEES   172 x 70mm Issued in 1997 **Cat.#42**
  Green / Green and reddish brown.
  King Birendra Bir Bikram Shah / Cow.
  "Commemorative Issue on the Special Occasion of Silver Jubilee of His Majesty's
  Accession."

500 RUPEES   158 x 70mm **Cat.#35**
  Brown, blue violet and multicolor / Brown and gold.
  King Birendra Bir Bikram Shah with coronation crown / Two
  tigers.
  Without (Cat.#35), and with windowed security thread (Cat.#35b).

1,000 RUPEES   172 x 70mm **Cat.#36**
  Blue, brown and multicolor.
  King Birendra Bir Bikram Shah with coronation crown and
  temple /Elephant.
  Without (Cat.#36), and with windowed security thread (Cat.#36b).

OUTMODED AND REDEEMABLE NOTES

*All older notes of all denominations are legal tender, but seldom
found in circulation.*

The Netherlands   Nederland •
Niederlande • Paises Bajos • Pays-Bas   **NLG**

Euro = 2.20371 gulden   Gulden = 100 cent.

The import and export of all currencies is free.   Jul1998

Alternative currencies: any major.

A BRIEF MONETARY HISTORY:
1 Jan 1999: Euro adopted at 2.20371 gulden.

Issuer: "DE NEDERLANDSCHE BANK", after 2002 "EUROPEAN CENTRAL BANK."

CURRENT NOTES

10 GULDEN   136 x 76mm Issued 4 Jan 1971 **Cat.#91**
25 April 1968 Blue and violet.
Frans Hals / Geometrical design.

10 GULDEN   136 x 76mm Issued 1 Sep 1997 **Cat.#99**
1 July 1997 Violet blue, red, yellow and multicolor.
Geometric designs, with bird (Ijsvogel) in watermark / Geometric designs.

25 GULDEN   141 x 76mm Issued 27 Mar 1990 **Cat.#100**
3 April 1989 Red and multicolor.
Big "25" and geometric designs / Geometric designs.

50 GULDEN   148 x 76mm Issued 7 Sep 1982 **Cat.#96**
4 Jan 1982 Yellow, orange and multicolor.
Sunflower and bee / Map and flowers.

100 GULDEN   154 x 76mm Issued 16 March 1981 **Cat.#97**
28 July 1977 Brown and multicolor.
Bird (Watersnip) / Bird head.

100 GULDEN   154 x 76mm Issued 7 Sep 1993 **Cat.#102**
9 Jan 1992 Brown, gold, metallic gray and orange brown.
"100" and geometrical designs / Geometrical designs.

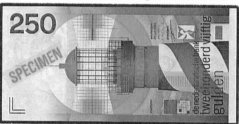

250 GULDEN   160 x 76mm Issued 7 Jan 1986 **Cat.#98**
25 July 1985 Purple and multicolor.
Lighthouse / Lighthouse and map.

1,000 GULDEN   160 x 76mm Issued 15 Jan 1973 **Cat.#94**
30 March 1972 Green.
Baruch d'Espinoza and Star of David / Geometrical design.

1,000 GULDEN   166 x 76mm Issued 2 April 1996 **Cat.#104**
2 June 1994 Green and gray.
Value and geometrical designs / Geometrical designs.

OUTMODED AND REDEEMABLE NOTES

5 GULDEN   136 x 76mm Issued 19 Dec 1966 Cat.#90
26 Apr 1966 Grayish green.
Vondel / Modern building.   rruu20250430

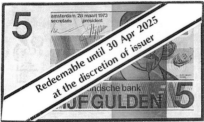

5 GULDEN   136 x 76mm Issued 23 Aug 1973 Cat.#95
28 Mar 1973 Green.
Joost van der Vondel / Geometric design.   rruu20250430

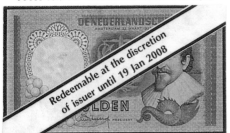

10 GULDEN   147 x 82mm Issued 27 Aug 1954 Cat.#85
23 March 1953 Blue, brown and green.
Hugo de Groot / Scales.   rruu20080119

25 GULDEN   155 x 86mm Issued 14 Feb 1956 Cat.#87
10 April 1955 Red, orange and brown.
Christiaan Huygens and planets / Geometrical design. rruu20080119

25 GULDEN   148 x 76mm Issued 15 Dec 1972 Cat.#92
10 Feb 1971 Red.
Jan Pietersz. Sweelinck / Geometrical designs. rruu20250430

100 GULDEN   168 x 98mm Issued 27 Aug 1954 Cat.#88
2 Feb 1953 Brown.
Erasmus / Geometrical design.   rruu20080119

100 GULDEN   154 x 76mm Issued 15 Dec 1972 Cat.#93
14 May 1970 Brown.
M. Adriaanszoon de Ruyter / Compass.   rruu20160723

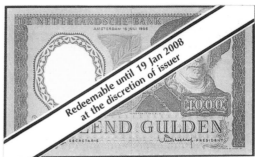

1,000 GULDEN   170 x 98mm Issued 16 July 1958 Cat.#89
15 July 1956 Brown and green.
Rembrandt van Rijn / Hand with paintbrush.   rruu20080119

Netherlands Antilles
Nederlandse Antillen • Niederlandische Antillen
• Antillas Neerlandesas • Antilles Néerlandaises **ANG**

Gulden = 100 cent.

Currency import-export restrictions:
Local currency in/out: NAf 200.
Foreign currency in/out: free.

Alternative currencies: any major.

Issuer: "BANK VAN DE NEDERLANDSE ANTILLEN"

CURRENT NOTES

5 GULDEN   147 x 66mm **Cat.#22**
1986-94 Blue and multicolor.
Bird (Troepiaal) / Bank seal.

©MRI BANKERS' GUIDE TO FOREIGN CURRENCY
P.O.Box 3174 HOUSTON TX 77253 USA

10 GULDEN 147 x 66mm **Cat.#23**
1986-94 Green and multicolor.
Bird (Kolibrie) / Bank seal.

10 GULDEN 147 x 66mm **Cat.#28**
1 Jan 1998 Green and multicolor.
Bird (Kolibrie) / Bank seal.
Improved version of the 1986 type, with gold foil seal and pearl essence printing.

25 GULDEN 147 x 66mm **Cat.#24**
1986-94 Red and multicolor.
Bird (Flamingo) / Bank seal.

25 GULDEN 147 x 66mm **Cat.#29**
1 Jan 1998 Red and multicolor.
Bird (Flamingo) / Bank seal.
Improved version of the 1986 type, with gold foil seal and pearl essence printing.

50 GULDEN 147 x 66mm **Cat.#25**
1986-94 Brown, orange and multicolor.
Bird (Andes mus) / Bank seal.

50 GULDEN 147 x 66mm **Cat.#30**
1 Jan 1998 Brown, orange and multicolor.
Bird (Andes mus) / Bank seal.
Improved version of the 1986 type, with gold foil seal and pearl essence printing. Not yet in circulation, except for a small amount released for testing purposes.

100 GULDEN 147 x 66mm **Cat.#26**
1986-94 Brown and multicolor.
Bird (Suikerdiefje) / Bank seal.

100 GULDEN 147 x 66mm **Cat.#31**
1 Jan 1998 Brown and multicolor.
Bird (Suikerdiefje) / Bank seal.
Improved version of the 1986 type, with gold foil seal and pearl essence printing.

250 GULDEN 147 x 66mm **Cat.#27**
1986-90 Violet and multicolor.
Bird (Caraibische spotlijster) / Bank seal.

OUTMODED AND REDEEMABLE NOTES

"Muntbiljeten" are redeemed by the Government. The following banknotes issued by the "Curaçaosche Bank" and the "Bank van de Nederlandse Antillen" may be redeemed by the Bank van de Nederlandse Antillen until the dates indicated. Older notes may be redeemable at their discretion.

| 1 GULDEN 1970 | Muntbiljet Cat.#15 | Redeemable without time limit |
| 2½ GULDEN 1970 | Muntbiljet Cat.#16 | Redeemable without time limit |

5 GULDEN 1962	31 Dec 2013	Cat.#1
5 GULDEN 1967-84	1 Jan 2020	Cat.#8
10 GULDEN 1962	31 Dec 2013	Cat.#2
10 GULDEN 1967-84	1 Jan 2020	Cat.#9
25 GULDEN 1962	31 Dec 2013	Cat.#3
25 GULDEN 1967-79	1 Jan 2020	Cat.#10
50 GULDEN 1962	31 Dec 2013	Cat.#4
50 GULDEN 1967-80	1 Jan 2020	Cat.#11
100 GULDEN 1962	31 Dec 2013	Cat.#5
100 GULDEN 1967-81	1 Jan 2020	Cat.#12
250 GULDEN 1962	31 Dec 2013	Cat.#6
250 GULDEN 1967	1 Jan 2020	Cat.#13
500 GULDEN 1962	31 Dec 2013	Cat.#7

New Caledonia
Nouvelle
Calédonie • Neukaledonien • Nueva Caledonia **XPF**

See C.F.P. francs.

New Zealand
Neuseeland • Nueva Zelanda • Nouvelle-Zélande NZD

Dollar(s) = 100 cent(s.)

The import and export of all currencies is free. Amounts over NZD10,000 must be declared.

A BRIEF MONETARY HISTORY
July 1967: dollar = 0.50 New Zealand pound.

Alternative currencies: any major.

Issuer: "RESERVE BANK OF NEW ZEALAND."

New Zealand currency is used in the Cook Islands, Niue, Pitcairn Island, Ross Dependency and Tokelau.

CURRENT NOTES

5 DOLLARS   135 x 66 mm **Cat.#177**
Orange brown and multicolor / Brown, reddish brown, grayish green and multicolor.
Sir Edmund Hillary, tractor and Mt Cook ' Yellow eyed penguin "Hoiho" and flora.

5 DOLLARS   **Cat.#185**
The release of a new polymer note is planned for October 1999.

10 DOLLARS   140 x 68mm Issued 10 May 1993 **Cat.#178**
Blue, pink and multicolor / Green, gray, blue and multicolor.
Kate Sheppard and camellias / Rives scene and blue ducks.

10 DOLLARS   140 x 68mm **Cat.#182**
Same, back changed to blue, green, gray and multicolor.

10 DOLLARS   140 x 68mm Due in October 1999 **Cat.#186**
Blue, pink and multicolor / Green, gray, blue and multicolor.
Kate Sheppard and camellias / River scene and blue ducks.
Printed in polymer, with two "windows."

10 DOLLARS   **Cat.#190**
A new polymer note will be issued later in 1999 to commemorate the millennium.

20 DOLLARS   145 x 70mm Issued 1 Sep 1992 **Cat.#179**
Green, yellow brown and multicolor.
Elizabeth II and "The Beehive" (Government building) / New Zealand falcon "Karearea" and mountain scene.

20 DOLLARS   145 x 70mm **Cat.#183**
Same, back changed to green and brown.
Counterfeits exist. Known serial numbers are EJ151396 and EU653443. Some notes were overprinted to commemorate the 70th birthday of Elizabeth II.

20 DOLLARS   145 x 70mm Issued 3 May 1999 **Cat.#187**
Green, brown, yellow and multicolor.
Elizabeth II and "The Beehive" (Government building) / New Zealand falcon "Karearea" and mountain scene.
Printed on polymer note with two "windows."

50 DOLLARS   150 x 72mm **Cat.#180**
Violet brown, orange, olive brown and multicolor / Violet, green, blue and multicolor.
Sir Apirana Ngata and meeting house / Kokako bird and forest.

50 DOLLARS   **Cat.#188**
A new polymer note will be issued in early 2000.

100 DOLLARS   155 x 74mm **Cat.#181**
Brownish red and multicolor / Brown, yellow, lilac red and multicolor.
Lord Rutheford of Nelson and Nobel Prize medal / Mohua bird and forest scene.
Counterfeits exist. Known serial numbers are AG520163 and AH321908.

100 DOLLARS   155 x 74mm Due 26 July 1999 **Cat.#189**
Brownish red and multicolor / Brown, yellow, lilac red and multicolor.
Lord Rutheford of Nelson and Nobel Prize medal / Mohua bird and forest scene.
Printed in polymer, with two "windows."

OUTMODED AND REDEEMABLE NOTES

All older notes of the Reserve Bank are redeemable. One pound is worth two dollars and 10 shillings equals 1 dollar.

Nicaragua   NIO

Córdoba(s) = 100 centavo(s.)

Hotel and international telephone charges must be paid with U.S. dollars.

The import and export of all currencies is free.

A BRIEF MONETARY HISTORY

15 Feb 1988: new córdoba (chanchero) = 1,000 córdobas
1990: córdoba oro established at par with U.S. dollar
4 Mar 1991: córdoba chanchero fixed at 5,000,000 per córdoba oro
1 May 1991: notes in córdobas chancheros are demonetized
1992: name changed from córdoba oro to córdoba.
Issuer: "BANCO CENTRAL DE NICARAGUA"

CURRENT NOTES

Smaller notes not listed because of low value.

1 CÓRDOBA ORO = 1 CÓRDOBA   156 x 67mm **Cat.#173**
1990 Violet blue and multicolor / Green and multicolor.
Francisco Hernández de Córdoba and cornfield / Arms.

1 CÓRDOBA   156 x 67mm **Cat.#179**
1995 Violet blue and multicolor / Green and multicolor.
Francisco Hernández de Córdoba and cornfield / Arms.

5 CÓRDOBAS   156 x 67mm **Cat.#174**
Lilac, olive green and multicolor / Green.
Indian chief Diriangén and sorghum plants / Rafaela Herrera firing cannonball at British warship.

5 CÓRDOBAS   156 x 67mm **Cat.#180**
1995 Lilac, olive green and multicolor / Green.
Indian chief Diriangén and sorghum plants / Rafaela Herrera firing cannonball at British warship.

10 CÓRDOBAS ORO = 10 CÓRDOBAS   156 x 67mm **Cat.#175**
1990 Green, violet blue and multicolor / Green and multicolor.
Miguel de Larreynaga and rice paddy / Arms.

10 CÓRDOBAS   156 x 67mm Issued 19 Aug 1996 **Cat.#181**
1996 Green and multicolor.
Miguel de Larreynaga / Arms.

20 CÓRDOBAS   156 x 67mm **Cat.#176**
Red, brown and multicolor / Green.
Augusto C. Sandino and coffee plant / Emmanuel Mongalo and fire in the Mesón de Rivas (1854).

20 CÓRDOBAS   156 x 67mm **Cat.#182**
1995 Red, brown and multicolor / Green.
Augusto C. Sandino and coffee plant / Emmanuel Mongalo and fire in the Mesón de Rivas (1854).

20 CÓRDOBAS   156 x 67mm Issued in mid-1998 **Cat.#187**
1997 Orange brown and light green / Orange brown and multicolor.
José Santos Zelaya / Arms.

50 CÓRDOBAS   156 x 67mm **Cat.#177**
Violet, lilac and multicolor / Green.
Dr Pedro J. Chamorro and plants / Toppling of Somoza's statue, and scene at election polls.

50 CÓRDOBAS   156 x 67mm **Cat.#183**
1995 Violet blue, yellow brown and brown / Black, dark blue, blue, green and multicolor.
Dr Pedro Joaquín Chamorro C. and plants / Value and arms.

100 CÓRDOBAS ORO ≒ **100 CÓRDOBAS**   156 x 67mm **Cat.#178**
1990-92 Blue, red and multicolor / Green and multicolor.
Ruben Darío and cotton field / Arms.

100 CÓRDOBAS ORO   156 x 67mm **Cat.#188**
1997 Blue, red and multicolor / Green and multicolor.
Ruben Darío / Arms.
Series A (1990) notes have 3 signatures. Series B (1992) have two signatures.

500 CÓRDOBAS   **Cat.#185**
A note of this value is held in reserve.

1,000 CÓRDOBAS   **Cat.#186**
A note of this value is held in reserve.

Niger   XOF

It uses notes issued by the "BANQUE CENTRALE DES ETATS DE L'AFRIQUE CENTRALE."

For description of notes and currency import-export restrictions see WEST AFRICAN STATES.

Alternative currencies: FRF, USD.

Nigeria   NGN

Naira = 100 kobo.

Currency import-export restrictions:
Local currency in/out: NGN 100.
Foreign currency in: free, must declare if amount exceeds US$ 10,000.
Out: up to the amount imported and declared.

Hotel bills must be settled with foreign currency, or exchange receipts must be produced.

Alternative currencies: GBP, USD.

A BRIEF MONETARY HISTORY
July 1959: Nigerian pound established at par with West African pound.
Jan 1973: naira = 0.50 Nigerian pound

Issuer: "CENTRAL BANK OF NIGERIA."

CURRENT NOTES

5 NAIRA   151 x 78mm Issued 23 April 1984 **Cat.#24**
Purple and brown violet.
Alhaji Sir Abubaker Tafawa Balewa / Dancers.
CAUTION: GREEN NOTES ARE WORTHLESS.

10 NAIRA   151 x 78mm Issued 23 April 1984 **Cat.#25**
Red and multicolor.
Alvan Ikoku / Two women.
CAUTION: LILAC NOTES ARE WORTHLESS.

20 NAIRA   151 x 78mm Issued 23 April 1984 **Cat.#26**
   Green.
   Gen. Murtalla Muhammed / Arms.
CAUTION: RED, VIOLET AND MULTICOLOR NOTES ARE WORTHLESS.

50 NAIRA   151 x 78mm Issued 23 April 1984 **Cat.#27**
   Blue, gray and multicolor.
   Four people / Farming scene and drum.

100 NAIRA   **Cat.#28**
   To be issued by end-1999. It will honor Chief Obafemi Awolowo.

200 NAIRA   **Cat.#29**
   To be issued in 2000. It will honor Alhaj Ahmadu Bello.

500 NAIRA   **Cat.#30**
   To be issued in 2000. It will honor Dr. Nnamdi Azikiwe.

Niue   NZD

New Zealand currency is used.

Currency import-export restrictions:
NZ currency import free, export NZ$ 100.
Foreign currency import free, export requires authorization from
a bank.

Northern Cyprus

In this part of Cyprus occupied by Turkey, both Turkish Lira and
Cypriot pounds are used. See Cyprus for details.

Northern Ireland
Nordirland • Irlanda del Norte • Irlande du Nord GBP

Sterling pound(s) = 100 penny (pence).

The import and export of local and foreign currencies are free.

Alternative currencies: Bank of England notes are current. All major
currencies are easily exchanged.

ISSUERS: BANK OF IRELAND, FIRST TRUST BANK, NORTHERN BANK,
ULSTER BANK.

CURRENT NOTES

5 POUNDS B. of Ireland   135 x 70mm Issued 24 Oct 1990 **Cat.#70**
   28 Aug 1990 Blue, violet and multicolor.
   Seated woman / The Queen's University in Belfast.

5 POUNDS B. of Ireland   135 x 70mm Issued 24 Oct 1990 **Cat.#78**
   1 July 1997 Blue, violet and multicolor.
   Seated woman / The Queen's University in Belfast.

5 POUNDS Northern Bank   135 x 70mm **Cat.#193**
   1988-90 Blue and multicolor.
   W. A. Traill, building and trolley car / "N", antenna and computer
   equipment.

5 POUNDS Ulster Bank   135 x 70mm **Cat.#332**
   1990-92 Brown and multicolor.
   Three vignettes / Arms.

5 POUNDS Ulster Bank 135 x 70mm Issued in Dec. 1998 **Cat.#335**
   1 July 1998 Brown and multicolor.
   Three vignettes / Arms.
   With ascending serial numbers and silver imprint.

10 POUNDS Bank of Ireland   141 x 75mm **Cat.#71**
   14 May 1991 Purple, maroon and multicolor.
   Seated woman / The Queen's University in Belfast.

10 POUNDS Bank of Ireland   141 x 75mm **Cat.#75**
1 July 1995 Blue, reddish brown and multicolor.
Seated woman / The Queen's University in Belfast.

10 POUNDS First Trust Bank   141 x 75mm **Cat.#132**
10 Jan 1994 Brown, gray green and multicolor.
Young man / The "Girona".

10 POUNDS Northern Bank
141 x 75mm Issued in Aug 1997 **Cat.#198**
24 Feb 1997 Brown and multicolor.
J.B. Dunlop / Pediment of City Hall, Belfast.

10 POUNDS Ulster Bank 141x75mm Issued in Nov 1997 **Cat.#335**
1 Jan 1997 Green and pale orange.
Three vignettes / Arms.
With windowed security thread reading "ULSTER BANK".

20 POUNDS Bank of Ireland   149 x 80mm **Cat.#72**
9 May 1991 Green, brown and multicolor.
Seated woman / The Queen's University in Belfast.

20 POUNDS Bank of Ireland   149 x 80mm **Cat.#76**
1995- Green, brown and multicolor.
Seated woman / The Queen's University in Belfast.

20 POUNDS First Trust Bank   149 x 80mm **Cat.#133**
1994 Purple, green and multicolor.
Woman / Chimney at Lacada Point.

20 POUNDS First Trust Bank   149 x 80mm **Cat.#138**
1998 Purple, green and multicolor.
Woman / Chimney at Lacada Point.
With a windowed security thread and a gold seal at top right.

20 POUNDS Northern Bank   149 x 80mm **Cat.#199**
21 Feb 1997 Purple and multicolor.
H. Ferguson / Pediment of City Hall, Belfast.

20 POUNDS Ulster Bank   149 x 80mm **Cat.#333**
1990 Purple and multicolor.
Three vignettes / Arms.

20 POUNDS Ulster Bank   149 x 80mm **Cat.#336**
1 Jan 1996 Purple and multicolor.
Three vignettes / Arms.
With ascending serial numbers and gold logo on front.

50 POUNDS Bank of Ireland   156 x 85mm **Cat.#73**
1 July 1995 Brown, olive and multicolor.
Seated woman / The Queen's University in Belfast.

50 POUNDS First Trust Bank   156 x 85mm **Cat.#134**
10 Jan 1994 Green and multicolor.
Man / Angel holding medal.

50 POUNDS Northern Bank   156 x 85mm **Cat.#196**
1990 Bluish green and black / Brown and olive.
Sir Samuel Davidson, tea dryer and centrifugal machine / "N",
antenna and computer.

50 POUNDS Northern Bank   156 x 85mm **Cat.#200**
A new note is planned for issue in October 1999.

50 POUNDS Ulster Bank 156x85mm Issued in Nov 1997 **Cat.#338**
1 Jan 1997 Olive green.
Three vignettes / Arms.
With a hologram.

100 POUNDS B. of Ireland 163x90mm Issued 1 May 1993 **Cat.#74**
1992 Red, brown and multicolor.
Seated woman / The Queen's University at Belfast.

100 POUNDS Bank of Ireland   163 x 90mm **Cat.#77**
1 July 1995 Dark red, reddish brown and multicolor.
Seated woman / The Queen's University at Belfast.

100 POUNDS First Trust Bank   163 x 90mm **Cat.#135**
10 Jan 1994 Brown olive and multicolor.
Man and woman / The Armada.

100 POUNDS Northern Bank   163 x 90mm **Cat.#197**
1990 Lilac, black and blue / Lilac, black and orange.
Sir James Martin, airplanes and Martin Baker ejection seat / "N",
antenna and computer.

100 POUNDS Northern Bank   **Cat.#201**
A new note is planned for issue in October 1999.

100 POUNDS Ulster Bank   163 x 90mm **Cat.#334**
1 Dec 1990 Purple and multicolor.
Three vignettes / Arms.

©MRI BANKERS' GUIDE TO FOREIGN CURRENCY
P.O.Box 3174 HOUSTON TX 77253 USA

OUTMODED AND REDEEMABLE NOTES

Old notes issued by :
Allied Irish Banks, Belfast;
Bank of Ireland, Belfast;
Belfast Banking Company, Belfast;
National Bank Ltd., Belfast;
Northern Bank, Belfast;
Provincial Bank of Ireland, Belfast;
and Ulster Bank, Belfast are redeemable.

Northern Mariana Islands

United States currency is used.

Norway
Norge/Noreg • Norwegien • Noruega • Norvège **NOK**

Krone(r) = 100 ør e.

Currency import-export restrictions:
The import and export of all currencies is free. Amounts exceeding
NOK 25,000 or its equivalent must be declared to Customs. *Jul1998*

Alternative currencies: any major.

Issuer: "NORGES BANK."

Norwegian currency is used in Bouvet Island, Jan Mayen, Peter I
Island, Queen Maud Land and Svalbard

CURRENT NOTES

50 KRONER   128 x 60mm Issued 20 January 1997 **Cat.#46**
"Edition VII" Green.
Fairy-tale writer Peter Christen Asbjørnsen and Osier band /
Water lilies and dragonfly.
After 1999 the serial number fluoresces under UV light.

100 KRONER   136 x 65mm Issued 15 Sep 1997 **Cat.#47**
"Edition VII" 1995 Purple brown and multicolor / Red and
multicolor.
Kirsten Flagstad / Main auditorium of Den Norske Opera.
After 1999 the date is in the bottom right corner of front. Both serial numbers
and date fluoresce under UV light.

200 KRONER   144 x 70mm Issued 1 Nov 1994 **Cat.#48**
1994- Blue, green and multicolor.
Christian Bilkeland / Map of Northern Europe.
After 1999 the date is in the bottom right corner of front. Both serial numbers
and date fluoresce under UV light.

500 KRONER   155 x 78mm **Cat.#44**
1991-98 Violet blue and multicolor / Light violet and multicolor.
Edvard Grieg / Floral pattern.

500 KRONER   152 x 75mm Issued 7 June 1999 **Cat.#49**
1999 Brown and multicolor / Brown, light orange red and
multicolor.
Sigrid Undste / Wreath of wheat and roses.

1,000 KRONER   155 x 78mm **Cat.#45**
1990- Reddish purple and multicolor.
C.M. Falsen / Heraldic lion, 1668.

1,000 KRONER   160 x 80mm **Cat.#50**
Reddish violet and bluish violet.
Christian M. Falsen.
New "Edition VII" note planned for release in early 2001.

OUTMODED AND REDEEMABLE NOTES

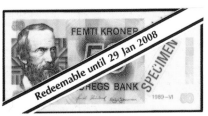

50 KRONER   136 x 66mm **Cat.#42**
1984-95 Green and multicolor.   *rruu20080129*
A.O. Vinje / Detail from entrance to Hylestad Stave Church.

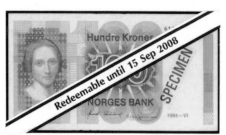

100 KRONER   145 x 78mm **Cat.#43**
1977-96 Reddish brown and multicolor.
Camilla Collett / Buckle.

rruu20080915

500 KRONER   172 x 90mm **Cat.#39**
1978-85 Green and multicolor.
Niels Henrik Abel / University of Oslo (1855).

rruu20020621

1,000 KRONER   172 x 90mm **Cat.#40**
1975-89 Violet, brown and multicolor.
Henrik Ibsen / "Lighthouse at Vardø."

rruu20010801

Oman   OMR

Rial(s) = 1000 baisa.

The import and export of local and foreign currencies are free.

Alternative currencies: any major.

A BRIEF MONETARY HISTORY
7 May 1970: rial Saidi established at rate of 21 Gulf rupees.
11 Nov 1972: name changed to rial Omani

Issuer: "CENTRAL BANK OF OMAN."

CURRENT NOTES

Caution!!!
This note
is worth only
1/10 of a rial

100 BAISA = **0.10 RIAL** 120 x 63mm Issued 18 Nov 1976 **Cat.#13**
Light brown and multicolor.
Crossed daggers emblem / Port Qaboos.

Caution!!!
This note
is worth only
1/10 of a rial

100 BAISA = **0.10 RIAL**   120 x 63mm **Cat.#22**
1987 Light Brown and multicolor.
Sultan Qaboos / Port Qaboos.

Caution!!!
This note
is worth only
1/10 of a rial

100 BAISA = **0.10 RIAL**   122 x 64mm **Cat.#31**
1995 Green and purple.
Sultan Qaboos and canal / Falcon, ibex and other animals.

Caution!!!
This note
is worth only
1/5 of a rial

200 BAISA = **0.20 RIAL** 132 x 65mm Issued 1 Jan 1985 **Cat.#14**
Purple and multicolor.
Crossed daggers emblem / Rustaq Fort.

Caution!!!
This note
is worth only
1/5 of a rial

200 BAISA = **0.20 RIAL**   132 x 65mm **Cat.#23**
1987 Violet and multicolor.
Sultan Qaboos / Rustaq Fort.

©MRI BANKERS' GUIDE TO FOREIGN CURRENCY
P.O.Box 3174 HOUSTON TX 77253 USA

200 BAISA = 0.20 RIAL   128 x 64mm **Cat.#32**
1995 Green, brown and blue.
Sultan Qaboos and airport / Port.

Caution!!!
This note
is worth only
1/5 of a rial

¼ RIAL   129 x 68mm Issued 18 Nov 1976 **Cat.#15**
Dark blue and brown.
Crossed daggers emblem / Jalali Fort.

¼ RIAL   135 x 70mm **Cat.#24**
1989 Gray blue and multicolor.
Sultan Qaboos / Modern Fishing Industry.

½ RIAL   137 x 73mm Issued 18 Nov 1976 **Cat.#16**
Green and violet.
Crossed daggers emblem / Sumail Fort.

½ RIAL   140 x 74mm **Cat.#25**
1987 Green, violet and multicolor.
Sultan Qaboos / Sultan Qaboos University.

½ RIAL   135 x 64mm **Cat.#33**
1995 Brown, rose and green.
Sultan Qaboos and fort / Nakhl and Al-Hazm forts.

1 RIAL   145 x 78mm Issued 18 Nov 1976 **Cat.#17**
Red and brown.
Crossed daggers emblem / Sohar Fort.

1 RIAL   145 x 78mm **Cat.#26**
1987 Red, olive brown and multicolor.
Sultan Qaboos / Sohar Fort.

1 RIAL   145 x 76mm **Cat.#34**
1995 Gray, purple brown and green.
Sultan Qaboos and stadium / Daggers and other traditional
objects.

5 RIALS   155 x 78mm Issued 18 Nov 1976 **Cat.18**
Lilac, blue and multicolor.
Crossed daggers emblem / Nizwa Fort.

5 RIALS   165 x 78mm **Cat.#27**
1990 Dark rose, brown violet and multicolor.
Sultan Qaboos / Nizwa Fort.

5 RIALS   152 x 76mm **Cat.#35**
  1995 Red and multicolor.
  Sultan Qaboos and building / View of city.

10 RIALS   165 x 78mm Issued 18 Nov 1976 **Cat.#19**
  Brown and multicolor.
  Crossed daggers emblem / Mirani Fort.

10 RIALS   165 x 78mm **Cat.#28**
  1987-93 Brown and multicolor.
  Sultan Qaboos / Mirani Fort.

10 RIALS   159 x 77mm **Cat.#36**
  1995 Brown, green and blue.
  Sultan Qaboos and tower / View of city.

20 RIALS   175 x 78mm Issued 18 Nov 1976 **Cat.#20**
  Gray blue, orange and multicolor.
  Sultan Qaboos / Central Bank.

20 RIALS   175 x 79mm **Cat.#29**
  1987-94 Gray blue and multicolor.
  Sultan Qaboos / Central Bank.

20 RIALS   166 x 77mm **Cat.#37**
  1995 Green and multicolor.
  Sultan Qaboos and building / Two buildings and industrial park.

50 RIALS   166 x 78mm **Cat.#21**
  ND, 1985-92 Olive, blue and multicolor.
  Sultan Qaboos / Jabreen Fort.
  There are two similar notes, without and with date. Both are current.

50 RIALS   174 x 77mm **Cat.#38**
  1995 Purple brown and multicolor.
  Sultan Qaboos, building and view of fort / View of city.

OUTMODED AND REDEEMABLE NOTES

Similar notes issued by "Sultanate of Muscat and Oman" are worthless.

5 RIALS Oman Currency Board.   *Cat.#11*
  Purple, blue and multicolor.
  Crossed daggers emblem / Nizwa Fort.

10 RIALS Oman Currency Board.   *Cat.#12*
  Brown, blue and multicolor.
  Crossed daggers emblem / Mirani Fort.

Pakistan Paquistán   **PKR**

Rupee(s) = 100 paisa.
Currency import-export restrictions:

Local currency in/out: Rp. 500 from India, Rp. 3,000 from other countries.
Foreign currency in and out: free.
Reconversion of unspent rupees is allowed provided receipts can be produced for previous exchange of foreign into local currency.

Alternative currencies: any major.

A BRIEF MONETARY HISTORY
April 1948: Pakistani rupee established at par with Indian rupee.

Notes of 2 rupees and up are issued by "STATE BANK OF PAKISTAN."

CURRENT NOTES

5 RUPEES   126 x 73mm **Cat.#28**
Sepia, tan and pink.
Muhammad Ali Jinnah / Khajak tunnel in Baluchistan.

5 RUPEES   128 x 73mm Issued 12 Aug 1997 **Cat.#44**
Mauve
Muhammad Ali Jinnah "Quaid-e-Azam" (The Great Leader) / Tomb of Shah Rukn-e-Alam.
Commemorative of 50 years of the creation of Pakistan.

10 RUPEES   140 x 73mm **Cat.#29**
Green and multicolor.
Muhammad Ali Jinnah / View of Mohanjodaro.

50 RUPEES   154 x 73mm **Cat.#30**
Purple and multicolor.
Muhammad Ali Jinnah / Gate of Lahore fort.

100 RUPEES   166 x 73mm **Cat.#31**
Red, orange and multicolor.
Muhammad Ali Jinnah / Islamic College, Peshawar.

500 RUPEES   176 x 73mm **Cat.#42**
Green and multicolor.
Muhammad Ali Jinnah / State Bank of Pakistan building.

1,000 RUPEES   176 x 73mm Issued 18 July 1987 **Cat.#43**
Blue and blue orange.
Muhammad Ali Jinnah / Tomb of Jahangir, Lahore.

OUTMODED AND REDEEMABLE NOTES

50 RUPEES   154 x 83mm **Cat.#22**
Blue.
Muhammad Ali Jinnah / Two sailing ships.
CAUTION: GREENISH BLUE NOTES ARE WORTHLESS.

100 RUPEES   164 x 92mm **Cat.#23**
Dark blue.
Muhammad Ali Jinnah / Mosque.
CAUTION: GREEN NOTES ARE WORTHLESS.

Palau   USD

United States currency is used.

Palestine   Palestina

Israeli and Jordanian currencies are used in the area under the Palestine Authority. There are plans to issue currency, but because Bank Israel has to approve first, and notify the Central Bank of Jordan one year in advance, it can be assumed that it will take a long time (April 1996.)

A theoretical Palestinian dinar (=1,000 fils) exists equal to 10 Israeli sheqalim. Postage stamps were issued denominated in this currency.

Notes issued before 1948 by the "Palestine Currency Board" denominated in pounds may be redeemed at par in the Bank of England. Their numismatic value is far higher. Only four of the outstanding 6 notes of 100 pounds notes are known.

Central Bank: PALESTINE MONETARY AUTHORITY

Panamá   PAB

Balboa(s) = 100 centésimo(s).

United States currency is used.

The import and export of all currencies are free.

A BRIEF MONETARY HISTORY
1904: balboa = US$ 1.

Papua New Guinea   Papua-Neuguinea •
Papua Nueva Guinea • Papouasie Nouvelle GuinéePGK

Kina = 100 toea.

Currency import-export restrictions:
Local currency in: free.
Local currency out: K 200 in notes and K 5 in coins.
Foreign currency in: free.
Out: up to amount imported and declared.

Alternative currencies: AUD, GBP, USD.

A BRIEF MONETARY HISTORY
1973 kina = 1 Australian dollar.

Issuer: "BANK OF PAPUA NEW GUINEA."

CURRENT NOTES

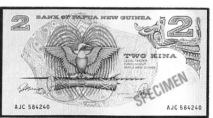

2 KINA   140 x 70mm **Cat.#5**
  Green and multicolor.
  Bird of Paradise / Artifacts.

2 KINA   140 x 70mm **Cat.#12**
  Green and multicolor.
  Bird of Paradise and artifacts / Artifacts.
  Printed on polymer, with round "window" at right.
  It commemorates the 9th South Pacific Games, Papua New Guinea 1991.

2 KINA   140 x 70mm Issued in early 1996 **Cat.#15**
  Green and multicolor.
  Bird of Paradise and artifacts / Artifacts.
  Printed on polymer, with round "window" at right.
  It commemorates the 20th Anniversary of the Bank of Papua and New Guinea.

2 KINA   140 x 70mm Issued in mid 1996 **Cat.#16**
  Green and multicolor.
  Bird of Paradise and artifacts / Artifacts.
  Printed on polymer, with round "window" at right.

5 KINA   145 x 73mm **Cat.#6**
Violet and multicolor.
Bird of Paradise / Mask.
Without and with windowed security thread (Cat.#14.)

10 KINA   150 x 75mm **Cat.#7**
Blue and multicolor.
Bird of Paradise / Bowl, ring, etc.

10 KINA   150 x 75mm Issued in Nov. 1998 **Cat.#17**
Blue and multicolor.
Bird of Paradise / Bowl, ring, etc.
Commemorates 25 years of the Bank of Papua New Guinea.

20 KINA   150 x 75mm **Cat.#9**
Red and multicolor.
Bird of Paradise / Boar's head.

50 KINA   150 x 75mm **Cat.#11**
Orange, yellow and multicolor.
Bird of Paradise and Parliament building / M. Somare,
headdresses and masks.

Paraguay   PYG

Guaraní(es) = 100 céntimo(s).
Minor unit coins are not used.

The import and export of all currencies is free.   July1998

Alternative currencies: ARS, BRL, UYU and any major.

A BRIEF MONETARY HISTORY
Oct. 1943: guaraní = 100 pesos fuertes.

Issuer: "BANCO CENTRAL DEL PARAGUAY."

CURRENT NOTES

Smaller notes not listed because of low value.

500 GUARANÍES   157 x 67mm **Cat.#200**
Blue.
Gen. Bernardino Caballero / Ship.
It is being replaced by a coin.

1,000 GUARANÍES   157 x 67mm **Cat.#201**
Purple.
Mariscal Francisco Solano López / "Oratorio de la Virgen."

1,000 GUARANÍES   157 x 67mm **Cat.#213**
Purple.
Mariscal Francisco Solano López / "Oratorio de la Virgen."

5,000 GUARANÍES   157 x 67mm **Cat.#202**
Red.
Carlos Antonio López / "Palacio de los López."
Without (Cat.#202) and with windowed security thread.

10,000 GUARANÍES   157 x 67mm **Cat.#203**
Brown.
José Gaspar Rodríguez de Francia / "14 de Mayo de 1811."

10,000 GUARANÍES   157 x 67mm **Cat.#215**
Serie 1998 Brown.
José Gaspar Rodríguez de Francia / "14 de Mayo de 1811."

50,000 GUARANÍES   157 x 67mm Issued ca.1990 **Cat.#210**
Blue, dark violet and multicolor / Black violet, olive green and multicolor.
"Soldado Paraguayo" / "Casa de la Independencia."
Cat.#210: with plain security thread.
Cat.#211: with plain windowed security thread.
Cat.#211A: with "cleartext" windowed security thread.

50,000 GUARANIES   157 x 67mm **Cat.#216**
Serie 1998 Blue, dark violet and multicolor / Black violet, olive green and multicolor.
"Soldado Paraguayo" / "Casa de la Independencia."
With "staircase" metallic impression in front.

100,000 GUARANÍES   157 x 67mm Issued 3 Aug 1998 **Cat.#217**
Serie 1998 Green, yellow brown and multicolor.
San Rice González de Santa Cruz / Represa de Itaipú.

OUTMODED AND REDEEMABLE NOTES

Older notes in guaraníes are redeemable.

Peru   Perú • Pérou   PEN

Nuevo(s) sol(es) = 100 céntimo(s).

Currency import-export restrictions:
Local currency in: free; out forbidden, but export permission may be obtained.
Foreign currency in: free.
Out: up to amount imported and declared.

Alternative currencies: any major.

A BRIEF MONETARY HISTORY
1985: 1,000 soles = 1 inti
1 July 1991: 1,000,000 intis = 1 nuevo sol

Issuer: "BANCO CENTRAL DE RESERVA DEL PERU."

CURRENT NOTES

10 NUEVOS SOLES   140 x 65mm Issued 1 June 1991 **Cat.#151**
1 Feb 1991-92 Green, brown and multicolor.
J. Abelardo Quiñones / Quiñones flying upside down, and his signature.

10 NUEVOS SOLES   140 x 65mm **Cat.#156**
1995 Green, brown and multicolor.
J. Abelardo Quiñones / Quiñones flying upside down, and his signature.

10 NUEVOS SOLES   140 x 65mm **Cat.#163**
1997 Green, brown and multicolor.
J. Abelardo Quiñones / Quiñones flying upside down, and his signature.
With iridescent planchettes, microlettering inside the "10" in the lower left of front and next to the portrait, and "cleartext" security thread.

20 NUEVOS SOLES   140 x 65mm Issued 1 June 1991 **Cat.#152**
1991-92 Orange, brown and multicolor.
Raul Porras Barrenechea and patio of San Marcos University / "Palacio de Torre Tagle."

©MRI BANKERS' GUIDE TO FOREIGN CURRENCY
P.O.Box 3174 HOUSTON TX 77253 USA

20 NUEVOS SOLES　　　140 x 65mm　**Cat.#157**
　　1994-95 Orange, brown and multicolor.
　　Raul Porras Barrenechea and patio of San Marcos University /
　　"Palacio de Torre Tagle."

20 NUEVOS SOLES　　　140 x 65mm　**Cat.#164**
　　1997 Orange, brown and multicolor.
　　Raul Porras Barrenechea and patio of San Marcos University /
　　"Palacio de Torre Tagle."
　　With iridescent planchettes, microlettering inside the "10" in the lower left of
　　front and next to the portrait, and "cleartext" security thread.

50 NUEVOS SOLES　　140 x 65mm　Issued 1 June 1991　**Cat.#154**
　　1 Feb 1991 Brown, gray and multicolor / Brown, grayish blue,
　　blue green and multicolor.
　　Abraham Valdelomar / Laguna de Huacachina.

50 NUEVOS SOLES　　　140 x 65mm　**Cat.#160**
　　16 June 1994 Brown, gray and multicolor / Brown, grayish blue,
　　blue green and multicolor.
　　Abraham Valdelomar / Laguna de Huacachina.

100 NUEVOS SOLES　　140 x 65mm　Issued 22 July 1992　**Cat.#155**
　　1991-92 Black blue, blue, lilac, green and multicolor.
　　Jorge Basadre / Biblioteca Nacional.

100 NUEVOS SOLES　　　140 x 65mm　Issued 2 Jan 1997　**Cat.#161**
　　1995 Black blue, blue, lilac, green and multicolor.
　　Jorge Basadre Grohmann / Biblioteca Nacional.

200 NUEVOS SOLES　　140 x 65mm　Issued 29 Aug 1997　**Cat.#162**
　　20 April 1995 Rose red and green.
　　Santa Rosa de Lima / Convent of Santo Domingo.

Philippines
Pilipinas • Philippinen • Filipinas　　　**PHP**

Piso = 100 sentimo(s).

Currency Import-export restrictions:
Local currency in/out: P 10,000. Larger amounts require authorization from the Bangko Sentral ng Pilipinas.
Foreign currency in: free.
Out: free, provided it is not foreign exchange obtained from the banking system. Reconversion at airports or other ports of exit free up to USD 200.00 or equivalent. Larger amounts may be reconverted in financial institutions with supporting receipts showing previous exchange of hard currency into pesos in the banking system.

Aug1998

Alternative currencies: any major.

Issuer: "BANGKO SENTRAL NG PILIPINAS."

CURRENT NOTES

5 PISO　　　160 x 66mm　**Cat.#168**
　　1949 Green and multicolor.
　　E Aguinaldo / Declaration of Independence.
　　With old (1949) or new (1993) seals. These notes are being replaced by a coin.

10 PISO　　　160 x 66mm　**Cat.#169**
　　1949 Brown and multicolor.
　　A. Mabini / Barasoain church.
　　With old (1949) or new (1993) Central Bank seals.

10 PISO　　　160 x 66mm　**Cat.#188**
　　1997 Brown and multicolor.
　　Apolinario Mabini and Andres Bonifacio / Barasoain church.

20 PISO   160 x 66mm **Cat.#170**
1949 Orange and multicolor.
M. L. Quezón / Malacañang Palace.
With old (1949) or new (1993) Central Bank seals.

50 PISO   160 x 66mm **Cat.#171**
1949 Red and multicolor.
S Osmeña / Old Executive House.
With old (1949) or new (1993) Central Bank seals.
In 1999 it was stamped to commemorate 50 years of the Central Bank.

100 PISO   160 x 66mm **Cat.#172**
Mauve and multicolor.
M A Roxas / New Central Bank building.
With old (1949) or new (1993; 1998) Central Bank seals.

100 PISO   160 x 66mm **Cat.#187**
1898-1998 Philippine Centennial Commemorative
Similar to the regular note, with commemorative mustard, gold, purple and
blue overprint at left of the front.

500 PISO   160 x 66mm **Cat.#173**
1949 Yellow and multicolor.
Benigno S. Aquino, Jr. / Scenes of his life, and allegorical groups.
With old (1949) or new (1993; 1998) Central Bank seals.

1,000 PISO   160 x 66mm **Cat.#174**
1949 Blue and multicolor.
José Abad Santos, Josefa Llanes Escoda and Gral Vicente Lim; and
torch / Banawe Rice terraces, the Manunggul and the Langgal.
With old (1949) or new (1993; 1998) Central Bank seals.

2,000 PISO   216 x 133mm **Cat.#190**
1998 Multicolor.
Installation of president José E. Estrada / President Fidel V.
Ramos and wife waving flag.
This note is sold at a premium.

100,000 PISO   356 x 216mm **Cat.#189**
1998 Green, yellow and brown.
"Unang Sigw sa Pugad Lawin" with the seal of the National
Centennial Commission and the BSP / Declaration of Philippine
Independence in Kawit, Cavite, June 12, 1898.
This note is sold at twice the face value in a limited issue of 1,000 notes.

Pitcairn Islands   NZD

New Zealand currency is used. Although the island has very few
inhabitants, coins were struck for the numismatic market.

Poland   Polska • Polen • Polonia • Pologne PLN

(New) złoty (złotych) = 100 (new) grosz(y).

The import of local or foreign currencies is free.
Out: free up equivalent of ECU 2,000 or to amount imported and
declared. In other cases a permit from the Ministry of Finance or
the President of the National Bank of Poland is required.
Reconversion allowed with supporting exchange receipts.

Alternative currencies: any major.

A BRIEF MONETARY HISTORY
Oct 1950: old złotych replaced. (1 to 3 new for each 100 old.)
Jan 1995: (new) złoty = 10,000 (old) złotych.

Issuer: "NARODOWY BANK POLSKI."

CURRENT NOTES

10 (NEW) ZŁOTYCH 120 x 60mm Issued in January 1995 **Cat.#173**
25 March 1994 Brown, green and multicolor.
Mieszko I / "Denar" from the reign of Mieszko I.

20 (NEW) ZŁOTYCH 126 x 63mm Issued in January 1995 **Cat.#174**
25 March 1994 Violet brown and multicolor.
Bolesław I Chrobry / "Denar" from the reign of Bolesław I
Chrobry.

50 (NEW) ZŁOTYCH 132 x 66mm Issued in January 1995 **Cat.#175**
25 March 1994 Blue violet, blue green and brown.
Kazimierz III Wielki / Eagle from a seal of Kazimierz III Wielki, orb
and scepter and view of medieval Cracow and Kazimierz.

100 (NEW) ZŁOTYCH   138 x 69mm Issued 1 June 1995 **Cat.#176**
25 March 1994 Olive green and multicolor.
Władysław II Jagiełło / Arms and Teutonic Knights' Castle in
Malbork.

200 (NEW) ZŁOTYCH   144 x 72mm Issued 1 June 1995 **Cat.#177**
25 March 1994 Brown and multicolor.
King Zygmunt I the Old / Eagle in hexagon from the Zygmunt's
Chapel in the Wawel Cathedral, and Wawel's court.

OUTMODED AND REDEEMABLE NOTES

*The following notes are redeemable until 31 Dec 2010; smaller notes
are omitted because of low value:*

{5,000 ZŁOTYCH} 1982-88 = 0.50 (NEW) ZŁOTY	*Cat.#150*
{10,000 ZŁOTYCH} 1987-88 = 1 (NEW) ZŁOTY	*Cat.#151*
{20,000 ZŁOTYCH} 1989 = 2 (NEW) ZŁOTE	*Cat.#152*
{50,000 ZŁOTYCH} 1989 = 5 (NEW) ZŁOTYCH	*Cat.#153*
{50,000 ZŁOTYCH} 1993 = 5 (NEW) ZŁOTYCH	*Cat.#159*
{100,000 ZŁOTYCH} 1990 = 10 (NEW) ZŁOTYCH	Cat.#154
{100,000 ZŁOTYCH} 1993 = 10 (NEW) ZŁOTYCH	Cat.#160
{200,000 ZŁOTYCH} 1989 = 20 (NEW) ZŁOTYCH	Cat.#155
{500,000 ZŁOTYCH} 1990 = 50 (NEW) ZŁOTYCH	Cat.#156
{500,000 ZŁOTYCH} 1993 = 50 (NEW) ZŁOTYCH	Cat.#161
{1,000,000 ZŁOTYCH} 1991 = 100 (NEW) ZŁOTYCH	Cat.#157
{1,000,000 ZŁOTYCH} 1993 = 100 (NEW) ZŁOTYCH	Cat.#162
{2,000,000 ZŁOTYCH} 1992 = 200 (NEW) ZŁOTYCH	Cat.#158
{2,000,000 ZŁOTYCH} 1993 = 200 (NEW) ZŁOTYCH	Cat.#163

Portugal   PTE

Euro = 200.482 escudos Escudo(s.)

Currency Import-export restrictions:
The import and export of local and foreign currency is free.
Customs declaration required on amounts over PTE 2,500,000 in
currency, coins, travellers checks and negotiable securities. Jul1998

Alternative currencies: any major.

A BRIEF MONETARY HISTORY:
1 Jan 1999: Euro adopted at 200.482 escudos.

Issuer: "BANCO DE PORTUGAL", after 2002 "EUROPEAN CENTRAL BANK."

CURRENT NOTES

500 ESCUDOS Ch. 13   125 x 68mm Issued 17 Sep 1997 **Cat.#187**
17 April 1997 Brown, reddish brown and multicolor.
João de Barros / Allegory of the Portuguese Discoveries.

1,000 ESCUDOS Ch.13 132 x 68mm Issued 22 Oct 1996 **Cat.#188**
18 April 1996 Purple, brown and multicolor.
Pedro Alvares Cabral / Cabral's vessel, his coat of arms and
Brazilian fauna.

2,000 ESCUDOS Ch.2   140 x 68mm Issued 15 Feb 1996 **Cat.#189**
21 Sep 1995- Blue, greenish blue, light brown and orange
brown.
Bartolomeu Dias / Caravel and compass.

5,000 ESCUDOS Ch.3   147 x 75mm Issued 15 Feb 1996 **Cat.#190**
5 Jan 1995 Green, purple brown and orange brown.
Vasco da Gama / Ship and encounter of Vasco da Gama with the
authorities of Calcutta.

10,000 ESCUDOS Ch.2 153 x 75mm Issued 22 Oct 1996 **Cat.#191**
2 May 1996 Reddish brown, brown and multicolor.
Infante D. Henrique and his seal / Vessel.

OUTMODED AND REDEEMABLE NOTES

20 ESCUDOS Ch. 7	Cat.#167 .	Redeemable until 30 May 2006
20 ESCUDOS Ch. 8	Cat.#173 .	Redeemable until 30 May 2006
20 ESCUDOS Ch. 9	Cat.#176 .	Redeemable until 30 May 2006
50 ESCUDOS Ch. 8	Cat.#168 ..	Redeemable until 30 Jun 2007
50 ESCUDOS Ch. 9	Cat.#174 ..	Redeemable until 30 Jun 2007
100 ESCUDOS Ch. 7	Cat.#169 .	Redeemable until 31 Mar 2007
100 ESCUDOS Ch. 8	Cat.#178 .	Redeemable until 31 May 2010
100 ESCUDOS Ch. 9	Cat.#179 ..	Redeemable until 31 Jan 2012
500 ESCUDOS Ch. 10	Cat.#170 ..	Redeemable until 29 Jan 2008
500 ESCUDOS Ch. 11	Cat.#177 .	Redeemable until 31 May 2010
500 ESCUDOS Ch. 12	Cat.#180	Redeemable until 30 Apr 2018
1,000 ESCUDOS Ch. 8A	Cat.#166 .	Redeemable until 30 Jun 1999
1,000 ESCUDOS Ch. 10	Cat.#172 ..	Redeemable until 30 Jan 2007
1,000 ESCUDOS Ch. 11	Cat.#175 ..	Redeemable until 31 Oct 2011
1,000 ESCUDOS Ch. 12	Cat.#181 .	Redeemable until 31 Dec 2017
2,000 ESCUDOS Ch. 1	Cat.#186 .	Redeemable until 31 Dec 2017
5,000 ESCUDOS Ch. 1	Cat.#183 .	Redeemable until 30 Nov 2012
5,000 ESCUDOS Ch.2&2A	Cat.#184 .	Redeemable until 31 Dec 2017
10,000 ESCUDOS Ch. 1	Cat.#185 .	Redeemable until 31 Dec 2017

Qatar Katar QAR

Riyal(s) = 100 dirhem(s).

The import and export of all currencies is free.   Jul1998

Alternative currencies: any major.

A BRIEF MONETARY HISTORY
1973: riyal established at par with Gulf rupee.

Issuer: "QATAR CENTRAL BANK."

CURRENT NOTES

1 RIYAL Qatar Central Bank   134 x 66mm **Cat.#14**
Purple brown and multicolor.
Legends and arms / Small boat out of water.

WARNING

Similar notes issued by the Qatar Monetary Agency are out of circulation, but still redeemable.

5 RIYALS Qatar Central Bank   140 x 68mm **Cat.#15**
Lilac red, purple and multicolor / Reddish brown, green and blue.
Legends and arms / Animal and arms.

10 RIYALS Qatar Central Bank   145 x 69mm **Cat.#16**
Green, blue and multicolor.
Legends and arms / National Museum.

50 RIYALS Qatar Central Bank   152 x 70mm **Cat.#17**
Purplish blue, olive brown and multicolor.
Legends and arms / Industrial scene.

100 RIYALS Qatar Central Bank   158 x 72mm **Cat.#18**
Brown, olive, orange red and multicolor / Green and olive.
Legends and arms / Qatar Central Bank building.

500 RIYALS Qatar Central Bank   165 x 74mm **Cat.#19**
Green, brown, purple brown and multicolor.
Legend and arms / Offshore oil drilling platform.
It has a 8 point star hologram.

OUTMODED AND REDEEMABLE NOTES

1 RIYAL Qatar Monetary Agency   134 x 66mm **Cat.#7**
Brown, green and multicolor.
Legends and arms / City street scene.   rruu20060622

1 RIYAL Qatar Monetary Agency   134 x 66mm **Cat.#13**
Purple brown and multicolor / Purple brown.
Legends and arms / Small boat out of water.   rruu20060622

5 RIYALS Qatar Monetary Agency   140 x 68mm **Cat.#8**
Lilac red, purple and multicolor / Reddish brown, green and blue.
Legends and arms / Animals and plants.   rruu20060622

10 RIYALS Qatar Monetary Agency   145 x 69mm **Cat.#9**
Green, blue and multicolor.
Legends and arms / National Museum.   rruu20060622

50 RIYALS Qatar Monetary Agency   152 x 70mm **Cat.#10**
Blue and multicolor.
Legends and arms / Industrial scene.   rruu20060622

100 RIYALS Qatar Monetary Agency   158 x 72mm **Cat.#11**
Green and multicolor.
Legends and arms / Qatar Monetary Agency building.   rruu20060622

500 RIYALS Qatar Monetary Agency   165 x 74mm **Cat.#12**
Blue, green and multicolor.
Legends and arms / Offshore drilling platform.   rruu20060622

Réunion   FRF

French currency is used now.

Notes of the Caisse Centrale de la France Libre, Caisse Centrale de la France d'Outre-Mer, Caisse Centrale de la France and Institut d'Émission des Départements d'Outre-Mer are redeemable only in St. Denis. Fifty old francs equal 1 new franc. These notes have high numismatic value.

Romania   Rumänien • Rumania • Roumanie **ROL**

Leu (lei) = 100 ban(i).
Minor unit coins are not used.

Currency Import-export restrictions:
Local currency in/out: 500,000 lei.
Foreign currency in/out: US$10,000 or equivalent.
Arriving visitors must deposit with Customs amounts exceeding USD10,000. Departing travellers must deposit amounts in excess of 500,000 lei.   Aug1998

Alternative currencies: any major.

A BRIEF MONETARY HISTORY
Aug 1947: new leu = 20,000 (old) lei
Jan 1952: new leu converted (rates between 20 to 400 1947 lei.)

Issuer "BANCA NAŢIONALA A ROMANIEI."

CURRENT NOTES

1,000 LEI   140 x 61mm Issued 1 June 1998 **Cat.#107**
1998 Blue, yellow, green, brown and multicolor.
Mihai Eminescu, lily flower and quill / Lime and blue flowers, and ruins of Histria ancient fort.

5,000 LEI   145 x 64mm Issued 1 June 1998 **Cat.#108**
1998 Violet brown, orange, blue and multicolor.
Lucian Blaga and daffodil / Crucifix and vine leaf.

10,000 LEI   162 x 78mm Issued 23 May 1994 **Cat.#105**
Feb 1994 Violet brown, reddish brown and multicolor.
Nicolae Iorga and snake god Glycon / Historical Museum in
Bucharest, statue of Fortuna and clay statue "Thinking man of
Hamangia".

10,000 LEI   **Cat.#109**
A smaller size note will be issued soon.

50,000 LEI   155 x 70mm Issued 20 Nov 1996 **Cat.#106**
1996 Violet blue, lilac and multicolor.
George Enescu / Bucegi mountains and fragment of "Oedip
Rege."

100,000 LEI   160 x 73mm Issued 1 June 1998 **Cat.#110**
1998 Red, green and multicolor.
Nicolae Grigorescu, mallow flowers and paintbrush / Village
house and peasant girl.

Russia   Rossiia • Russland • Rusia • Russie   **RUB**

(New) ruble(s) = 100 (new) kopek(s).

Currency import-export restrictions:
Local currency in/out: up to 500 times the minimum wage.
Foreign currency in: free, **must** declare.
Out: up to amount imported and declared.

Alternative currencies: any major.

A BRIEF MONETARY HISTORY
Dec 1947: (new) ruble = 10 (old) rubles.
Jan 1961: (new) ruble = 10 rubles of 1947.
1 Jan 1998: new ruble = 1,000 rubles of 1993-95.

Issuer: "Банк России" (Russian Bank).

Some of the republics of the Russian Federation issue
banknotes and coupons, which circulate locally.

CURRENT NOTES

5 (NEW) RUBLES   137 x 60mm Issued 2 Jan 1998 **Cat.#267**
1997 Green and multicolor.
Monument to the 1,000th anniversary of Russia and Sofia
Cathedral in Novgorod / View of the fortress wall with the
Novgorod Kremlin towers.

10 (NEW) RUBLES   150 x 65mm Issued 2 Jan 1998 **Cat.#268**
1997 Olive green and multicolor.
Bridge across the Enisey river and chapel in Krasnoyarsk /
Krasnoyarsk hydroelectric dam.

50 (NEW) RUBLES   150 x 65mm Issued 2 Jan 1998 **Cat.#269**
1997 Brown, violet, blue and multicolor.
Statue symbolizing the Neva river, in the Stock Exchange plaza
in St. Petersburg / The Stock Exchange in St. Petersburg.

100 (NEW) RUBLES   150 x 65mm Issued 2 Jan 1998 **Cat.#270**
1997 Purple, brown and multicolor.
Quadriga on portico of the Bolshoi Theater in Moscow / Bolshoi
Theater.

©MRI Bankers' Guide to Foreign Currency
P.O.Box 3174 Houston TX 77253 USA

500 (NEW) RUBLES   150 x 65mm Issued 2 Jan 1998 **Cat.#271**
1997 Violet brown and blue.
Statue of Peter the Great and view of the port of Arkhangelsk / Monastery in Solovetsky Island.

OUTMODED AND REDEEMABLE NOTES

Smaller notes not listed because of low value.

Caution!!!
This note is worth only 5 rubles

{5,000 RUBLES} = **5 (NEW) RUBLES**   152 x 68mm **Cat.#258**
1993-94 Brown, red, blue and multicolor.   ru31dec01
Flag atop the House of Government in the Kremlin / The Kremlin.
There is a variety with the date 1994 in small numbers at left of front side.

Caution!!!
This note is worth only 1 ruble

{5,000 RUBLES} = **5 (NEW) RUBLES**   137 x 60mm **Cat.#262**
1995 Green and multicolor.
Monument to the 1,000th anniversary of Russia and Sofia Cathedral in Novgorod / View of the fortress wall with the Novgorod Kremlin towers.   ru31dec01

Caution!!!
This note is worth only 10 rubles

{10,000 RUBLES} = **10 (NEW) RUBLES**   152 x 68mm **Cat.#259**
1993-94 Brown violet, green and multicolor.   ru31dec01
Flag atop the house of Government in the Kremlin / The Kremlin.
There is variety with the date 1994 in small numbers at the left of front side.

Caution!!!
This note is worth only 10 rubles

{10,000 RUBLES} = **10 (NEW) RUBLES**   150 x 65mm **Cat.#263**
1995 Olive green and multicolor.
Bridge across the Enisey river and chapel in Krasnoyarsk / Krasnoyarsk hydroelectric dam.   ru31dec01

WARNING

1993 and 1995 notes are redeemable at the ratio of 1,000 to a new ruble.

Caution!!!
This note is worth only 50 rubles

{50,000 RUBLES} = **50 (NEW) RUBLES**   152 x 68 **Cat.#260**
1993-94 Lilac brown, green and multicolor.   ru31dec01
Flag atop the house of Government in the Kremlin / The Kremlin.
There is a variety with the date 1994 in small numbers at the left of front side.

Caution!!!
This note is worth only 50 rubles

{50,000 RUBLES} = **50 (NEW) RUBLES**   150 x 65mm **Cat.#264**
1995 Brown, violet, blue and multicolor.
Statue symbolizing the Neva river, in the Stock Exchange plaza in St. Petersburg / The Stock Exchange in St. Petersburg.ru31dec01

Caution!!!
This note is worth only 100 rubles

{100,000 RUBLES} = **100 (NEW) RUBLES**
150 x 65mm Issued 30 May 1995 **Cat.#265**
1995 Purple, brown and multicolor.
Quadriga on portico of the Bolshoi Theater in Moscow / Bolshoi Theater.   ru31dec01

Caution!!!
This note is worth only 500 new rubles

{500,000 RUBLES} = **500 (NEW) RUBLES**
150 x 65mm Issued 17 March 1997 **Cat.#266**
1995 Violet brown and blue.
Statue of Peter the Great and view of the port of Arkhangelsk / Monastery in Solovetsky Island.   ru31dec01

©MRI BANKERS' GUIDE TO FOREIGN CURRENCY
P.O.BOX 3174 HOUSTON TX 77253 USA

Rwanda   Ruanda   RWF

Franc(s) = 100 centime(s).
Minor unit coins are not used.

Currency Import-export restrictions:
Local currency in/out: free up to equivalent of USD 100.
Declaration required for larger amounts.
Foreign currency in: free.
Out: up to amount imported and declared.

Alternative currencies: USD.

A BRIEF MONETARY HISTORY
1960: Rwanda-Burundian franc = Belgian Congo franc.
1964: Rwandan franc = Rwanda-Burundian franc.

Issuer: "BANQUE NATIONALE DU RWANDA."

CURRENT NOTES

100 FRANCS   135 x 70mm Cat.#19
1982- Purple and multicolor.
Zebras / Woman carrying baby.
"Amafranga" on back before 1989. Since 1989 "Amafaranga."

500 FRANCS   130 x 74mm Issued in January 1995 **Cat.#23**
1 Dec 1994 Grayish blue and light pink.
Mountains / Water buck.

500 FRANCS   Issued in May 1999 **Cat.#26**
New note in circulation dated 1 December 1998. Details not
available.

1,000 FRANCS   130 x 74mm Issued in January 1995 **Cat.#24**
1 Dec 1994 Reddish brown.
Mountains / Buffaloes and bananas.

1,000 FRANCS   Issued in May 1999 **Cat.#27**
New note dated 1 December 1998 in circulation. Details not
available.

5,000 FRANCS   130 x 74mm Issued in January 1995 **Cat.#25**
1 Dec 1994 Reddish brown and light blue.
Mountains / Lion.

5,000 FRANCS   Issued in May 1999 **Cat.#28**
1 Dec 1998 Black, red and green on light red
Group of dancers / Modern building.

Saharan Arab Democratic Republic   RAD Saharaui • DAR Saharawi

The sovereignty of this former Spanish territory is under dispute.
Coins in pesetas are produced for collectors. The "peseta saharaui"
is the official monetary unit since February 1996.

St Helena   Ste-Héléne   SHP

Pound(s) = 100 penny (pence).
Parity: GBP 1.00

The import and export of all currencies is free.   6AUG1998

Alternative currencies: GBP.

Issuer: "GOVERNMENT OF ST HELENA."

CURRENT NOTES

5 POUNDS   153 x 73mm **Cat.#7**
Blue and multicolor.
Elizabeth II and view of island / Arms.

5 POUNDS   135 x 70mm **Cat.#11**
Blue and multicolor.
Elizabeth II and view of island / Arms.

©MRI Bankers' Guide to Foreign Currency
P.O.Box 3174 Houston TX 77253 USA

10 POUNDS   160 x 80mm **Cat.#8**
  Light red.
  Elizabeth II and view of island / Arms.

20 POUNDS   163 x 85mm **Cat.#10**
  Light brown.
  Elizabeth II and view of island / Arms.

OUTMODED AND REDEEMABLE NOTES

50 PENCE = 0.50 POUND   140 x 60mm *Cat.#5*
  Purple.
  Elizabeth II and view of island / Arms.
  Notes with serial numbers 170,001 to 200,000 are worthless.

1 POUND   153 x 73mm *Cat.#9*
  Olive brown.
  Elizabeth II and view of island / Arms.
  Notes with serial numbers 350,001 to 400,000 are worthless.

St Kitts and Nevis   St Kitts-und- Nevis •

S. Cristóbal y Nevis • Saint Christophe et Nevis   XCD

East Caribbean currency is used.

Currency import-export restrictions:
Local or foreign currency in/out: free. Amounts over XCD 250,000 or equivalent (USD92,593) require approval of the Ministry of finance. Declaration required for the import and export of XCD 10,000 or equivalent (USD 3,704) in other currencies.   Aug1998

United States dollars are widely accepted. Alternative currencies: CAD, DEM, FRF, GBP.

St Lucia   XCD

East Caribbean currency is used.

Currency import-export restrictions:
Import free. Export up to amount imported and declared.

United States dollars are widely accepted. Alternative currencies: CAD, DEM, FRF, GBP.

St Martin   Sint Maarten   ANG/FRF

French and Netherlands Antilles currencies are legal tender in the respective portions of the island. U.S. dollars are used widely.

Alternative currencies: all major.

St Pierre & Miquelon   FRF

French currency is used now. Older notes of the Caisse Centrale de la France Libre and Caisse Centrale de la France d'Outre-Mer are redeemable only in St. Pierre at the ratio of 1 nouveau franc for 50 old francs. All have a high numismatic value.

St Vincent & the Grenadines   XCD

East Caribbean currency is used.
Currency import-export restrictions:
Local currency in: free.
Out: XCD 50.
Foreign currency in: free.
Out: up to amount imported and declared.

United States dollars are widely accepted. Alternative currencies: CAD, DEM, FRF, USD.

Samoa   WST

Tālā = 100 sene

Currency import-export restrictions:
Local currency in: free.
Local currency out: 2,000 tala.
Foreign currency in: free, export up to amount brought in.

Alternative currencies: AUD, GBP, NZD, USD.

A BRIEF MONETARY HISTORY
July 1967: tālā = 0.30 Western Samoan pound.
Up to 1985: tala pegged to New Zealand dollar.
March 1985: tala was linked to basket of currencies.
Issuer: "CENTRAL BANK OF SAMOA."

CURRENT NOTES

2 TĀLĀ   140 x 72mm **Cat.#25**
  Blue and multicolor.
  Wood carver / Hut and palm tree.

2 TĀLĀ   140 x 70mm **Cat.#31**
  Violet brown, lilac blue, olive green and multicolor.
  Malietoa Tanumafili and view of Apia / Six seating people.
  Printed in polymer, with a transparent window.

5 TĀLĀ   140 x 72mm **Cat.#26**
  Red and multicolor.
  Child writing / Small port city.

10 TĀLĀ   140 x 72mm **Cat.#27**
  Brown and multicolor.
  Man picking bananas / Shoreline.

20 TĀLĀ   140 x 72mm **Cat.#28**
  Brown and multicolor.
  Fisherman with net / Round building.

50 TĀLĀ   140 x 72mm **Cat.#29**
  Green and multicolor.
  H.H. Malietoa Tanumafili II, National Museum / Man
  performing traditional knife dance.

100 TĀLĀ   140 x 72mm **Cat.#30**
  Olive brown, lilac brown and multicolor.
  Malietoa Tanumafili, flag and "Fono House" (Parliament) / Harvest
  scene.

OUTMODED AND REDEEMABLE NOTES

*All older notes of all denominations issued by the Monetary Board of
Western Samoa are redeemable.*

San Marino   ITL

Italian currency is used.

©MRI BANKERS' GUIDE TO FOREIGN CURRENCY
P.O.Box 3174 HOUSTON TX 77253 USA

São Tomé and Príncipe

São Tomé e Príncipe • São Tomé und Príncipe •
Sto. Tomé y Príncipe • Saint-Thomas et Prince **STD**

Dobra(s) = 100 centimo(s).
Minor unit coins are not used.

Currency import-export restrictions:
Local currency in/out: forbidden.
Foreign currency in: free, may declare.
Out: up to amount imported and declared.
Some establishments require payment in U.S. dollars or CFA francs.

Alternative currencies: FRF, GBP, PTE, USD.

A BRIEF MONETARY HISTORY
1976 dobra = 1 escudo.

Issuer: "BANCO CENTRAL DE S.TOMÉ E PRINCIPE"

CURRENT NOTES

5,000 DOBRAS　　　129 x 67mm Issued 5 Aug 1997 **Cat.#65**
22 Oct 1996 Violet brown, rose, green and multicolor / Purple, rose and multicolor.
Rei Amador and bird (Papa figo) / Esplanade and modern building.

10,000 DOBRAS　　　136 x 67mm Issued 5 Aug 1997 **Cat.#66**
Green, azure and orange brown.
Rei Amador and bird (Óssobô) / Bridge with palm trees and mountain in background.

20,000 DOBRAS　　　143 x 67mm Issued 5 Aug 1997 **Cat.#67**
22 Oct 1997 Red, olive, green, brown, azure and multicolor.
Rei Amador and bird (Camussela) / Village by the sea.

50,000 DOBRAS　　　150 x 67mm Issued 5 Aug 1997 **Cat.#68**
22 Oct 1997 Brown and multicolor.
Rei Amador and bird (Conóbia) / Building.

OUTMODED AND REDEEMABLE NOTES

Smaller notes not listed because of low value.

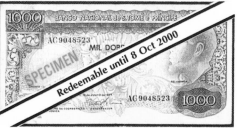

1,000 DOBRAS B.N. de S.Tomé e Príncipe　　　160 x 80mm **Cat.#55**
1977-89 Blue and multicolor.
Rei Amador and bananas / Man cutting fruit off tree.　　*ru8oct2000*

1,000 DOBRAS B.C. de S.Tomé e Príncipe　　　160 x 80mm **Cat.#63**
26 Aug 1993 Violet, blue and multicolor.
Rei Amador and bananas / Man cutting fruit off tree.　　*ru8oct2000*

Saudi Arabia

Saudi-Arabien • Arabia Saudita • Arabie Saoudite **SAR**

Riyal(s) = 100 halala(s).

Currency import-export restrictions:
Local currency in/out: 100,000 riyals.
Foreign in/out: Israeli currency forbidden. Other free.

Alternative currencies: all major.

Issuer: "SAUDI ARABIAN MONETARY AGENCY."

CURRENT NOTES

1 RIYAL　　　134 x 62mm **Cat.#21**
Brown and multicolor.
Fahd and coin / Desert flowers.

5 RIYALS　　　145 x 66mm **Cat.#22**
Purple and multicolor.
Fahd and dhows / Oil refinery at Ras Tanura.

10 RIYALS   150 x 68mm **Cat.#23**
Black, brown, purple and multicolor.
Fahd and Murabba palace / Palm grove.

20 RIYALS   152 x 69mm **Cat.#28**
Grey, brown, blue and red / Grey, brown and blue.
Abdul Aziz and Qiba Mosque / Annur Mountain.

50 RIYALS   155 x 70mm **Cat.#24**
Green and multicolor.
Fahd and Dome of the Holy Rock in Jerusalem / View of Al-Aqsa
Mosque in Jerusalem.

100 RIYALS   160 x 72mm **Cat.#25**
Brown violet and multicolor.
Fahd and old part of the Prophet Mosque in Medina / Holy
Mosque in Medina.

200 RIYALS   163 x 73mm **Cat.#31**
Green, grey, brown and red / Grey, brown and green.
Abdul Aziz and Al Mussmack Palace / Al Mussmack Palace gate.
Commemorative of the centennial of the kingdom.

500 RIYALS   166 x 74mm **Cat.#26**
Lilac blue and multicolor.
Abdul Aziz ibn Saud and view of the Holy Kaaba / Holy Mosque
of Makkah.

OUTMODED AND REDEEMABLE NOTES

All older notes are redeemable by the Saudi Arabia Monetary
Authority.

1 RIYAL   130 x 66mm Issued 19 April 1977 **Cat.#16**
Brown and multicolor.
Faisal and Jabal al-Nur mountain in Mecca / Dhahran airport.

5 RIYALS   152 x 70mm Issued 19 April 1977 **Cat.#17**
Green, brown and multicolor.
Faisal and irrigation canal / Jisan Dam.

10 RIYALS   164 x 74mm Issued 1 Oct 1977 **Cat.#18**
Purplish brown and multicolor.
Faisal and offshore drilling platform / Oil refinery.

50 RIYALS   177 x 82mm Issued 9 Oct 1976 **Cat.#19**
Green and multicolor.
Faisal and Holy Prophet's Mosque in Medina, with green dome
and adjoining minaret / Other view of same mosque.

100 RIYALS   182 x 85mm Issued 9 Oct 1976 **Cat.#20**
Blue and multicolor.
Abdul Aziz ibn Saud and al-Haram mosque at Mecca / Interior of
Holy Prophet's Mosque in Medina.

50 POUNDS Clydesdale Bank plc   155 x 85mm **Cat.#225**
22 March 1996 Green, brown and multicolor.
Adam Smith / 18th century artifacts.
Small size, it replaces the larger 1989 type.

100 POUNDS Bank of Scotland   164 x 90mm **Cat.#123**
17 July 1995 Red and multicolor.
Sir Walter Scott / Leisure and Tourism.
Issued to commemorate the Bank's Tercentenary.

100 POUNDS Clydesdale Bank plc   164 x 90mm **Cat.#223**
1991 Red and multicolor.
Lord Kelvin / University of Glasgow Lecture room.
Larger notes dated before 1985 are outmoded.

100 POUNDS Clydesdale Bank plc   164 x 90mm **Cat.#228**
2 Oct 1996 Lilac, purple and multicolor.
Lord Kelvin / Glasgow University.
With windowed security thread and gold foil seal.

100 POUNDS Royal Bank of Scotland   164 x 90mm **Cat.#350**
1987- Pink and multicolor.
Lord Ilay / Balmoral Castle.

OUTMODED AND REDEEMABLE NOTES

Coins are replacing one pound notes.

Old notes from these banks are redeemable:
Bank of Scotland
British Linen Bank,
The Clydesdale Bank Ltd.
Clydesdale & North of Scotland Bank Ltd.
Commercial Bank of Scotland, Limited,
The National Bank of Scotland, Ltd.
National Commercial Bank of Scotland, Ltd.
North of Scotland & Town & Country Bank, Limited,
North of Scotland Bank Ltd.,
Royal Bank of Scotland and
The Union Bank of Scotland, Limited.

Senegal Sénégal   XOF

It uses notes issued by "BANQUE CENTRALE DES ETATS DE L'AFRIQUE DE L'OUEST."

For description of notes and currency import-export restrictions see WEST AFRICAN STATES.

Alternative currencies: FRF, USD.

Serbia   Srpska • Serbien • Serbie

It uses Yugoslavian dinars.

Seychelles Seychellen   SCR

Rupee(s) = 100 cent(s).

Currency import-export restrictions:
Local currency in: free; out: SCR 100.
Foreign currency in/out: free.   2JUN1997
Visitors must settle their hotel and travel expenses with hard
currency or with rupees with proof of exchange in banks.

Alternative currencies: DEM, GBP, USD.

Issuer: "CENTRAL BANK OF SEYCHELLES."

CURRENT NOTES

10 RUPEES   130 x 65mm Cat.#32
Dark blue, green, orange red and multicolor.
Building, four people in uniform and man with flags / People
dancing.

10 RUPEES   150 x 75mm Issued 18 May 1998 **Cat.#36**
Blue, green, brown and multicolor.
Coco-de-Mer palm and black spotted trigger fish / Hawksbill
turtle, Fairy Terns and Coco-de-Mer palm.

25 RUPEES   140 x 70mm Cat.#33
Purplish brown and multicolor.
Building, two people with coconuts and man / Ox driven mill.

25 RUPEES   150 x 75mm Issued 18 May 1998 **Cat.#37**
Dark purple, deep pink and multicolor.
"Wrights gardinia" flower and lion fish / Seychelles blue pigeon,
coconut crab and Bi-Centennary monument.

50 RUPEES   150 x 75mm Issued 18 May 1998 **Cat.#38**
Green, brown and multicolor.
Orchid "Paille en Que" and Angel fish / Flightless white troathed
rail or "Tiomitio", yellow fin tuna and the Clock Tower.

100 RUPEES   150 x 75mm Issued 18 May 1998 **Cat.#39**
Red and multicolor.
Pitcher plant and Vielle Babone Cecile / Giant land tortoise and
bridled tern.

OUTMODED AND REDEEMABLE NOTES

*All older notes issued by the Government of Seychelles, Republic of
Seychelles, Seychelles Monetary Authority and Central Bank of
Seychelles are redeemable.*

*Red "fish" notes of 100 RUPEES of the Seychelles Monetary Authority
are redeemable at the Central Bank, provided their serial numbers
are A000,001 to A300,000.*

Sierra Leone   SLL

Leone(s) = 100 cent(s).
Prices are still quoted in "pounds". One "pound" equals 2 leones.
Minor unit coins are not used.

Currency import-export restrictions:
Local currency in or out: Le 50,000.
Foreign currency in: free, provided it is not from countries which
prohibit its export. Declaration optional.
Foreign currency out: free to USD 5,000 or to amount imported and
declared.   Aug1998

Alternative currencies: GBP, USD.

A BRIEF MONETARY HISTORY
Aug 1964: leone = 0.50 West African pound

Issuer: "BANK OF SIERRA LEONE."

CURRENT NOTES

Smaller notes not listed because of low value.

500 LEONES   160 x 74mm **Cat.#19**
27 April 1991 Green, red and multicolor.
Dr J Saidu Momoh and building / Two ships.

500 LEONES   160 x 74mm Issued in January 1996 **Cat.#24**
27 April 1995 Green, reddish brown and multicolor.
Kai Londo / Two ships.

1,000 LEONES   160 x 74mm Issued in July 1993 **Cat.#20**
4 Aug 1993 Red, yellow and multicolor.
Bai Bureh / Antenna.

5,000 LEONES   160 x 74mm Issued in July 1993 **Cat.#21**
4 Aug 1993 Blue, violet and multicolor.
Senge Pieh / Dam.

Singapore Singapur • Singapour   **SGD**

Dollar(s) = 100 cent(s).

The import and export of local and foreign currencies are free.

Alternative currencies: all major.

A BRIEF MONETARY HISTORY
12 June 1967: Republic of Singapore currency notes were issued.
Malayan Currency Union ceased.

Issuer: "BOARD OF COMMISSIONERS OF CURRENCY, SINGAPORE."

CURRENT NOTES

2 DOLLARS   132 x 63mm Issued in 1992 **Cat.#28**
Purple and multicolor.
"Tongkang" boat / Chingay procession.

5 DOLLARS   133 x 66mm Issued in 1989 **Cat.#19**
Green, violet and multicolor.
"Twakow" boats / PSA container terminal.

10 DOLLARS   143 x 69mm Issued 1 March 1988 **Cat.#20**
Red and multicolor.
Barter trading vessel "Palari" / Public housing.

25 DOLLARS   141 x 79mm Issued in mid-1996 **Cat.#33**
Reddish brown, green and multicolor.
Monetary Authority of Singapore building / View of the financial
district skyline.
Commemorative of 25 years of the Monetary Authority of Singapore.

50 DOLLARS   155 x 74mm Issued in 1987 **Cat.#22**
Blue and multicolor.
Coaster vessel "Perak" / Benjamin Sheares Bridge.
Without (Cat.#22) and with windowed security thread (Cat.#22b).

50 DOLLARS   155 x 74mm   **Cat.#32**
Slate, red, yellow and multicolor.
Coaster vessel / Benjamin Sheares Bridge.
With "cleartext" windowed security thread reading "$50 SINGAPORE" in four languages.

100 DOLLARS   165 x 77mm Issued in 1985 **Cat.#23**
Brown and multicolor.
Passenger liner "Chusan" / Changi Airport.
Without (Cat.#23), and since 1995 with windowed "Cleartext" security thread which reads "$100 SINGAPORE" in 4 official languages.

500 DOLLARS   175 x 83mm Issued 1 March 1988 **Cat.#24**
Green and multicolor.
General cargo vessel "Neptune Sardonys" / People from the Armed Forces and Civil Defence Force.

1,000 DOLLARS   185 x 88mm Issued 22 Oct 1984 **Cat.#25**
Purple and multicolor.
Container ship "Neptune Garnet" / Ship repair yard.

10,000 DOLLARS   203 x 133mm Issued in 1987 **Cat.#26**
Red and multicolor.
General bulk carrier "Neptune Canopus" / 1987 National Day parade.

OUTMODED AND REDEEMABLE NOTES

All older and commemorative notes of all denominations are legal tender, but seldom found in circulation.

Slovakia   Slovenská Republika •
Slowakei • Eslovaquia • Slovaquie   **SKK**

Koruna (koruny or korún) = 100 halierov (halier).
Minor unit coins are not used.

Currency import/export restrictions:
Local or foreign in/out: 150,000 Kr. or equivalent.
Larger amounts must be declared to Customs. (Effective 1 Dec 1996.)

Visitors must show on arrival a credit card or USD15 or equivalent in cash for each day of stay.

Alternative currencies: CZK and all major.

A BRIEF MONETARY HISTORY
1993: 1 Slovak koruna = 1 federal Czechoslovak koruna.

Issuer: "NÁRODNA BANKA SLOVENSKÁ."

CURRENT NOTES

20 KORÚN   128 x 65mm Issued 30 Sep 1993 **Cat.#20**
1993- Dark gray, green and yellow.
Prince Pribina / Castle of Nitra and a part of coral necklace.

50 KORÚN   134 x 68mm   Issued 30 Aug 1993   **Cat.#21**
1993- Dark gray and blue.
St. Cyril and St. Metod / Allegory of the old Slavonic alphabet "Hlaholika".

100 KORÚN   140 x 71mm   Issued 30 Sep 1993   **Cat.#22**
1993- Dark grey, red, yellow and orange.
Madonna by master wood-carver Pavel of Levoča / City hall in Levoča and church of St. Jacob.
Back changed from yellow to red orange in 1996 notes.

200 KORÚN   146 x 74mm   Issued in September 1995   **Cat.#26**
1 Aug 1995   Green, rose and gray.
Anton Bernolák / View of Trnava.

200 KORUN   146 x 74mm   Issued 10 May 1999   **Cat.#30**
A similar note with improved security devices was issued May 10. Details not available.

500 KORÚN   152 x 77mm   Issued 15 Nov 1993   **Cat.#23**
1993- Dark gray and brown.
Ludovít Štúr / Castle of Bratislava and church of St. Nicholaus.
Those dated 1996 have the back changed from brown to brown and blue.

500 KORUN   152 x 77mm   **Cat.#31**
A similar note with improved security devices is planned in 2000.

1,000 KORÚN   158 x 80mm   Issued 29 Oct 1993   **Cat.#24**
1993- Magenta, purple and dark gray.
Andrej Hlinka / Madonna of church of Liptovské Sliače near Ružomberok, and church of St. Andrew in Ružomberok.

1,000 KORUN   158 x 80mm   **Cat.#32**
A similar note with improved security devices will be issued in September 1999.

5,000 KORÚN   164 x 83mm   Issued 22 May 1995   **Cat.#29**
3 April 1995   Orange brown, olive and multicolor.
Milan Rastislav Štefánik / Štefánik's grave on Bradlo Hill, Ursa Major constellation and pasque-flower.

5,000 KORUN   164 x 83mm   **Cat.#33**
A similar note with improved security devices will be issued in June 1999.

Slovenia
Slovenija • Slowenien • Eslovenia • Slovénie   SIT

Tolar(jev) = 100 stotins (stotinov).

Currency import-export restrictions:
Local: in or out 300,000 tolars or up to equivalent of DM 3,000.
Foreign in/out: free. Declaration required for amounts above the equivalent of SIT 2,200,000. Residents require prior approval for the export of amounts exceeding DEM 3,000 or equivalent.   Jul1998

Alternative currencies: DEM, GBP, ITL, USD.

A BRIEF MONETARY HISTORY
9 Oct 1991: unit = 1 Yugoslavian dinar
1992: tolar = 1 unit

Issuer: "BANKA SLOVENIJE."

CURRENT NOTES

Smaller notes not listed because of low value.

20 TOLARJEV   126 x 63mm   Issued 28 Dec 1992   **Cat.#12**
15 Jan 1992   Olive brown, orange and green.
Janez Vajkard Valvasor / Two angels.

50 TOLARJEV   132 x 66mm   Issued 19 March 1993   **Cat.#13**
15 Jan 1992   Black, violet, orange brown and multicolor / Dark blue, violet and brown.
Jurij Vega / Solar system and façade of the Academy of Sciences and Arts of Ljubljana.

100 TOLARJEV   138 x 69mm Issued 30 Sep 1992 **Cat.#14**
15 Jan 1992 Dark olive and multicolor/ Multicolor.
Painter Rihard Jakopič / Detail from painting "Sun" and
"Jakopičev paviljon".

200 TOLARJEV   144 x 72mm Issued 22 Feb 1993 **Cat.#15**
1992- Brown, gray, green and multicolor.
Iacobus Gallus / Musical score and façade of the Slovene
Philharmonic.

500 TOLARJEV   150 x 75mm Issued 30 Sep 1992 **Cat.#16**
15 Jan 1992 Dark olive, rose red, orange multicolor.
Architect Jože Plećnik / Façade of National and University Library
in Ljubljana.

1,000 TOLARJEV   156 x 78mm Issued 30 Sep 1992 **Cat.#17**
15 Jan 1992 Olive brown, green, yellow green and multicolor.
Poet France Prešeren / Poem "Zdravica".

1,000 TOLARJEV   156 x 78mm Issued 13 Dec 1993 **Cat.#18**
1 June 1993 Olive brown, green, yellow green and red orange.
Poet France Prešeren / Poem "Zdravica".

5,000 TOLARJEV   156 x 78mm Issued 13 Dec 1993 **Cat.#19**
1 June 1993 Red, green and brown.
Painter Ivana Kobilca / National Gallery façade.

5,000 TOLARJEV   156 x 78mm Issued 10 Feb 1998 **Cat.#21**
8 Oct 1997 Red, green and brown.
Painter Ivana Kobilca / National Gallery façade.

10,000 TOLARJEV   156 x 78mm Issued 15 March 1995 **Cat.#20**
28 June 1994 Lilac brown and orange brown.
Writer Ivan Cankar / Chrysanthemum.

OUTMODED AND REDEEMABLE NOTES

Smaller notes not listed because of low value.

50 (UNITS) = 50 TOLARJEV   *150 x 73mm Cat.#5*
   Olive.
   Mountains / Value.

100 (UNITS) = 100 TOLARJEV   *150 x 73mm Cat.#6*
   Reddish brown and olive/Orange brown.
   Mountains / Value.

200 (UNITS) = 200 TOLARJEV   *150 x 73mm Cat.#7*
   Green and grayish brown.
   Mountain / Value.

500 (UNITS) = 500 TOLARJEV   *150 x 73mm Cat.#8*
   Lilac / Lilac.
   Mountain / Value.

1,000 (UNITS) = 1,000 TOLARJEV   *150 x 73mm Cat.#9*
   Green and gray.
   Mountain / Value.

5,000 (UNITS) = 5,000 TOLARJEV   *150 x 73mm Cat.#10*
   Lavender.
   Mountain / Value.

Solomon Islands

Salomonen • Islas Salomones • Iles Salomon   **SBD**

Dollar(s) = 100 cent(s).

Currency import-export restrictions:
Local currency in: free; out: S I$ 250.
Foreign currency in: free.
Out: up to amount imported and declared.

Alternative currencies: AUD, GBP, USD.

A BRIEF MONETARY HISTORY
1977: 1 dollar = 1 Australian dollar.

Issuer: "CENTRAL BANK OF SOLOMON ISLANDS."

CURRENT NOTES

2 DOLLARS   139 x 70mm **Cat.#13**
Grayish green and multicolor.
Arms / Fishermen with spears.
Without (Cat.#13) and with "cleartext" security thread and ascending serial numbers (Cat.#18) It may be replaced by a coin.

5 DOLLARS   144 x 72mm **Cat.#14**
Blue and multicolor.
Arms / Long boats and hut.
Without (Cat.#14) and with "cleartext" security thread and ascending serial numbers (Cat.#19).

10 DOLLARS   147 x 74mm **Cat.#15**
Purple, brown violet and multicolor.
Arms / Shell money making.
Without (Cat.#15) and with "cleartext" security thread and ascending serial numbers (Cat.#20).

20 DOLLARS   153 x 77mm **Cat.#16**
Brown, orange and multicolor.
Arms / Dancers.
Without (Cat.#16) and with "cleartext" security thread and ascending serial numbers (Cat.#21).

50 DOLLARS   159 x 80mm **Cat.#17**
Green, violet and multicolor.
Arms / Butterflies and reptiles.
Without (Cat.#17) and with "cleartext" security thread and ascending serial numbers and violet added to back (Cat.#22).

100 DOLLARS   **Cat.#23**
A new note is being planned.

OUTMODED AND REDEEMABLE NOTES

All older notes of all denominations with Elizabeth II are legal tender, but seldom found in circulation.

©MRI BANKERS' GUIDE TO FOREIGN CURRENCY
P.O.BOX 3174 HOUSTON TX 77253 USA

Somalia   Soomaaliya • Somalía • Somalie   SOS

Shilin = 100 sent(i).
Small unit coins are not used.

In view of the chaotic situation and absence of an effective government structure, it is doubtful that currency restrictions are enforced.

Currency import-export restrictions:
Local currency in/out: Sh. 1,000.
Foreign currency in: free, must declare.
Out: up to amount imported and declared.

Alternative currencies: ETB; KES; AED and USD.

A BRIEF MONETARY HISTORY
22 May 1950: somalo established at par with East African shilling.
1 July 1960: name changed to scellino(i).
1975: name changed to shilin soomaali.

Notes carry the name of: "CENTRAL BANK OF SOMALIA."

CURRENT NOTES

Smaller notes not listed because of low value.

1,000 SHILIN   154 x 76mm **Cat.#37**
1990- Lilac, orange and greenish blue / Multicolor.
Women weaving baskets / Row of buildings and port of Mogadishu.
Forgeries abound.

There are reports that new notes were printed.

Somaliland   Somalilandia • Somalilande

Somaliland shilling.

Visitors must exchange US$50.00 upon arrival.

A BRIEF MONETARY HISTORY
Somaliland shilling introduced December 1994 at 1,000 Somali shillings.

Issuer: "BAANKA SOMALILAND"

CURRENT NOTES

Smaller notes not listed because of low value.

100 SHILIN   135 x 61mm **Cat.#5**
1994- Brown, red and multicolor.
Building / Herd of sheep with ship in background.

500 SHILIN   145 x 66mm **Cat.#6**
1994- Dark green, violet gray and multicolor / Violet blue and multicolor.
Building / Herd of sheep with ship in background.

South Africa   Suid Afrika •
Südafrika • Africa del Sur • Afrique du Sud   ZAR

Rand = 100 cent(s).

Currency import-export restrictions:
Local currency in/out: R 5,000. No limits to or from Lesotho, Namibia or Swaziland.
Foreign currency in: free, must declare.
Out: up to amount imported and declared.   Jul1998

Alternative currencies: all major.

A BRIEF MONETARY HISTORY
1961: rand = 0.50 South African pound.

Issuer: "SOUTH AFRICAN RESERVE BANK."

South African currency is used in Lesotho, Namibia and Swaziland.

CURRENT NOTES

10 RAND   128 x 70mm Issued ca. October 1993 **Cat.#123**
Green and brown.
Rhinoceros / Ram's head.

20 RAND   134 x 70mm Issued ca. April 1993 **Cat.#124**
Violet brown and multicolor.
Elephants / Open pit mining.

©MRI BANKERS' GUIDE TO FOREIGN CURRENCY
P.O.BOX 3174 HOUSTON TX 77253 USA

50 RAND　　　140 x 70mm　Issued in 1992　**Cat.#125**
Reddish lilac, brown and multicolor.
Lion and pride of lions by water / Petrochemical complex.

100 RAND　　　146 x 70mm　Issued 2 April 1994　**Cat.#126**
Gray, violet brown and orange.
Buffaloes / Tourism motif, showing zebras.

200 RAND　　　152 x 70mm　Issued 1 Oct 1994　**Cat.#127**
Lilac brown, orange and green.
Leopards / Bridge and antenna.

OUTMODED AND REDEEMABLE NOTES

No South African currency has to date been demonetized and all banknotes of previous issues are regarded as legal tender, even though they are withdrawn from circulation after a new series has been issued. One South African pound equals two Rands.

Spain　España • Spanien • Espagne　　ESP

Euro = 166.386 pesetas　Peseta(s)

Currency import-export restrictions:
Local or foreign currency in: free, declaration needed for amounts over ESP 1,000,000 or equivalent.
Out: declaration required for amounts over ESP 1,000,000 or equivalent; form may be filed with Customs, Banco de España or any commercial or savings bank or credit cooperatives.　　Jul1998

Alternative currencies: all major.

A BRIEF MONETARY HISTORY:
1 Jan 1999: Euro adopted at 166.386 pesetas.

Issuer: "BANCO DE ESPAÑA", after 2002 "EUROPEAN CENTRAL BANK."

CURRENT NOTES

1,000 PESETAS　　　138 x 76mm　**Cat.#158**
23 Oct 1979　Green and multicolor.
Benito Pérez Galdós / Mountains and map.
It will be withdrawn from circulation soon.

1,000 PESETAS　　130 x 65mm　Issued in 12 Oct 1994　**Cat.#163**
12 Oct 1992　Green and multicolor.
Hernán Cortés / Francisco Pizarro.
Commemorates the 5th Centennial of the Discovery of America by Columbus.

2,000 PESETAS　　　138 x 68mm　Issued in May 1993　**Cat.#162**
24 April 1992　Red and multicolor.
José C Mutis observing flower / Royal Botanical Garden gate and title page of Mutis' "Historia de los Árboles…"
Commemorates the Fifth Centennial of the Discovery of America by Columbus.

2,000 PESETAS　　138 x 68mm　Issued in late 1995　**Cat.#164**
24 April 1992　Red and multicolor.
José C Mutis observing flower / Royal Botanical Garden gate and title page of Mutis' "Historia de los Árboles…"
Modified portrait and horizontal serial number removed.

5,000 PESETAS   156 x 85mm **Cat.#160**
23 Oct 1979 Ochre violet and multicolor.
Juan Carlos / Royal palace.

5,000 PESETAS   146 x 71mm Issued in 1993 **Cat.#165**
12 Oct 1992 Ochre and multicolor.
Columbus / Astrolabe.
Commemorates the Fifth Centennial of the Discovery of America by Columbus.

10,000 PESETAS   165 x 85mm **Cat.#161**
24 Sep 1985 Blue and multicolor.
Juan Carlos / Prince of Asturias and view of the Escorial.

10,000 PESETAS   154 x 74mm Issued 20 July 1995 **Cat.#166**
12 Oct 1992 Violet blue and multicolor.
Juan Carlos and building / Jorge Juan and blueprint of a caravel.
Commemorates the Fifth Centennial of the Discovery of America by Columbus.

OUTMODED AND REDEEMABLE NOTES

Important Notice

Since the early 1990's the value of all notes issued in Burgos since 1936, and in Madrid since 1940, was restored. These can be redeemed at any branch of the Banco de España. Early notes in nice condition have great numismatic value.

Smaller notes not listed because of low value.

25 PESETAS	Burgos	21 de noviembre de 1936	Cat.#99
25 PESETAS	Burgos	20 de mayo de 1938	Cat.#110
25 PESETAS	Madrid	9 de enero de 1940	Cat.#116
25 PESETAS	Madrid	19 de febrero de 1946	Cat.#130
25 PESETAS	Madrid	22 de julio de 1954	Cat.#147
50 PESETAS	Burgos	21 de noviembre de 1936	Cat.#100
50 PESETAS	Burgos	20 de mayo de 1938	Cat.#111
50 PESETAS	Madrid	9 de enero de 1940	Cat.#117
50 PESETAS	Madrid	31 de diciembre de 1951	Cat.#142

100 PESETAS	Burgos	21 de noviembre de 1936	Cat.#101
100 PESETAS	Burgos	20 de mayo de 1938	Cat.#112
100 PESETAS	Madrid	9 de enero de 1940	Cat.#118
100 PESETAS	Madrid	19 de febrero de 1946	Cat.#131
100 PESETAS	Madrid	2 de mayo de 1948	Cat.#136
100 PESETAS	Madrid	7 de abril de 1953	Cat.#144
100 PESETAS	Madrid	19 de noviembre de 1965	Cat.#150
100 PESETAS	Madrid	17 de noviembre de 1970	Cat.#152
200 PESETAS	Madrid	16 de setiembre de 1980	Cat.#156
500 PESETAS	Burgos	21 de noviembre de 1936	Cat.#102
500 PESETAS	Burgos	20 de mayo de 1938	Cat.#113
500 PESETAS	Madrid	9 de enero de 1940	Cat.#119
500 PESETAS	Madrid	21 de octubre de 1940	Cat.#124
500 PESETAS	Madrid	19 de febrero de 1946	Cat.#132
500 PESETAS	Madrid	15 de noviembre de 1951	Cat.#140
500 PESETAS	Madrid	22 de julio de 1954	Cat.#148
500 PESETAS	Madrid	23 de julio de 1971	Cat.#153
500 PESETAS	Madrid	23 de octubre de 1979	Cat.#157
1,000 PESETAS	Burgos	21 de noviembre de 1936	Cat.#103
1,000 PESETAS	Burgos	20 de mayo de 1938	Cat.#114
1,000 PESETAS	Madrid	9 de enero de 1940	Cat.#120
1,000 PESETAS	Madrid	21 de octubre de 1940	Cat.#125
1,000 PESETAS	Madrid	19 de febrero de 1946	Cat.#133
1,000 PESETAS	Madrid	4 de noviembre de 1949	Cat.#138
1,000 PESETAS	Madrid	31 de diciembre de 1951	Cat.#143
1,000 PESETAS	Madrid	29 de noviembre de 1957	Cat.#149
1,000 PESETAS	Madrid	19 de noviembre de 1965	Cat.#151
1,000 PESETAS	Madrid	17 de setiembre de 1971	Cat.#154
2,000 PESETAS	Madrid	22 de julio de 1980	Cat.#159
5,000 PESETAS	Madrid	6 de febrero de 1976	Cat.#155

Sri Lanka   LKR

Rupee(s) = 100 cents.
Lakh(s) = 100,000 rupees.

Currency import-export restrictions:
Obtain Exchange Control form "D" on arrival.
Local currency in/out: SL Rs 1,000.
Foreign currency in: free, must declare amounts over USD 10,000 or equivalent in convertible currencies.
Out: must declare USD 10,000 or equivalent in convertible currencies.
Reconversion into cash, only at exit points (Katunayake Airport / Colombo Port).
Other banks and forex dealers can supply only checks or transfers.
In all cases supporting receipts are needed.

Alternative currencies: All major, AED, SAR.

Issuer: "CENTRAL BANK OF SRI LANKA", formerly "CENTRAL BANK OF CEYLON."

CURRENT NOTES

10 RUPEES Central Bank of Ceylon,   127 x 67mm **Cat.#92**
  or Central Bank of Sri Lanka   **Cat.#96**
1982-89 Olive green and multicolor.
"Octagon, Temple of the Tooth Relic Kandy" / Shrine.

©MRI BANKERS' GUIDE TO FOREIGN CURRENCY
P.O.BOX 3174 HOUSTON TX 77253 USA

10 RUPEES　　　　　123 x 62mm **Cat.#102**
1991-94 Green, yellow, brown and multicolor.
Lion stone carving / Presidential Secretariat building and flowers.

10 RUPEES　　　　　123 x 62mm **Cat.#108**
1995 Green, yellow, brown and multicolor.
Lion stone carving / Presidential Secretariat building and flowers.
With improved security devices.

20 RUPEES Central Bank of Ceylon　137 x 70mm **Cat.#93**
or Central Bank of Sri Lanka　　　　　　　　　　**Cat.#97**
1982-90 Violet, lilac and multicolor.
"Moonstone Anuradhapura" / Shrine.

20 RUPEES　　　　　130 x 65mm **Cat.#103**
1991-94 Purple, red and multicolor.
Traditional Sinhalese mask / Two youths fishing, and sea shells.

20 RUPEES　　　　　130 x 65mm **Cat.#109**
1995 Purple, red and multicolor.
Traditional Sinhalese mask / Two youths fishing, and sea shells.
With improved security devices.

50 RUPEES Central Bank of Ceylon.　145 x 74mm **Cat.#94**
1982 Blue and multicolor .
"Raja Maha Vihare, Kelaniya" / Ruins.

50 RUPEES Central Bank of Sri Lanka.　145 x 74mm **Cat.#98**
1989 Blue and multicolor .
"Raja Maha Vihare, Kelaniya" / Ruins.

50 RUPEES　　　　　136 x 68mm **Cat.#104**
1991-94 Blue, orange and multicolor.
Head of a Sri Lankan Kandyan dancer / Floral design.

50 RUPEES　　　　　136 x 68mm **Cat.#110**
1995 Blue, orange and multicolor.
Head of a Sri Lankan Kandyan dancer / Floral design.
With improved security devices.

100 RUPEES Central Bank of Ceylon　155 x 76mm **Cat.#95**
1982 Orange and multicolor.
Lion / Parliament.

100 RUPEES Central Bank of Sri Lanka　155 x 76mm **Cat.#99**
1987-90 Orange and multicolor.
Lion / Parliament.

100 RUPEES　　　　　144 x 72mm **Cat.#105**
1991-94 Orange and brown.
Decorative pot and moonstone / Tea pluckers.
Earlier notes have brown and orange back, later ones are orange.

100 RUPEES   144 x 72mm **Cat.#111**
  1995 Orange and brown.
  Decorative pot and moonstone / Tea pluckers.
  With improved security devices.

200 RUPEES   146 x 74mm Issued 4 Feb 1998 **Cat.#114**
  1998-02-04 Blue and light orange,
  Building and allegories of progress during 50 years of
  Independence / Building and allegories of the National Heritage.
  Printed on polymer. It commemorates 50th Independence Anniversary. Some,
  with red serial numbers, were issued in special folders. Regular notes have black
  serial numbers.

500 RUPEES Central Bank of Ceylon   165 x 79mm **Cat.#89**
  1981-85 Purple and multicolor.
  Elephant / Temple.

500 RUPEES Central Bank of Sri Lanka   165 x 79mm **Cat.#100**
  1987-90 Purple and multicolor.
  Elephant / Abhayagiri Stupa, Anuradhapura.

500 RUPEES   150 x 75mm **Cat.#106**
  1991-94 Brown, violet, brown orange and multicolor.
  Two drummers and a dancer / "Ruwanve-lisaya Dagoba
  Anuradhapura" building behind columns and vegetation.

500 RUPEES   150 x 75mm **Cat.#112**
  1995 Brown, violet, brown orange and multicolor.
  Two drummers and a dancer / "Ruwanve-lisaya Dagoba
  Anuradhapura" building behind columns and vegetation.
  With improved security devices.

1,000 RUPEES Central Bank of Ceylon   175 x 83mm **Cat.#90**
  1981 Green and multicolor.
  Dam / Peacock and mountains.

1,000 RUPEES Central Bank of Sri Lanka   175 x 83mm **Cat.#101**
  1987-90 Green and multicolor.
  Victoria Dam / Peacock and University of Ruhuna.

1,000 RUPEES   156 x 78mm **Cat.#107**
  1991-94 Brown, green, purple and multicolor.
  Two elephants / Octagon of the Temple of the Tooth in Kandy
  and peacocks.

1,000 RUPEES   156 x 78mm **Cat.#113**
  1995 Brown, green, purple and multicolor.
  Two elephants / Octagon of the Temple of the Tooth in Kandy
  and peacocks.
  With improved security devices.

OUTMODED AND REDEEMABLE NOTES

Notes of 1; 2 and 5 Rupees not listed because of their low value.

The following notes are redeemable:

10 RUPEES 1953-54 Green and violet . . . . *Cat.#34*
10 RUPEES 1956-63 Green and violet . . . . *Cat.#40*
10 RUPEES 1964 Green and violet . . . . *Cat.#64*
10 RUPEES 1968-77 Green and violet . . . . *Cat.#69*
10 RUPEES 1979 Green and multicolor . . . . *Cat.#66*

20 RUPEES 1979 Green and multicolor . . . . *Cat.#67*

50 RUPEES 1970 Blue on multicolor . . . . *Cat.#77*
50 RUPEES 1972-74 Purple and greenish blue . . . . *Cat.#79*
50 RUPEES 1979 Blue, brown and multicolor . . . . *Cat.#68*

100 RUPEES 1970 Violet brown and multicolor . . . . *Cat.#78*
100 RUPEES 1971-75 Purple, gray and multicolor . . . . . . *Cat.#80*
100 RUPEES 1979 Gold, green and multicolor . . . . *Cat.#69*

Sudan Sudán • Soudan SDD

Dinar = 100 piastres

It is unclear whether the import and export of local and foreign currencies are free. Currency Declarations may have to be filed.

Alternative currencies: GBP, USD.

A BRIEF MONETARY HISTORY
April 1957: Sudanese pound created at par with Egyptian pound.
1992: dinar = 10 pounds; both currencies coexist.
March 1999: the dinar becomes the only currency.
Issuer: "BANK OF SUDAN."

CURRENT NOTES

Smaller notes not listed because of low value.

25 DINARS 140 x 65mm **Cat.#53**
  1992 Olive green and brown.
  Large building / Circular design.

50 DINARS 140 x 65mm **Cat.#54**
  1992 Blue, olive and brown.
  Large building / Value.
  There are two slightly different varieties.

100 DINARS 140 x 65mm **Cat.#55**
  1994 Blue, orange brown, brown violet and multicolor / Lilac brown, purple brown and multicolor.
  Building / Building.
  Without or with windowed security thread.

1,000 DINARS 140 x 65mm **Cat.#57**
  1996 Green, yellow brown and purple.
  Building / Building.

Suriname SRG

Gulden = 100 cent.
Minor unit coins are not used.

Currency import-export restrictions:
Local currency in/out: Sf 100.
Foreign currency in: free, must declare.
Out: up to amount imported and declared.
Arriving visitors must convert NLG 300 or equivalent at SRG 53 per USD1.00.
Reconversion allowed, provided SRG 50 or more were spent per day of stay.

Alternative currencies: FRF, NLG, USD.

Issuer: "CENTRALE BANK VAN SURINAME."

CURRENT NOTES

Smaller notes not listed because of low value.

100 GULDEN 145 x 69mm Issued in 1993 **Cat.#49**
  9 July 1991 Purple brown, red and green.
  Central Bank of Surinam building / Open mining and toucan.

500 GULDEN　　　145 x 69mm Issued in 1993 **Cat.#50**
9 July 1991 Brown, red, green and multicolor / Multicolor.
Central Bank of Surinam building / Oil drilling and toucan.

1,000 GULDEN　　　145 x 69mm Issued in 1993 **Cat.#51**
1 July 1993 Gray, red and green on rose.
Central Bank of Suriname building / Harvest scene.

2,000 GULDEN　　　145 x 69mm **Cat.#52**
1 June 1995 Gray, red and green.
Central Bank of Suriname building / Logging scene.

5,000 GULDEN　　　145 x 69mm Issued in early 1998 **Cat.#53**
5 October 1997 Violet, green, red and multicolor.
Building / Bird and banana bunches.

10,000 GULDEN　　　145 x 69mm Issued in early 1998 **Cat.#54**
5 October 1997 Green, red, rose and multicolor.
Building / Bird and industrial complex.

OUTMODED AND REDEEMABLE NOTES

Notes dated 1986 are redeemable until 31 July 2023.

Swaziland　　Swasiland • Suazilandia　　**SZL**

Lilangeni (emalangeni) = 100 cent(s).
Parity: ZAR 1.00. South African rand are widely used.

Currency import-export restrictions:
Local currency in/out: E 500. Unlimited to or from South Africa and Lesotho.
Foreign currency: import free, export up to amount declared on entry.　　　Jul1998

Alternative currencies: GBP, USD, ZAR.

A BRIEF MONETARY HISTORY
1974: 1 lilangeni = 1 South African rand.

Issuer: "CENTRAL BANK OF SWAZILAND."

CURRENT NOTES

5 EMALANGENI　　　138 x 63mm **Cat.#14**
Green and multicolor.
Mswati III / Swazi Regiment.

5 EMALANGENI　　　138 x 63mm **Cat.#19**
Green olive and multicolor.
Mswati III / Swazi regiment.

5 EMALANGENI　　　148 x 69mm Issued in 1995 **Cat.#23**
Green olive, brown and multicolor.
Mswati III / Swazi regiment.

10 EMALANGENI　　　144 x 66mm **Cat.#15**
Violet blue and multicolor.
Mswati III / Luphohlo hydroelectric complex.

10 EMALANGENI　　　148 x 67mm **Cat.#20**
　Violet blue and multicolor.
　Mswati III (New portrait) / Hydroelectric complex.
　Without (Cat.#20) and with windowed security thread (Cat.#26).

20 EMALANGENI　　　150 x 69mm **Cat.#21**
　Purple and multicolor.
　Mswati III / Agricultural products.

20 EMALANGENI　　　150 x 69mm **Cat.#17**
　Same as previous note, with triangular overprint to
　commemorate the 21st Birthday of King Mswati.

20 EMALANGENI　　　150 x 69mm **Cat.#21**
　Magenta and multicolor.
　Mswati III / Cattle and truck.
　Without (Cat.#21), and with windowed security thread (Cat.#27).

50 EMALANGENI　　　157 x 72mm **Cat.#22**
　Orange red, orange brown, green and multicolor.
　Mswati III / Central Bank building.

50 EMALANGENI　　　152 x 70mm **Cat.#26**
　1 April 1995 Orange red, orange brown, green and multicolor.
　Mswati III / Central Bank building.
　With a continuous holographic band at right.

100 EMALANGENI　　　156 x 70mm **Cat.#27**
　6.9.1996 Brown and multicolor.
　Mswati III / Rock formation.

200 EMALANGENI　　　161 x 70mm **Cat.#30**
　8.9.1998 Green and lilac brown.
　Mswati III / Traditional Swazi village.
　Commemorative of the 30th Independence Anniversary. With a continuous
　holographic band at right.

OUTMODED AND REDEEMABLE NOTES

*All older notes issued by the Monetary Authority of Swaziland and
the Central Bank of Swaziland are legal tender, but seldom found in
circulation.*

Sweden
Sverige • Schweden • Suecia • Suède　　　**SEK**

Krona (kronor) = 100 öre.

The import and export of local and foreign currencies are free.

Alternative currencies: all major.

Issuer: "SVERIGES RIKSBANK."

CURRENT NOTES

20 KRONOR　　　131 x 72mm Issued in 1991 **Cat.#61**
　Violet and multicolor.
　Selma Lagerlöf / Scene from "Nils Holgersson's Wonderful
　Journey through Sweden."

20 KRONOR   121 x 67mm Issued 15 Sep 1997 **Cat.#63**
Violet and multicolor.
Selma Lagerlöf / Scene from "Nils Holgersson's Wonderful Journey through Sweden."

50 KRONOR   120 x 77mm Issued 22 March 1996 **Cat.#62**
Olive green, rose and light brown / Olive green, light brown and multicolor.
Soprano Jenny Lind, musical score, theater scene and rose / Silver harp.

100 KRONOR   141 x 72mm Issued in 1986 **Cat.#57**
Blue green, brown violet and multicolor.
Carl von Linné and plants / Bee pollinating a flower, based on a photograph by Lennart Nilsson.

500 KRONOR   150 x 82mm Issued in 1989 **Cat.#59**
Gray blue and reddish brown.
Karl XI / Christopher Polhem.

1,000 KRONOR   161 x 82mm Issued in 1989 **Cat.#60**
Brown black and multicolor.
Gustav Vasa / Harvest and threshing from "History of the Nordic Peoples" by Olaus Magnus.

OUTMODED AND REDEEMABLE NOTES

Important Notice

Older demonetized notes may be exchanged at the discretion of the Sveriges Riksbank.
There is a modest fee for this service.

500 KRONOR   152 x 81mm Issued in 1989 **Cat.#58**
Blue and multicolor.
Kàrl XI / Christopher Polhem.

Switzerland

Schweiz/Suisse/Svizra/Svizzera • Suiza   **CHF**

Franc(s) = 100 centime(s).

The import and export of all currencies is free.   Jul1998

Alternative currencies: all major.

Issuer: "BANQUE NATIONALE SUISSE-BANCA NAZIONALE SVIZZERA-SCHWEIZERISCHE NATIONALBANK-BANCA NAZIUNALA SVIZRA."

CURRENT NOTES

10 FRANCS   137 x 66mm Issued 5 Nov 1979 **Cat.#180**
1979-90 Reddish brown and multicolor.
Leonhard Euler / Water turbine.

10 FRANCS   127 x 74mm Issued 8 April 1997 **Cat.#186**
Yellow, brown, green and multicolor.
Le Corbusier / The "Modulor" and architectural designs.

©MRI BANKERS' GUIDE TO FOREIGN CURRENCY
P.O.Box 3174 HOUSTON TX 77253 USA

20 FRANCS   148 x 70mm Issued 4 April 1979 **Cat.#181**
1979-89 Blue and multicolor.
Horace-Benédict de Saussure and hygrometer / Group of alpinists and ammonite.

20 FRANCS   75 x 138mm Issued 1 October 1996 **Cat.#187**
Lilac red
Arthur Honegger / Designs related to his "Pacific 231" symphony.

50 FRANCS   159 x 74mm Issued 4 April 1979 **Cat.#182**
1978-87 Green and multicolor.
Konrad Gessner / Owl, plant (Primula Auricula) and stars.

50 FRANCS   148 x 74mm Issued 3 Oct 1995 **Cat.#188**
Green and multicolor.
Sophie Taeuber-Arp / Some of her designs.

100 FRANCS   170 x 78mm Issued 4 Oct 1978 **Cat.#183**
1976-91 Blue violet and multicolor.
Francesco Castelli, known as Borromini / Church of St. Ivo.

100 FRANCS   159 x 74mm Issued 1 Oct 1998 **Cat.#189**
Blue.
Alberto Giacometti / Four of his sculptures.
The "100" in position D is made of very tiny holes visible through the light.

200 FRANCS   74 x 170mm Issued in October 1997 **Cat.#190**
Brown, yellow and gray.
Charles Ferdinand Ramuz / Diableret massif, Lake Geneva and manuscripts of his works.
The "200" in position D is made of very tiny holes visible through the light.

500 FRANCS   181 x 82mm Issued 4 April 1977 **Cat.#184**
1977-92 Brown and multicolor.
Albrecht von Haller / Anatomical figure and plant.

©MRI BANKERS' GUIDE TO FOREIGN CURRENCY
P.O.BOX 3174 HOUSTON TX 77253 USA

1,000 FRANCS   192 x 86mm Issued 4 April 1978 **Cat.#185**
1978-93 Violet and multicolor.
Auguste Forel / Ants and anthill.

1,000 FRANCS   74 x 182mm Issued 1 April 1998 **Cat.#191**
Violet and multicolor.
Jacob Burckhardt / Historical scenes.
The "1000" in position "D" is made of very tiny holes visible through the light.

OUTMODED AND REDEEMABLE NOTES

5 FRANCS   125 x 70mm **Cat.#151**
1913-52 Brown.
Man / Value.   rruu20000430

10 FRANCS   137 x 75mm Issued 1 Oct 1956 **Cat.#174**
1955-77 Reddish brown and purple.
Keller / Flower.   rruu20000430

20 FRANCS   153 x 85mm Issued 29 March 1956 **Cat.#175**
1954-76 Blue and multicolor.
Dufour / Flower.   rruu20000430

50 FRANCS   173 x 95mm Issued 14 June 1957 **Cat.#176**
1955-74 Green and multicolor.
Girl / Apple harvest.   rruu20000430

100 FRANCS   190 x 105mm Issued 14 June 1957 **Cat.#177**
1956-73 Blue and multicolor.
Boy and lamb / Saint Martin of Tours sharing his cape. rruu20000430

500 FRANCS   210 x 115mm Issued 14 June 1957 **Cat.#178**
1957-74 Reddish brown and multicolor.
Woman / Fountain of Youth.   rruu20000430

1,000 FRANCS   230 x 125mm Issued 14 June 1957 **Cat.#179**
1954-74 Purple.
Woman / Dance of Death.   *rruu20000430*

Syria   Syrien • Siria • Syrie   **SYP**

Pound(s) = 100 piastre(s).

Currency import-export restrictions:
Local currency in: free;
Local currency out: LS 5,000 for Syrian travelers to Jordan and Lebanon; forbidden otherwise.
Foreign currency in: free, must declare amounts over US$5,000.
Foreign currency out (foreigners only): free to US$5,000 or amount imported and declared on arrival, minus money changed, with supporting receipts. Those considered to be Syrian citizens are limited to US$2,000. (Effective Jan 6, 1992). No reconversion allowed.

Non-residents must settle their bills with convertible currencies.

Alternative currencies: all major.

Issuer: "CENTRAL BANK OF SYRIA."

CURRENT NOTES

50 POUNDS   155 x 75mm **Cat.#103**
1977- Brown, black, green and multicolor.
Dam and ancient statue / Citadel.

50 POUNDS   **Cat.#106**
New type to be issued soon.

100 POUNDS   167 x 80mm **Cat.#104**
1977- Green and multicolor.
Ruins and statue of Zenobia / Grain silos.

100 POUNDS   **Cat.#107**
New type to be issued soon.

200 POUNDS   160 x 75mm **Cat.#108**
1997 Red and multicolor,
Monument of Salahedin Al-Ayoubi and tomb of the Unknown Soldier / Cotton, weaving and Energy plant.

500 POUNDS   180 x 85mm **Cat.#105**
1958- Brown, purple and multicolor.
Ugaritic relics / Cuneiform chart and golden bowl.

500 POUNDS   **Cat.#109**
New type to be issued soon.

1,000 POUNDS   170 x 75mm Issued 29 March 1998 **Cat.#110**
1997 Light brown, green and blue.
Hafez Al-Assad / Agriculture, Industry and Services.

OUTMODED AND REDEEMABLE NOTES

Old notes dated since 1958 are valid, but seldom found in use.

Taiwan - Republic of China   TWD

Yuan (NT$) = 100 cent(s).

Currency import-export restrictions:
Local currency in/out: NT$ 40,000.
Larger amounts require a permit from the Central Bank of China.
Foreign currency in and out: free, amounts over USD 5,000 must be declared to customs.

Alternative currencies: all major.

A BRIEF MONETARY HISTORY
15 June 1949: New Taiwan dollar = 40,000 Taiwan dollars.

Issuer: "THE CENTRAL BANK OF CHINA."

CURRENT NOTES

50 YUAN   164 x 69mm Issued 9 Oct 1972 **Cat.#982**
Violet, purple and light blue.
Dr Sun Yat-sen / Chungshan building.

50 YUAN   166 x 72mm Issued 15 June 1999 **Cat.#990**
Purple and multicolor / Red.
Two banknotes / Central Bank of China main building.
Commemorative of the 50th anniversary of the creation of the NT dollar.
Printed on polymer, with a golden optical variable device in a "window."

100 YUAN   162 x 69mm Issued 13 Feb 1988 **Cat.#989**
Red and multicolor.
Dr Sun Yat-sen / Chungshan building.

100 YUAN   **Cat.#991**
A new note will be issued in the near future.

500 YUAN   170 x 75mm **Cat.#987**
Brown, reddish brown and multicolor.
Chiang Kai-Shek / Chungshan building.

500 YUAN   **Cat.#992**
A new note will be issued in the near future.

1,000 YUAN   170 x 75mm Issued 15 June 1982 **Cat.#988**
Blue violet and multicolor.
Chiang Kai-Shek / Presidential office.

1,000 YUAN   **Cat.#993**
A new note will be issued in the near future.

2,000 YUAN   **Cat.#994**
A new note will be issued in the near future.

OUTMODED AND REDEEMABLE NOTES

Notes of the following types are legal tender, but rarely found in circulation.

Tajikistan   Tadschikistan • Tadjikistan   TJR

Tajik ruble(s) = 100 tanga
Minor unit coins are not used.

Alternative currencies: DEM, RUB, USD.

A BRIEF MONETARY HISTORY
10 May 1995: Tajik ruble introduced at 100 Russian rubles.

Issuer: National Bank of the Republic of Tajikistan.

CURRENT NOTES

Smaller notes not listed because of low value.

200 RUBLES   120 x 60mm Issued 10 May 1995 **Cat.#7**
1994 Olive green and purple brown.
Arms and value / Building with flag.

500 RUBLES   120 x 60mm Issued 10 May 1995 **Cat.#8**
1994 Lilac brown and light green.
Arms and value / Building with flag.

1,000 RUBLES   **Cat.#9**
1994 Printed but not issued.

Tanzania   Tansania • Tanzanie   TZS

Shilingi = 100 senti.
Minor unit coins are not used.

Currency import-export restrictions:
Local currency in/out: forbidden to visitors.
Foreign currency in: it is free to import convertible notes, must declare on a special currency declaration form.
Out: up to amount imported and declared.
Visitors may reconvert up to Sh. 7,000 with proof of exchange.
Many services (as National Park entry fees, better hotels, air and hydrofoil tickets, etc.) require payment in hard currency. It is advisable to carry smaller notes, otherwise change will be given back in shilingi.

Alternative currencies: DEM, GBP, USD.

A BRIEF MONETARY HISTORY
June 1966: Tanzanian shilling = East African shilling.

Issuer: "BENKI KUU YA TANZANIA."

CURRENT NOTES

200 SHILINGI   135 x 67mm Issued 25 May 1993 **Cat.#25**
Black, orange red and brown.
Pres. Mwinyi / Two fishermen.
CAUTION: Large size notes are legal tender, but outmoded.

500 SHILINGI   138 x 69mm Issued 28 Jan 1993 **Cat.#26**
Black, green and multicolor.
Pres Mwinyi and zebra / Cloves harvest scene.
CAUTION: Large size notes are legal tender, but outmoded.

500 SHILINGI   138 x 69mm Issued 10 March 1997 **Cat.#30**
Black, green and multicolor.
Giraffe and zebra / Cloves harvest scene.

1,000 SHILINGI   142 x 71mm Issued 28 Jan 1993 **Cat.#27**
Green, orange, brown and multicolor.
Pres. Mwinyi and elephants / Industrial buildings and door to the Peoples Bank of Zanzibar.
CAUTION: Large size notes are legal tender, but outmoded.

1,000 SHILINGI   142 x 71mm Issued 10 March 1997 **Cat.#31**
Green, orange, brown and multicolor.
Giraffe and elephants / Industrial building and door to the Peoples Bank of Zanzibar.
CAUTION: Large size notes are legal tender, but outmoded.

5,000 SHILINGI   145 x 73mm Issued 25 Jan 1995 **Cat.#28**
Brown and multicolor.
Pres. Mwini and rhinoceros / Giraffes with Mount Kilimajaro and Zanzibar Chest in background.

5,000 SHILINGI   145 x 73mm Issued 10 March 1997 **Cat.#32**
Brown and multicolor.
Giraffe and rhinoceros / Giraffes with Mount Kilimanjaro and Zanzibar chest in background.

10,000 SHILINGI   150 x 75mm Issued 25 Jan 1995 **Cat.#29**
Violet blue and multicolor.
Pres. Mwini and lion / Bank of Tanzania Head Office building and Zanzibar House of Wonder.

10,000 SHILINGI   150 x 75mm Issued 10 March 1997 **Cat.#33**
Violet blue and multicolor.
Giraffe and lion / Bank of Tanzania Head Office building and Zanzibar House of Wonder.

©MRI BANKERS' GUIDE TO FOREIGN CURRENCY
P.O.BOX 3174 HOUSTON TX 77253 USA

OUTMODED AND REDEEMABLE NOTES

Older large size notes with portrait of Pres. Mwini are still redeemable.

Thailand Tailandia • Thailande   THB

Baht = 100 satang.

Currency import-export restrictions:
Local currency in: free.
Local currency out: B50,000, or 500,000 for travelers to neighboring countries.
Foreign currency in: free.
Out: up to amount imported.

Alternative currencies: all major.

Issuer: "BANK OF THAILAND."

CURRENT NOTES

20 BAHT   139 x 72mm Issued 2 Nov 1981 **Cat.#88**
Green and multicolor.
King Bhumibol / Statue of Taksin the Great.

20 BAHT   **Cat.#104**
A polymer note may be issued in the future.

50 BAHT   144 x 72mm Issued 20 Sep 1985 **Cat.#90**
Blue and multicolor.
King Bhumibol / Statue of Rama VII.
Regular issue (Cat.#90), and with small text commemorating the 90th Birthday of the Queen Mother.

50 BAHT   144 x 72mm Issued in December 1996 **Cat.#99**
Blue, violet, yellow and multicolor.
King Bhumibol / Statue of Rama VII.
Polymer note commemorative of the 50th Anniversary of King Bhumibol's accession to the throne.

50 BAHT   144 x 72mm Issued in August 1997 **Cat.#103**
Blue, dark green, rose and multicolor.
King Bhumibol / Statue.

100 BAHT   150 x 72mm Issued in Oct 1994 **Cat.#97**
Red, brownish red and orange brown.
King Bhumibol / Statues, schoolchildren, book and monk teaching children.

500 BAHT   159 x 80mm Issued 5 Nov 1987 **Cat.#91**
Violet and multicolor.
King Bhumibol / Statue of Rama I.
There is a variety with small text commemorating the 90th Birthday of the Queen Mother.

500 BAHT   156 x 71mm Issued in 3 April 1996 **Cat.#101**
Violet and multicolor.
King Bhumibol / Statues of Kings Rama I and Rama II and palace.
There is a variety with small text commemorating the 50th Anniversary of King Bhumibol's accession to the throne.

500 BAHT   170 x 91mm Issued 9 July 1996 **Cat.#102**
Olive green, yellow and multicolor.
King Bhumibol seated on the Royal Mobile Throne, and emblem
of Golden Jubilee celebrations / King Bhumibol while performing
various activities.
Printed on polymer, to commemorate King Bhumibol Golden Jubilee.

1,000 BAHT   166 x 80mm Issued 10 August 1992 **Cat.#92**
Type 14.
Gray, brown, orange and multicolor.
King Bhumibol / The King and Queen.
Cat.# 92 with watermark King's head. Cat.#96 with watermark Queen's head. It
has a commemorative text in back.

1,000 BAHT   **Cat.#105**
A commemorative note honoring the 60th anniversary of King
Bhumibol's coronation is planned for December 1999.

OUTMODED AND REDEEMABLE NOTES

*All older notes of all types are still legal tender, but seldom found in
circulation.*

60 BAHT   159 x 159mm **Cat.#93**
Brown and multicolor.
Rama IX seated on throne / The King and Queen.
It honors the King's 60th birthday.

Togo   XOF

It uses notes issued by "BANQUE CENTRALE DES ETATS DE L'AFRIQUE
DE L'OUEST."

For description of notes or currency import-export restrictions see
WEST AFRICAN STATES.

Alternative currencies: FRF, USD.

Tokelau   NZD

New Zealand currency is used.

Alternative currencies: GBP, USD.

Tonga   TOP

Pa'anga = 100 seniti.

Currency import-export restrictions:
The import and export of all currencies is free for non-resident visitors. A declaration is required when the amount exceeds TOP 1,000 or its equivalent.

Jul1988

Alternative currencies: AUD, GBP, NZD, USD.

A BRIEF MONETARY HISTORY
1967: 1 Pa'anga = 0.50 Tongan pound.

Issuer: "NATIONAL RESERVE BANK OF TONGA."

CURRENT NOTES

1 PA'ANGA N.R.B. of Tonga   150 x 70mm **Cat.#31**
Olive, brown and orange.
Taufa'ahau / River and palms.

2 PA'ANGA N.R.B. of Tonga   150 x 70mm **Cat.#32**
Red and brown.
Taufa'ahau / Women making Tapa cloth.

5 PA'ANGA N.R.B. of Tonga   150 x 70mm **Cat.#33**
Purple and multicolor.
Taufa'ahau / Ha'amonga archway.

10 PA'ANGA N.R.B. of Tonga   150 x 70mm **Cat.#34**
Bluish green and dark violet brown.
Taufa'ahau / Royal Palace.

20 PA'ANGA Government of Tonga   150 x 70mm **Cat.#23**
1985-89 Orange and multicolor.
Taufa'ahau / Tonga Development Bank.

20 PA'ANGA N.R.B. of Tonga   150 x 70mm **Cat.#29**
Orange and multicolor.
Taufa'ahau / Tonga Development Bank.

50 PA'ANGA Kingdom of Tonga   150 x 70mm **Cat.#24**
1988-89 Brown, green and multicolor.
Taufa'ahau / View of the Harbor.

OUTMODED AND REDEEMABLE NOTES

All older notes are redeemable.

Trans-Dniester Republic

Republica Nistriana • Dniestr (Rive Gauche)

Ruble.

A BRIEF MONETARY HISTORY
Early 1994: Russian notes validated with an adhesive stamp are placed in circulation.
August 1994: "new" ruble = 100 "old" rubles.

Alternative currencies: DEM, MDL, RUR, USD.

Issuer: "TRANS-DNIESTER REPUBLICAN BANK."

The Trans-Dniester region (Transnistria) is part of the Republic of Moldova. After some political circumstances proclaimed itself an independent entity. It is not recognized by the United Nations or other international organizations.

CURRENT NOTES

Smaller notes not listed because of low value. Some notes circulate at multiples of face value.

50,000 RUBLIEI 124 x 58mm Issued 29 Aug 1996 **Cat.#30**
1996 Blue.
Suvorov / New Parliament building.

{1,000 RUBLIEI} = **100,000 RUBLIEI**
123 x 57mm Issued in 1995 **Cat.#26**
1994 Violet and purple.
Suvorov / New Parliament building.

100,000 RUBLIEI 123 x 57mm Issued 29 Aug 1996 **Cat.#31**
1996 Lilac brown.
Suvorov / New Parliament building.

{50,000 RUBLIEI} = **500,000 RUBLIEI**
130 x 62mm Issued in April 1996 **Cat.#28**
1995 Brown.
Drama and Comedy Theater / Portrait.

500,000 RUBLIEI 123 x 57mm Issued 1 June 1997 **Cat.#32**
1997 Lilac brown and light aquamarine.
Suvorov / New Parliament building.

Trinidad & Tobago Trinité et Tobago **TTD**

Dollar(s) = 100 cent(s).

Currency import-export restriction:
Local: Declaration required for amounts over TTD 20,000.
Foreign: Declaration required for amounts over USD 5,000.

Alternative currencies: all major.

A BRIEF MONETARY HISTORY
Dec. 1964: Trinidadian dollar established at par with BWI (Eastern Caribbean) dollars.

Issuer: "CENTRAL BANK OF TRINIDAD AND TOBAGO."

CURRENT NOTES

1 DOLLAR 156 x 66mm **Cat.#30**
Red.
Arms and birds / Central Bank and offshore oil rig.

1 DOLLAR 156 x 66mm **Cat.#36**
Red and multicolor.
Arms and birds / Building and oil refinery.

5 DOLLARS 156 x 66mm **Cat.#31**
Green.
Arms, branches and leaves / Central Bank and crane.

5 DOLLARS 156 x 66mm **Cat.#37**
  Green and multicolor.
  Arms and bird / Building and women working.

10 DOLLARS 156 x 66mm **Cat.#32**
  Brown.
  Arms and bird / Central Bank and factory.

10 DOLLARS 156 x 66mm **Cat.#38**
  Brown and multicolor.
  Arms and bird / Financial complex and port scene.

20 DOLLARS 156 x 66mm **Cat.#33**
  Purple.
  Arms and flowers / Central Bank and cocoa pods.

20 DOLLARS 156 x 66mm **Cat.#39**
  Purple and multicolor.
  Arms and hummingbird / Building and steel drums.

100 DOLLARS 156 x 66mm **Cat.#35**
  Blue.
  Arms and branch with leaves / Central Bank, huts and palm trees.

100 DOLLARS 156 x 66mm **Cat.#40**
  Blue and multicolor.
  Arms and bird / Building and oil rig.

OUTMODED AND REDEEMABLE NOTES

1 DOLLAR *156 x 66mm* *Cat.#26*
  Red
  Elizabeth II and arms / Central Bank building and offshore rig.

5 DOLLARS *156 x 66mm* *Cat.#27*
  Green.
  Elizabeth II and arms / Central Bank building and crane.

10 DOLLARS *156 x 66mm* *Cat.#28*
  Brown
  Elizabeth II and arms / Central Bank building and factory.

20 DOLLARS *156 x 66mm* *Cat.#29*
  Purple.
  Elizabeth II and arms / Central Bank building and cocoa pods.

50 DOLLARS *156 x 66mm* *Cat.#34*
  Brown and multicolor.
  Arms and hummingbird / Central Bank building and net fishing.

Tunisia   Tunisie • Tunesien • Túnez   **TND**

Dinar(s) = 1,000 millim.

Currency import-export restrictions:
Local currency in/out: forbidden.
Foreign currency in: free, must declare amounts over D 500 or
equivalent if re-export is intended.
Out: up to amount imported and declared. Reconversion allowed to
30 % of amount exchanged, with a limit of D 100.
It is advisable to keep all exchange receipts until departure.

Alternative currencies: DEM, FRF, GBP, USD.

A BRIEF MONETARY HISTORY
Dec. 1958: 1 dinar = 1,000 francs.

Issuer: "BANQUE CENTRALE DE TUNISIE"

CURRENT NOTES

5 DINARS   160 x 80mm **Cat.#79**
3 Nov 1983 Reddish brown and lilac.
Habib Bourguiba / Hydroelectric dam.

5 DINARS   136 x 70mm Issued 7 Nov 1993 **Cat.#86**
93-11-7 Green and olive / Green, olive and reddish brown.
Hannibal and military Punic port / Allegory of "7 novembre
1987."

10 DINARS   170 x 84mm **Cat.#80**
3 Nov 1983 Blue, lilac and multicolor.
Habib Bourguiba / Central Bank of Tunisia building.

10 DINARS   170 x 84mm **Cat.#84**
20 March 1986 Yellow brown and green.
Habib Bourguiba / Offshore oil rig.

10 DINARS   145 x 73mm Issued 7 Nov 1994 **Cat.#87**
1994-11-7 Black, green and orange.
Ibn Khaldoun / Book with "7 Novembre..."

20 DINARS   180 x 90mm **Cat.#77**
15 Oct 1980 Blue, brown and multicolor.
Habib Bourguiba / Port and amphitheater in Monastir.

20 DINARS   180 x 90mm **Cat.#81**
3 Nov 1983 Blue and green.
Habib Bourguiba / Harbor.

20 DINARS   153 x 76mm Issued 9 Nov 1992 **Cat.#88**
1992-11-7 Mauve, blue, red and yellow.
Kheireddine Ettounsi on horseback and dome of Sidi Merhez
mosque / Allegory of "7 novembre 1987."

30 DINARS   161 x 79mm Issued 9 Nov 1997 **Cat.#89**
1997-11-7 Orange brown, brown and multicolor.
Poet Aboul Kacem Chebbi / Farming, artisans and children
drinking water.

©MRI BANKERS' GUIDE TO FOREIGN CURRENCY
P.O.Box 3174 HOUSTON TX 77253 USA

OUTMODED AND REDEEMABLE NOTES

5 DINARS 160 x 80mm **Cat.#71**
15 Oct 1973 Brown, lilac and multicolor. rruu20031231
Habib Bourguiba / Tourism, architecture and archaeology.

5 DINARS 160 x 80mm **Cat.#75**
15 Oct 1980 Brown and multicolor.
Habib Bourguiba / Buildings, bridge and hills. rruu20031231

10 DINARS 170 x 84mm **Cat.#72**
15 Oct 1973 Lilac and multicolor. rruu20031231
Habib Bourguiba / Youth, transportation and archaeology.

10 DINARS 170 x 84mm **Cat.#76**
15 Oct 1980 Blue green and yellow brown.
Habib Bourguiba / Reservoir. rruu20031231

Turkey Turkiye • Turkei • Turquía • Turquie **TRL**

Lira = 100 kuruş.
Minor unit coins are not used.

Currency import-export restrictions:
Local currency in: free; out up to equivalent of US$ 5,000.
Foreign currency in: free, may declare.
Out: free to US$ 5,000 or more if declared on entry. Aug1998

Alternative currencies: all major.

Issuer: "TÜRKİYE CUMHURİYET MERKEZ BANKASI."

CURRENT NOTES

50,000 LIRA 152 x 76mm Issued 15 May 1989 **Cat.#203**
Green and multicolor.
Atatürk / Parliament.
There are two very similar varieties. It is being replaced by a coin.

100,000 LIRA 158 x 76mm Issued 11 Nov 1991 **Cat.#205**
Brown, green and multicolor.
Atatürk and his equestrian statue / Group of children offering
flowers to Atatürk.
It is being replaced by a coin.

100,000 LIRA 158 x 76mm Issued 12 Aug 1996 **Cat.#206**
Brown, green and multicolor / Light brown and multicolor.
Atatürk and his equestrian statue / Group of children offering
flowers to Atatürk.
Without optical variable ink impression on top right and with lithographed back.
It is being replaced by a coin.

250,000 LIRA 158 x 76mm Issued 2 Oct 1992 **Cat.#207**
Blue, lilac and multicolor.
Atatürk / "Red Tower" in Alanya.

250,000 LIRA   158 x 76mm Issued 16 March 1998 **Cat.#213**
Blue, lilac and multicolor / Blue.
Atatürk / "Red Tower" in Alanya.
Modified version, without the "optical variable ink" triangle in front, and back
offset in blue instead of intaglio blue and lilac.

500,000 LIRA   160 x 76mm Issued 18 March 1993 **Cat.#208**
Purple and multicolor.
Atatürk / "Çanakkale Şehitleri Anıtı" (Monument to the Çanakkale
Martyrs".

500,000 LIRA   160 x 76mm **Cat.#212**
Purple and multicolor.
Atatürk / "Çanakkale Şehitleri Anıtı" (Monument to the Çanakkale
Martyrs".
Without optical variable ink impression on top, and with lithographed back.

1,000,000 LIRA   160 x 76mm Issued 16 Jan 1995 **Cat.#209**
Claret red and grayish blue.
Atatürk / Atatürk dam in Şanlı Urfa.

5,000,000 LIRA   162 x 76mm Issued 6 Jan 1997 **Cat.#210**
1997 Brown and reddish brown.
Atatürk / View of Anıtkabir, the Mausoleum of Atatürk in Ankara.

OUTMODED AND REDEEMABLE NOTES

Old notes of 5,000; 10,000 and 20,000 lira are redeemable.

Turkmenistan   TMM

Manat = 100 tenge.
Minor unit coins are not used.

Alternative currencies: DEM, RUB, USD.

A BRIEF MONETARY HISTORY
Nov. 1993: manat established at rate of 500 Russian rubles.

Issuer: "TÜRKMENISTANYŇ MERKEZI DÖWLET BANKY." (Central
Government Bank of Turkmenistan), now "TÜRKMENISTANYŇ MERKEZI
BANKY." (Central Bank of Turkmenistan).

CURRENT NOTES

Smaller notes not listed because of low value.

1,000 MANAT   156 x 78mm **Cat.#8**
1995 Green and light red.
Pres. Niyazov and building / Horse inside triple circle.

5,000 MANAT   156 x 78mm Issued in mid 1996 **Cat.#9**
1996 Violet brown, mauve and multicolor.
Pres. Niyazov and building / Coat of arms.

10,000 MANAT   156 x 78mm Issued in 1996 **Cat.#10**
1996 Olive, brown and multicolor.
Pres. Niyazov and building / Coat of arms.

10,000 MANAT   156 x 78mm **Cat.#11**
1998 Olive, brown, blue and multicolor.
Pres. Niyazov and building / Mosque.

©MRI BANKERS' GUIDE TO FOREIGN CURRENCY
P.O.Box 3174 HOUSTON TX 77253 USA

Turks & Caicos   USD

United States currency is used.
The import and export of local and foreign currencies are free.

Tuvalu   AUD

Australian currency is used. The import and export of all currencies is free up to the equivalent of AUD 200.

Alternative currencies: GBP, USD.

Uganda   Ouganda   UGX

Shilling(s) = 100 cent(s).
Minor unit coins are not used.

Currency import-export restrictions:
The import and export of all currencies is free.   Aug1998

Alternative currencies: ATS, BEF, CAD, CHF, DEM, DKK, ESP, FRF, GBP, ITL, JPY, KES, NLG, PTE, SEK, TZS, USD.

A BRIEF MONETARY HISTORY
Aug 1966: 1 Ugandan shilling = 1 East African shilling
1987: new shilling = 100 shillings

Issuer: "BANK OF UGANDA."

CURRENT NOTES

Smaller notes not listed because of low value.

200 SHILLINGS   152 x 74mm **Cat.#32**
1987-96 Brown and multicolor.
Arms / Textile factory.

500 SHILLINGS   152 x 74mm Issued 15 Dec 1994 **Cat.#33**
1991- Dark brown, purple brown, green and multicolor.
Elephant / Municipal building and "The Uganda's Independence Monument" at left.
Since 1994 with windowed security thread.

1,000 SHILLINGS   152 x 74mm Issued 15 Dec 1994 **Cat.#34**
1991 Green, reddish brown and multicolor.
Farmer at left, maize garden at center / Grain silo.
Since 1994 with windowed security thread.

5,000 SHILLINGS   152 x 74mm Issued 14 Feb 1994 **Cat.#37**
1993 Red, green and multicolor.
Lake Bunyonyi and terraces / Kaawa Ferry.

10,000 SHILLINGS   152 x 74mm Issued 10 Oct 1995 **Cat.#38**
1995 Red, green, brown and multicolor.
Stylized musical instruments / Owen Falls dam and kudu.

20,000 SHILLINGS   **Cat.#39**
It may be issued soon.

Ukraine   Ukraïna • Ucrania   UAH

Hryvnia(s) = 100 kopiyka(s).

Currency import/export restrictions:
Local currency in: UAH 85 provided proof of previous export is produced; out UAH 85.
Foreign currency in: free up to USD 50,000 or its equivalent. Out: free up to USD 1,000 or its equivalent. Larger amounts only if previously imported and declared.
Reconversion requires proof of previous exchange declared in form N° 322. It is recommended to keep these records very carefully, as it is reported that Customs officials are very strict.   Jul1998

Alternative currencies: DEM, GBP, RUB, USD.

A BRIEF MONETARY HISTORY
1991: 1 karbovanets = 1 Soviet ruble.
2 Sep 1996: 1 hryvnia = 100,000 karbovanets

Issuer: "Національний Банк України" (National Bank of Ukraine).

CURRENT NOTES

1 HRYVNIA　　135 x 70mm Issued 2 Sep 1996 **Cat.#103**
1992 Olive green, yellow and blue.
Prince Volodymyr / Ruins of Khersones.

1 HRYVNIA　　133 x 66mm Issued 2 Sep 1996 **Cat.#108**
1994 Brown, light green and gray.
Price Volodymyr / Ruins of Khersones.

2 HRYVNIAS　　135 x 70mm Issued 2 Sep 1996 **Cat.#104**
1992 Brown and multicolor.
Yaroslav the Wise / Cathedral of St. Sophia in Kyiv.

2 HRYVNIAS　　133 x 66mm Issued 1 Sep 1997 **Cat.#109**
1995 Purplish brown, reddish brown and multicolor.
Yaroslav the Wise / Cathedral of St. Sophia in Kyiv.

5 HRYVNIAS　　135 x 70mm Issued 2 Sep 1996 **Cat.#105**
1992 Blue and multicolor.
Iliynska church in Subotov / Portrait.

5 HRYVNIAS　　133 x 66mm Issued 1 Sep 1997 **Cat.#110**
1994- Blue, green and multicolor.
Iliynska church in Subotov / Portrait.

10 HRYVNIAS　　135 x 70mm Issued 2 Sep 1996 **Cat.#106**
1992 Violet and multicolor.
Ivan Mazepa / Kiev-Pechersk Monastery.

10 HRYVNIAS　　133 x 66mm Issued 1 Sep 1997 **Cat.#111**
1994 Reddish brown, violet and multicolor.
Ivan Mazepa / Kiev-Pechersk Monastery.

20 HRYVNIAS　　135 x 70mm Issued 2 Sep 1996 **Cat.#107**
1992 Brown and multicolor.
Ivan Franko / Opera House in Lviv.

20 HRYVNIAS　　133 x 66mm Issued 1 Sep 1997 **Cat.#112**
1995 Brown, green, lilac and multicolor.
Ivan Franko / Opera House in Lviv.

50 HRYVNIAS　　133 x 66mm Issued 2 Sep 1996 **Cat.#113**
Violet, yellow and multicolor.
Mikhaylo Hrushevski / Ukrainian Verkhovna Rada (Parliament.)

100 HRYVNIAS　　133 x 66mm Issued 2 Sep 1996 **Cat.#114**
Green, brown, lilac and pink.
Taras Shevchenko / Cathedral of St. Sophia in Kyiv.

©MRI BANKERS' GUIDE TO FOREIGN CURRENCY
P.O.Box 3174 HOUSTON TX 77253 USA

United Arab Emirates
Vereinigte Arabische Emirate • Emiratos Árabes Unidos • Union des Emirats Arabs **AED**

Dirham = 100 fils

The United Arab Emirates dirham is the common currency of Abu Dhabi, Ajman, Dubai, Fujairah, Ras al Khaima, Sharjah and Umm al Qaiwain.

The import and export of local and foreign currencies are free.

Alternative currencies: all major.

Issuer: "UNITED ARAB EMIRATES CENTRAL BANK."

CURRENT NOTES

5 DIRHAMS   143 x 60mm **Cat.#7**
  Brown and multicolor.
  Harbor / Sharjah Market.

5 DIRHAMS   143 x 60mm Issued ca. April 1994 **Cat.#12**
  1993 Brown and orange.
  Building / Harbor.

10 DIRHAMS   145 x 62mm **Cat.#8**
  Green and multicolor.
  Dagger / View of an ideal farm.

10 DIRHAMS   145 x 62mm Issued ca. April 1994 **Cat.#13**
  1993 Green and multicolor.
  Dagger / View of an ideal farm.

20 DIRHAMS   150 x 63mm Issued in late 1999 **Cat.#20**
  1997 Green, blue and multicolor / Green.
  Dubai Creek Golf and Yacht Club / Dhow.
  Commemorative of the Accession Day of President Sheikh Zayed bin Sultan Al Nahyan, and the National Day.

50 DIRHAMS   150 x 63mm **Cat.#9**
  Purple, olive and multicolor.
  Oryx / Al Jahilie Fort.

50 DIRHAMS   150 x 63mm Issued in mid-1995 **Cat.#14**
  1995 Purple and multicolor.
  Oryx / Al Jahilie Fort.

100 DIRHAMS   155 x 66mm **Cat.#9**
  Red, black and multicolor.
  Al Fahidie Fort / Dubai Trade Centre.

100 DIRHAMS   155 x 66mm Issued ca. April 1994 **Cat.#15**
  1993 Red, olive green and multicolor.
  Al Fahidie Fort / Dubai Trade Centre.

100 DIRHAMS   155 x 66mm **Cat.#xxx**
  1998 Red, olive green and multicolor.
  Al Fahidie Fort / Dubai Trade Centre.
  Similar to the 1993 note, without the "100" over the watermark area on front.

200 DIRHAMS   157 x 67mm **Cat.#16**
  1989 Brown, green and multicolor.
  Sharia Court building and Zayed Sports City / U.A.E. Central Bank building.

500 DIRHAMS   160 x 68mm **Cat.#11**
Blue, brown and multicolor.
Falcon head / Mosque in Dubai.

500 DIRHAMS   160 x 68mm Issued ca. April 1994 **Cat.#17**
1993 Green, violet brown and multicolor.
Falcon head / Mosque in Dubai.

500 DIRHAMS   160 x 68mm Issued in late 1996 **Cat.#18**
1996 Green, violet brown and multicolor.
Falcon head / Mosque in Dubai.
With silver seal at left.

1,000 DIRHAMS   163 x 70mm **Cat.#20**
1998 Brown, green and multicolor.
Al Hosn palace in Abu Dhabi / Abu Dhabi cornice.
Commemorative of the Accession Day of President Sheikh Zayed bin Sultan Al
Nahyan, and the National Day. With a holographic band at right.

United Kingdom   Vereinigtes
Königreich • Reino Unido • Royaume-Uni   **GBP**

Current notes are listed under England, Northern Ireland and
Scotland.

OUTMODED AND REDEEMABLE NOTES

Old notes from the "United Kingdom of Great Britain and Ireland"
and "United Kingdom of Great Britain and Northern Ireland" are
redeemable at the Bank of England.

British Military Authority

Issued during World War II, are payable in Sterling at the Bank of
England, the Treasury's redemption agent. These notes are worth
more when in good condition.

Notes issued for the "British Armed Forces" are worthless.

Smaller notes not listed because of low value.

{1 SHILLING} = **0.05 POUND**   114 x 72mm **Cat.#M2**
Gray on violet.
Lion over crown / Value.

{2 SHILLINGS 6 PENCE} = **0.125 POUND**   114 x 72mm **Cat.#M3**
Green on pink.
Lion over crown / Value.

{5 SHILLINGS} = **0.25 POUND**   114 x 72mm **Cat.#M4**
Brown on blue and green.
Lion over crown / Value.

{10 SHILLINGS} = **0.50 POUND**   138 x 77mm **Cat.#M5**
Blue on olive and lilac.
Lion over crown / Value.

1 POUND   148 x 84mm **Cat.#M6**
Violet on light brown.
Lion over crown / Value.

United States of America
Vereinigte Staaten • Estados Unidos de Norte
América • États-Unis d'Amérique   **USD**

Dollar = 100 cent(s).

Currency import-export restrictions:
Local or foreign: free. Import or export of US$10,000 or equivalent
must be declared to Customs on form "Report of International
Transportation of Currency."

There is an embargo on transactions with Cuba, Iran, Iraq, Libya and
North Korea. Rules differ for each country. Bringing in small
amounts of their currency may not be a violation, while importing
large quantities, or doing business with these countries to obtain it
is a violation.

Alternative currencies: all major.

©MRI BANKERS' GUIDE TO FOREIGN CURRENCY
P.O.Box 3174 HOUSTON TX 77253 USA

All notes issued by the "United States of America" are valid. The bulk of currency in use now is issued by the Federal Reserve Banks. The branch letter and district number must match. Their list is:

1	A	Boston, Massachusetts
2	B	New York, New York
3	C	Philadelphia, Pennsylvania
4	D	Cleveland, Ohio
5	E	Richmond, Virginia
6	F	Atlanta, Georgia
7	G	Chicago, Illinois
8	H	St. Louis, Missouri
9	I	Minneapolis, Minnesota
10	J	Kansas City, Missouri
11	K	Dallas, Texas
12	L	San Francisco, California

Counterfeit notes

"Know your Money" is a very useful booklet with information on how to detect counterfeit dollar bills. It is available gratis from:

United States Secret Service
1800 G Street NW
Washington DC 20223.

Dubious dollar bills may be verified by calling the Secret Service. From outside the USA call them at:

Bangkok: (66-2) 252-5040 ext. 2651
Bogotá: (57-1) 315-1319
Bonn: (49-228) 339 2587
Hong Kong: (852-2) 2810-5560
London: (44-171) 499 9000 ext.2846 or 2847
Manila: (63-2) 521-7116
Nicosia: (357-2) 476-100 ext.2549
Ottawa: 514-398-9488
Paris: (33-1) 4076 0758
Rome: (39-6) 46741, ext. 2736,

or their headquarters in Washington: 202-435-6300
Additional offices will open soon at the American Embassies in Nicosia, Ottawa and Santafé de Bogotá.

In the United States call the local office listed in your phone book.

Once you give them the Series, district letter and plate numbers found in the front, and the plate number located in the lower right corner of the back, they can check their database and tell you whether your note is a known forgery.

Mutilated notes

Mutilated currency is redeemable when clearly more than 50% (at least 51%) is present.
To redeem it, send it by Registered or Insured mail to:

Operations, OCS
Bureau of Engraving and Printing
13th and C. Sts., Room 344
P O Box 37048
Washington DC 20013

Local issues

In several small cities circulate notes issued by local associations. These are denominated in "hours": one hour being $10. These notes are intended for use strictly inside the area in which were issued.

CURRENT NOTES

All current notes are Black / Green.

1 DOLLAR   156 x 65mm **Cat.#443**
George Washington / Great Seal of the United States.
A golden-colored coin will replace this note in 2000.

2 DOLLARS   156 x 65mm **Cat.#461**
Thomas Jefferson / Congress in session.

5 DOLLARS   156 x 65mm **Cat.#444**
Abraham Lincoln / Lincoln Memorial.

5 DOLLARS Series 1993   156 x 65mm **Cat.#491**
Abraham Lincoln / Lincoln Memorial.
With security thread, and microlettering around the portrait frame.

5 DOLLARS   **Cat.#499**
New note with improved features expected in 2000.

10 DOLLARS   156 x 65mm **Cat.#445**
Alexander Hamilton / Treasury building.

10 DOLLARS   156 x 65mm **Cat.#486**
Series 1990-
Alexander Hamilton / Treasury building.
With security thread and microlettering around the portrait frame.

10 DOLLARS   **Cat.#500**
New note with improved features expected in 2000.

20 DOLLARS   156 x 65mm **Cat.#446**
Andrew Jackson / The White House.

20 DOLLARS   156 x 65mm **Cat.#487**
Series 1990-95
Andrew Jackson / The White House.
With security thread and microlettering around the portrait frame.

20 DOLLARS 156 x 65mm **Cat.#501**
Series 1996
Andrew Jackson / The White House.

50 DOLLARS 156 x 65mm **Cat.#447**
Ulysses S. Grant / Capitol building.

50 DOLLARS 156 x 65mm **Cat.#488**
Series 1990-93
Ulysses S. Grant / Capitol building.
With security thread and microlettering around the portrait frame.

50 DOLLARS 156 x 65mm **Cat.#502**
Series 1997.
Ulysses S. Grant / Capitol building.

100 DOLLARS 156 x 65mm **Cat.#448**
Benjamin Franklin / Independence Hall.

100 DOLLARS 156 x 65mm **Cat.#495**
Series 1990-93
Benjamin Franklin / Independence Hall
With security thread and microlettering around the portrait frame.
Some were forged by printing each side on thin paper and the security thread inside. Both halves are then pasted.

100 DOLLARS 156 x 65mm **Cat.#503**
1996 Black and green.
Benjamin Franklin / Independence Hall.
The "100" in the lower right of the front changes colors from black to green.

OUTMODED AND REDEEMABLE NOTES

All large or small size notes issued by the United States of America are redeemable.

This includes:

Fractional currency of 1862-74,
United States Notes of 1862 to 1966,
Gold Certificates of 1863 to 1923,
Silver Certificates of 1878 to 1957,
Interest Bearing Notes of 1861-64,
Compound Interest Treasury Notes of 1864-65,
Refunding Certificates of 1879,
Coin notes of 1890-91,
Federal Reserve Notes since 1914,
National Bank Notes.

500 DOLLARS 156 x 65mm *Cat.#425*
William McKinley / Value.

1,000 DOLLARS 156 x 65mm *Cat.#426*
Grover Cleveland / Value.

5,000 DOLLARS 156 x 65mm *Cat.#427*
James Madison / Value.

10,000 DOLLARS 156 x 65mm *Cat.#428*
Salmon P. Chase / Value.

©MRI BANKERS' GUIDE TO FOREIGN CURRENCY
P.O.BOX 3174 HOUSTON TX 77253 USA

Uruguay   UYU

Peso(s) uruguayo(s) = 100 centésimo(s).

The import and export of local and foreign currencies are free.

Alternative currencies: ARS, BRL, CLP, PYG and all major.

A BRIEF MONETARY HISTORY
1975: nuevo peso = 1,000 pesos oro
1993: peso uruguayo = 1,000 nuevos pesos.

Issuer: "BANCO CENTRAL DEL URUGUAY."

CURRENT NOTES

Caution!!!
This note
is worth only
5 pesos uruguayos

{5,000 NUEVOS PESOS} = **5 PESOS URUGUAYOS**
159 x 74mm **Cat.#65**

Brown, blue and multicolor.
Brig. Gen. J. A. Lavalleja / "Jura de la Constitución de 1830."

5 PESOS URUGUAYOS   159 x 74mm Issued in Dec 1997 **Cat.#81**
Brown, blue and multicolor.
Brig. Gen. J. A. Lavalleja / "Jura de la Constitución de 1830."

5 PESOS URUGUAYOS   **Cat.#83**
A new note is being planned.

Caution!!!
This note
is worth only
10 pesos uruguayos

{10,000 NUEVOS PESOS} = **10 PESOS URUGUAYOS**
159 x 74mm **Cat.#67**

Blue and multicolor.
"Plaza de la Democracia" / Arms of Uruguay's 19 departments.

10 PESOS URUGUAYOS 159 x 74mm Issued in late 1995 **Cat.#73A**
Blue and multicolor.
"Plaza de la Democracia" / Arms of Uruguay's 19 departments.
There are two varieties, without and with "Decreto Ley Nº14316".

10 PESOS URUGUAYOS   Issued in May 1999 159 x 74mm **Cat.#84**
1998 Slate and light rose.
Eduardo Acevedo Vásquez / Facultad de Agronomía.

Caution!!!
This note
is worth only
20 pesos uruguayos

{20,000 NUEVOS PESOS} = **20 PESOS URUGUAYOS**
159 x 74mm **Cat.#69**

1989-91 Green, lilac and multicolor.
Juan Zorrilla de San Martín / Manuscript and allegory of Victory.

20 PESOS URUGUAYOS 159x74mm Issued in August 1995 **Cat.#74**
1994 Green, lilac and multicolor.
Juan Zorrilla de San Martín / Manuscript and allegory of Victory.

Caution!!!
This note
is worth only
50 pesos uruguayos

{50,000 NUEVOS PESOS} = **50 PESOS URUGUAYOS**
159 x 74mm **Cat.#70**

1989-91 Red and multicolor.
José Pedro Varela / Monument.

50 PESOS URUGUAYOS   159 x 74mm Issued in Sep 1995 **Cat.#75**
1994 Red and multicolor.
José Pedro Varela / Monument.

100 PESOS URUGUAYOS 159 x 74mm Issued 31 Aug 1995 **Cat.#76**
1994 Violet and multicolor.
Eduardo Fabini / Sculpture of Pan playing a "siringa."

200 PESOS URUGUAYOS 159 x 74mm Issued in late 1995 **Cat.#77**
1995 Brown, lilac, green, orange and multicolor.
Pedro Figari / "Baile Antiguo."

500 PESOS URUGUAYOS 159 x 74mm Issued in Aug 1995 **Cat.#78**
1994 Blue violet, green, violet and multicolor.
Alfredo Vázquez Acevedo / "Universidad de Montevideo."

1,000 PESOS URUGUAYOS
            159 x 74mm Issued 15 April 1996 **Cat.#79**
1995 Olive green, brown and rose red.
Juana de Ibarbourou / Palm tree and books in the back.

OUTMODED AND REDEEMABLE NOTES

Notes of 1,000 and 2,000 nuevos pesos, which are only worth 1 and
2 pesos uruguayos can be redeemed at the Central Bank.

Uzbekistan   Usbekistan • Ouzbékistan   **UZS**

Sum = 100 tyyn.

Currency import/export restrictions:
Local currency in: free; out: free, declaration required.
Foreign currency in: free, declaration required. Out: free up to USD
1,200 or equivalent. Declaration required. Larger amount require
prior permission. Reconversion requires proof of prior exchange.
Certain hotel charges, visa fees and airplane tickets must be paid
with U.S. dollars.

July1998

Alternative currencies: DEM, RUB, USD.

A BRIEF MONETARY HISTORY
Nov. 1993: "sum" coupons issued.
1 July 1994: "sum-note" = 1,000 "sum-coupons"

Issuer: "Ўзбекистон Республикаси Марказий Банки" (Central
Bank of the Republic of Uzbekistan).

CURRENT NOTES

Smaller notes not listed because of low value.

10 SUM   142 x 69 Issued 1 June 1994 **Cat.#76**
1994 Violet, grayish blue and multicolor.
Arms and value / Timurids Mausoleum (Guri Amir) in Samarkand.

25 SUM   142 x 69 Issued 1 June 1994 **Cat.#77**
1994 Dark blue, brown and multicolor.
Arms and value / Architectural ensemble "Shohi Zinda" in
Samarkand.

50 SUM   142 x 69 Issued 1 June 1994 **Cat.#78**
1994 Brown and orange.
Arms and value / Esplanade in Reghistan in Samarkand.

100 SUM   142 x 69 Issued 1 June 1994 **Cat.#79**
1994 Brown, blue, lilac and green / Purple.
Value and peacocks / "Drujba Narodov" palace in Tashkent.

200 SUM   144 x 78mm Issued in 1 March 1997 **Cat.#80**
1997 Green, blue, yellow, orange and multicolor.
Arms / Mythological beast.

Vanuatu   VUV

Vatu (No minor unit).

The import and export of local and foreign currencies are free.

Alternative currencies: AUD, FRF, GBP, USD.

A BRIEF MONETARY HISTORY
1981: vatu = New Hebrides franc

Issuer: "RESERVE BANK OF VANUATU", formerly "CENTRAL BANK OF VANUATU."

CURRENT NOTES

200 VATU   135 x 68mm Issued in 1995 **Cat.#8**
Purple, green and multicolor / Purple, light orange brown and multicolor.
Coat of arms / Statue of family life, "Traditional parliament in session" and Vanuatu flag.
A small number were overprinted with a legend commemorative of 15 years of independence.

500 VATU Central Bank of Vanuatu   140 x 70mm **Cat.#2**
Red and multicolor.
Man holding spear / Native carvers.

500 VATU Reserve Bank of Vanuatu   140 x 70mm **Cat.#5**
Red and multicolor.
Man holding spear / Native carvers.

1,000 VATU Central Bank of Vanuatu   150 x 75mm **Cat.#3**
Black and multicolor.
Man holding spear / Sailboat.

1,000 VATU Reserve Bank of Vanuatu   150 x 75mm **Cat.#6**
Black and multicolor.
Man holding spear / Sailboat.

5,000 VATU Central Bank of Vanuatu   160 x 79mm **Cat.#7**
Brown lilac and multicolor.
Man holding spear / "Gol" dive.

OUTMODED AND REDEEMABLE NOTES

{100 FRANCS} = 100 VATU   140 x 76mm **Cat.#18**
Issued by "Institut d'Emission d'Outre-Mer", overprinted "Nouvelles Hébrides." Redeemable at the Reserve Bank of Vanuatu.

100 VATU   130 x 65mm **Cat.#1**
Green and multicolor.
Man holding spear / Cattle.

{500 FRANCS} = 500 VATU   150 x 81mm **Cat.#19**
Issued by "Institut d'Emission d'Outre-Mer", overprinted "Nouvelles Hébrides." Redeemable at the Reserve Bank of Vanuatu.

{1,000 FRANCS} = 1,000 VATU   *160 x 86mm Cat.#17*
Issued by "Institut d'Emission d'Outre-Mer", overprinted "Nouvelles Hébrides." Redeemable at the Reserve Bank of Vanuatu.

Vatican City
Stato della Città del Vaticano • Vatikan   **ITL**

Italian money is used.

Venezuela   **VEB**

Bolívar(es) = 100 céntimo(s).
Minor unit coins are not used.

Currency import-export restrictions:
The import and export of local currency in relatively small amounts are free.
Foreign currency in: must declare amounts over USD 10,000 or equivalent.
Foreign currency out: must declare amounts over USD 5,000 or equivalent.

Alternative currencies: all major.

Issuer: "BANCO CENTRAL DE VENEZUELA."

CURRENT NOTES

Smaller notes not listed because of low value.

100 BOLIVARES   157 x 69mm **Cat.#55**
1972- Brown and multicolor.
Bolívar / National Capitol.
These are being replaced by coins.

500 BOLIVARES   157 x 69mm **Cat.#67**
1981- Blue, purple and multicolor.
Bolívar / Orchids.
These are being replaced by coins.

1,000 BOLIVARES 157 x 69mm Issued in November 1991 **Cat.#73**
8 Aug 1991 Lilac brown and multicolor / Lilac brown, olive green and multicolor.
Simón Bolívar and page of Independence Declaration on background / Scene of signature of Declaration of Independence.

1,000 BOLIVARES   157 x 69mm **Cat.#76**
17 March 1994 Lilac brown and multicolor / Lilac brown, olive green and multicolor.
Simón Bolívar and page of Independence Declaration on background / Scene of signature of Declaration of Independence.
Like Cat.#73, but value at bottom right of front printed with optical variable ink.

2,000 BOLIVARES   157 x 69mm Issued in Oct. 1995 **Cat.#74**
1994-96 Green, violet black and multicolor.
Antonio José de Sucre / Military scene (Battle of Ayacucho.)

2,000 BOLIVARES   157 x 69mm **Cat.#77**
1997 Green, violet black and multicolor.
Antonio José de Sucre / Military scene (Battle of Ayacucho.)
Similar to the 1994-96 type, with "2000" in bottom left corner in black instead of brown and green.

5,000 BOLIVARES   157 x 69mm Issued in Oct. 1995 **Cat.#75**
12 May 1994 Brown, orange brown and multicolor.
Simón Bolívar / Historic scene (Declaration of Independence.)

10,000 BOLIVARES 157 x 69mm Issued in late Nov. 1998 **Cat.#78**
10 Feb 1998 Olive brown, red and dark olive.
Simón Bolívar / Teatro Teresa Carreño.

20,000 BOLIVARES   **Cat.#79**
Its issue is planned for 1999.

50,000 BOLIVARES   **Cat.#80**
Its issue is planned for 1999.

OUTMODED AND REDEEMABLE NOTES

All older notes issued by the Central Bank of Venezuela are valid.

Vietnam   VND

New đồng = 100 xu = 10 hao.
Minor unit coins are not used.

Currency import-export restrictions:
Local currency in/out: forbidden without special permission.
Foreign currency in: free, must declare.
Out: up to amount imported.
Visitors are required to pay hotel bills, airline tickets and certain other items in foreign currency.

Alternative currencies: CAD, FRF, GBP, THB, USD.

A BRIEF MONETARY HISTORY
Jan 1955: Vietnamese đong replaces Indochinese piastre.
1959: new đồng (North) = 1,000 đồng (North)
1975: new South Viet Nam đồng = 500 piastres (South)
1978: Viet Nam đồng = 1 new đồng (North) or 0.80 new South Vietnam đồng.

Issuer: "NGAN HÀNG NHÀ NƯỚC VIẾT NAM." (State Bank of Vietnam).

CURRENT NOTES

Smaller notes not listed because of low value.

2,000 ĐỒNG   134 x 64mm Issued 4 March 1988 **Cat.#103**
1987 Purple brown and multicolor.
Ho Chi Minh and arms / Industrial plant.

2,000 ĐỒNG   134 x 64mm Issued 1989 **Cat.#107**
1988 Brownish purple on brown and multicolor.
Ho Chi Minh and arms / Women in a textile factory.

5,000 ĐỒNG   134 x 64mm Issued 4 March 1988 **Cat.#104**
1987 Dark blue and multicolor.
Ho Chi Minh and arms / Offshore oil rigs.

5,000 ĐỒNG   134 x 64mm Issued in 1993 **Cat.#108**
1991 Blue and multicolor.
Ho Chi Minh / Electrical lines.

10,000 ĐỒNG   140 x 68mm Issued 4 May 1992 **Cat.#109**
1990- Orange red and multicolor / Orange red, brown and multicolor.
Ho Chi Minh and arms / Boat.

20,000 ĐỒNG   140 x 68mm Issued in February 1993 **Cat.#110**
1991 Blue green and multicolor.
Ho Chi Minh / Packing factory.

50,000 ĐỒNG   140 x 68mm Issued in February 1993 **Cat.#111**
1990- Dark Olive green and multicolor.
Ho Chi Minh / Port.
Those dated 1994 are slightly different.

Negotiable bank cheques

The State Bank of Vietnam issues "Negotiable bank cheques" in values of 100,000 through 5,000,000 đong. The cheques have an expiration date, and are mainly used between banks and businesses. These are not used by the public.

West African States

États de l'Afrique de l'Ouest • Westafrikanische Staten • Estados del África Occidental   **XOF**

Franc(s) CFA West = 100 centime(s).
Minor unit coins are not used.
Parity: FFR 0.01

Common currency for several former West African countries, which are identified by the following letters:

B Benin,
C Burkina Faso,
A Ivory Coast,
D Mali,
H Niger,
K Senegal,
S Guiné-Bissau,
T Togo.

Currency import-export restrictions:

Residents, between countries of the West African Monetary Union:
Local or foreign currency: import and export free.

Residents, to and from countries of the Central African States (Cameroon, Central African Rep., Chad, Congo, Equatorial Guinea and Gabon); France and the Comores:
Local currency: free, must declare.
Foreign currency in: free, must declare to Customs and convert in the official market in 8 days any amount over CFA f 25,000 (50,000 for Burkina Faso, Niger and Senegal)
Foreign currency out: free up to equivalent of CFA f 500,000 (CFA f 1,000,000 for Burkina Faso, Niger and Senegal.)

Non Residents:
CFA francs: in or out, free, must declare.
Foreign currency in: must declare.
Out: free up to the equivalent of CFA fr 250,000; more if declared on arrival.

Alternative currencies: FRF, USD.

Issuer: "BANQUE CENTRALE DES ETATS DE L'AFRIQUE DE L'OUEST."

CURRENT NOTES

500 FRANCS   140 x 74mm Issued 1 Oct 1979 **Cat.#6**
1981-91 Green and multicolor.
Old man and cattle / Pineapple and aerial view.

500 FRANCS   140 x 80mm Issued 2 Sep 1991 **Cat.#10**
1991- Multicolor.
Portrait of Samori Touré / Man driving farming machine.
The first two digits of the serial number indicate the year of issue.

1,000 FRANCS   149 x 80mm Issued 22 June 1981 **Cat.#7**
1981-90 Yellow, brown and multicolor.
Statue, open pit mine and woman's head / Wood carver and carving.

1,000 FRANCS   147 x 80mm Issued 20 Jan 1992 **Cat.#11**
1991- Violet brown on yellow, brown and multicolor.
Workmen hauling bags, and woman's head / Twin statues and mask, two women with baskets, and elevated river storage bins.
The first two digits of the serial number indicate the year of issue.

2,000 FRANCS   **Cat.#15**
The introduction of this denomination is being considered.

2,500 FRANCS   154 x 80mm Issued 2 Nov 1992 **Cat.#12**
1992- Lilac, brown and multicolor.
Woman's head and hydroelectrical installation / Cocoa bean harvest and statue.
The first two digits of the serial number indicate the year of issue.

5,000 FRANCS   159 x 85mm Issued 3 April 1978 **Cat.#8**
1977-92 Blue and multicolor.
Woman and fishing scene / Carvings, fishing boats and mask.

5,000 FRANCS   161 x 80mm Issued 19 Sep 1994 **Cat.#13**
1992- Blue, brown and multicolor.
Uranium refining and treating plant and West African dancer / Pottery market.
The first two digits of the serial number indicate the year of issue.

10,000 FRANCS   168 x 92mm Issued 1 Oct 1976 **Cat.#9**
Reddish brown and multicolor.
Young woman / Textile machine and two workers.

10,000 FRANCS   168 x 80mm Issued 19 Sep 1994 **Cat.#14**
1992- Reddish brown, Green and multicolor.
Traditional West African chief and BCEAO building / Woman crossing bridge.
The first two digits of the serial number indicate year of issue.

OUTMODED AND REDEEMABLE NOTES

All older notes issued by "Banque de l'Afrique Occidentale", "Institut d'Emission de l'A.O.F. et du Togo" and "Banque Centrale des Etats de l'Afrique de l'Ouest" are redeemable.

Yemen Jemen   YER

The Arab and People's Democratic Republics merged in 1990.

Rial(s) = 100 fils.
Minor unit coins are not used.

Currency import-export restrictions:
Local currency in/out: forbidden.
Foreign currency in: free, must declare amounts over US$ 2,000 if reëxport is intended.
Out: free under US$ 2,000 or up to amount declared and imported.

Hotel bills and airline tickets must be paid with convertible currency.

Alternative currencies: GBP, SAR, USD.

Issuer: "CENTRAL BANK OF YEMEN."

CURRENT NOTES

Smaller notes not listed because of low value.

20 RIALS   145 x 75mm **Cat.#14**
Purple, blue and multicolor.
Sculpture of god of Grapes / Terraces.

20 RIALS   145 x 75mm Issued 4 Dec 1986 **Cat.#19**
Purple, blue and multicolor.
Sculpture of god of Grapes / City view.

20 RIALS   145 x 75mm **Cat.#25**
Brown and multicolor.
Sculpture of god of grapes / Port of Aden and boat.

20 RIALS   145 x 75mm **Cat.#26**
Brown and multicolor.
Sculpture of god of grapes / City view.

50 RIALS   150 x 70mm Issued 15 Aug 1973 **Cat.#15**
Olive and multicolor.
Statue / Old building.

50 RIALS   150 x 70mm Issued 10 Feb 1993 **Cat.27**
Olive and multicolor.
Statue / City in the Hadramaut.
Without or with Arabic inscription on back.

100 RIALS   150 x 75mm Issued 1 March 1976 **Cat.#16**
Lilac and multicolor.
Child and mythical beast / City and mountain.

100 RIALS   150 x 75mm Issued 15 May 1979 **Cat.#16A**
Lilac and multicolor.
Child and mythical beast / Building.

100 RIALS   150 x 75mm Issued 15 Aug 1984 **Cat.#21**
Lilac and multicolor.
City view / View of Sana'a.

100 RIALS   150 x 75mm Issued in May 1993 **Cat.#28**
Lilac and multicolor.
Mountainside scene / View of Sana'a.

200 RIALS   155 x 75mm Issued 11 March 1996 **Cat.#29**
Green and lilac.
Man with sword and knife / City by sea.

500 RIALS   155 x 80mm Issued 15 Feb 1997 **Cat.#30**
Dark blue, orange brown and multicolor.
Central Bank building / Ruins of Queen of Sheba's palace in
Mareb.

1,000 RIALS   157 x 85mm **Cat.#31**
Olive green, green and light salmon / Brown and green.
Castle of Sayoun / View of old Sana'a.

OUTMODED AND REDEEMABLE NOTES

*Older notes issued by the Central Bank of Yemen are redeemable.
Notes in "buqshas" are fractional and without practical value.*

Yugoslavia
Jugoslavija • Jugoslawien • Yougoslavie   **YUM**

New (super) dinar(a) = 100 para.

Currency import-export restrictions:
Local currency in/out: Not available.
Foreign currency in: free, must declare.
Out: up to amount imported.

Alternative currencies: the German mark is the de-facto currency.
United States dollars are easily exchanged.

A BRIEF MONETARY HISTORY
1Jan1966: new dinar = 100 dinars
3Jan1990: new dinar = 10,000 dinars
26Dec/31Dec1991: Old notes exchanged at par for new notes, to
deny value to Yugoslavian notes remaining in Slovenia and Croatia.
1992: new (denominovani) dinar = 10 dinars
Oct. 1993: 1 (October) dinar = 1,000,000 dinars
Jan. 1, 1994: (1994) dinar = 1,000,000,000 (October) dinars
Jan. 1994: "super" dinar = 1 German mark; old currency declared
worthless.

Issuer: "NARODNA BANKA JUGOSLAVIJE."

CURRENT NOTES

5 NEW DINARA   131 x 62mm Issued 5 Dec 1994 **Cat.#148**
3 March 1994 Brown and purple.
Nikola Tesla / Museum Nikola Tesla in Belgrade.

10 NEW DINARA   135 x 64mm   Issued 5 Dec 1994   **Cat.#149**
3 March 1994   Brown and reddish brown.
Petar II Petrovič Njegoš / Monastery in Cetinje.

20 NEW DINARA   139 x 66mm   Issued 3 Aug 1994   **Cat.#150**
3 March 1994   Brown and olive green.
Poet and painter Djura Jakšić / Monastery in Vraczevshnitza.

50 NEW DINARA   143 x 68mm   Issued 31 July 1996   **Cat.#151**
June 1996   Dark greenish blue and gray.
Miloš Obrenovich / His palace.

100 NEW DINARA   148 x 70mm   Issued 9 June 1997   **Cat.#152**
October 1996   Light brown.
Dositej Obradovic / Monastery of Hopovo.

Zambia   Sambia • Zambie   ZMK

Kwacha = 100 ngwee.
Minor unit coins are not used.

Currency import-export restrictions:
Local currency in/out: equivalent to 100 U.S.dollars.
Foreign currency in/out: free, declaration required for amounts over US$5,000.
Reconversion allowed to up to USD 2,000 or equivalent.

Alternative currencies: GBP, USD.

A BRIEF MONETARY HISTORY
1968: kwacha = 0.50 Zambian pound.

Issuer: "BANK OF ZAMBIA."

CURRENT NOTES

Smaller notes not listed because of low value.

500 KWACHA   145 x 70   **Cat.#39**
1992   Brown, blue and multicolor.
Eagle and baobab tree / Elephant head, cotton field and workers, and Freedom statue.

1,000 KWACHA   145 x 70mm   Issued in May 1996   **Cat.#40**
Red, green, orange and multicolor.
Eagle and baobab tree / Animal, tractor and Freedom statue.

5,000 KWACHA   145 x 70mm   Issued in May 1996   **Cat.#41**
Violet, brown and multicolor.
Eagle and baobab tree / Lion head, plant and Freedom statue.

10,000 KWACHA   145 x 70mm   Issued in May 1996   **Cat.#42**
Green, brown and multicolor.
Eagle and baobab tree / Porcupine, harvest scene and Freedom statue.

Zimbabwe Simbabwe ZWD

Dollar(s) = 100 cent(s).

Currency import-export restrictions:
Local currency in/out: Z$ 500.
Foreign currency in: free, must declare.
Out: up to amount imported.
Hotel bills must be paid in convertible currency.
Reconversion requires presentation of exchange certificates.

Alternative currencies: GBP, USD.

A BRIEF MONETARY HISTORY
1970: dollar = 0.50 Rhodesian pound.

Issuer: "RESERVE BANK OF ZIMBABWE."

CURRENT NOTES

Smaller notes not listed because of low value.

5 DOLLARS   140 x 73mm **Cat.#2**
1980-94 Green and multicolor.
Matapos Rocks / Two women grinding grain.
Two watermarks, with side or frontal view of bird.

5 DOLLARS   139 x 68mm Issued 27 Jan 1997 **Cat.#5**
1997 Brown, orange red and purple / Brown, green and light red.
Matapos Rocks / Mountain landscape.

10 DOLLARS   146 x 77mm **Cat.#3**
1980-94 Red and multicolor.
Matapos Rocks / View of Harare and Eternal Flame.

10 DOLLARS   142 x 70mm Issued in early December 1997 **Cat.#6**
1997 Green, purple brown, red and multicolor.
Balantyne Rocks and leaf / Chilolo Cliffs.

20 DOLLARS   152 x 81mm **Cat.#4**
1980-94 Blue and multicolor.
Matapos Rocks / Elephant and Victoria Falls.

20 DOLLARS   145 x 72mm Issued in early December 1997 **Cat.#7**
1997 Green, blue, orange and multicolor.
Balantyne Rocks and two buffalos / Victoria Falls.

50 DOLLARS   148 x 74mm Issued ca. March 1994 **Cat.#8**
1994 Dark brown, olive green and red.
Matapos Rocks / Great Zimbabwe ruins.

100 DOLLARS   151 x 76mm Issued in early 1995 **Cat.#9**
1995 Dark brown and multicolor.
Matapos Rocks / Kariba Dam and reservoir

OUTMODED AND REDEEMABLE NOTES

All older notes in pounds issued by Bank of Rhodesia and Nyasaland and the Reserve Bank of Rhodesia are redeemable at the ratio of 2 dollars for each pound. Later notes in dollars are also redeemable.

Travelers Checks

Acceptance of Travelers Checks

To prevent losses be prudent when cashing travelers checks.

First inspect the original signature. If it looks overwritten, the checks may have been stolen, and the thief wrote a new signature over the original one.

You don't always have to call the issuer, but for larger transactions it is better to obtain an authorization code by calling the numbers listed in the next page. You will receive an approval code. Write it on one of the checks.

Write in the back of one check the full name of the presenter, the passport number, or other identification, the birth date, and other details you may find useful. If problems arise, you can prove you exercised due care when cashing the checks.

Witness the countersigning. Make sure the signature is done in a normal fashion and that it is in the same handwriting and name of the original one. If the customer seems to be drawing the signature, it may be the checks are stolen, and that a false or stolen piece of identification is used.

Signatures are acceptable in any alphabet, characters or language.

If the checks are presented already signed and countersigned, ask the customer to sign them again on the back, and witness and compare the signatures.

If the customer presents checks lacking the first signature, maybe the selling agent didn't ask for a signature at the time of purchase. Call the issuer to verify if they were reported stolen. You can ask to see the original purchase receipt. If everything is in order, just ask your customer to sign them in both places.

If after you accepted travelers checks you find a countersignature missing, type in the space where that signature should have been:

**"Absence of signature guaranteed
by** (your Company name)"

Do not cash checks presented by someone other than the original owner, unless recourse is available.

Reiseschecks Annahme

Beim Wechseln von Reiseschecks soll man vorsichtig sein, um einem eventuellen Verlust zu vermeiden.

Bevor man die Reiseschecks annimmt, soll man die Originalunterschrift genau betrachten. Sieht es aus, als ob die Unterschrift überschrieben ist, so ist es möglich, daß die Reiseschecks gestohlen sind und daß der Dieb eine neue Unterschrift über die Originalunterschrift gesetzt hat.

Es ist nicht immer nötig, den Aussteller anzurufen, aber für größere Geschäfte könnte man eine Genehmigungsnummer verlangen. Die entsprechenden Telefonnummern finden Sie auf den nächsten Seite. Diese Genehmigungsnummer trägt man dann auf einem der Schecks ein.

Auf der Rückseite einer der Schecks trägt man dann folgendes ein: Den vollständigen Name des Vorlegers, Reisepaßnummer oder Nummer anderer Ausweise, Geburtsdatum und andere Einzelheiten, die man für wichtig hält.

Prüfen Sie, ob die Unterschrift mit dem Original übereinstimmt. Man sollte sich überzeugen, daß die Unterschrift auf normale Weise erfolgt und daß Handschrift und Name mit dem Original übereinstimmen.

Wenn der Kunde Schecks ohne die erste Unterschrift vorlegt, ist es möglich, daß der Verkäufer den Kunden nicht beauftragt hat, die Schecks zu Zeit des Ankaufs zu unterschreiben. Wenn man die Verkaufsstelle anruft, kann man erfahren, ob die Schecks gestohlen sind. Sie können auch die Originalquittung verlangen. Wenn alles stimmt, verlangen Sie, daß der Kunde alle Schecks in Ihrer Gegenwart zwei mal unterzeichnet.

Unterschriften sind in jeder Form annehmbar.

Wenn ein Scheck schon mit der zweiten Unterschrift vorgelegt wird, verlangen Sie eine nochmalige Unterzeichnung auf der Rückseite des Schecks, und dann vergleichen Sie die Unterschriften.

Sollten Sie Reiseschecks akzeptiert haben, wobei der Kunde einige nicht unterzeichnet hat, dann trägt man mit der Schreibmaschine folgendes ein:

**"Absence of signature guaranteed
by** (Ihr Firmename)

Schecks, die von anderen Personen als dem Originalbesitzer vorgelegt werden, kann man nur annehmen, wenn ein Regreß möglich ist.

Aceptación de cheques de viajero

Sea prudente al aceptar cheques de viajero, y evitará pérdidas.

Antes de aceptarlos, revise la firma original. Si parece sobrescrita, puede ser que sean robados, y que el ladrón escribió otra firma encima de la original, para pasarlos.

No es necesario llamar al emisor para cada operación, pero conviene hacerlo para cantidades grandes. Use los números de teléfono que siguen, y obtendrá un código de autorización, que deberá escribir en el dorso de uno de los cheques.

Escriba siempre en el dorso de uno de los cheques el nombre del cliente, número de pasaporte u otra identificación, fecha de nacimiento, y cualquier otro dato que sea pertinente. Si surgiera algún problema, Ud. puede demostrar que fue prudente al aceptar los cheques.

El cliente debe firmar delante suyo. Asegúrese que la contrafirma es igual a la original. Si le parece que el cliente está dibujando su nombre en vez de firmarlo, puede tratarse de cheques robados, que son pasados con un documento falso o robado.

Las firmas pueden estar en cualquier idioma, alfabeto o caracteres.

Si el cliente presenta un cheque que ya está contrafirmado, pídale que lo vuelva a firmar al dorso, y compare las firmas.

Si los cheques no tienen la primera firma, puede ser que el agente vendedor no le pidió al cliente que los firmase. Ud. puede pedir el recibo de compra, o llamar al emisor para verificarlos. Si todo está en orden, pida al cliente que ponga ambas firmas.

Si después de cambiar cheques de viajero Ud. descubre que por error falta la contrafirma en alguno, escriba en el lugar donde va la firma:

**"Absence of signature guaranteed
by** (nombre de su compañía)"

Cambie cheques presentados por terceras personas solamente si las conoce, y tiene recurso.

©MRI Bankers' Guide to Foreign Currency
P.O.Box 3174   Houston TX 77253   USA

To verify Travelers Checks:

Most issuers offer toll free telephone numbers, or accept collect calls from anyone to verify whether travelers checks are reported lost or stolen.

Since they will ask you for it, make a list of the checks sorted by denomination and serial number before you call.

American Express Company

Afghanistan	Call Bahrain direct** 00-973-256834
Anguilla	Toll-free 1-800-221-7282
Antigua	Toll-free 1-800-221-7282
Argentina	Toll free 54-1-312-0900
Australia, except Sydney,	Toll-free 1-800-251-902
Sydney	Collect (61-2) 886-0689
Austria	Toll-free 0660-6840
Bahamas	Toll-free 1-800-221-7282
Bahrain	(973)-25-68-34
Bangladesh	Call India direct** 011-687-5930
Barbados	Toll-free 1-800-221-7282
Belgium	Toll-free 0800-12112
Bermuda	Toll-free 1-800-221-7282
Bhutan	Call India direct** 011-687-5930
Brazil, São Paulo	Toll-free (000)-811-543-0555
British Virgin Islands	Toll-free 1-800-221-7282
Brunei	call collect Singapore 65-738-3383
Cambodia	call collect* Hong Kong 852-800-2403
Canada	Toll-free 1-800-268-9824
Cayman Islands	call USA Collect 801-964-6665
Chile	call USA Collect 801-964-6665
China	Call Australia collect 61-2-886-0689
Costa Rica	call USA Collect 801-964-6665
Denmark	Toll-free 800-10100
Dominican Republic	Toll-free 1-800-221-7282
Finland	Toll-free 9800-12000
France	Toll-free 0800-90-8600
Paris	01.47.77.77.77
Germany	Toll-free 013-085-3100
Grenada	call USA Collect 801-964-6665
Hong Kong (collect)	call collect 852-288-59332
India	call direct 011-687-5930
Indonesia	Toll-free 001-800-61005
Ireland	Toll-free 1-800-626000
Israel-Tel Aviv	Toll-free*** 1-7744-08694
Italy	Toll-free 1678-72000
Japan	Toll-free 0120-030-130
Korea	Collect 822-394-0066
Laos	Call direct** Hong Kong 852-800-2403
Macau	Call direct** Hong Kong 852-800-2403
Malaysia	Toll-free 800-0463
Maldives	Call India direct** 011-687-5930
Marshall Islands	Call direct** Hong Kong 852-800-2403
México	Toll-free 1-800-221-7282
Mongolia	Call direct** Hong Kong 852-800-2403
Montserrat	Call USA collect 1-801-964-6665
Myanmar	call collect Singapore 65-738-3383
Nepal	Call India direct** 011-687-5930
The Netherlands	Toll-free 06022-0100
New Zealand	Toll-free 0800-44-1068
Norway	Toll-free 800-11000
Panamá	Call USA collect 1-801-964-6665
The Philippines	Toll-free 1-800-611-0087
Portugal	Toll-free 0505-44-9080
Puerto Rico and U.S. Virgin Islands	Toll-free 1-800-221-7282
St. Kitts & Nevis	Toll-free 1-800-221-7282
Singapore	Toll-free 1-800-738-3383
Spain	Toll-free 900-99-4426
Sri Lanka	Call India direct** 011-687-5930
Sweden	Toll-free 020-795-155
Switzerland	Toll-free 155-0100
Taiwan	Toll-free 800-616-1389
Thailand	Collect 662-273-0022
Turkey	Toll-free 00-800-449-14820
United Kingdom	Toll-free 0800-521313
USA	Toll-free 1-800-525-7641
Uruguay	Call USA Collect 1-801-964-6665
Venezuela	Call USA Collect 1-801-964-6665
Vietnam	Call Hong Kong direct** 852-800-2403

African countries	Call Collect UK 44 1273 571-600
Other Asian countries:	call collect Hong Kong 852-288-59332
Other European countries:	call collect England (44) 1273-571-600
Middle East	Call Bahrain collect/direct** 973 256-834
Other South American/Caribbean countries:	
	call collect USA 1-801-964-6665

* To call collect from these countries you must dial 001 to reach an operator.
** These countries do not allow collect calls. Ask for reimbursement of charges.
*** A local charge will be incurred.

Citicorp

Australia	Collect (2) 239-9533
Australia	Toll-free (2) 008-02272
Germany	Collect (49-641) 84888
Hong Kong	Collect (5) 821-7215
Japan	Collect 3 501 1348
Other Countries	Collect USA 813-623-1709
Singapore	Collect 223-1009
Taiwan	Collect (2) 716-9739
USA	Toll-free 800-645-6556
United Kingdom	Collect (44-171) 982-4040

Interpayment Systems Ltd.

Australia	Toll-free 1-800-127-477
Austria	Toll-free 0660-7320
Belgium	Toll-free 0800-7-1645
Brazil	Toll-free 000-811-784-0553
Canada and the Caribbean	Toll-free 1-800-732-1322
Cyprus	Toll-free 080-91028
Denmark	Toll-free 800-1-77-46
France	Toll-free 0591-5617
Germany	Toll-free 0130-82-4719
Greece	Toll-free 00-800-4412-8455
Hong-Kong	Toll-free 800-2495
Hungary	Toll-free 00-800-11117
Israel	Toll-free 177-440-8338
Italy	Toll-free 1678-70987
Luxembourg	Toll-free 0800-2119
México	Toll-free 95-800-010-0588
The Netherlands	Toll-free 06-022-2431
New Zealand	Toll-free 0800-44-0110
Norway	Toll-free 800-11-815
Portugal	Toll-free 0505-44-8307
Singapore	Toll-free 800-4481-114
South Africa	Toll-free 0800-99-8174
Spain	Toll-free 900-97-4447
Sweden	Toll-free 020-792-221
Switzerland	Toll-free 155-7262
Turkey	Toll-free 00-800-44-91-4899
United Kingdom	Toll-free 0800-515884
USA	Toll-free 1-800-732-1322
From other countries call collect	UK 44-1733 318949
By Fax	UK 44-1733-503670
or	USA 1-212-858-8607

Mastercard

Toll-free	USA 800-223-7668
or, after hours	USA 800-223-7373
or call collect	USA 609-987-7442

Thomas Cook / Mastercard

Australia	Toll free 1-800-127-495
Austria	0660-6266
Belgium	Toll-free 0800-1-2121
Cyprus	Toll free 080-91029
Denmark	Toll-free 80 01 01 10
France	Toll-free 05 90 8330
Germany	Toll-free 0130 85 9930
Greece	Toll-free 00-800-4412-8366
Hong Kong	Toll-free 800-2505
Hungary	Toll-free 00-800-11501
Israel	177-440-8424
Italy	Toll-free 1678 72050
Luxembourg	Toll-free 0800-2123
México	Toll-free 95-800-223-7373
The Netherlands	Toll-free 06 022 8630
New Zealand	Toll-free 0800-44-0112
Norway	Toll-free 800 11 005
Portugal	0505-44-9095
Singapore	Toll-free 800-4481-115
South Africa	Toll-free 0800-99-8175
Spain	Toll-free 900 99 4403
Sweden	Toll-free 020 795 110
Switzerland	Toll-free 155 0130
Turkey	Toll-free 00-800-44-91-4895
UK	Toll-free 0800-622101
Other countries call Collect	UK (44 1733) 318950
or Collect	USA 609-987-7300 / 609-987-7442
USA, Canada and Caribbean	
	Toll-free 800-223-9920 / 800-223-7668 / 800-223-7373
FAX	UK (44 1733) 502370 USA 609-987-7494
Telex UK	32200

Thomas Cook - Visa

Austria	Toll-free 0660-6102
Belgium	Toll-free 0800-1-5446
Brazil	Toll-free 000-811342-0552
Canada and the Caribbean	Toll-free 1-800-227-6811
Denmark	Toll-free 800-10448
France	Toll-free 0591-5613
Germany	Toll-free 0130-81-4070
Greece	Toll-free 00-800-4412-1863
Italy	Toll-free 1678-74155
México	Toll-free 95-800-257-3381
The Netherlands	Toll-free 06-022-5484
The Philippines	Toll-free 1-800-257-3381
Portugal	Toll-free 0505-44-1857
Spain	Toll-free 900-97-4414
Sweden	Toll-free 020-793-108
Switzerland	Toll-free 155-8450
Thailand	Toll-free 001-800-11-342-0662
United Kingdom	Toll-free 0800-895-078
From other countries call collect	UK 44 171 937-8091
Fax	UK 44 1733 503670

VISA

Austria	Vienna (0222) 54-1146
Belgium	Aalst (053) 77-6593
Denmark	Toll-free 800 100 31
France	Toll-free 05-423711
Germany	Frankfurt (069) 29-5178
italy	Rome (06) 679-5691
Japan	03-282-8115
The Netherlands	Amsterdam (020) 43-7025
New Zealand	64 (04) 474-9299
Portugal	Lisbon (01) 88-4109
Spain	Madrid (91) 401-2212
Sweden	Stockholm (08) 21-0011
Switzerland	Zurich (01) 302-0809
United Kingdom	call collect London (0171) 937-8091
USA	Toll-free 800-227-6811
in California	Toll-free 800-632-0520
In Alaska	Toll-free 800-227-6830
Or call collect USA	415-574-7111

Australian dollars

AMERICAN EXPRESS CO.

20 DOLLARS	Lilac blue and blue
50 DOLLARS	Same
100 DOLLARS	Same
200 DOLLARS	Same

THOMAS COOK / MASTERCARD

50 DOLLARS	Blue and multicolor
100 DOLLARS	Same
200 DOLLARS	Same

Earlier issues remain valid.

Issued by Thomas Cook Australia Pty. Limited, G.P.O. Box 990H, Melbourne, Victoria, 3001, Australia.

VISA

20 DOLLARS	Blue and multicolor
50 DOLLARS	Same
100 DOLLARS	Same
200 DOLLARS	Same

©MRI BANKERS' GUIDE TO FOREIGN CURRENCY
P.O.Box 3174 HOUSTON TX 77253 USA

British pounds

CITICORP

10 POUNDS	. . . .	Green, black and orange brown
20 POUNDS	. . . .	Same
50 POUNDS	. . . .	Same
100 POUNDS	. . . .	Same
500 POUNDS	. . . .	Same

Earlier series remain valid.

THOMAS COOK / MASTERCARD

10 POUNDS	. . . .	Blue and multicolor
20 POUNDS	. . . .	Same
50 POUNDS	. . . .	Same
100 POUNDS	. . . .	Same
200 POUNDS	. . . .	Same

Issued by Thomas Cook Travellers Cheques Ltd., P.O.Box 36, Peterborough PE3 6SB, England. Earlier issues remain valid.

TRAVELLERS CHEQUE ASSOCIATES
AMERICAN EXPRESS CO

10 POUNDS	. . . .	Lilac blue and blue
20 POUNDS	. . . .	Same
50 POUNDS	. . . .	Same
100 POUNDS	. . . .	Same
200 POUNDS	. . . .	Same
500 POUNDS	. . . .	Same

Earlier series remain valid.

VISA

VISA Travelers checks issued by **"Bank of Credit and Commerce International"** cannot be cashed. These must be sent for collection by the original purchaser, along with the purchase receipt, to: Visa, Box 8066, San Francisco CA 94128, USA.

10 POUNDS	. . . .	Blue and multicolor
20 POUNDS	. . . .	Same
50 POUNDS	. . . .	Same
100 POUNDS	. . . .	Same
500 POUNDS	. . . .	Same

Canadian dollars

AMERICAN EXPRESS CO.

20 DOLLARS	. . . .	Lilac blue, blue and red
50 DOLLARS	. . . .	Same
100 DOLLARS	. . . .	Same
500 DOLLARS	. . . .	Same

Earlier series remain valid.

THOMAS COOK / MASTERCARD

20 DOLLARS	. . . .	Blue and multicolor
50 DOLLARS	. . . .	Same
100 DOLLARS	. . . .	Same

Issued by Thomas Cook Canada Ltd., P.O.Box 2209, Sta. "P", Toronto, Ont. M5S 2T2, Canada. Earlier series remain valid.

VISA

20 DOLLARS	Blue and multicolor
50 DOLLARS	Same
100 DOLLARS	Same
500 DOLLARS	Same

Cypriot pounds

BANK OF CYPRUS (LONDON) LIMITED

10 POUNDS	Greenish blue
20 POUNDS	Greenish blue
50 POUNDS	Greenish blue

Issued by Bank of Cyprus (london) Limited, 27/31 Charlotte Street, London 1P 2HJ.

ECU European currency unit

SOCIETE DU CHEQUE DE VOYAGE
EN ECU - AMERICAN EXPRESS CO.

These were discontinued around 1986, but may be reintroduced in the future.

THOMAS COOK / MASTERCARD

50 ECUS	Blue and multicolor
100 ECUS	Same

Issued by and redeemable at Euro Travellers Cheque ECU Ltd., P.O.Box 36, Peterborough, PE3 6SB, England.

French francs

SOCIETE FRANCAISE DU CHEQUE DU VOYAGE
AMERICAN EXPRESS CO.

100 FRANCS	Lilac blue and blue
200 FRANCS	Same
500 FRANCS	Same
1,000 FRANCS	Same

Earlier series remain valid.

THOMAS COOK / MASTERCARD

200 FRANCS	Blue and multicolor
500 FRANCS	Same
1,000 FRANCS	Same

Earlier series remain valid. Issued by Franchèque S.A., B.P. 46-16, 75761 Paris Cedex 16, France.

VISA

100 FRANCS	Blue and multicolor
200 FRANCS	Same
500 FRANCS	Same
1,000 FRANCS	Same

German marks

AMERICAN EXPRESS CO.

50 DEUTSCHE MARK	Lilac blue and blue
100 DEUTSCHE MARK	Same
200 DEUTSCHE MARK	Same
500 DEUTSCHE MARK	Same

Earlier series remain valid.

CITICORP

50 DEUTSCHE MARK	Green, black and yellow brown
100 DEUTSCHE MARK	Same
200 DEUTSCHE MARK	Same
500 DEUTSCHE MARK	Same
1,000 DEUTSCHE MARK	Same

THOMAS COOK / MASTERCARD

50 DEUTSCHE MARK	Blue and multicolor
100 DEUTSCHE MARK	Same
200 DEUTSCHE MARK	Same
500 DEUTSCHE MARK	Same

Earlier series remain valid. Issued by Thomas Cook Travellers Cheques Ltd., P.O.Box 36, Peterborough PE3 6SB, England.

VISA

50 DEUTSCHE MARK	Blue and multicolor
100 DEUTSCHE MARK	Same
200 DEUTSCHE MARK	Same
500 DEUTSCHE MARK	Same

Hong Kong dollars

HONGKONG BANK
THOMAS COOK / MASTERCARD

200 DOLLARS	Blue and multicolor
500 DOLLARS	Same
1,000 DOLLARS	Same

Earlier series are still valid. Issued by HongKong and Shanghai Thomas Cook Ltd., P.O.Box 64, 1 Queen's Road Center, Hong Kong.

VISA

100 DOLLARS	Blue and multicolor
200 DOLLARS	Same
500 DOLLARS	Same
1,000 DOLLARS	Same

Italian lire

BANCA COMMERCIALE ITALIANA

10,000 LIRE	Brown
25,000 LIRE	Green
50,000 LIRE	Brownish red
100,000 LIRE	Bluish green

WARNING

Italian Travelers Checks lose value one year after issue.

BANCA NAZIONALE DEL LAVORO

50,000 LIRE	....	Bluish green
100,000 LIRE	....	Pink

MONTE DEI PASCHI DI SIENA

10,000 LIRE	....	Brown
25,000 LIRE	....	Green
50,000 LIRE	....	Red
100,000 LIRE	....	Blue

Japanese yen

AMERICAN EXPRESS CO.

5,000 YEN	....	Lilac blue and blue
10,000 YEN	....	Same
20,000 YEN	....	Same
50,000 YEN	....	Same

Earlier series remain valid.

CITICORP

5,000 YEN	....	Green, black and orange brown
10,000 YEN	....	Same
20,000 YEN	....	Same
50,000 YEN	....	Same

MITSUI BANK / THOMAS COOK
MASTERCARD

10,000 YEN	....	Blue and multicolor
20,000 YEN	....	Same
50,000 YEN	....	Same
100,000 YEN	....	Same

Issued by The Mitsui Bank Limited, P.O.Box Tokyo Central 208, Tokyo, Japan. Earlier series remain valid.

VISA

5,000 YEN	....	Blue and multicolor
10,000 YEN	....	Same
20,000 YEN	....	Same
50,000 YEN	....	Same

Netherlands guilders

AMERICAN EXPRESS CO.

100 GULDEN	....	Blue and multicolor
200 GULDEN	....	Same
500 GULDEN	....	Same

THOMAS COOK / MASTERCARD

100 GULDEN	....	Blue and multicolor
200 GULDEN	....	Same
500 GULDEN	....	Same

Issued by Euro Travellers Cheque Nederland Ltd., P.O.Box 36, Peterborough PE3 6SB, England.

New Zealand dollars

VISA

50 DOLLARS	....	Blue and multicolor
100 DOLLARS	....	Same
200 DOLLARS	....	Same

Norwegian kroner

VISA

500 KRONER	....	Blue and multicolor

Portuguese escudos

VISA

1,000 ESCUDOS	....	Blue and multicolor
5,000 ESCUDOS	....	Same
10,000 ESCUDOS	....	Same

Saudi riyals

AMERICAN EXPRESS CO.

50 RIYALS	....	Lilac blue and green
100 RIYALS	....	Same
500 RIYALS	....	Same
1,000 RIYALS	....	Same

Singaporean dollars

VISA

50 DOLLARS	....	Blue and multicolor
100 DOLLARS	....	Same
500 DOLLARS	....	Same

©MRI BANKERS' GUIDE TO FOREIGN CURRENCY
P.O.Box 3174 HOUSTON TX 77253 USA

South African rand

> **WARNING**
>
> Rand travellers cheques cannot be negotiated outside the South African Monetary Area unless endorsed "Available anywhere in the world."

**THE STANDARD BANK OF SOUTH AFRICA LIMITED
DIE STANDARD BANK VAN SUID-AFRICA BEPERK**

20 RAND	Gray/Blue
50 RAND	Dark blue, brown and green
100 RAND	Green/Blue
200 RAND	Purple/Blue
500 RAND	Yellow/Blue

Spanish pesetas

CENTRAL HISPANO
(Banco Central Hispanoamericano)

5,000 PESETAS	Lilac
10,000 PESETAS	Blue
15,000 PESETAS	Brown

VISA

1,000 PESETAS	Blue and multicolor
5,000 PESETAS	Same
10,000 PESETAS	Same

Issued by Banco Atlántico, S.A., Gran Vía 48, 28013 Madrid, Spain.

Swiss francs

SWISS BANKERS/AMERICAN EXPRESS CO.

50 CHF	Lilac blue and blue
100 CHF	Same
200 CHF	Same
500 CHF	Same

Earlier series issued by the American Express and by Swiss Bankers remain valid.

VISA

50 CHF	Blue and multicolor
100 CHF	Same
200 CHF	Same
500 CHF	Same

United States dollars

AMERICAN EXPRESS CO.

10 DOLLARS	Lilac blue and blue
20 DOLLARS	Same
50 DOLLARS	Same
100 DOLLARS	Same
500 DOLLARS	Same
1,000 DOLLARS	Same

Earlier series remain valid.

In May 1992 American Express introduced dual signature travelers checks. Signed at time of purchase by both buyers, may be countersigned and cashed by either one.

CITICORP

10 DOLLARS	Green, black and orange brown
20 DOLLARS	Same
50 DOLLARS	Same
100 DOLLARS	Same
500 DOLLARS	Same
1,000 DOLLARS	Same

MASTERCARD

10 DOLLARS	Blue and multicolor
20 DOLLARS	Same
50 DOLLARS	Same
100 DOLLARS	Same
500 DOLLARS	Same

Issued by MasterCard International, Travelers Cheque Division, P.O.Box 1296, Radio City Station, New York, NY 10101, USA.

THOMAS COOK / MASTERCARD

20 DOLLARS	Blue and multicolor
50 DOLLARS	Same
100 DOLLARS	Same
500 DOLLARS	Same
1,000 DOLLARS	Same

Issued by Thomas Cook Inc., Travelers Cheque Division, 3 Independence Way, Princeton, NJ 08540, USA. Earlier issues are valid.

VISA

VISA travelers checks issued by **"Bank of Credit and Commerce International"** cannot be cashed. They must be sent for collection by the original purchaser, along with the purchase receipt, to: Visa, Box 8066, San Francisco CA 94128, USA.

10 DOLLARS	Blue and multicolor
20 DOLLARS	Same
50 DOLLARS	Same
100 DOLLARS	Same
200 DOLLARS	Same
500 DOLLARS	Same
1,000 DOLLARS	Same